Red Guards and Workers' Militias in the Russian Revolution

Red Guards
and Workers' Militias in the
Russian Revolution

REX A. WADE

Stanford University Press, Stanford, California
1984

Stanford University Press, Stanford, California
© 1984 by the Board of Trustees of the Leland Stanford Junior University
Printed in the United States of America
ISBN 0-8047-1167-4
LC 82-60488

Acknowledgments

Acknowledging the assistance of others is perhaps the pleasantest part of writing a book. I have been especially fortunate in the support I have received from numerous people and organizations. The early research was facilitated by several months in Helsinki, Finland, under a Senior Fellow grant from the National Endowment for the Humanities and a Fulbright-Hayes travel grant. An IREX award provided an opportunity for research in the Soviet Union. An American Council of Learned Societies grant allowed a semester of reduced teaching in which to write. Librarians everywhere have been very helpful—I would mention especially those at the University of Helsinki library, the Hoover Institution, and the State Historical, Lenin, and Academy of Sciences libraries in the Soviet Union. The Russian Bibliographer at the University of Hawaii library, Patricia Polansky, owns my special gratitude; no researcher was ever better served by a knowledgeable and helpful librarian.

More colleagues have helped than I could possibly list. Their generosity in time and in passing on pieces of information is greatly appreciated. Many of them have provided critiques of the work, either through reading all or parts of the manuscript or by comments on papers about the Red Guards delivered at scholarly conferences; William Rosenberg, Alexander Rabinowitch, Ronald Suny, and Allan Wildman deserve special thanks. Tsuyoshi Hasegawa kindly lent the manuscript of his now published *The February Revolution*, and David Collins of Leeds University lent me his unpublished and otherwise unavailable doctoral dissertation on the Red Guard. The generosity of both men is greatly appreciated. Finally, my colleague at the University of Hawaii, Donald J. Raleigh, not only read the manuscript but shared many hours of discussion about the Revolution.

I have been extraordinarily fortunate in the help I have received in the preparation of the work for publication. Gwen Agina typed the early drafts, and Janet Agena typed the later material and final version, helped with proofreading and indexing, and kept me reasonably on schedule toward the end. Suzie Ajifu and Dawn Kaneshiro also helped in preparation of the manuscript. To all four, for their cheerfulness as well as work, I am indebted. My association with Stanford University Press continues to be a pleasure. J. G. Bell, the Editor, mixed forbearance of missed deadlines with periodic prods and has been supportive throughout. Peter Kahn has been a most able and pleasant editor with whom to work.

Finally, I, like many authors, am deeply indebted for the sacrifices made by my wife, Beryl, and children. All three children, Beth, Doug, and Stephanie (especially the last), hastened the book by asking periodically if it was finished yet. To them it is dedicated.

R.A.W.

Contents

Eight pages of photographs follow p. 132

Note on Spelling and Dates

Spelling is a simplified version of the Library of Congress transliteration system. Names and words with a common English spelling are used in the latter form (Trotsky, Soviet, Kerensky, Alexander). Russian place names in the text, especially of Petrograd districts, sometimes are modified, and in some instances rather arbitrary decisions were made whether to use noun or adjective forms (Petrogradskii district, but Vyborg rather than Vyborgskii district). Clarity of identification and ease to the reader were the guiding principles for these modifications. Where such changes were made in the text, strict transliteration was adhered to in the bibliographic materials (Kharkov in the text, but Khar'kov or Khar'kovskii in the notes).

All dates are according to the Russian calendar. In 1917 the Julian calendar in use in Russia was thirteen days behind the Gregorian calendar in use in the West.

Red Guards and Workers' Militias in the Russian Revolution

Introduction

"[The Vyborg] proletariat took into its own hands all the
administration of the district. I, as the appointed 'commissar
of the [Soviet] Executive Committee,' was only an assistant
in that tremendous self-assertiveness exhibited by the proletariat in the district."

—A. G. Shliapnikov,
speaking of the February Revolution

During my years of studying the Russian Revolution of 1917, I
gradually developed an uneasy feeling that the extensive and varied
writings on the subject—my own included—have tended to concentrate too much on the top political figures at the expense of the
lower levels of society. The major figures seemed to function in a
vacuum, as though suspended in midair, and the "dark masses"
were largely unknown, their attitudes accepted by later historians
to be as depicted by the political parties and the top political leaders—the Trotskys, Miliukovs, and Kerenskys. Both Western and
Soviet historians have tended toward this distortion, with the result
that readers have gotten little sense of how Ivan Ivanovich, the man
in the Russian street, perceived the Revolution and his role in it. My
concern about this omission has proved to be shared by other historians of the Revolution, many of whom have encouraged and lent
support to the writing of this book.

One happy by-product of the post-Stalin era in the USSR is that
historians there now give more attention to the local levels of political and other activity in the Revolution. Valuable document collections and many volumes of memoirs by participants, especially at
the factory and district level, have been published, and this has
greatly assisted the Western historian, whose use of most Soviet
archival materials is either severely limited or refused altogether.

Coupled with contemporary 1917 sources and publications of the
1920's, these Soviet works have helped to make possible the study
of the lower levels of popular participation in the Revolution of
1917. Still, when I first began my research I assumed that the material would be very limited, so I merely planned several articles on
various aspects of the problem, to be completed quickly. The first
article was on the district soviets (*raionnye sovety*) of Petrograd.[1]
To my surprise, there was much more material available than I had
expected, and turning next to workers' armed bands, I soon realized that I could not do justice to the topic in even a long article.
Therefore I began to rethink the project, and the result is the present book.

This volume is, on one level, a history of the workers' militias and
Red Guard in 1917, the story of voluntary armed bands and their
role in the outcome of the Russian Revolution.* One of the overriding concerns of the Russian Revolution, as of any revolution, was
the problem of armed force. During the first days of the Revolution
there was a general concern with the question and a unanimity of
opinion—the people must be armed in order to maintain public order and resist a possible tsarist counterattack. This era of common
assumptions was short-lived, however, as the fear of a tsarist counterrevolution gave way to deep-seated class and political antagonisms, and as conflicting views of the goals of the Revolution became more clearly articulated. Some people hoped for a quick
return to "normalcy," including the disbanding of armed groups,
whereas others—especially among the industrial working class—
felt deeply that their own possession of arms was not only a right
but an absolute prerequisite for the defense of their newly found
liberties. A. G. Shliapnikov, addressing a group of Vyborg-district
workers on February 28 about the actions of the Petrograd Soviet,
found arms and the organization of a militia to be the questions
that interested them most.[2] Nothing moved them to action more

---

* The term "militia" (*militsiia*) came into use immediately in the February Revolution and was adopted—and is still used in the Soviet Union—in place of the word
police. As we shall see, it had a wider range of meanings than simply "police," including that of a special paramilitary armed citizens' force for protection of the public order or of the interests of a particular group. The term "Red Guard" was
adopted from a Finnish organization of that name formed during the Revolution of
1905 and the subject of considerable interest thereafter, including a book by G. V.
Plekhanov.

surely than the threat of the loss of arms and of their own armed defense forces.

It did not take long in the rapidly developing—or deteriorating— situation of 1917 for this sense of the need for arms to defend one's liberties or viewpoint to take on more concrete forms. For the workers especially, a fear of counterrevolution helped create a feeling of the need not only to be armed but also to be organized for the defense of their rights against a class foe. And from here it was only a short step to the conception that such armed forces were necessary not merely to defend freedoms already won but to move Russia forward toward the goal of a government more attuned to the workers' aspirations—that is, as a force to be used in a new revolution. Moreover, one is struck by the workers' unquestioned assumption—fed by the Social Democratic parties, especially the Bolsheviks—that they represented the true interests of the Revolution in a way no other group did. Nor can one fail to notice a basic reality of political life in Russia in 1917: as Russian society lost its cohesiveness, as the power of the government became weaker with each passing day, and as the unreliability of the army as a force for internal power became more apparent, armed groups that were determined to enforce their viewpoint and that possessed even the rudiments of organization and leadership came to wield enormous power, power completely out of proportion to their size. And when such groups were located in Petrograd, they were a particularly potent force. Despite the crumbling of government authority in the provinces and the beginnings of separatist movements among the nationalities, Petrograd remained the center of political decision-making, and actions there influenced all of Russia. An armed force in Petrograd could sway the course of any new political revolution, since it was likely to begin there, as the February Revolution had. Moreover, the development of armed bands in Petrograd was imitated in the provinces, and these groups could be a powerful force bringing the rest of the country in the direction taken by the capital.

This volume is, however, more than just a history of worker armed bands. As I studied these bands I found them to be an excellent means of exploring an issue long debated among both participants and historians—the issue of spontaneity versus leadership in the Revolution. The armed bands were a complex combination of spontaneity, voluntaristic action, and initiative from below inter-

acting with ideas derived from outside political ideologies and attempts at control or influence by political parties. The relationship
between the mass of the population and would-be leaders is one of
the main problems of any revolutionary movement, and the Russians of the nineteenth century grappled with it over and over. It
was one of the main causes for the split among the Populists in the
1870's, and was inherited by their Socialist Revolutionary (SR) suc-
cessors, by the Marxists, and even by the liberals. The Russian
Marxists especially gave a great deal of attention to this issue, both
in theory and in practice. Several historians, most notably Leopold
Haimson,[3] have argued persuasively that the intelligentsia in general and the Marxists in particular came to use "consciousness"
(*soznatel'nost'*) and "elemental spontaneity" (*stikhiinost'*) as terms
to describe the respective characteristics of the leaders and the
masses, and to see these on the one hand as conceptual categories
for explaining the world around them and on the other as the
two poles of "awareness" and "feeling" that somehow had to be
brought closer together in order to achieve a successful revolution
and construct a new society. Different interpretations of these two
attributes were critical in the conflict that led to the split of the Social Democratic Party into Bolsheviks and Mensheviks and in Lenin's thinking about how to organize the new state after 1917.

Given the importance of the term "spontaneity" in the history of
the Revolution and in our story, and the many connotations it car-
ries in the historical literature, I want to clarify how it is used in this
book. At the outset let me say that I am not concerned with the
controversy over the extent to which "spontaneity" adequately conveys the nuances of the Russian word *stikhiinost'*. Rather, I will dis-
regard—save for this passage—its revolutionary polemical history
and will employ it as a good English word useful in analyzing
the Russian Revolution of 1917, particularly the process of self-
organization of armed bands. Several types of actions might be
characterized as spontaneous in our usage: (1) complete spontaneity, in the sense of efforts on the part of individuals previously
unassociated, or only loosely associated, to organize themselves
without any instructions from outside into local bodies of authority
in order to act in the face of momentous social and political events;
(2) efforts on the part of people belonging to some existing social

entity (school, association, factory) and acting through its facilities to organize local bodies of authority composed primarily of people belonging to that entity, but operating without its formal sanction or traditional leadership and beyond its normal functions; (3) the self-authorized formation of local bodies of authority by some previously existing nongovernmental organization acting beyond its traditional sphere of competence; and (4) the formation of local bodies of authority (e.g. Red Guards) by low-level political leaders (e.g. factory or district party members) at least partly influenced by general party doctrine but acting on their own initiative, and whose actions or ideas about the role of these organizations are not guided by any central party leadership. I would also consider as spontaneous any example of extensive self-organization and initiative that was nonetheless responsive to appeals, urgings, or directives of higher authoritative political bodies (such as the Petrograd Soviet or a central party leadership). I would contrast this with efforts to organize a militia or other body by a central authority (such as the Petrograd Soviet or the City Duma*) using its own agents. In an extremely fluid situation, as we will see, the dividing line between spontaneous and directed action is often almost impossible to distinguish precisely, especially in retrospect. Spontaneous activity rarely leaves extensive or clear records.

The Revolution, by releasing the pent-up frustrations of the "dark masses," brought to a head the problems of leadership and organization, of how to harness the spontaneity of the masses. For one thing, the initial revolution in 1917 was made by those spontaneous masses, especially by the soldiers and the industrial workers, with only a minimal role played by intelligentsia leadership groups. Immediately, however, the masses looked for leadership and direction, whether from the State Duma, from the radical intelligentsia of the Petrograd Soviet, or from spokesmen arising out of their own ranks. Yet they also clung to their own autonomy. Thus, meshing spontaneity and leadership emerged as a basic problem for the Revolution from its beginning. This was the more difficult in

---

* The Petrograd City Duma (city council) was elected on a limited franchise before the Revolution and democratized in 1917 by the addition of representatives from the lower classes. Many other cities had similar *dumy*. The State Duma, however, was the lower house of the legislature formed in 1906; it is hereafter referred to simply as "the Duma."

that Russia lacked any substantial tradition of orderly public life, and had virtually no experience of the mass of the population participating in the political life of the country. The voluntary restraints on anarchistic self-assertion that exist in more developed political cultures were extremely weak in Russia. Moreover, there was the inescapable fact that in Russia in 1917 these "dark masses" were armed. Large numbers of individuals acquired arms in 1917, and when they began to organize themselves or be organized into armed bands a potent political force was created that made the problems of leadership more critical but no easier to solve. Most of these armed bands, formed at factories, were very much locally oriented and jealous of their autonomy, yet felt a need for some sort of larger structure, some kind of sanction or central leadership. This proved, in Petrograd especially, very difficult to achieve. The repeated efforts to do so, and the problems involved, make these groups an excellent case study of popular aspirations and the problems of leadership and spontaneity.

These armed bands also provide a good vehicle for studying the secondary and tertiary levels of political leadership, the group Tsuyoshi Hasegawa has so aptly dubbed "the sub-elite."[4] This is the leadership at the point where the masses and the political parties touched, where popular aspirations came into contact with party programs, where the leaders emerging from the workers interacted with the professional revolutionaries. The nature of this level of leadership, and of its relations with both higher political officials and the worker masses below, will be a recurring theme.

The armed groups were very sensitive to the ebb and flow of revolution: more than any other identifiable organization or grouping, their fortunes changed with the various periods of revolutionary crisis and relative quiescence. Factory committees, supply commissions, district soviets—all had ongoing and reasonably well defined functions and institutional bases. Strike committees and other ad hoc organizations came and went as needed. The workers' militia and Red Guard, however, had more permanence than the latter organizations but less stability than the former. Their fortunes rose and fell with the revolutionary crises and the mood of the populace, reflecting the degree of political intensity at any given moment and the extent to which the working class felt that its interests demanded the ultimate political expression—a rallying to arms. Thus a study in detail of the formation of armed bands in the Revolution should help considerably our understanding of the social psychology of the Russian Revolution and contribute to a better understanding of the revolutionary process in general. The creation of these armed bands, their own self-assertiveness, the efforts to harness or control them, and their own efforts to seek political support and leaders to express and even define their interests—these are the main issues of this book.

The book is divided into two parts. The longer first part is a detailed study of the armed bands in Petrograd, an effort to get the fullest possible understanding of their organization, nature, aspirations, and role. The second part studies similar armed bands in the rest of the country. Two chapters in this part study the Red Guard in the provincial cities of Saratov and Kharkov to provide a basis for comparison with the Petrograd "model." These cities were chosen for reasons of geography, comparability in size, and availability of good sources on this subject. The third chapter provides an overview of the workers' militias, *druzhiny*,* and Red Guards in Russia, noting especially where similarities with and differences from the three "model" cities occur. This particular overall structure has been chosen in preference to the more commonly used eclectic pattern—drawing material helter-skelter from all over Russia, with a citation first from Petrograd, then from Astrakhan, then from Voronezh—that aims at building up a composite picture of the topic.[5] The problem with the latter approach is that though it gives an impression of completeness, it in fact fails to present a coherent image of any real organization that actually existed. What emerges is an artificial Red Guard that never existed anywhere, and not only is a certain reality sacrificed, but we are robbed of the ability to see the organization develop. The dynamics are lost.

The approach used in this book will, I hope, allow us to get a better picture of the Red Guard by studying a few actual workers' militias and Red Guard organizations in detail, tracing their evolution and role in the Revolution, and thereby gaining a sense of their dynamics. At the same time, this approach throws into sharper focus the similarities and dissimilarities across Russia. To the possi-

---

* *Druzhiny* (singular *druzhina*) were armed bands ("detachments" is the closest English translation) that took their name from the princely military retinues of early Russia. Members were called *druzhiniki*.

ble objection that Russia was a very diverse country and that any selection of cities is bound to be unrepresentative, there are, I think, adequate responses. First, one must acknowledge that the charge is partly true but that the problem of "representativeness" is probably unsolvable. Second, in view of the overwhelming importance of Petrograd and its Red Guard in the Russian scheme in 1917, it must be singled out for special study in order properly to examine the role of any group in the Revolution. After that, a study in detail of a couple of other cities allows comparison to see how typical Petrograd was and also allows a glimpse into revolutionary dynamics in provincial cities.

I hope that this approach will bring into sharper focus both the diversity and similarity in the Revolution across Russia, facilitating comparisons. Fundamentals of revolution and class conflict did impose some constraints on patterns of behavior for all inhabitants of the former Russian Empire, but local peculiarities existed also. I hope, too, that my approach will provide another benefit. In the West the Revolution has been studied only sketchily outside of Petrograd.[6] The chapters on Saratov and Kharkov do not pretend to be comprehensive studies, but they do provide pictures of the Revolution in those two cities. Because they are less well known than Petrograd, considerable information about the Revolution in general—the composition of their soviets, for example—has been included. Thus those chapters focus less narrowly on the workers' militia and Red Guard and should have additional usefulness as partial histories of the Revolution in two provincial cities.

1
The Coming of the Revolution

"The strikers . . . were dispersed in one place but quickly gathered in other places, showing themselves to be exceptionally stubborn." —*Police report, February 24, 1917*

Russia entered upon the Industrial Revolution late among the major European powers, really only in the 1880's and 1890's. Nonetheless, by the outbreak of war in 1914 a significant industrial capacity existed and also an important industrial working class. Russian industrialization, coming relatively late and involving extensive government subsidy and foreign investment, created certain special features in the economy and society, the most striking of which—and the most important for us—was the formation of very large factories and their concentration in a few places. The process tended to "organize" the workers by gathering them into large factories and subjecting them to the discipline and interdependence of the workshop. That many workers lived in barracks provided by the factory reinforced this "organization." Even when they lived in private quarters, this typically took the form of apartment buildings in working-class districts, usually in the same area as the factory, under conditions of serious crowding. Thus their nonworking as well as working experience tended to shape a sense of identity, of class-consciousness, and to group the workers in a way that would permit political mobilization under the right circumstances. Moreover, younger and single workers especially tended to live in barracks or factory-provided housing, and it was these workers who, as we shall see, were most likely to join armed bands such as the Red Guard in 1917. This concentration and "organization," added to the fact that industry tended to be concentrated in major cities, especially but not exclusively in the capitals—Petrograd and Moscow—meant that workers were able to exercise an influence completely out of proportion to their numbers in the overall population when their discontents exploded into disorders. They represented a group much more dangerous to the existing political and social order than the vastly more numerous peasantry.

Virtually all Russian cities with any significant industrial activity tended to have clearly delineated factory and working-class districts. This was true of Petrograd as well. In the chapters that follow we will refer frequently to the districts (*raiony*) of Petrograd—to their workers' militias, to their Red Guard units and staffs, and to other aspects of their local organization, including soviets. These districts represented an important level of organization and self-organization. Therefore, we should look briefly at them and their socioeconomic characteristics.[1] In 1917 there were about 19 such districts in Petrograd, although the number varied from time to time because of shifting boundaries, consolidations, and divisions. Some, especially on the edges of the city, were known by more than one name. Generally the districts coincided with well recognized geographic and historical areas and/or with the old police districts. Some, in turn, were divided into two to four subdistricts (*podraiony*) that coincided with the former police subdistricts. On March 9, 1917, 51 such subdistricts existed.[2]

Most Petrograders still lived close to their place of work. Public transportation developed late in the capital, served the outlying factory areas poorly, and was expensive in relation to worker income. (It is easy for the modern reader to forget that for the poorer classes the tram was a luxury, a symbol of those better off; hence the symbolism in the descriptions of the overturning and stopping of trams during the February Revolution.) The tendency to live close to one's place of work gave the districts their distinctive social characteristics, but even working-class districts had a mixed population owing to the presence of factory owners and managerial personnel. For the same reason, the better areas also housed a large lower-class population: restaurant and food workers, shop clerks, workers in small manufacturing or craft enterprises, service workers, and menials and unskilled workers of all kinds. Moreover, the extreme housing shortage of Petrograd, even before the war worsened it, contributed to this intermixing as the cellars and garrets of better housing blocks were rented to poor folk.[3] Still, the city did have distinct socioeconomic districts, and especially large factory and working-class districts. Socially and economically the districts broke down into three broad groupings. One group in the center of the city was primarily upper and middle class in composition, with a large number of government buildings. This encompassed especially the region on the left bank of the Neva River stretching back to the Fontanka Canal, although upper-class sections existed also east of the Fontanka and along the riverfront in the Vasil'evskii and Petrogradskii districts. A second area of much more mixed population, with larger lower-class and industrial areas as well as middle-class and some upper-class sections, stretched between the Fontanka and Obvodnyi canals on the left side of the Neva and included the island districts of Vasil'evskii and Petrogradskii across the Neva. Surrounding the city on all sides lay the factory and working-class districts. These three general groupings deserve closer inspection. (See Maps 1 and 2.)

There were three districts in the city center with almost no significant factories or industrial working class, although they had, as all districts did, a considerable miscellaneous lower-class population: these were the Admiralty, Spasskii, and Kazanskii districts. They occupied all but the western edge of the region between the Neva River and the Fontanka Canal. The heart of this area was the region stretching from the Winter Palace, the Admiralty Building, and the General Staff Building along the Nevskii Prospect, the most imposing and important street of the city and the symbol of privileged Russia. Here were to be found palaces, luxury shops and restaurants, and fashionable apartments. The area to the east of Gorkhovaia Street, reaching to Liteinyi Prospect and beyond, was especially fashionable. Some sections toward the western edges of these districts and along the Fontanka Canal could be considered inner-city slums, but the lower-class elements here were not organized by factory, were politically insignificant, and played little role in the Revolution or in the history of the Red Guard.

These three districts were bordered on all sides by several others of a more mixed population, including some with factories. On the western, or downriver, side, completing the area enclosed by the Fontanka Canal, was the Kolomenskii district. It, with the above three, made up the old Second City District. The Kolomenskii dis-

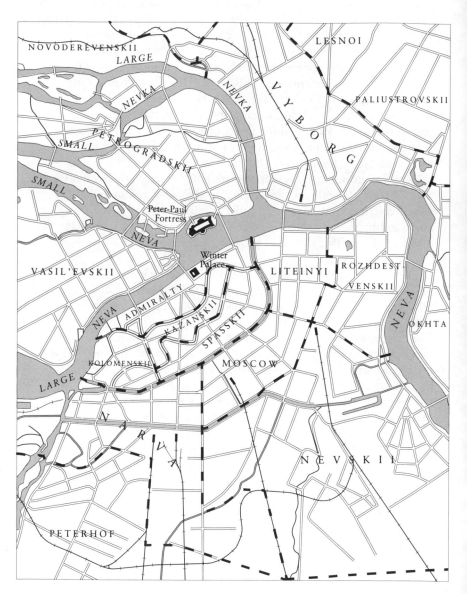

MAP 1. Petrograd in 1917, showing district boundaries.

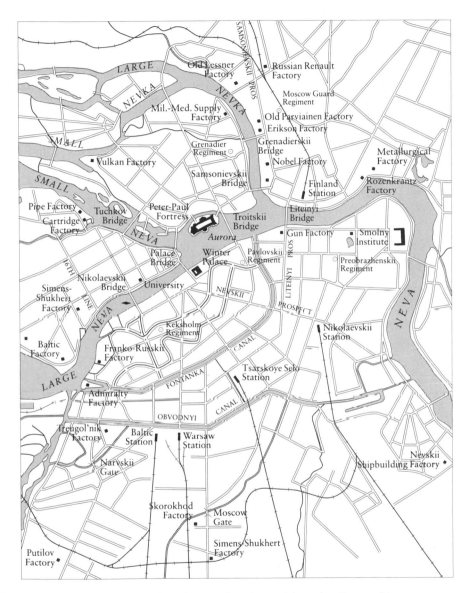

MAP 2. Petrograd in 1917, showing locations of factories discussed in the text.

trict had a considerable middle-class and even some upper-class population in the east, but it became industrial in the west, near the waterfront. There, where the Neva flows into the Gulf of Finland, were three large shipbuilding concerns—the Franko-Russkii, the Admiralty, and the New Admiralty—employing a total of about 20,000 workers, who lived in the area. On the upriver side of the three center districts, east of the Fontanka Canal, were two districts of mixed but somewhat more pedigreed population, the Liteinyi and the Rozhdestvenskii. The western part of the Liteinyi district along Liteinyi Prospect was one of the most fashionable areas of the city. However, because the Liteinyi Bridge connected to the radical Vyborg district across the Neva, the region was the scene of many disorders and demonstrations in 1917 as workers from Vyborg poured into the city center. The two districts did have a few factories, mostly small, but including at least two important ones, the Gun Factory and a branch of the Petrograd Cartridge Factory. They accordingly did provide small working-class components for militias and Red Guard units. The two districts housed a number of military barracks, especially Imperial Guard regiments. The Rozhdestvenskii district included two famous buildings that in 1917 housed the Petrograd Soviet: the Tauride Palace and the Smolny Institute.

South of the Liteinyi and Spasskii districts, between the Fontanka and Obvodnyi canals, lay the Moscow district. It also was of very mixed character. Its first subdistrict, abutting Nevskii Prospect and the Fontanka, was still a fairly fashionable area, whereas its fourth subdistrict joined the southwest industrial districts and contained a number of factories, though it was still not heavily industrial. Generally it had more of a middle-class character than the others we have discussed so far. South of the Rozhdestvenskii and Moscow districts lay the large and sprawling Nevskii district (sometimes, especially before 1917, called the Aleksandrovskii or Aleksandro-Nevskii). Its northern boundary was the Nevskii Prospect, and hence the upper part of the district had a better reputation than the more industrial and even semirural areas across the Obvodnyi Canal. The Nevskii, Moscow, Rozhdestvenskii, and Liteinyi districts made up the First City District.

The Obvodnyi Canal represented something of a boundary south of which Petrograd became more industrial and working-class. This area was mostly of fairly recent settlement, having grown up with the industrial surge of the late nineteenth century. A number of factories were strung along the Neva River, the most important of which was the Nevskii Shipbuilding and Mechanical Factory, the largest in the Nevskii district. Further south, upstream, was the giant Obukhov Steel Factory, with some 12,000 workers, which dominated the ill-defined and semirural area that in 1917 came to be called by the same name as the factory and had its own district soviet. Moving inland across sparsely populated areas, we find significant factories appearing again in the western part of the Nevskii district. Most of these lay near Zabalkanskii Prospect and its extension, the Moscow Highway, the main road south out of the city. Here, at Zabalkanskii Prospect, the industrial parts of the Moscow and Nevskii districts abutted two major industrial districts, the Narva and, south of it, the Peterhof. In the latter district lay the Putilov works, the largest factory complex in Russia, with numerous metalworking shops and a shipbuilding shop. The Narva and Peterhof districts, stretching south from the Fontanka Canal along the Gulf of Finland, were heavily industrial and working class, especially the southern parts. Peterhof as a separate district was just emerging, and sometimes the entire district was called the Peterhof-Narva or simply the Narva district (the Bolshevik Party organization continued to combine both areas under the term "Narva district committee"). Sometimes parts of this area were referred to as the "Moscow Gate" district and other parts as the "Moscovo-Narva." Boundaries in this area were in general ill-defined, especially in popular usage. This southwestern part of the city—the Peterhof, Narva, and western sections of the Moscow and Nevskii districts—housed one of the two main concentrations of industrial workers in Petrograd. A key problem in the creation of any large-scale worker movement was how to link these workers with those of the other main worker districts north of the city center, on the right bank of the Neva.

On the north side (right bank) of the Neva River, the two island districts of Vasil'evskii and Petrogradskii were mixed in population. The former is an island formed by the branching of the Neva into the Small and Large Neva rivers. Intended by Peter the Great to be a major focal point of his city, it was the site of many important public and business institutions, including the University, the Stock Exchange, the Academy of Sciences, and the Academy of Arts. As a result the area near the Neva and along Bolshoi Prospect, especially near the island's eastern tip, was quite fashionable. As one moved north and west inland the character changed, becoming first more middle and lower-middle class along Srednyi Prospect, and then distinctly lower class along Malyi Prospect and in the west near the harbor area. Baedeker's 1914 guide to Russia states that "the inner parts of the Vasili Ostrov [Vasil'evskii Island] offer no attractions to the stranger."[4] If not for the tourist, the island is interesting for the social historian because of the great diversity of population it contained—aristocrats, merchants large and small, craftsmen, a large settlement of foreigners, university and other students, and large numbers of workers. The social differentiations and mix are still remarkably visible in its buildings to the person who walks the island today. Most of the industrial workers came from the large factories, especially the Pipe Factory, with 20,000 workers, near the harbor area. Workers of this district played a significant role in 1917. To the east lay the Petrogradskii district, composed of Petrograd Island itself and a number of small islands. Its dominant structure is the Peter-Paul Fortress, facing the Winter Palace from across the Neva. The district encompassed a wide social scale, from fashionable sections of villas and dachas (the latter mostly on the northern islands), through sizable areas of middle-class residences, to a number of important factories, some quite large, located especially northeast along the Large Nevka River, which separated the district from the neighboring Vyborg district.

The Vyborg district is dismissed as "unattractive" by Baedeker with only a few lines in small print.[5] The reason for this unattractiveness, however, makes it very important for us—its heavy industrial concentration. Its factories fill the pages that follow: Baranovskii, Old and New Lessner, Old and New Parviainen, Erikson, Metallurgical, and others. It was the most heavily working-class of all the districts of Petrograd, and the most radical. Here began the initial strikes and demonstrations leading to the February Revolution, here alone the Bolsheviks controlled the district soviet from the beginning, and here large and active Red Guard detachments were formed. The phrase "the Vyborg workers" carried with it a particular ring, heartening or disheartening according to the outlook of the hearer. Its workers tended to be higher skilled than those of other districts, to have a greater sense of class identity, and to play a more central role in many of the activities of 1917, from demonstrations to Bolshevization. North and east of Vyborg, and often lumped together with it, were several ill-defined and semirural districts, each with a few large factories to provide the nucleus for organization and armed workers' bands: Okhta and Porokhovskii (east of the Neva just before it bends to run west to the sea), and Paliustrovskii, Lesnoi, and Novoderevenskii (running on around the northern outskirts of Vyborg). They, like a few nearby towns with large manufacturing establishments—Sestroretsk with its large arms factory, for example—play a small role in the Revolution, providing support to the main workers' districts and movements in Petrograd.

The city, then, was large and diverse, but with certain socially and economically well-defined areas whose location influenced behavior in times of unrest. Especially important was the overriding fact of a city center that was largely governmental and upper to middle class ringed by great industrial and working-class districts. In times of turmoil the workers from all directions gravitated to the center of the city, to march down Nevskii Prospect, the symbol of privileged Russia, and to hold demonstrations on the great squares along that and other major streets. This was more than symbolic, however, for the central core of the city also separated the northern and southern working-class districts, and only by invading it could the workers link up. The same phenomenon existed on a smaller scale on Vasil'evskii Island: the industrial workers could link up with workers from other districts only by passing through the governmental and fashionable part of the island.

The size and nature of the working class in Petrograd and in Russia as a whole have been extensively debated, but some generally accepted estimates exist that are adequate for our purposes. A. G. Rashin, in probably the most reliable study of the Russian working class to 1914, estimates 12,415,000 nonagricultural wage workers of all kinds in 1913. He includes domestic servants, handicraft workers, restaurant workers, and others who could not be considered "proletarian" but who certainly would be among the disaffected lower classes supporting revolutionary activity in 1917. His figures show about 7–8 million employed in reasonably large factories, mines, or other enterprises—and thus in a position to be mobilized for political and armed action. This figure includes 3,350,000 he identifies as factory and mine workers, 1,500,000 construction workers, and 1,400,000 transportation and communication workers.[6] It is these workers rather than the assorted urban poor, shop clerks, handicraft workers, and servants, that would have an impact on the Revolution and contribute to the Red Guard and other armed bands. This figure increased considerably by 1917, although exactly comparable figures are not available. L. S. Gaponenko has calculated that there were about 9.5 million industrial workers (including rail and water transport and construction workers), plus another million unskilled workers and day laborers, in 1917.[7] Thus there was a significant increase in the working class overall.

These workers were concentrated primarily in certain areas of European Russia. Petrograd and its environs formed perhaps the most compact industrial center, with about 417,000 industrial workers in 1917. The largest area was Moscow and the sprawling Central Industrial Region encompassing the surrounding provinces, especially to the northeast around Vladimir and Nizhnii Novgorod. This area numbered about 1,030,000 workers in 1917. A third major region was in the Ukraine, especially the industrial area stretching from Kharkov through the mining districts of the Donbas, with 893,000 workers. A fourth center was in the Urals, involving especially mining and metallurgy, with about 357,000 workers. A final region stretched along the middle and lower Volga (including the cities of Kazan, Saratov, and Tsaritsyn); it employed 128,000 in mixed industry, including a great deal of agricultural processing.[8] All of these areas increased their industrial work force during the war, although the largest increases came in the industries producing for defense and so especially affected the metalworking areas, including Petrograd and Kharkov (metalworking factories employed 13.6 percent of factory workers in 1913 but 25.3 percent in 1917). Petrograd had 242,600 factory workers in 1914 but 392,000 by January 1, 1917, an increase of 62 percent; moreover, there were another 24,200 in large factories just outside the capital (figures vary slightly by author, but all are in general agreement).[9] In Kharkov the population grew by 55.9 percent, most of which represented industrial increases, whereas for the Ukraine as a whole the industrial and mining work force grew 28 percent between 1914 and 1917. Consumer-related industries and regions strong in them, by contrast, declined or grew slowly.

The wartime growth of the work force increased the tendency toward heavy concentration of workers in a few large factories. In Petrograd, as an example, the average size of factories rose from 536 workers in 1913 to 974 in 1917, and the number of factories employing over 100 workers rose from 362 to 414 during the same period. In 1917, 71.4 percent of all Petrograd workers were in factories of over 1,000; 38 factories employing over 2,000 workers each accounted for about two-thirds of all workers. Some factories were enormous: figures for the Putilov Factory in 1917 range from 26,000 to over 30,000 workers, about double its 1914 size; the Pipe Factory had about 20,000, about triple its 1914 size; the Obukhov Steel Factory had 11,000–12,000; and the Petrograd Cartridge Factory had about 12,000. Several factories were in the 4,000–8,000 range. Moreover, the great bulk of the Petrograd workers were in the highly skilled metalworking industry—in 1917, about 237,369 workers, 60.4 percent of the total.[10] Put differently, the metalworkers, a skilled, organized, and traditionally radical work force, grouped in large factories, increased about 136 percent in Petrograd between 1914 and 1917.

The size and composition of the Petrograd working class deserve special attention because of the role it played in the Revolution and our story. Its size was about the same at the time of the February and October revolutions, but this masked two significant shifts in 1917. First there was an increase of 10–12 percent by midsummer, the result primarily of the reduction of the work day to 8 hours combined with a need to maintain defense-related production. Then there was a decline that brought the figures at about the time of the October Revolution back to what they had been in January. This decline had its causes in the growing shortage of materials and the labor disputes that increased so sharply in the late summer and fall, both of which forced either partial or complete shutdowns of factories.[11] Obviously, a 10–12 percent shrinkage in jobs had an impact on worker attitudes and politics in the fall.

Not only the size and concentration, but also the social composition of this work force changed between 1914 and 1917, a result of the draft of workers for the army combined with the growth of industry. In Petrograd, for example, some 40,000 workers were mobilized between 1914 and 1916—about 17 percent of the prewar industrial work force. With the loss of these workers and the addition of enough to total the 392,000 in the city by January 1, 1917, we can see that almost half the industrial workers of the capital were new. Where did they come from? The general categories are obvious: women, children coming of working age, peasants from the countryside, and refugees from the war zones. I. P. Lieberov argues that most were peasants—50–75 percent of them. Many were women and youths under age 18, whose percentage in the work force increased enormously by the beginning of 1917, women making up 33.3 percent and under-18 males a little over 8 percent (adult males were only 58.5 percent). Unfortunately, we cannot distinguish what proportion of the women and youths were previous residents of Petrograd and what were a part of the new peasant influx. Some 10–13 percent of the work force consisted of 40,000–50,000 Polish and Baltic workers, usually evacuated along with their factories. There were also what Lieberov calls "bourgeois elements": shopkeepers, merchants' sons, intelligentsia, prosperous peasants, etc. He estimates them at 25,000–30,000, or 7 percent. A last and relatively small group were soldiers assigned to work in Petrograd factories—3,695 on January 1, 1917, some of whom were former workers.[12] Thus, the working force had a major component of new persons; or, put differently, only about half the workers had been in the factories before the war. Much the same picture seems to hold for the country as a whole, although it varies in detail from place to place. Generally, women and youths were more important in the work force outside Petrograd, especially in Moscow and the textile industries of the Central Industrial Region.[13]

What impact did this changing composition have on the attitudes and behavior of the working class? It meant that a significant number of workers had only a short tradition of industrial labor and discipline. Though this picture is contrary to the one some Soviet historians like to portray of a hardened and experienced proletariat, it does not necessarily make the workers less revolutionary. Most of the new ones were drawn from the same sources that had previously provided recruits for the factories, and in any case the displaced peasants and women (often with husbands in the army) brought with them traditional discontents heightened by the new problems of urban and industrial adjustment. The role of displaced peasants in urban unrest has been extensively, though inconclusively, treated in historical studies of the development of Russian industry and urbanization, and we will look at this question as it affected the Red Guard in Chapter 8.

The poverty, job insecurity, and terrible working and living conditions of the worker in Russia are so well known that it is not necessary to chronicle them here, with statistics that themselves are inadequate in drawing the dismal picture. We will, however, examine the extent to which the economic situation worsened during the war years, and how that might have influenced behavior in 1917. It has been traditional to emphasize the rapid inflation of the war years as a factor worsening conditions. In fact, the situation varied a great deal by industry and area, and the inflation was not so sharp as is usually assumed: real wages dropped only about 9 percent overall, and in defense factories actually increased slightly.[14] However, there were two factors at work that hid this and shaped attitudes and actions. First, workers believed that their standard of living and real wages had fallen more than they had. A police report of October 1916 showed that Petrograd workers felt their wages had only doubled while prices had tripled, and only one in 50 of those questioned felt satisfied with his standard of living. A January 1917 Moscow report on attitudes of carpenters, mechanics, and manual laborers showed that they felt prices had increased twice as much as wages.[15] Whatever was happening, then, workers *believed* that their economic condition had worsened appreciably, and this is what shaped their actions. Second, food and other consumer goods became increasingly scarce and increased the sense of deprivation and discontent. Workers and their families found that they had to wait long hours in food lines after working 11–13 hours. These problems sometimes provoked strikes or work stoppages, and provided a source of complaints and an opportunity for agitation, spreading of rumors, and clashes with the police. Moreover, fear that the already short food supply would diminish further raised the specter of real starvation. The problem of supplies—both foodstuffs and raw materials to keep the factories going—was a major concern both before and during 1917, and was a fundamental cause of unease and unrest. Indeed, in the winter of 1916–17 a number of factories closed for lack of supplies. Another figure dramatizes the problem: importation of bread products to Petrograd fell in 1917 to 44 percent of its 1914 figure, and this against an increase in consumers.[16]

Housing conditions, always difficult and often wretched, deteriorated during the war as a result of the influx of additional workers and the lack of maintenance or new construction. The city numbered about 2.5 million in 1917, an increase of about 200,000 since 1914, mostly workers and refugees. On February 26, 1917, 100,700 refugees from Poland, the Baltic, and other front areas were registered in Petrograd; as we have seen, 40,000–50,000 were Polish and Baltic factory workers.[17] Not surprisingly, it was the working-class districts that had to absorb most of this population. The crowding was terrible: there were instances of two or three families sharing a room, and many people shared beds or slept on a bench or on the floor in a corner. Paving, electricity, and running water still had not extended from the city center to some working-class districts, and the maintenance problem is graphically illustrated by a March 1916 action of the Petrograd city authorities exempting landlords from mandatory upkeep of their properties except where the roof was collapsing.[18]

Economic distinctions among the workers have often been cited—or asserted—as a factor in political behavior before and during 1917. Salaries did vary by skill and profession: Z. V. Stepanov states that average work pay ranged from 60 to 140–50 rubles a month at the beginning of 1917, but that the number of workers in the higher pay scales was quite small, from 1–2 percent to 4–5 percent, depending on the branch of industry. The largest numbers of highly paid workers were in metalworking and printing factories. Although Stepanov feels the need—following prerevolutionary Russian Marxist literature—to talk about a "workers' aristocracy" that provided an avenue for "bourgeois ideology and politics among the proletarian class," he acknowledges that this very small group had no significant impact.[19] Indeed, the metalworking factories Stepanov cites as having a relatively large proportion (4–5 percent) of highly paid workers include both the Obukhov Factory, which remained Menshevik-SR and politically moderate until October 1917, and the Parviainen Factory, which was a leader in radicalism and Bolshevik influence. Overall one finds little evidence that internal economic distinctions played any significant role in worker politics in 1917, and there is no evidence of it as a factor in determining Red Guard or workers' militia membership. Also, workers showed remarkable unity across pay lines: the early demands for wage increases usually stressed improving the pay of the lowest, unskilled categories vis-à-vis the higher, skilled categories.

A somewhat similar conclusion, at least for political implications, can be drawn from literacy rates. In 1918, 88.9 percent of male workers and 64.9 percent of female workers in Petrograd were literate. For the country, the figures were 79.2 percent and 44.2 percent, respectively. The metalworkers and printers, the great majority of Petrograd workers, had an even higher literacy rate. The significant factor, however, was not literacy versus illiteracy, but rather the level of literacy. Though most male workers were literate (and males made up the Red Guard), the level was uniformly low. A study of 724 metalworkers at the Putilov Factory in 1918 showed that whereas only 5.5 percent were completely illiterate, a mere 9.6 percent had finished the three-year rural or four-year city schools. Moreover, only two men in the sample had more than four years of education.[20] These figures suggest that internal divisions based on educational level were insignificant. They do emphasize, though, the importance of those "simple slogans" I. M. Liapin cites as uniting diverse workers under Bolshevik leadership in the Red Guard.[21] Indeed, the significant divisions were not within the industrial working class—although one must recognize that within so large a group various levels of cultural development, political sophistication, and personal viewpoints existed—but between a relatively homogeneous working class and the rest of society, "privileged Russia." Differing jobs, levels of income, and amounts of education may help to explain who emerged as leaders within the industrial working class, and even the varying responses of the workers to issues, but these differences paled before the gap between workers and "the bourgeoisie." There was a deep-seated feeling of injustice and hardship, of being mistreated and oppressed, that transcended internal distinctions. Workers, whether skilled or unskilled, found themselves in a condition of general poverty and powerlessness in relation to the other urban classes.

Government policies for dealing with worker discontents had never been very enlightened and were even less so during the war. The main approach was repression. To the traditional arrests, banishments, and fines were added in 1916 the threat of being sent to the front in disciplinary battalions. Moreover, wartime laws provided punishment for actions hindering war production, including worker activities or protests that closed factories or slowed production. Many factories were under the direct supervision of military authorities, and Petrograd was in the area under martial law. In September 1916, General Frolov in Petrograd ordered that workers engaged in work stoppages in factories producing for defense be tried by court-martial. This order was apparently not enforced, but it does show the government attitude and the kind of threat that hung over workers. In addition, workers in defense-related factories who had been given draft deferments once it became obvious that the war would be a long one were threatened with the loss of their deferments for political or economic protests. The deputy head of the Petrograd police claimed in December 1915 that fear of being sent to the front had been a major factor in preventing a general strike and remained a major deterrent to labor unrest.[22] It did not, of course, deter the growth of resentment against "privileged society," nor did it stop worker agitation: for example, about 2,000 workers were mobilized into the front army after a strike at the Putilov Factory in February 1916.

To any discussion of causes of worker unrest one must of course add general war-weariness, which spread over all the belligerent countries in 1917, but seems to have come especially early and been especially strong in Russia. Enthusiasm for the war had evaporated quickly among almost all social strata as Russia absorbed tremendous casualties. Expressions of this ranged from Paul Miliukov's celebrated "stupidity or treason" attack on the government in the Duma session of November 1, 1916, to the alarming army desertion rates of 1916. For the workers the war brought conscription, the maiming or death of friends and relatives, harsher work discipline under the threat of military punishment, a scarcity of goods, a decline in purchasing power, and deteriorating living conditions. The strike figures show their response in stark relief. On the eve of the war there had been a sharp increase in strikes and disorders, but the outbreak of fighting brought a dramatic end to this. The figures soon turned upward again, however, with 1,688,000 man-days lost in 1915, and 4,749,000 lost in 1916.[23] The strikes in Petrograd in late 1916 were especially severe, and there were even instances of soldiers in reserve regiments encouraging the workers.

Any discussion of the background to the events of the Revolution of 1917 must include an assessment of the workers' experiences and remembrances of the Revolution of 1905, especially in regard to armed bands. In 1905–6 a large number of fighting detachments (mostly commonly called *druzhiny*) were formed in Russia: L. T. Senchakova lists 312 cities, towns, villages, railroad stations, and other places where such units are known to have existed.[24] Often they were mainly defensive, protecting workers' meetings, demonstrations, or strikes, and expelling police agents, but sometimes they took the offensive, attacking police, government officials, employers, and landowners, and staging bank raids. They frequently were a means for workers to press their demands on factory management or to defend gains already made. Sometimes their functions included protecting the persons and property of the citizenry in general. Most of the 1905 *druzhiny* saw little fighting, but there were important exceptions, notably the famous Moscow uprising of December 1905 and actions in places such as Rostov-on-the-Don, Kharkov, Odessa, and the Urals region. In St. Petersburg, *druzhiny* played a less conspicuous role in 1905–6, but they did exist.[25]

The importance of the *druzhiny* of 1905–6 for us, however, rests not so much with their actions as with the memory they left behind. Much as the creation of the soviets of 1905 helped to prepare the way for their immediate establishment in 1917, so the rapid formation of workers' armed bands in 1917 is indebted to their existence in 1905. Not only top party leaders but also lesser figures remembered and discussed the events of 1905. Many of the Bolshevik factory and district leaders in 1917 had been active in 1905, often in fighting *druzhiny*,[26] and no doubt the same was true in other parties. A number of 1917 participants and early writers on the topic later claimed that the 1905 *druzhina* activities were a source of inspiration in 1917, and newspaper articles and worker resolutions in 1917 suggest they were a vivid memory.[27] The very term "Red Guard" came from 1905 and the example of the Finnish Red Guard led by Captain Johan Kock. The experience of 1905, however, seems to have been more important as an inspiration and a source of some leaders than as a source of veteran fighters in 1917. Age worked against the latter: a *druzhinik* of 19 in 1905 would by 1917 be 31, and the great majority of guardsmen in 1917 were 30 or under. Marriage, family responsibilities, and other factors also reduced the number of "fighters from 1905" in the 1917 armed detachments. A sample cited by G. A. Tsypkin supports these conclusions: of 2,000 former Moscow Red Guards, only 72, or 3.6 percent, had participated in fighting *druzhiny* in 1905.[28] There are indications, however, that those active both in 1905 and in 1917 played a disproportionate role as organizers and leaders in the latter year.[29] Finally, not the least important feature of the *druzhiny* of 1905 was in providing an object lesson in failure, confirming in many workers the feeling that their own strong armed units were essential to the final triumph of the Revolution and that the soldiers ultimately were not reliable, since they had been used to suppress worker movements in 1905.

For all the strains that existed as 1917 began in Russia, there was little expectation of imminent revolution. Talk of the need for a change, perhaps even a palace coup, was widespread, but it was generally believed that there would not be any revolution until after the war. Lenin's statement to a group of Swiss workers in January 1917 that "we of the older generation may not live to see the decisive battles of the coming revolution"[30] was only the most famous expression of a widely held sentiment. When the events of late February, which at first appeared to be only another instance of a familiar type of urban disorder, blossomed into full-scale revolution, everyone was caught by surprise. That the revolution came so directly from spontaneous and uncoordinated events left a permanent stamp on its character and subsequent development: popular self-assertion became its key feature, and the difficulty of controlling and directing that newfound self-assertion one of its main problems.

It is not our purpose to trace in detail the beginning of the February Revolution; rather, I want to present a brief sketch in order to aid the reader who may not be familiar with it and to set upon the stage some people, groups, and events that are important in understanding what follows about the workers' militias and the Red Guard.[31] January and February 1917 witnessed an upswing in strike activity, longer and more surly lines at stores (especially bread shops), and growing apprehension about the supply situation. These came together in late February to provide the impetus for the disorders and demonstrations that led to the Revolution. On Women's Day, February 23, a socialist "holiday," rallies and fiery speeches at some factories met with a ready response from women workers, who were angry at having to wait in long bread lines after up to 12 and 13 hours of labor with no assurance of getting any bread. These women, mostly textile workers, demanded that metalworkers in nearby factories support their demonstrations. This snowballed from factory to factory in the Vyborg and Petrogradskii districts. Meanwhile, across town, over 20,000 workers locked out of the Putilov Factory the day before in a labor dispute were on the streets demonstrating and rioting. All told, around 100,000 workers were out of the factories on the 23d. The more militant, chanting the demand for bread, tried to cross the river and demonstrate in the city center, but this led to sharp clashes with police. There also was considerable vandalism and breaking into food shops that day.

The socialist political parties had little to do with the events of February 23. They had decided to downplay Women's Day. It was pressure from below that led to the demonstrations, with local party members in the factories joining in after it became obvious that the workers were ready for action with or without them. On the evening of the 23d, however, the local party leaders gathered in various places and generally agreed to support and encourage a broad strike movement focusing on demands for bread and peace. They were thus endorsing what the workers were already doing. The Bolshevik Vyborg district committee was especially supportive, going further than either the Party's Petersburg Committee or its Russian Bureau of the Central Committee.* Government authorities, though they took some security measures, did not expect the riots of February 23 to continue.

On the morning of the 24th, the Vyborg factories were the scene of innumerable meetings and speeches. Both veteran party members and previously nonpolitical people who emerged as spur-of-the-moment leaders urged strikes and demonstrations. Workers from one factory often converged on another to urge or demand that its workers come out also, a process that continued through the February days and was also used by insurgent soldiers against still uncommitted units on February 27. Two-thirds of the Vyborg work-

---

* The Bolsheviks retained the usage "Petersburg Committee" for their all-city grouping when the capital was renamed Petrograd in 1914. They claimed that the name change was an expression of chauvinism. The Russian Bureau of the Central Committee was a Party organization composed of those members of the Central Committee who were in Russia, as opposed to those who were in exile abroad (Lenin and most of the top leadership).

ers struck on the 24th, and the movement spread to virtually all the other working-class districts until there were about 200,000 strikers, the largest number since the outbreak of the war. By noon, despite the efforts of the police to block them (especially on the bridges over the Neva), large groups of demonstrators had begun to reach Nevskii Prospect and other main thoroughfares of central Petrograd. The crowds noticed, and were emboldened by, the obvious reticence not only of the garrison soldiers but also of the much-feared Cossacks. The passivity of the latter, the lack of vigor with which they followed commands to break up crowds, their obvious confusion and even friendliness—all were signs of what was to come and indirectly assisted the growth of the demonstrations. By the end of the 24th it was obvious to the authorities that a crisis of major proportions existed, but just how it would develop remained unclear. Neither the authorities nor the revolutionary parties had much of a grasp of what was happening, and the latter were not providing significant leadership or direction, despite the participation of many party members in the turmoil.

When the workers assembled at their factories on Saturday the 25th the mood was much more aggressive. Many had prepared for battle with the police by putting on thick clothes and padding and by arming themselves with knives, bolts, pieces of metal, and other crude weapons. At the Liteinyi Bridge, Vyborg workers again met police blocking them. This time, however, when mounted police led by Colonel Shalfeev attacked, the workers cut Shalfeev off, pulled him from his horse, and killed him. This marked the beginning of systematic attacks on police outposts and stations in the Vyborg district, and on policemen throughout the city. Moreover, on this day the worker ranks were swelled by students and middle class elements. Soldiers and Cossacks increasingly showed reluctance to take action, and often even assisted demonstrators directly or indirectly. The most spectacular event occurred at Znamenskii Square on Nevskii Prospect, where Cossacks not only did not assist police in breaking up the demonstration but attacked the police, killing Police Inspector Krylov, the commander. In other instances, however, troops did obey orders, even firing into the crowds. Still, many in the crowds—and some police agents reporting on them—sensed revolution. The balance rested with the troops: could the government maintain control of this means of coercion? This question, already posed in the streets, was now forced by receipt of a telegram from Nicholas II at the front commanding that the disorders be stopped immediately. General S. S. Khabalov, the military commander of Petrograd, issued a proclamation forbidding street gatherings and warning that the use of arms by troops was now authorized. The government began preparations to control the streets the next day with armed force. This would test the discipline of the troops and, with that, decide the outcome of the "crisis."

February 26 dawned clear and crisp upon a city turned into an armed camp. The fresh light snow that had fallen during the night softened but did not fundamentally alter the impression created by the sight of large numbers of soldiers positioned to control the main streets of the city center. With the factories closed—it was Sunday—the workers were deprived of their normal focus of organization and took longer to get formed into demonstrations. The bridges from the Vyborg and Petrogradskii districts into the city center were raised, but the workers easily crossed the Neva on the thick ice. Once across, however, they had a nasty shock: the troops fired on them. Some dozens were killed in several incidents, and many more were wounded. Many of the local party leaders, such as those of the Bolshevik Vyborg district committee, feared this signaled the end of the movement. What effect the shooting might have had on the workers and their strikes and demonstrations can never be known, however, for by the next morning the situation had changed dramatically because of the impact the shooting had on the morale and discipline of the troops.

February 27 proved to be the critical day. Workers and others resumed mass demonstrations and attacks on police and other symbols of authority, but the context was different. From the beginning of the day the government was deprived of the ability to make large-scale use of troops because the soldiers mutinied. This began about 8 A.M., when the training detachment of the Volynskii Guard Regiment, after a feverish night of discussing the shooting in which they had been involved the previous day, rebelled, shot their commander, and rushed to other units to urge their support. Gradually throughout the day other units joined them, often after being "invaded" by insurgents. Most soldiers wandered about aimlessly, but some joined workers in attacks on centers of authority. Units that had not rebelled mostly were kept in their barracks out of fear that they might. By mid-afternoon the streets were in the hands of disorderly mobs that lacked clear direction or purpose beyond attacks on the police, prisons, and other symbols of tsarist repression. There was a great deal of looting and other violent activity, not just on the part of the criminals set free when the prisons were stormed but also on the part of the mob, composed as it was of impoverished, alienated, armed people—soldiers or civilians—who found themselves in command of a city and without any significant restraints on their actions.

The military and civilian authorities showed great ineptitude in responding to the situation and failed to take any serious and coordinated countermeasures using the police and troops still at their disposal. Those police still on the streets were withdrawn around noon. Most changed into civilian clothes and slipped away. A few barricaded themselves on rooftops or upper floors of buildings and fired on the crowds, but this did little except cause confusion. They were hunted down and dealt with summarily. The few disjointed efforts to use some of the troops still obeying orders were futile and only added to the confusion and the bloodshed. It seems fair to say that on the afternoon of the 27th Petrograd was the scene of innumerable skirmishes, demonstrations, attacks on buildings, and lootings, each largely unconnected with any other and led by ad hoc leaders who had little or no contact with other leaders. No one had even a halfway complete picture of what was going on throughout the city, or of the outcome of it all. This confusion and breakdown of public safety was one of the main reasons for the formation of volunteer armed militias in the Revolution.

Despite the fact that no one led or coordinated any significant part of the rebellion taking place in the streets, or even understood just what was happening, there were men willing—and some eager—to provide leadership as it became clearer that the old order might be crumbling. Thus there emerged on the evening of the 27th two centers of political authority for the Revolution: the Temporary Committee of the State Duma, and the Petrograd Soviet of Workers' Deputies (the phrase "and Soldiers" was inserted on March 1). The events up to the evening of the 27th represented a genuine mass uprising, with only local leaders in the factories and barracks giving any kind of direction even to a small part of it. Now Duma members and intelligentsia socialists began to try to provide comprehensive leadership and to channel the energy of a populace in revolt. In a sense what existed was a new version of the old gap between the small educated elites and the broad masses of the population, between consciousness and spontaneity. The problem was how to bridge it and bring the two together.

The Petrograd Soviet was formed in response not only to the obvious need for leadership on the 27th, but to repeated demands from the workers themselves dating back to the 24th and 25th.[32] As the strike movement developed after the 23d, factory militants apparently harked back to the Soviet of 1905, which had originated as a central strike committee. Already on the 24th and 25th some factories began to choose deputies and to pressure socialist leaders and Duma members to help them: the rank and file in the streets were far ahead of the socialist intelligentsia, as they would be frequently in 1917. By the 27th it became apparent that this was more than a massive strike, that a revolution was taking place and might succeed, and that organizing political power was a pressing need. In the early afternoon a group of socialists met in the Tauride Palace, the seat of the Duma, formed a Temporary Revolutionary Committee of the Soviet of Workers' Deputies, and issued an appeal to workers and soldiers to elect deputies for a Soviet meeting at 7:00 that evening. An assortment of intelligentsia radicals, workers, and soldiers finally gathered and began around 9:00 P.M. Three Duma socialists were elected officers: Nikolai Chkheidze, a Georgian Menshevik, became chairman, a post he held into September; and Mikhail Skobelev, a Menshevik, and Alexander Kerensky, a Trudovik,* were chosen vice-chairmen. An Executive Committee was elected, and it quickly came to dominate the unwieldy Soviet plenum, whose membership grew to 3,000 in late March. That domination wavered only on a few occasions, most notably when the Menshevik-SR coalition that controlled the Soviet lost power to the Bolsheviks in September and Trotsky replaced Chkheidze as chairman. The Executive Committee in turn grew eventually to 90 members and had much of its decision making preempted by its smaller Bureau, which also had the advantage of being composed only of the dominant faction. Both executive bodies were composed pri-

---

* The Trudoviks (Toilers), moderate agrarian socialists, were a parliamentary offshoot of the Socialist Revolutionaries (SRs), the main agrarian socialist party. As 1917 progressed Kerensky was usually called an SR.

marily of professional revolutionaries and intelligentsia socialists. In the first days of the Revolution the Executive Committee met constantly, in often chaotic conditions as demands and problems pressed the harried members. Soviet "policy" often was whatever some editorial writer in *Izvestiia*, the official Petrograd Soviet newspaper,* or Executive Committee member at some meeting personally felt and said. At first party lines were blurred and the leaders were mostly new or second-rank men, the main party leaders and theorists being in exile. Only with the return of the more important leaders from Siberian or foreign exile in late March and early April did party lines become firmer. It was in late March that the block of more moderate Menshevik-SR socialists led by Irakli Tsereteli took firm control of Soviet policies and gave them greater coherence.

On February 27, despite the mass confusion and lack of reliable information, the Executive Committee and the Soviet immediately began to try to cope with some of the most pressing issues, especially food supply and the organization of the mutinied soldiers (both to defend the city against an expected tsarist counterattack and to prevent them from looting and pillaging). This same meeting first raised the matter of a workers' militia. Nonetheless, the intelligentsia leaders quickly and firmly took a position that the Soviet, although performing some governmental functions in the emergency, was not a government. The Menshevik and Marxist view that this was the liberal, bourgeois stage of the revolution predominated, assisted, it must be said, by both a realistic assessment of their own weaknesses and a clear aversion to exercising direct governmental power and responsibility in the chaotic situation. The Soviet leaders consequently supported the creation of a new government composed primarily of Duma liberals. In the long run this created an unworkable duality, with the Provisional Government having responsibility but little power and the Petrograd Soviet exercising real authority but declining formal responsibility. In the short run, however, as Hasegawa has persuasively argued, the new government of "respectable" Duma leaders helped the Revolution succeed, since it stayed the hand of the generals, who probably would have used disciplined front-line troops to crush by force a government of little-known radicals.[33]

---

* Many newspapers in 1917 were called *Izvestiia*, for it was the most common title used for newspapers of local soviets. Unless otherwise qualified, *Izvestiia* throughout this book refers to the Petrograd newspaper.

What was this government of Duma leaders? The Duma, created as the lower house of a two-house legislature following the Revolution of 1905, was far from representative of Russian society. Still, it had been the most important center of legal political activity and, from 1915, had been increasingly critical of the government. Its call for a cabinet of ministers responsible to the Duma had been unsuccessful but had led to extensive discussions of who might compose such a government. Thus the Duma leaders were not totally unprepared to assume political responsibility, nor did they lack some aura of being spokesmen for popular aspirations. Nonetheless, they were not revolutionaries (with a few exceptions) and were reluctant to respond to the crisis until it was clear that it was completely out of the control of the government. Indeed, the Duma members found themselves in a quandary during the last week of February. They could not ignore what was going on around them, yet they had no way to do anything about it. Then, on the evening of the 26th, Nicholas prorogued the Duma. When the deputies learned this on the morning of the 27th, they were both confused and angered. While they discussed what to do, the mutiny of the troops spread around them. Finally, about mid-afternoon, they met "privately" and unofficially. After a long debate, around 5:00 P.M. they agreed to form a "Temporary Committee of the State Duma" (Duma Committee hereafter). Their concern was to try to control, channel, and limit the revolution, which was already pouring into the Tauride Palace as demonstrating workers, soldiers, and others seeking some sort of broader leadership made their way there. By late afternoon the building and surrounding area were filled with thousands of people of all kinds in search of some authority and guidance. Army units began to arrive, in part or in whole. Mikhail Rodzianko, the Duma Committee chairman, the Kadet leader Miliukov, Chkheidze, Kerensky, and others found themselves being called out of the chamber to address the crowds and to try to answer questions about what was happening. Finally, knowing that the Soviet was meeting, the Duma Committee decided late in the evening to take responsibility for governance and restoring order in Petrograd. Early on the 28th the Duma Committee and its own committees and commissions began to try to cope with the immediate problems of the soldiers and the food supply, and with the larger question of forming a new government.

The Duma Committee moved into its position of authority reluctantly, whereas the Petrograd Soviet responded more eagerly but with a great deal of uncertainty about just what its role might be. The leaders of the two groups soon began negotiations about the formation of a government. Shortly after midnight on the morning of March 2, representatives of the two bodies began serious bargaining, which proved easier than either had expected. The two main issues were the composition of the government and its initial statement of policy. The second issue was quickly resolved. The Soviet delegation presented a list of minimum demands it had prepared, mostly guarantees of civil liberties. The Duma leaders readily agreed, and these became the basis for the first announcement of "policy" by the new government. The composition of the government was only a little more difficult because the Soviet leaders conceded that the ministers should come from the liberal Duma elements. As noted earlier, they considered this the "liberal, bourgeois" stage of the revolution and felt that they could not join the government. Therefore, they rejected the Duma Committee proposal to include Kerensky and Chkheidze in the government. Finally agreement was reached on a government headed by Prince Georgii Lvov, a liberal humanitarian but not a Duma member. The rest of the membership was drawn mostly from the liberal and moderate Duma leaders. Kerensky, however, persuaded the Soviet to authorize him to join the government. He thus became the only socialist (albeit a very moderate one) and Soviet member in the government.

Most of the members of the new Provisional Government, announced on March 2, felt that the main work of the revolution had been accomplished by the overthrow of Nicholas II and his government and looked forward to consolidating the gains already made. They took a very restrictive view of the duties and authority of the Provisional Government: it was a transitory regime whose duty was to cope with pressing questions and hold the country together until a Constituent Assembly could form a definitive government. Such a legalistic view was morally commendable, but not entirely practical. Even more of a problem for the creation of any stable government, however, was the attitude of the Petrograd Soviet. Rejecting formal responsibility, the Soviet nonetheless claimed the right to veto government actions and to demand that certain policies be followed. Even though the Soviet helped to form the Provisional Government, it declined to join and gave it only qualified support. This conditional support weakened the Provisional Government, which faced extreme difficulties because of the Soviet's influence over the soldiers, workers, and peasants throughout Russia and especially in the capital. The real locus of power and authority, to the extent that one existed after February, was the Soviet. This was the origin of the famous *dvoevlastie*, the "dual authority" of a formal government with responsibility but little real power and an unofficial body with power but little official responsibility. This institutional cleavage spread throughout the country. It was reinforced by an intellectual cleavage between socialists and nonsocialists, by a we–they frame of mind that was strong among the Soviet leaders, who could not shake their traditional class-struggle orientation and their mistrust of the bourgeoisie. Moreover, this attitude was even stronger among the industrial workers, with their deep distrust of "privileged society" and growing sense of class distinctiveness. Indeed, in many ways the *dvoevlastie* was only an institutionalized expression of this attitude, and the workers' militia and Red Guards an even more militant expression of it.

2

Spontaneity and Leadership:
February

"Sometimes one met civilian armed detachments, workers
and students, with or without soldiers. These were the newly
created militia, or, rather, self-appointed volunteers; to them
Petersburg was very much indebted for the rapid establishment of order and safety."
                                    —N. N. Sukhanov

The creation of armed bands, of "militia," was both a spontaneous
popular reaction to the events of the last week of February 1917
and the result of a conscious effort on the part of the leaders
thrown up by the Revolution. At first, during the days of strikes
and demonstrations from February 23 to February 26, neither the
crowd nor its would-be leaders seem to have made much effort to
form armed groups. E. N. Burdzhalov, in his detailed account of
the February Revolution, is emphatic that the workers who went on
strike, formed the mass demonstrations, and came into conflict
with police and troops "advanced into the revolutionary struggle
without arms and without having organized fighting detachments
of the kind organized by Moscow workers in the December 1905
fight." This unarmed revolution could triumph only by winning
over units of the garrison.[1] Another Soviet historian cites police records as showing 11 instances of use of arms by demonstrators on
February 25, seven involving revolvers, three involving bombs, and
one a grenade.[2] His claim that these isolated cases represent the
transition to armed insurrection seems a gross exaggeration, however. Armed confrontations with police and soldiers took place accidentally and, at first, were defensive. Gradually aggressive attacks
upon the police became more frequent, with workers falling upon

isolated policemen, beating them up and taking their arms. By late on the 25th policemen were seen only in groups. Though workers avidly seized arms where possible and in a few places even replaced the police on the streets (as apparently happened by the 26th in the area around the Putilov Factory in the Peterhof district),[3] these were transitory and ad hoc groupings. Even on the 26th, when the government took more vigorous measures against the demonstrators and used troops and police to fire on the crowds, the use of arms by the workers was still only sporadic.

The leaders of the revolutionary parties who were in Petrograd apparently did not consider arming the workers a pressing matter and did not make much of any effort in this direction; indeed, they often discouraged it. Memoirs of the more important figures suggest not only some pessimism about the outcome of the disorders and a slowness in reacting, but also small concern with this specific matter. When the Bolshevik Party organizations—the Russian Bureau of the Central Committee, the Petersburg Committee, and the Vyborg district committee—undertook to assess events on the 25th, their various suggestions about how to direct and broaden the revolution did not include forming armed workers' groups. After the clashes of the 26th, however, and the arrest of most of the Petersburg Committee, this issue intruded itself on their meetings and assessments. A gathering of Bolsheviks and Mezhduraiontsy* on Vasil'evskii Island February 26 discussed collecting arms for forming fighting *druzhiny*. The same day the Russian Bureau of the Central Committee and some other local Bolsheviks met in the Vyborg district to discuss what needed to be done. Some present suggested that they get arms, organize fighting *druzhiny*, and with their help overpower the defenders of the autocracy. The majority, however, overruled this as impractical, arguing that the revolution could triumph only through winning over parts of the army garrison.[4] The Bolshevik Party, then, as late as the evening of the 26th did not undertake to organize armed workers' detachments, although it did talk about possibly erecting street barricades and calling a Soviet of Workers' Deputies of the 1905 type. Even on the morning of the 27th, when troops of the garrison were mutinying,

---

* The *Mezhduraionnyi komitet* (Interdistrict Committee) was an organization of Social Democrats in Petrograd who had refused to join either the Bolshevik or the Menshevik factions. It merged with the Bolsheviks in July 1917.

the Party hesitated; A. G. Shliapnikov, probably the leading Bolshevik at liberty in Petrograd, responded to a demand for arms by Vyborg-district workers with a reaffirmation of the position that the success of the revolution lay not in forming fighting *druzhiny* of workers but in winning over the soldiers.[5] Though Shliapnikov quite possibly was correct, it is clear that the lower-level worker leaders and the workers themselves were far more eager to take up arms and organize themselves for their use than were the party leaders.

The shift toward extensive use of arms by workers, students, and others came on February 27, after the first mutinies brought troops into the streets and made arms widely available. There still does not seem to have been much in the way of organized armed bands; rather, that day witnessed workers, soldiers, and others spontaneously combining to achieve a specific objective, such as taking a police station, and then dissolving. M. Rafes saw and described such a situation at the Duma building, where a soldier and former student at Petrograd University, Fedor Linde, climbed onto a fence, called for soldiers and for civilian volunteers, and proceeded to organize detachments to seize strategic points. The detachments chose their own commanders from among former soldiers, noncommissioned officers, and others with experience at the front. All this was completely improvised, without direction from any important political center or figure.[6] This type of crowd initiative appears to have been at the heart of all the armed bands formed on the 27th, and most descriptions of them fit this one by Sukhanov, who on the afternoon of the 27th "met automobiles and trucks in which stood and sat soldiers, workers, students, upper-class girls with and without medical emblems. God knows from where, to where, and for what reason they went. Rifles were present in large numbers." However, he notes, although arms were distributed widely and armed workers were widespread, there was no organized strength.[7] Indeed, what occurred that day were the first rudimentary efforts at short-term organization, but aimed more at rounding up the remaining police, who had almost completely disappeared from the streets since midday on the 27th, than in establishing a permanent armed body or an order-keeping force to replace them.

The arms available to these bands varied widely. Some had a number of rifles (military and sporting), whereas others were armed with revolvers or even sabers. Often not all members had arms. Weapons were acquired from a variety of sources: individual soldiers, police, and plundered storehouses. A regiment's coming over to the revolution was often accompanied by the opening of its arms stores and the distribution of the contents among the crowd, civilians as well as soldiers. One diarist records that in the Petrogradskii district on the evening of the 27th a truck with workers and soldiers in it pulled up to a knot of workers and began to distribute arms,[8] probably taken from some barracks or military store. It is worth noting, because it is important for the future, that an unrecorded but large number of arms fell into the hands of individuals, especially workers, on February 27 and 28. These were retained by them, only a few later being turned over to any kind of authority, governmental or revolutionary. The long-run implications of this were not then apparent; the immediate problem was arming and mobilizing for defense of the revolution.

Although most armed bands formed on February 27 were transitory and spontaneous, there were some efforts at forming permanent, better organized groups. Surprisingly enough, the earliest examples come from the outlying districts rather than the central city or main workers' districts. The reason seems to lie in the need to secure the revolution and maintain some degree of public safety in areas where troops in revolt played a minor role. An unusually good picture of revolutionary self-organization comes from the events in the Obukhov district on the southern edge of the city. The revolution there was "secured" late on the 27th with the aid of a truckload of soldiers and workers from the center of the city. Then an ad hoc "revolutionary committee" was set up and "armed workers' detachments" organized (in practice, this meant that at least one person in each detachment had to be armed). The detachments were sent out to secure public order and disarm any police they found. They were specifically warned, however, to avoid the Obukhov Factory guards, who apparently had not yet been disarmed or won over. The committee acted on its own, ignorant of any decisions taken by the Petrograd Soviet—or perhaps even of the Soviet's existence. Indeed, its decision to organize armed patrols preceded by several hours the Petrograd Soviet Executive Committee's decision to appeal to the workers to organize militias.[9]

The main push for organizing volunteer armed bands came on

the 28th, from two directions. On the one hand, spontaneous formation continued at the local level and forced recognition from the "higher ups." On the other, central political bodies began to pay attention to this matter and to play a role. As a result of these twin efforts, the armed bands emerged as a permanent force from February 28 on. Four central political bodies can be identified as operating by February 28 to try to give some direction to the armed bands springing up in the city: (1) the newly formed Petrograd Soviet; (2) the Petrograd City Duma; (3) the Committee for Military-Technical Assistance; and (4) the Temporary Committee of the State Duma. Of these, the Petrograd Soviet and the City Duma played the most important role in the long run, so we will look at them first. Later in this chapter we will turn back to the self-organizing efforts, and finally we will examine the interplay of the two.

The question of what to do about the armed bands, about public order, and about organizing a workers' militia thrust itself upon the Petrograd Soviet during its inaugural meeting, which opened around 9 P.M. on February 27. The meeting was chaotic, being frequently disrupted by excited soldiers who insisted on announcing the adherence of their units to the Revolution. At some point, probably about 10:30 or 11:00 P.M. but perhaps later, the Menshevik M. A. Brounshtein proposed to the Soviet that it send directives to each factory to form a militia consisting of 100 men for every 1,000 workers. This directive would be carried to each district of the city by the deputies when they returned home. He also proposed the appointment of commissars to each district "to restore order and to direct the struggle against anarchy and pogroms." After some discussion the proposal was accepted, apparently by general consent rather than by vote. The Soviet meeting did not do anything about implementing the decision, although just before the meeting adjourned about 4 A.M. on the 28th the deputies were reminded of the importance of agitational and organizational work in their own districts. Presumably this work included forming militias, and some deputies did in fact play a role in forming militia units on the 28th.[10]

The real task of implementing the militia resolution was left to the Executive Committee of the Petrograd Soviet, which opened its first meeting just after the Soviet adjourned, i.e. shortly after

4 A.M. on February 28. It worked out a directive to the districts that called on them to organize a militia on the basis of 100 militia-men for each 1,000 workers. Several places around the city were designated as gathering points where militiamen were to receive arms and instructions: the worker medical-fund offices (*bol'ni-chnye kassy*) of the Parviainen Factory in the Vyborg district and the Putilov Factory in the Peterhof-Narva district; the labor ex-changes in the Petrogradskii and Vasil'evskii Island districts; the workers' evening school in the Nevskii district; and two factory caf-eterias in the Moscow and Rozhdestvenskii districts. This list of places ringed the central part of the city formed by the Neva and the Fontanka Canal, and it included only districts with a significant industrial labor force. The units were to go to the gathering points around midday, after receiving this appeal. However, the issue of *Izvestiia* with the proclamation came out only that afternoon. At the same meeting A. G. Shliapnikov was empowered by the Execu-tive Committee to take responsibility for all questions connect-ed with the arming of the workers.[11] Since Shliapnikov had not favored arming the workers on the 26th, one can only wonder whether he now gave it high priority among the many demands on his time. Judging from his own memoirs he did not, nor did he pro-vide the central leadership implied in this charge.

The same meeting of the Soviet Executive Committee also "noted some candidates for commissars" to the districts, as Sukhanov put it.[12] Apparently some deputies of the Petrograd Soviet were sent to various places and assisted in the formation of local militias, either as special tasks or as part of the larger job of organizing against the expected tsarist counterrevolution. Shliapnikov states that some five or six commissars met after the Executive Committee meet-ing—that is, considerably after 4 A.M. on the 28th—to discuss their tasks, especially the problems of armed strength in the dis-tricts. The discussion, he notes, was of a purely theoretical nature.[13] He himself went from there to a meeting of Vyborg-district Bolshe-viks instead of taking up his duties as commissar. His own memoirs show him not to have done much as a commissar, but to have acted primarily as a Bolshevik leader and member of the Petrograd So-viet. The only commissar who actually took a vigorous role in organizing a district was A. P. Peshekhonov in the Petrogradskii district, although he was not appointed until noon of the 28th. Two other commissars are known by name: S. Ia. Surin, a well-known Socialist Revolutionary (SR) assigned to the Lesnoi district on the northern edge of the city,[14] and V. A. Trifonov, a Bolshevik, who was named to the Vasil'evskii Island district.[15] Trifonov will play an important role later in the Red Guard, but his activities (if any) as commissar are not known and appear to have been minimal. It is an interesting sidelight on how the Soviet functioned in those first hectic hours that Shliapnikov, besides being put in overall charge of militia organization, should also be made commissar to the Vyborg district. The two tasks were mutually exclusive, as one demanded that he be at the Tauride Palace and the other that he work in the Vyborg district. Moreover, the Soviet apparently did not consider the extent to which his Party work as the leading Bolshevik in Petrograd might interfere with the fulfillment of either Soviet-appointed task.

Besides the commissars, other members of the Soviet were sent out for special tasks, and the presence of a representative from the Petrograd Soviet is frequently mentioned in reports about the decision to form a militia unit. For example, Mikhail Skobelev, the vice-chairman of the Soviet and a Menshevik member of the Duma, gave a speech at the Peter-Paul Fortress on February 28 in which he urged the organization of a militia.[16] Similarly, the Soviet call for formation of militia units is often cited in local resolutions establishing them. The Soviet itself followed up its general appeal with a new resolution on March 1 calling for the organization of a workers' militia and calling on "officer-socialists" to assist in forming and training units.[17] This resolution apparently met with a singular lack of response from the "officer-socialists."[18]

In discussing these Soviet activities it should be emphasized that the Soviet leaders were swamped with work and gave little or no thought to permanent organization or functions. They were concerned with the immediate task of mobilizing armed strength to meet an expected attack from tsarist forces—especially an anticipated assault from the front—and with the most pressing immediate problems of basic public order in the city, including how to cope with drunks, random shooting, and looting. The rapid triumph of the Revolution, so clear in retrospect, was not yet certain. Memories of 1905 and other failures were still fresh, and many expected that after a valiant effort they might well fail and be arrested or shot. Moreover, events crowded upon them in a confusing rapidity that prevented systematic activity and often forced them merely to try to respond to whatever crisis or person was most immediate or persistent: for example, it was Brounshtein's personal insistence that put the militia problem on the Soviet agenda in the first place. The various accounts of the Soviet's meetings suggest a lack of clarity about just what these self-formed militia units were supposed to do, and one is struck by the vagueness of the first Soviet statements. The appeal published February 28 calling for militia formation says nothing about the units' functions. Keeping public order seemed clearly implied, but were they expected to fight troops supporting the tsar? The vagueness reflected in part the pressure of time, but in part also the recognition by Soviet leaders that they in fact had little control over what these groups were doing or would do, or even over the extent to which they were formed. The leaders could do little but exhort the workers at this stage.

The efforts of the Petrograd Soviet to encourage the creation of a militia not only met with an enthusiastic response but were anticipated by a popular drive in the same direction. It is extremely difficult to measure the relative degree of complete spontaneity as against response to directions from above, but spontaneity there certainly was, of all the types described in the Introduction, in all districts of the city, and among all social classes. Early memoirists are in general agreement in stressing the spontaneous and self-directing nature of the first organizational efforts, especially in formation of armed workers' detachments. The most they claim for the political parties is that their local leaders gave some political direction to these strivings, or that their prior schooling of the Petrograd proletariat was influential, but some of the earliest writers scarcely claim even that. The first Bolshevik historian-memoirist of the militia–Red Guard movement, G. P. Georgievskii, writing in 1918 or 1919, emphasized the workers' drive to arm and organize themselves immediately: ". . . instinctively, no one directed, no one pushed the working class toward this, but rather they themselves felt that there was a threat, that they needed to arm themselves." [19] Vladimir Malakhovskii, a prominent figure in and writer on the workers' militias and Red Guard, is even more explicit that the workers "immediately, not waiting for the call of leaders and parties, knew that for strengthening the victory an armed guard was necessary."[20] Indeed, throughout their history down to October, the workers' militias and Red Guard for the most part were to be locally organized and directed. They are perhaps the example par excellence of local initiative and assertiveness in the Revolution. At this point the Soviet's role was mostly to exhort and to give legitimacy; the formation was coming from the workers themselves.

Alongside the "workers' militias" there began to appear on the 28th also a "City Militia" organized under the auspices of the City Duma. The City Duma played an important role in stimulating local organization of militia patrols in the first days, although its intent was quite different from that of the Soviet. It appealed to all social classes without distinction and was concerned solely with public order. The City Duma discussed the question of organization of a citywide militia on the evening of February 28, and Dmitrii Kryzhanovskii, an architect, reported on the need to form a militia to safeguard life and property. The City Duma accordingly named him commander (*nachal'nik*) of the City Militia and set up a committee to aid him in its formation. The committee set to work that very evening. The same session chose commissioners for the districts of the city and established a number of centers for their work and for the collection of arms for the militia. It is instructive to compare the locations designated by the City Duma with those named by the Soviet earlier the same day. Whereas the Soviet named districts that were heavily working-class, the City Duma was more all-inclusive, including the upper- and middle-class Kazanskii district as well as working-class districts, including Vyborg. What is most striking is the difference in specific gathering places. Whereas the Petrograd Soviet named distinctly working-class assembly points, the City Duma chose clearly public locations, although perhaps with a slight middle-class flavor. Thus in the Petrogradskii district, for example, the Soviet named the labor exchange whereas the City Duma designated the Elite Theater and the aquarium gardens; in the Nevskii district the Soviet named a workers' night school, and the Duma the Balobinskaia Hotel. Other Duma-designated locations listed by Z. S. Kel'son include two schools, a theater, and an auction hall.[21] The City Duma leaders were thinking in terms of a general, all-citizen problem of public safety; the Soviet leaders instinctively thought along class lines.

The commissioners appointed by the City Duma on February 28—

apparently about four to seven for each district—scattered across the city that night to begin the work of organizing local political life, including a militia. The exact nature of their work has not been recorded, unfortunately, but apparently they were successful in establishing themselves and providing some order to the growth of the militia in certain parts of the city, especially the city center. Most commissioners were from the middle class, often City Duma members. A very large percentage were lawyers, but there were also such diverse figures as the actor G. G. Ge, Professor Voronov of the Technological Institute, a dentist, a prince, and students.[22] Kel'son describes one, giving a good picture of the kind of forceful, colorful person who came to the fore so frequently in those days. This was V. G. Botsvadze, a student at the Medical-Technological Academy. Energetic, decisive, with a flair for the dramatic, he had participated—on a white horse, no less—in the storming of the prisons on the Vyborg side on February 27. On the 28th he was appointed a deputy commissioner for Vyborg's first subdistrict by the City Duma, along with another student and two City Duma members, both of whom soon dropped out. As head of the militia there, Botsvadze regularly came to the City Militia headquarters, armed from head to foot and accompanied by a couple of similarly attired workers, and in a strong Georgian accent threatened to shoot unless he were given arms and money. This so unnerved the hapless Kryzhanovskii that he invariably gave in with the result that Botsvadze got almost half the arms dispensed by the City Militia office.[23] Botsvadze was a popular commissar in a predominantly Bolshevik workers' area, but he also held authorization from the City Militia (and sought its approval when he resigned in May). This sort of local leader who emerged in the chaos and spontaneous activity of the February Revolution and who then was "authorized" by an agency such as the City Duma to do what he was already doing must have been quite common (if not always so colorful). Yet it also is clear that this higher approval was sought and often felt to be essential. Botsvadze's example underscores the complexity of relationships among governmental agencies, spontaneously created local bodies, and self-proclaimed leaders in 1917.

Meanwhile, the central office of the militia at the City Duma busied itself with various tasks of organizing what was in fact (and what they largely considered to be) a new police force, including such mundane but essential tasks as providing distinguishing symbols of authority. For the latter, dozens of ladies, mostly wives of City Duma members, sewed white armbands with the red initials "G. M." (*Gorodskaia Militsiia*, "City Militia") and identification numbers. A couple of dozen Boy Scouts between 10 and 15 turned up at the City Duma and volunteered for service as messengers both inside the militia office and with the districts. People appeared, did a job or two, and disappeared. Some unknown person brought several thousand identification cards from some printshop, as well as thousands of placards proclaiming "this building protected by the militia." Appeals were issued calling for the help of the population in the work of the militia by joining, turning over arms, or volunteering in other ways. Various groups seconded this call. Indeed, the number of volunteers for this patriotic and revolutionary duty got so large that even registering them became almost impossible. Kel'son, who was trying to put the operation of City Militia headquarters on an orderly basis, later commented that it seemed as if almost the entire adult population of Petrograd was joining. Most apparently never actually did anything, or else performed one or two tasks or patrols and then left.[24] Still, the basis for a city militia, or police, was laid down and became a reality in the following days.

Two other organizations played a role in getting militia patrols on the streets on February 28 and March 1. One of these was the Committee for Military-Technical Assistance (hereafter abbreviated CMTA), an existing group representing various scientific and technical associations. It issued two appeals for the organization of a militia on February 28, which were published both in the *Izvestiia revoliutsionnoi nedeli** of that date and as separate broadsheets. In a declaration headed "Citizens!," the CMTA asserted that only by a quick restoration of order in the streets would final victory be secured, and it called on the people to assist in the establishment of order and to obey the patrols. It outlined a system of patrols that included an automobile with a white flag which would make the rounds of the patrol points each hour and report the results to the "bureau." The patrols were to deal with drunks and prevent reckless shooting, looting, and arson. The CMTA's appeal was the first

---

* This was a newspaper issued by a committee of journalists during the interval between the disappearance of the old newspapers in the revolutionary turmoil and the appearance of new ones (or the reappearance of the old ones) about March 1.

set of published instructions for the organization and functioning of a militia, and as such probably influenced militias being formed by other groups. As an existing organization willing to step into the vacuum of street-level leadership, the CMTA almost certainly played a significant role. Kel'son certainly suggests that it did.[25] The CMTA itself appears to have concentrated on organizing militia patrols of students from the technological schools, where several units were in fact formed on February 28 and March 1. Indeed, immediately after the appeal headed "Citizens!" was another addressed to students and calling on them to join "organizations for maintaining order in Petrograd." If the CMTA did in fact organize the students, its role was not negligible, for Kel'son emphasizes (and other references bear him out) that students were very active in the first flush of militia activity and that student or student-led patrols were among the first on the streets. In some instances their professors also took part. Student activity on other than an individual basis quickly waned, however. Distinctly student militia units soon disappeared altogether except for one in the Petrogradskii district that continued for some time as part of the City Militia.[26]

Finally, one must mention the activity of the Temporary Committee of the State Duma and of its Military Commission. Although the Duma Committee did not undertake to form a militia, it did issue a number of appeals and instructions that contributed to the early formation of armed bands. At 2:00 A.M. on the 28th it appealed to the residents of Petrograd to protect public institutions and equipment, government buildings, factories, and other places. About the same time it issued an appeal to the population to "organize yourselves."[27] This would have been before the Petrograd Soviet's call was issued. M. A. Karaulov, a Cossack member of the Duma Committee, published on March 1 a set of rules for "military units and the people's militia" to follow in making arrests that listed categories of people subject to arrest: drunks, burglars, arsonists, people shooting in the air and otherwise disrupting order, former police, and people making illegal arrests and searches. The order also listed places to take those arrested.[28] Karaulov's rules are strikingly similar to those set forth by various spontaneously formed militia units and, given their date of publication, may have influenced them. Though the similarity in content may simply have grown out of the same set of problems, a statement from such an authoritative body probably was welcomed and used by many of the self-constituted militia patrols of the first days.

The activity of the Duma Committee in the area of public order centered in its Military Commission, formed under the direction of Colonel B. A. Engel'hardt as a merger of commissions appointed on the 27th by both the Petrograd Soviet and the Duma Committee whose functions duplicated each other. It began to try to regulate the disposition of armed units on the morning of the 28th. Most of the Military Commission's efforts focused on the garrison, but some directives were to civilians. The Military Commission also authorized D. A. Kryzhanovskii to "organize on behalf of the public organizations of Petrograd a City Militia for the purpose of maintaining order on the streets of Petrograd"; but as this was dated 1:15 A.M. on March 1, it postdated the City Duma's action.[29] This suggests that some of the Military Commission directives were an effort to "legitimize" existing groups and actions. The Temporary Committee of the State Duma and its Military Commission played a role in providing security on February 28 and March 1, but they had little impact on the volunteer armed bands being formed, especially among the workers, and soon were eclipsed by the City Duma and the Petrograd Soviet. The Temporary Committee of the State Duma itself ceased to play an important political role soon after the formation of the Provisional Government on March 2.

Several organizations, then, moved on the 28th into the void left by the collapse of the old authorities. They were concerned mostly with securing a modicum of public order. One has only to read the newspapers of the time and the better memoir accounts to grasp the combination of exaltation and fear—fear for personal security as well as for the political future—in people's minds in those days. The crash of the old order brought the destruction not only of the hated political police but also of the ordinary police who protected individuals and property. The sense of insecurity was heightened as word spread that the destruction of the prisons on the 27th had released ordinary criminals along with the "politicals." This, combined with the tremendous surge of self-assertion released by the Revolution, led to the creation of voluntary militia units with no or only the slightest encouragement from above. It is notable that all of the political bodies except the Soviet limited their concerns to preserving public order. Only the Soviet suggested a broader political and social role for the militias, and did so only faintly. Indeed, some of the militia groups showed a sharper political consciousness than the "central" bodies. A look at some of the first of them will help us to understand their origins and nature and their relationship (or lack thereof) to the political organizations. Such a survey underscores their self-constituted, spontaneous nature—the urge so characteristic of Russians in 1917 to create organizations to represent their interests.

Many of the early efforts to organize a militia were appeals to the population in general, lacking any clear class lines, since these tended in any case to be obscured in the revolutionary euphoria and the sense of common cause and danger. For example, there were frequent calls for a "people's" (narodnaia) militia. The kinds of militia formed during the first two or three days can be broken down into three broad social types: those of heterogeneous composition, those made up almost entirely of workers, and those composed mainly of students or students and soldiers. In addition, there were three main types of institutional or geographical bases for the militias: factories, schools or other semipublic institutions, and "resident's" or "citizen's" committees in various localities. Some examples will help to illustrate the variety of militia organizations that were formed, as well as the variety of their objectives.

The developments on Vasil'evskii Island are especially instructive. Representative of the student-soldier-type militia is the one formed by the Organizational Committee of the Mining Institute on February 28. This committee, composed of three professors and 15 students, was formed on the 28th and by its own description "entered into relations with the Temporary Revolutionary Government [Duma Committee] and was confirmed the evening of February 28 by the commandant of the State Duma [probably the Military Commission]." It appears that the Organizational Committee acted independently and then got Duma sanction. According to its own later report, it chose a militia commission that from the evening of February 28 took upon itself responsibility for providing armed security in parts of the island.[30] Patrols were formed consisting of 10 soldiers of the Finland Regiment and one student, who acted as commander (the regiment's officers, like most of those in Petrograd, disappeared for a time on the 27th and 28th). Through these patrols and some stationary posts the militia commission of the Mining Institute maintained armed security in the area from the "harbor to the 4th and 5th lines [streets]," that is, across almost the entire island except the eastern tip around the Bourse and the University. The patrols, the report said, maintained order by stopping disorderly shooting, taking arms from youths and drunkards, arresting police, stopping and checking passing autos, and generally putting things in order and settling disputes. To change patrols, the student commander went to the Mining Institute and secured a replacement for himself, who then went to the barracks of the Finland Regiment and got a replacement patrol of soldiers to take over the arms and duties of the retiring patrol.[31] At about the same time a similar militia, this one using the sailors of the Second Fleet, was organized by an ad hoc committee for maintenance of order and patrolled part of the same area of Vasil'evskii Island, near the harbor.[32] The practice of using soldiers or sailors commanded by a student, worker, or other civilian was extremely common at first and dates from February 27, when the mutinying soldiers, seeking guidance and leaders in the absence of their officers, often turned to or just accepted the leadership of individuals who acted in an authoritative manner.

This type of militia, though among the first to be organized, was really little more than simply using army units for police duty. A workers' militia in the strict sense was formed at the Petrograd Cable Factory, also located in the harbor area of Vasil'evskii Island. Learning about the militia organized by the ad hoc committee using sailors, the factory committee on February 28 or March 1 decided to ask a general factory meeting to approve a militia of volunteers, at a ratio of 100 for each 1,000 workers, up to a total of 270. It also introduced a demand that was to be a major bone of contention between the militias and the factory owners—that militiamen be paid regular work salaries if being on duty caused them to miss work. The general meeting of the workers approved this on March 1, and 103 people signed up immediately.[33] Workers from the Cable Factory and some other factories in the area eventually organized a permanent commissariat of workers' militia in the harbor subdistrict of Vasil'evskii Island. A number of other workers' militias were organized about the same time on the island. One centered around the Pipe Factory and eventually became the second subdistrict commissariat of workers' militia.

A very different type of militia emerged in the first subdistrict on Vasil'evskii Island, the eastern end that included a large number of government offices, the Bourse, the University, and some middle-class housing. Here a "residents' committee" was established to supervise activities in the area and a militia was formed under a justice of the peace named Drozdov. Although the composition of this militia is not indicated, it clearly was not made up of workers, for its existence caused continued agitation in the Vasil'evskii Island Soviet of Workers' Deputies at least until the second week of March. This militia eventually came under the control of the City Militia. Kel'son also indicates the existence of a student-based militia at the University, which may have been part of Drozdov's but probably was distinct.[34]

The militia on Vasil'evskii Island, then, originated in different ways and from varied sources. Even after the first days of the Revolution passed and some regularity developed, this diversity persisted and the island came to be divided into areas patrolled by a militia under the authority of the City Militia and by militias giving allegiance to autonomous workers' militia commissariats. This pattern seems to have reflected the socioeconomic differences between neighborhoods and resulting different political outlooks. What is striking is that almost all the militia centers seem to have been self-constituted, with little outside involvement beyond the possible influence of the various appeals of February 28.

Just to the east across the Little Neva was the Petrogradskii district, where a unique situation developed on February 28 when A. P. Peshekhonov, a Popular Socialist* leader and future minister in the Provisional Government, established a commissariat with the official sanction of both the Soviet and the Temporary Committee of the State Duma. By his own account, he had just returned to the Tauride Palace about noon on the 28th when "one of the SDs" asked him to go as Soviet commissar to the Petrogradskii district. Peshekhonov's account makes it clear that he was not among the commissars who had met immediately following the Petrograd Soviet Executive Committee meeting earlier that morning. After a moment of hesitation—he suspected a maneuver to get him out of the Soviet—he accepted. Being aware of the activities of the Duma

* A small agrarian socialist party.

Committee, he also sought out its approval. This he received in rather casual form from the Kadet leader, Paul Miliukov, who responded to Peshekhonov's request by saying, "Well, go ahead if you find that this suits you." It would hardly have suited Miliukov, who probably could not have conceived of removing himself from what he considered the center of political activity to work in one of the districts. Peshekhonov, on the other hand, true to his populist heritage, was excited by this chance to immerse himself in the "thicket" of the Revolution. Gathering up some intelligentsia, radicals, soldiers, and Petrogradskii-district workers who were at the Palace, he obtained a truck and proceeded to the district. There he and his assistants set up the commissariat at the Elite movie theater, strategically located at the main intersection of the district, on the corner of Bol'shoi and Kamenoostrovskii prospects, and began the multitude of tasks of local government.[35]

In his memoir, Peshekhonov lays heavy stress on the problem of maintaining public order and personal security. He makes two points about the need for some sort of police—points frequently encountered in other authors. The first is that during the early days of the Revolution there was widespread theft and assaults, which naturally caused great fear among the common populace, the more so as they were often carried out under the guise of "requisitions" or searches for counterrevolutionaries. The second is that in the early revolutionary enthusiasm there was a willfulness and arbitrariness of almost anarchistic proportions that led to many searches, attacks, "arrests," and other violent acts without criminal intent against persons and property. During the first days the newly established organs of local authority were besieged by people bringing in "arrested" persons; Peshekhonov calls it an "epidemic of self-authorized arrests." He cites as an excellent if slightly humorous example the state of affairs following an announcement by the Duma Committee chairman, Mikhail Rodzianko: Peshekhonov found in the commissariat holding room one man who had been "arrested" for criticizing and another "arrested" for praising him. The fielding of a militia in the Petrogradskii district allayed some fears and brought a quick decline in arbitrary arrests and searches there. It took a little longer to bring robbery and other criminal activity under control, for some of it was apparently well organized and armed.[36] The organizing of the militia was done by V. M.

Shakh, a Menshevik, whom Peshekhonov called his "most active assistant."[37] Peshekhonov acknowledged that the militia initially was not much to brag about, being poorly disciplined and managed by a "Social Democrat comrade" (Shakh) who tried—wrongly in Peshekhonov's view—to give it a class composition and outlook. Nevertheless, he insisted, it did the essential job and had the virtue of a "high moral level," of being composed of people of good quality.[38] Unfortunately, Peshekhonov does not identify its social composition or just what he meant by "people of good quality."

A unique feature of the militia in the Petrogradskii district is that even where independent and spontaneously created units were formed, they soon were brought under the direction of Peshekhonov's commissariat. For example, a group of intelligentsia independently organized a militia, as did a local citizens' group on Krestovskii Island, but both were soon merged with Peshekhonov's militia. When a "commandant" for the Petrogradskii district surfaced, a prince and Grenadier Regiment officer apparently appointed by the Military Commission of the Duma Committee, he too was quickly incorporated into the commissariat to help organize duty schedules. In addition there were irregular bands, such as one led by a student that besieged the commissariat demanding arms.[39] Some of these bands simply disappeared, whereas others merged into the commissariat's militia, which in turn eventually became part of the City Militia. There also were militia units formed at factories in the Petrogradskii district, some spontaneously, such as that formed at the Military-Medical Supply Factory.[40] However, these too apparently came under the direction of the district commissar, and there is no clear evidence of any completely independent workers' militia in the district for any length of time during the first days of the Revolution. Startsev notes that "worker-militiamen of the Petrogradskii district did not form their own commissariats," and that "they all received their verification not from commissariats of workers' militia, as on Vasil'evskii Island, but from the district commissariat of city militia under the signature of Commissar V. M. Shakh," i.e., Peshekhonov's assistant.[41] Apparently, then, Peshekhonov's commissariat was able to establish a degree of control over militias in the Petrogradskii district that did not exist elsewhere. Indeed, Peshekhonov alone among the numerous commissars and commandants appointed by the Soviet and the Duma Committee managed—

or even made a concerted effort—to set up an all-encompassing district center of authority, including a centralized militia. This commissariat functioned as the organ of local government for just under three weeks, by which time the local political situation had changed greatly and new political bodies were well established.

Militia patrols sprang up in other parts of the city, composed of varied social elements. Generally the militias reflected the composition of the local population. In the socially mixed areas this added to the confusion and shifting character of the early volunteer bands. For example, in the Liteinyi district near the city center the workers of the Petrograd Cartridge Factory on February 28 organized a militia commanded by one Sergei Komarov to guard the factory. However, this formation soon merged into the City Militia of the fourth subdistrict under a Commissar Shekhter, named by the City Duma. This militia had a mixed social composition.[42] Another militia of mixed composition was organized in the Kolomenskii district on the evening of February 28 by an apparently self-constituted "supply (*prodovol'stvennaia*) commission" of six people. It announced that a "militia of soldiers and citizens under the direction of Lieutenant Grachev" would keep order, and the militia set up patrols and devoted considerable time to taking away drunks.[43]

In the heavily industrial Vyborg district, by contrast, we find the formation of militia units with an entirely proletarian outlook and composition. In these working-class areas the political role of the militia, stated mostly as "defense of the revolution," is more evident. A meeting of workers at the medical fund office of the Old Parviainen Factory on the morning of the 28th to organize political authority in the area set up a militia committee for the district. It was composed entirely of workers and headed by one Diumin, a metalworker. The *Izvestiia* appeal for creation of militias had not yet appeared on the street, but in view of the fact that the medical fund office of the Parviainen Factory had been designated as a gathering point by the Soviet, it may have been carried by word of mouth. Thus we cannot tell to what extent the actions at the medical fund office were a response to the Soviet appeal and to what extent completely spontaneous. There certainly was considerable local initiative and self-determination, however, for Shliapnikov says that the militia committee had been set up and arms were being collected and distributed before he arrived at the meeting as the Soviet's commissar. Shliapnikov, in fact, repeatedly stresses worker initiative, *samostoiatel'nost'*. The Bolshevik Party role was not that of a mover and organizer, he states, but merely that of an agency to give political guidance; as Soviet commissar he was only assisting in *samostoiatel'nost'*. The Vyborg militia committee issued an appeal by its own authority (on a press it had seized) for those possessing arms to come to the militia center to be organized into militia detachments to maintain order, or at least to turn over the arms to the militia for its needs. It is interesting as an illustration of the spirit of the time that the appeal, although written in the most radical district and the only one to be firmly pro-Bolshevik from the beginning, used the term "citizens" and not "workers." [44] It is indicative of the extent of local initiative that also on February 28 a *komendatura** of militia was set up by the Vyborg District Soviet (organized that day), with N. I. Kuchmenko as commander. [45] As the soviet itself was largely of local spontaneous origin, the development speaks strongly of worker initiative. And as noted earlier, it was from the Vyborg district that the Bolshevik Petersburg Committee had been importuned for arms on the morning of the 27th.

During the next two or three days workers' militias sprang up in most of the factories of the district, many of them apparently independent of the militia committee or *komendatura*. Drawing on memoir accounts in Soviet archives, Startsev describes a militia formed by the factory committee of the Rozenkrants Factory by March 1, which with the militias of other factories nearby made up the militia commissariat in Vyborg's first subdistrict. He lists militia organizations by March 1 also at the New Lessner, New Parviainen, and Erikson factories, which formed with other detachments Vyborg's second subdistrict militia commissariat. Soldiers from the Moscow Guard Regiment and the First Machine Gun Regiment also took part in this second subdistrict militia. [46] It appears that the numerous factories of the Vyborg district one by one formed militia units during the first week of the Revolution.

In the neighboring Lesnoi district on the northeast outskirts of the city a militia detachment of 200 was formed at the Aivaz Factory, apparently under the influence of the Soviet appeal. Students from the nearby Polytechnic Institute also participated in the mili-

---

* Literally, a commandancy or commander's office. The term is often used in 1917 to designate a district or citywide militia command or organizing office.

tia, either in this one or their own.[47] Further east yet in the Po-rokhovskii district on the very edge of the city, the workers of the factories located in that semirural area met in a mass meeting at 9:00 A.M. on the 28th to choose a "temporary executive committee of the Porokhovskii district." It set up a number of commissions, including one for a militia that in turn established a workers' militia drawing on the local factories. The militia undertook to secure lo-cal control by disarming the remaining police, establishing patrol posts, and winning over the military regiments quartered in the area.[48] This is the earliest known instance of a militia established clearly in response to the resolution of the Petrograd Soviet—and again news of the resolution had to have been verbal, since the meeting took place several hours before *Izvestiia* appeared. Pre-sumably the message was carried by one of the Soviet deputies re-turning home. Still, the establishment of a functioning militia re-quired extensive local initiative, even if responding to the call of the Soviet. The leaders of the militia are not known, but the factories were strongly Menshevik and the district soviet was overwhelm-ingly Menshevik and anti-Bolshevik down to October.[49] On the other side of the city, workers' militias in the industrial Peterhof district centered on the massive Putilov works. The medical fund office of the Putilov Factory had been named in the Soviet appeal as a gathering point for militia, and apparently was so used. However, in this huge factory of about 30,000 workers, the earliest and most spontaneous organization of workers' detachments seems to have taken place in various shops. The election of an organized militia, as against transitory ad hoc armed groups, appears to have coin-cided here as in many other places with the election of deputies to the Soviet.[50]

There are numerous other examples of local creation of militia organizations, workers' and others. Kel'son cites examples of spe-cial militias organized at a wide variety of places, including major shopping arcades and markets such as the Gostinyi Dvor, the Apra-kin Dvor, and the Mariinskii market. Whether these groups were meant to patrol a larger area or just to maintain the security of these shops is not clear. Militia commissariats were established wherever an interested group came together: in factory medical fund offices, workers' cafeterias, schools, former police stations, movie theaters, an auction hall, hotels, even in private apartments.[51]

Out of public spirit and private fears, for the defense of the Revolution and its advancement, to handle drunks or disarm defenders of the old regime, to cope with thieves and other common criminals who had been let out of jail along with everyone else on the 27th— for all imaginable motives a great surge of organizing armed "militia" bands swept the city. The spontaneity and resulting chaos of a multitude of armed bands thrilled the hearts of revolutionaries and tormented the leaders trying to harness the revolutionary tide.

The long-run implications of these spontaneous armed bands were not yet clear by March 1, but that they posed a serious problem for any new government trying to establish its authority soon became apparent. The large numbers of arms distributed from military and police stores to the population could not easily be collected, nor the armed groups forced to disband. Moreover, many of them, especially among the workers, were to continue in existence, strengthen themselves, and become a source of armed support for worker demands, economic and political. At this time, however, most citizens of the capital probably viewed them much as Sukhanov did when, in the quote at the outset of this chapter, he paid tribute to their rapid establishment of order and safety in the city.[52] Yet the safety and order provided by such groups was a tentative and, for many, illusory thing. The events of the last week of February not only destroyed the tsarist regime but unleashed forces of spontaneity and self-organization that could not readily be harnessed or directed. The ability of the government and political groups to do so would be critical to the outcome of the Revolution. The interplay of such efforts with the continuing self-assertion of the workers as expressed in these armed bands will be the focus of our attention in the following chapters.

3

City Police or Workers' Guards?

"The workers of the Cable Factory, having heard the report
of our representatives to the Council of Workers' Militia
about the organization of the people's [city] militia, . . . see
in such an organization the campaign of the bourgeoisie
against the workers' militia."
—*Resolution of a general meeting, March 12*

By March 2 the Revolution was triumphant. The Provisional Government announced its existence and issued a brief program. Nicholas II, isolated and abandoned, abdicated. These two events set the stamp of finality upon the success of the February Revolution. Russia now faced the task of establishing a new order in the country. The problems were overwhelming and were never successfully solved by the Provisional Government. Forming a central government was relatively easy, whatever its effectiveness; but establishing new norms of local government among a citizenry unaccustomed to participation in the public life of the state was much more arduous, complicated as it was by the tremendous wave of self-assertion and self-organization that swept the country. In no realm was the problem more difficult, more reflective of the basic divisions of Russian society, or more pressing than in that of regulating the numerous armed bands still springing to life and establishing a new police system.

The creation of a new police or public-order system was handicapped by several factors. First, it had been one of the demands of the Petrograd Soviet in the negotiations leading to the formation of the Provisional Government that the police be transformed into a people's militia subject to local authorities. The Provisional Government's acceptance of this demand was embodied in its program statement, Point 5 of which called for "the substitution of a people's militia for the police, with elective officers responsible to the organs of local self-government."[1] As a matter of local administration, with the central government playing little or no role, the public-order system would thus be very much dependent upon the vigor and effectiveness of local authorities. Second, the intelligentsia tradition of "innocent faith in the perfectibility of man [and] the detestation of violence and coercion"[2] made it both seemingly less pressing and in fact more difficult for the new government and Soviet leaders to face the problem of developing new organs of public order. And third, some groups, especially among the industrial workers, resisted the establishment of any effective new municipal police and maintained their own armed bands.

In Petrograd the problem was staggering. By March 2 a bewildering array of militias, *druzhiny*, and other armed groups existed, and more were being created daily. An estimated 20,000 men were under arms in Petrograd in these organizations by mid-March,[3] and there were still other individuals with arms. Despite the diversity, it was nonetheless obvious by March 2 that two main militia groups existed—those sponsored by the new City Militia administration, and those that called themselves workers' militias or some variant thereof and, though lacking any central organization, felt themselves distinct from the City Militia and even hostile toward it. In an effort to find a way to avoid possible clashes between armed groups and duplication of efforts, and generally bring some order, two Menshevik members of the Petrograd Soviet, V. P. Piatiev and one Chernev, approached Kel'son at the City Duma that day and announced that they had been sent by the Soviet for "contact." Kel'son and Chernev made a round of workers' militia centers in an effort to get their agreement on spheres of influence and activity for workers' militias and the City Militia. They also attempted, with partial success, to get local workers' militias to agree to accept the overall authority of the City Militia administration. Kel'son and Chernev also drew up "regulations" for militiamen, setting forth who could make arrests, conditions under which militiamen could use firearms, their various responsibilities, and other details. A meeting on March 3 of 50 district militia commissars, from both the City Militia and the workers' militias (but apparently mostly from the former) approved these regulations, which were printed and distributed throughout the city the next day.[4] Though such a result was probably unintended, the efforts of Kel'son and Chernev were in fact the first step toward institutionalizing the bifurcation of the militia.

By March 3, then, two main militia groups were recognized. Each had been encouraged in its development and sanctioned by a larger body—the Petrograd Soviet in the one case and the City Duma in the other. They embodied two very different outlooks. The City Militia administration viewed its organization as basically a popular, nonpartisan police force entrusted with maintaining public safety. The workers' militias and the Petrograd Soviet, by contrast, already looked upon their organizations as much more political and distinctly class-oriented (even if this sentiment was not yet clearly articulated), and at least by implication insisted that the City Militia also was in some way partisan. The workers especially mistrusted the basic concept of a neutral police force. Their experience with the tsarist police led them to look upon the police as agents of the political authorities and backers of the factory management. Moreover, to the extent that they had been influenced by Marxist theories or were now being led by Marxist intelligentsia, that also led them to reject the idea of a neutral police. Neither experience nor theory prompted them to accept it. The City Militia officials, on the other hand, tended to view the separate workers' militias as temporary, a stage to be succeeded in time by a single City Militia responsible to the city government. Symbolic of the gulf that existed between the two was the response when Dmitrii Kryzhanovskii, head of the City Militia, opened the meeting of March 3 with the greeting "gentlemen"; several voices responded "here there are no gentlemen."[5]

The problem posed by the existence of two types of militia and two conceptions of what a militia should be was vigorously debated during the week following March 3, with the question of an independent workers' armed force at stake. The first forum was a conference of representatives of various militia organizations on March 5. A. G. Shliapnikov, who was sent as the representative of the Petrograd Soviet Executive Committee, estimates an attendance of three to four hundred, about half workers and the rest largely soldiers, students, and military cadets. Shliapnikov was asked to make a report on the subject on behalf of the Petrograd Soviet. This caused him a slight problem, for the Soviet had not really discussed

the issue and did not have an official position. He readily solved
this by giving his own views as those of the Soviet, a not uncommon
procedure for Soviet "spokesmen" during the first weeks of the
Revolution. Shliapnikov claims he argued that the militia in Petrograd must be working-class in composition and must be viewed not
simply as an order-keeping body but rather as an armed expression
of working-class goals and as an instrument to defend the Revolution and, if need be, to move it forward. Although this smacks of
later embellishment and exaggeration, a speech that was even partially so class-oriented and that presented the militia as a political
weapon rather than merely an order-keeping body would have been
adequate to call forth the strong opposition he says it met from the
students and others. Their objections reflected not only social val-
ues but also the widespread mood of that time, which stressed "all-
citizen" solutions and tended to blur class and other sentiments.
There also were objections to having an armed, or at least heavily
armed, militia—the British constabulary was sometimes held as a
model in these debates. Worker resistance to disarming or to sub-
merging themselves in a larger citywide militia was strong, however, and the meeting ended without agreement.[6] The discussion
was to be resumed in a second meeting on March 7.

Between the meetings of March 5 and 7 efforts were made to
clarify—or establish—the position of the Soviet and the workers'
militia representatives, without a great deal of success. A discussion
in the Petrograd Soviet on March 5 showed sentiment in favor of
a workers' militia, and the Executive Committee was charged to
work out a report, in cooperation with district militia representatives, and to compile instructions for the militiamen.[7] However, the
tenor of the Executive Committee when it took up the question on
March 7 was rather different, for it was prepared to accept the possibility of joining the workers' militia to the City Militia on the condition that the Soviet would have the right to approve candidates
for militiamen.[8] The latter was an extremely important qualifier,
but it was in line with the broad Soviet view that it should have the
right to approve the membership of all organizations, from the government on down, so as to exclude those persons felt to be politically unreliable. It was a version of the qualified support that the
Soviet extended to the Provisional Government, and it had the
effect of formally sanctioning a unified militia while at the same

time requiring a procedure that in practice made a unified militia an impossibility. And even at that, the Executive Committee's resolution only affirmed the "possibility" of a merger; it did not commit the Soviet to one. It probably reflects an ambivalence in the minds of the Soviet leaders: they wanted both a unified militia (in their new role as guardians of order) and armed workers' bands (an expression of their old revolutionary instincts). This duality of attitude bedeviled Soviet thinking about the militia from March to September.

The same day that the Executive Committee met, March 7, a meeting between workers' militia representatives from six districts or subdistricts and representatives of the Soviet Executive Committee was held at the Liteinyi district militia commissariat. It is not clear whether this took place before or after the Executive Committee meeting, but it was a lively session covering many topics. The business included reports on organizational problems, on the status of the militia, and on the arms question, and discussion of small but pressing problems such as the continuing existence of disorderly groups using arms for "requisitions" in outlying areas. Most important, however, was the issue of the militia's role in the new Russia. The participants clearly felt the tasks of the workers' militia to be much wider than those of the City Militia. Though sharing the latter's function of maintaining order and public security, the workers' militia was also seen as having a duty to serve as a cadre that, together with the revolutionary army, could repulse any counter-revolutionary efforts. Hence it needed to retain its own independent organization and "be a bulwark for political positions that have been taken and to come out in all situations where the interests of the democracy are threatened." Still, recognizing that there must be some cooperation, or at least contact, with the City Militia, the representatives agreed to attend the forthcoming conference. They also expressed a need for more central coordination of the purely workers' militia in the form of a unifying organizational center. Reflecting the overwhelming local orientation and initiative in militia work, they resolved to form such a center at the militia section of the commissariat of the Petrogradskii district, not at the Petrograd Soviet.[9] The sentiments expressed at this meeting were more radical than those in the Soviet discussions and indicate that workers' militiamen had a more militant view of their organization and a more suspicious attitude toward city officials than did the Soviet leaders. Local sentiment already was running well ahead of official positions.

The different attitudes came into clearer focus when the city conference on the militia resumed on the 7th. It was again chaired by Kryzhanovskii and again composed of representatives of the workers' militias as well as of the City Militia. A draft of basic principles drawn up by a special commission was laid before the delegates. The main feature of the draft was a carefully worked out democratic procedure for regulating the militia: in each district there would be a committee for the militia elected by all the citizens of that district; the committee in turn would send representatives to a citywide council of the militia, which, with the addition of two representatives elected by the militiamen, would be the main organ for supervision of the militia. This proposal met with protests, especially from the workers' militiamen, who objected that it would take too long to set up. They apparently were also afraid that it would mean the loss of their own autonomy and ability to run their own affairs—a paramount concern throughout 1917 in any discussion of the organization of the militia. Finally the conference decided, on the recommendation of V. M. Shakh, the Menshevik militia leader from the Petrogradskii district, to send the draft off to a "committee of professors" for further study, thereby effectively scuttling it.[10] Shakh recommended for the time being a very different scheme of organization: in each subdistrict there would be a council elected by the militiamen, not the citizenry, and this council in turn would elect delegates to a district council, from which members would be sent to a city council. The city council, then, responsible for the organization and direction of the militia, would be composed almost entirely of militiamen. The only outsiders would be individuals co-opted by the council (and then only up to one-seventh of the total membership), plus a number of representatives—equal to those co-opted—who could be sent from the Petrograd Soviet. Election of these councils would begin immediately and be completed by March 13, when the city council of militia would be organized.[11] This proposal, which removed the militia from public control, passed.

Having forced this system on the conference, the workers' militiamen then got themselves exempted from even its minimal controls by passing a proposal that would preserve their own autonomous existence within the City Militia. They would take City Militia identifying armbands, but would add their own distinctive red emblems. Moreover, they were allowed the option either of participating directly in the elections at the subdistrict level (whenever they were assured, as an *Izvestiia* article put it, "of adequate numbers") or of sending representatives straight to the district council. This plan, as the *Izvestiia* account noted, gave the "proletarian militia" the advantages of being connected with the City Militia while allowing it to preserve its independence. It guaranteed that the militia would not be separated "from the demands of the revolutionary movement." [12]

   This organizational structure, specifically rejecting a militia controlled by a publicly elected body in favor of a militia responsible basically only to itself, was ironic coming as it did from those who claimed to be defenders of a revolution against the tsarist tradition of a police force not responsible to public opinion. Yet it reflected the sharp social antagonisms of Russia and was an early expression of a fundamental attitude of the workers throughout 1917—the determination not to have "their" organizations brought under any kind of nonproletarian control or influence. The militia problem threw this issue into especially sharp relief, and this conference was one of the few places, and the earliest, where the question of generally elected versus class-based institutions was so clearly posed. Moreover, because it involved arms it was extremely emotional; at stake was much more than a mere council or other forum for speeches and resolutions! Here too was an early example of a contradictory attitude held by working-class organizations in 1917 that proved crucial for the development of the Revolution: while insisting loudly on democracy, they rejected any "all-people" body or solution that might result in a nonworking-class or nonsocialist majority. Majority and democracy were equated only if the workers were the majority. This position also was an early manifestation of the attitude that identified their own interests with that of "the people" and themselves as "the democracy," the dogmatism that "we" represent the right and democracy, quite aside from whether "we" represent a numerical majority. This notion, so frequently traced to Leninism, seems to have had very strong emotional roots in the Russian working class quite aside from Leninism. It suggests that from the outset, peaceful, nonviolent political development was unlikely, and points to the importance of armed force for the future of the Revolution.

The arrangements worked out at the conference on the 7th were hardly adequate. The next day, March 8, the Executive Committee of the Petrograd Soviet decided that the question of the militia needed to be reconsidered.[13] This was apparently the origin of a report on militia organization given in the Petrograd Soviet plenum on March 10 by E. Sokolovskii, a Menshevik-Internationalist who played an active role in the Soviet during the early period. He stressed that the relations between "our militia" and the City Militia were bad, and though most of the speakers that followed him expressed their support for continuing an independent workers' militia, the issue was apparently left unsettled when the chairman intervened with a suggestion to resolve the question by first organizing the City Militia well and then removing any counterrevolutionary elements that might have gotten in (again, the notion of Soviet control over membership). Meanwhile, workers must participate in the district elections for militia councils to ensure democratic control. With this the Soviet dropped the issue, preferring to let things develop.[14]

The efforts to set up clear lines of authority and to unite the workers' militia and the City Militia after the March 7 meeting were only partially successful. Some workers' militia units accepted the authority of the city officials, but many defied both city and Soviet efforts toward unification. Although the prestige of the Soviet was great, it frequently had difficulty in gaining the workers' acceptance of unpopular decisions—as when it urged a return to work after the February Revolution without being able to give a solid guarantee of an eight-hour day—and they resisted on this issue as well. Moreover, on the militia issue the Soviet leadership itself was ambivalent: it was inclined to unite the two groups, with the workers' militia maintaining considerable autonomy, but because of rank-and-file resistance it never clearly articulated or pushed the matter. Indeed, in many workers' quarters there was strong resistance to any measures that would weaken the independence or hegemony of the workers' militia. Thus, for example, on March 12 a general meeting of the Petrograd Cable Factory workers resolved that "having heard the report of our representatives to the council of workers' militia [March 7 meeting] about the organization of the people's [city] militia, constructed on the basis of elected representatives from each apartment building, we see in such an organization the campaign of the bourgeoisie against the workers' militia. The campaign started by the bourgeois City Duma calls forth our strong protest." Instead, they argued, at a time when the struggle for a democratic republic and against monarchist remnants continued, the workers' militia must be strengthened.[15] More mildly, but to the same point, the Peterhof District Soviet, after hearing a report of its militia commission on March 8 about the "interference of the City Militia in the affairs of the district," decided to send Comrade Fedorov to the City Militia central office with a proposal that the workers' militia continue to patrol the areas they had held before there was a City Militia, i.e., that each militia maintain its present territorial domain.[16] The workers, then, though not averse to some form of cooperation, resisted all efforts to eliminate or seriously reduce the autonomy of their armed forces.

Worker determination to maintain arms and their own units is hardly surprising, given their historic grievances and the general uncertainties of Russia in 1917. Though the major political and economic crises of 1917 that encouraged vigorous efforts at arming themselves developed only later and will be traced in greater depth in Chapter Five, problems already existed that deserve comment at this point to make more explicable the workers' insistence on maintaining their separate armed forces. Already in March some very serious disputes had emerged between labor and management. The struggle for the eight-hour day was one of the first, and revealed clearly that workers were ready to press further in their demands than were their official leaders. The rapid emergence of factory committees—and management's grudging acceptance of them as the workers' spokesmen—provided a vehicle through which workers could and did press various issues, including a minimum wage for the lowest-paid categories, general wage increases, improvement of working conditions, and the maintenance of a factory workers' militia. One grievance that is often overlooked but is important in comprehending the workers' outlook was the frequent insistence that managers and foremen treat workers civilly and respect their dignity. "Crude" treatment of workers was a frequent charge leveled against those foremen, technicians, and managers whom the workers expelled from the factories after February. This demand by the workers has not received the attention from historians that the similiar demand of the soldiers—so dramatically embodied in Order No. 1—has received. Nonetheless, it was just as deeply felt by the workers, had a not dissimilar effect on relations with superiors, and reflected especially well the workers' expectation of a better life and determination to gain a greater control over it.[17]

All of these worker attitudes and many other issues soon came to be lumped together under the concept of "worker control" (*rabochii kontrol'*). This term has created confusion in Western writing, for the English "control" is not quite a cognate of the Russian. "Supervision" or "surveillance," used sometimes, do not do the task either. In fact, "worker control" was an elastic and changing concept in 1917, meaning mere supervision or worker input at some times, and real administration and running of the factory at others. At first it meant mainly a right of worker involvement in factory affairs, including helping to maintain efficient and continuing production, having a voice in working conditions, preventing sabotage, ejecting objectionable personnel, and having access to financial data of the plant. Although the process varied by factory, it often expanded to include control over hiring, the shipment of finished goods, and the acquisition of raw materials; in some places workers countersigned management orders and even made vital decisions about production and keeping the factory operating. Ultimately, in some instances workers took over the factory and ran it through their factory committees. In short, "worker control" was a multifaceted expression of a new role of involvement and assertion for workers in Russian society.[18]

For the workers and their factory committees, then, the presence of factory-based armed units gave emphasis to their demands. Although overt use of arms to settle work issues was very rare in the spring, the threat was already there. Indeed, the whole coercive relationship between workers and management was reversed. Now the workers had arms and some organizational basis for their use, whereas management had lost its factory guards and the ultimate threat of government police and troops. The factory guards now were the workers themselves, and the City Militia was too weak to assist employers even if it wanted to. Moreover, even if the Provisional Government were willing to use force to back up management, its soldiers were hardly reliable for such a task. The balance of power had tipped dramatically. Given past injustices and current hardships, plus the general distrust of "privileged Russia," we can understand the determination of the more militant workers to maintain their own armed forces and the support they mustered from their fellows. Whatever internal divisions existed among the workers—skilled and unskilled, old-timers and newcomers—paled into insignificance when they confronted the upper strata of society and especially their employers and overseers.

As a result of worker resistance to being wholly incorporated into the City Militia or to giving up arms, by mid-March the militia situation settled into a complex organizational pattern that was to last until October. In general, in working-class districts one found almost exclusively workers' militias, usually organized around the factory and placing as much emphasis upon safeguarding the factory grounds as upon patrolling the city area around it. In the middle-class districts in the city center, by contrast, one found a regular paid City Militia, composed of varied social elements, maintaining order and striving to create a Western-type nonpolitical police force. This neat dichotomy, however, breaks down on close examination. Some factory-based workers' militia units accepted directions from and subordinated themselves to the City Militia authorities, although they retained varying degrees of autonomy. Others rejected all subordination. Within the City Militia there were units made up largely of workers but operating strictly within the City Militia framework. Many districts were divided between workers' militia and City Militia commissariats by subdistricts. In some subdistricts even further division took place as certain streets, buildings, and areas were patrolled by autonomous workers' militia units while other streets and buildings were guarded by the City Militia. In such areas there were parallel militia structures, with an ad hoc territorial division of the subdistrict. Finally, though these lines of division and authority generally followed those established during the February Revolution, there was some shifting and reorganizing, as well as recurring efforts by city officials to close down or more tightly control worker units.

At this point, let us look more closely at the two types of militia and how they functioned. During March city officials pushed ahead with efforts to create a regular citywide militia to perform basic police functions. At the head of the new City Militia structure was a commander (*nachal'nik*) chosen by the City Duma and directly responsible to it; Kryzhanovskii continued in this post. A special council was established to advise him, composed of one representative from each district and several officials of the City Militia. The main feature of the militia itself, however, was its extreme decentralization. After an electoral process was established at a meeting of district representatives (the militia council?) on March 17, each of the city's 51 subdistricts organized a meeting of militiamen to elect a subdistrict council and militia commissar. In places where a separate workers' or other militia already existed, its members were invited to join in electing the subdistrict council and commissar. The council then in turn chose representatives to a district council, which elected a commissar for the district as a whole.[19] Effective control of the police power was thus left in local hands. Even so, groups could stay outside the subdistrict organization if they wished. This local autonomy, which is not surprising in the first days, was perpetuated later by revisions in the militia structure that gave primary responsibility for direction of the militia to the district *dumy* once they were created.

One obvious result of this structure is that even if a full unification of the militia had been achieved and independent workers' militias had disappeared, the central city government would still have had little control over the police. Even more significantly, the Provisional Government had none. This fact, which has not always been appreciated when evaluating the government's response to major crises in Petrograd, is of considerable importance: short of using the army, the government had no police or other armed force at its disposal to deal with antigovernment activities. Thus it could not make a "moderate" response to crises or even arrest individuals; it had to either call out troops or else depend on an ill-formed militia it did not control. Kel'son is quite correct in repeatedly stressing that the criticism of the City Militia authorities for their failure to develop an effective and disciplined police force was unfair because they did not have direct authority over it; much of the real control was dispersed through the districts and subdistricts. Indeed, City Militia and government officials did not even have any good method of information gathering. The reports from the district commissars did not give that assessment of the mood of the populace that the old police had routinely provided. Kel'son cites as an example that when Minister-President Prince Lvov wanted a report of what was going on in the city during the July Uprising, the militia commander sent Kel'son on a motorcycle to survey things and report.[20] Sometimes the government even had to rely on Bolshevik local militia commissars to find out about Bolshevik activities!

The administrative system, then, encouraged local militia commissariats pretty much to go their own way and to take on the political coloration and practices they desired. Moreover, there appears to have been continued friction between the various types of militia. One newspaper's satirical attack on the City Militia represented Kryzhanovskii as responding to a question about the inability of the militia to guard against Bolshevik disturbances by stating that the various district militia commissariats were too busy defending themselves against each other to fulfill that task.[21] The existence of a large number of semi-independent militia commissariats, especially when added to the continued existence of workers' militia units completely outside the City Militia structure, boded ill for efforts to restore orderly life in the capital. It reduced to a hollow mockery the assumption of some of those working on militia questions, such as N. A. Lenskii, that the political life of the country was returning to normal and that they could proceed with the formation of a British-type constabulary.[22]

Turning to the workers' militias, we find that their structure was even more highly decentralized and varied than that of the City Militia. The base of the workers' militia normally was the factory, where its members were chosen by election or were volunteers. Commonly the militia was supervised, or even organized, by a special militia commission of the factory committee. Support from the factory committees was essential in the face of efforts to disband the workers' militias or to incorporate them into the City Militia, and the workers' militias in turn gave the factory committees armed backing—or the threat thereof—in confrontations with management. These factory-based militias had their own commander, either elected by the militiamen or appointed by the factory committee. Representatives from the factory militias organized the subdistrict workers' militia commissariat, which was nominally responsible to the City Militia officials and, after their formation, to the district *dumy*. The functions of a subdistrict commissariat tended to be what each made them. The only extensive surviving protocols of a subdistrict workers' commissariat, the first Vyborg, set up the regulations for service by its militiamen, fixed the number of posts and patrols, set the number of militiamen (900 in this case—rather a lot for such a small area), and claimed that the commissariat would see to the matter of arms.[23] Other testimony, scattered through many memoirs, indicates that these commissariats were responsible for seeing to the training and provisioning of militiamen, for establishing and taking disciplinary measures, and for performing numerous civil registry tasks that had been the province of the old police. Obviously, the vigor and efficiency with which these tasks were carried out varied widely. Apart from this, the district and subdistrict workers' commissariats often were dependent upon the factory militia commissions or commanders to send the militiamen out for duties. The problem was compounded by high turnover among worker-militiamen, who tended to have little interest in day-to-day police work and to serve only a short time. Startsev claims that of 470 workers from the Metallurgical Factory in Vyborg's first subdistrict who served during the period from March to July, only ten served all four months. There were never more than 140 on the rolls at one time.[24]

At first glance one might assume that the district soviets would provide definite direction for the workers' militias, especially in the more heavily working-class districts, since they took a considerable interest in and claimed a share in the supervision of both workers' militias and the City Militia. In fact, however, their involvement only further complicated the matter, both because they were outside the formal line of institutional organization and responsibility and because their involvement varied so much by time and place, depending upon the composition and vigor of each soviet. Moreover, almost all district soviets recognized the legal authority of the City Militia officials, even when they ignored or opposed them in practice; and after the district *dumy* were established the district soviets also recognized their authority in militia affairs, although again they often violated that authority. Still, in the working-class districts the soviets' role tended to be considerable. The Vasil'evskii Island District Soviet was particularly active in supervising the function of the militia there, as were the Vyborg and some other soviets. Generally, district soviets (1) attempted to insure that the militias functioned well and were "democratic" (i.e., overwhelmingly worker and autonomous), (2) defended the workers' militias against city officials and factory management, and (3) tried to settle disputes among the militiamen. The district soviets were generally recognized as having some legitimate voice in militia affairs, yet they never really established themselves as the responsible directing agency. The militias, whether factory or united in some sort of sub-district or even district commissariat, retained their own autonomy in fact and often in theory as well. The locus of authority remained at the factory level, and various attempts to overcome this, as we will see in the following chapters, generally failed. A neat line of authority and responsibility for all workers' militias was never worked out between February and October; instead, confusion was the norm.

Diversity of nomenclature—both at the time and in later litera-ture—further complicates the problem of trying to clarify the struc-ture of the workers' armed bands.* One source of confusion is the distinction between "factory" and "workers'" militia. The two terms were often used interchangeably, but a slight distinction did exist, and took on more substance with the passage of time. Though both were based at a factory, a "workers' militia" usually patrolled a geographic territory and performed general security functions, whereas a "factory militia" often had the more limited responsibility of safeguarding the factory grounds and property. In fact, however, a factory militia often policed the area around its fac-tory and provided patrols to the local militia commissariat, whether workers' or city; conversely, units called "workers' militia" often performed factory guard duty. Another distinction was the assump-tion that the factory management had some say in the "factory mi-litia," even if it amounted to nothing more than the obligation to recognize it as the factory guard and to pay its members, whereas it had virtually no say in the matter of the "workers' militia," al-though it was often forced to pay salary to workers serving in it. Two other terms were used, less frequently, at this time—"workers' guard" and "fighting *druzhina*." Neither appears to have had clear special connotations, the choice of names being a matter of local inspiration at the time of formation. They simply were alternative

---

* Because of the variety of terms used in 1917, when reporting or summarizing contemporary accounts the term used by the author or document in question is used here also.

names for workers' self-organized armed bands. Despite the more belligerent sound, "fighting *druzhina*" (*boevaia druzhina*) was usually a defensive group with the same connotations as workers' militia or Red Guard (see Chapter Four), and was not normally seen as a special combat or offensive unit. Sometimes there existed within a single factory two separate organizations, in which case different names denoted different functions: one participant recalls that at the Metallurgical Factory there was both a factory militia and a fighting *druzhina*,[25] although he does not make clear their different functions. Similarly, the Admiralty Factory in September had both a Red Guard and a factory militia,[26] the former with broad functions of advancing and protecting worker interests, the latter with more narrow factory security functions. More important than any formal differences of function among the various groups, whatever they happened to be called, is the fact that they all represented worker self-organization and self-assertion, and all saw themselves as defenders of worker interests against the factory managers and the "bourgeoisie" in general.

Although most proletarian militia units were formed at factories or in a district and thus had a distinct territorial base, there were some that did not. These were formed along trade-union lines. The earliest and best known of these was the "Fighting *Druzhina* of Printers." Relatively small with only 100 men, it was formed by the Printers Union and apparently was well organized and armed. According to its own regulations, it existed "for the needs of the profession of printers and for the defense of the revolution." The printing plants had been special centers of concern during and just after the February Revolution, with many arbitrary seizures, and the printers apparently felt the need for their own armed force to protect themselves. The Printers' *Druzhina* had a decentralized structure, the key unit being the "ten." Each "ten" elected its own commander and was autonomous in its internal affairs. The elected commanders made up a council to direct the affairs of the *Druzhina*, provide instructors, issue instructions, and so forth, under the general authority of the Printers Union. Interestingly enough, the regulations gave considerable space to the responsibilities of members and the self-discipline expected of them, and included provisions for expulsion. It is not accidental that the printers later played a leading role in efforts to organize and discipline the various armed workers' bands.[27] Some other trade-union-based militias existed, though they were not so common in Petrograd as they were in some provincial towns. One example was the Construction Workers' Union Red Guard,[28] and it is possible that a trade-union-based militia of tailors and dressmakers existed, since an announcement in *Izvestiia* on March 5 summoned members of those trades to a meeting, one point of whose agenda was the organization of a militia.

In the face of the early, spontaneous, and rapid development of various kinds of armed groups, the major political parties were quickly obliged to consider their response to the situation and to take some kind of position on it—even if doing so had little effect in practical terms. The Bolsheviks especially, who after their initial hesitation had encouraged the workers to form armed bands, began to turn their attention to the broader issues involved once the immediate task of securing the revolution was completed. Several questions emerged: What was the purpose of these bands? What about their organizational structure (and especially their affiliation with the City Militia)? And what should be their relationship to other bodies, particularly the socialist parties? The Bolshevik Petersburg Committee took up these questions on March 3, at the first regular meeting of the reconstituted Committee. It charged comrades Chernomor (Ia. Ia. Ozol') and Mikhail Kharkharev to organize a military-militia commission and to put a draft for the organization of proletarian militia cadres before the Petersburg Committee for discussion in the shortest possible time. It is ironic, given the historic trouble of the Bolshevik Party with police infiltration, that Chernomor was later unmasked as having been a tsarist police provocateur and shot in 1924.[29] The early debates of the Petersburg Committee, however, merely underscored the fact that the members' views remained unfixed.[30] They normally took up the issue in connection with an ongoing concern with district-level political organization, and their discussions in fact had little immediate impact on what was happening among the workers' militia units in the factories and districts.

If discussion of the workers' militia was sporadic and usually in the context of local organizational problems, this may reflect in part indecision on the basic questions of the Party's attitude toward the Provisional Government, the nature of the revolution, and at what "stage" the revolution then stood. Once one went beyond pragmatic problems of defense and public order, a broader vision of the role of worker armed bands depended on working out these questions, and the Party had not yet done so. Still, some Bolshevik leaders began to address the issue publicly and in doing so to establish a Party position. The first major public statement on the militia question by the Bolsheviks came in a long unsigned article in *Pravda*, the Bolshevik newspaper, on March 8. It referred approvingly to the Petersburg Committee's March 3d resolution to strengthen the "proletarian militia cadres" and warned against letting the workers' militia movement fade away. Acknowledging that the workers' militia had restored order in the workers' districts, it argued that the organization of the militia had stopped halfway. The militia should not be viewed as a temporary organization for the needs of the moment, but must become a regular, strong workers' army. It must be a unified, democratic, autonomous organization, but with close ties to the Bolshevik Party through representatives in the Bolshevik district committees and the Petersburg Committee. *Pravda* insisted that the workers must not lay down their arms, for they were the cadres of the new revolutionary army. The new City Militia was repudiated on the grounds that it was being created by the old, and hence untrustworthy, city administration. The article continued with a call for strengthening and arming "new cadres of the revolutionary militia" and concluded, "The revolution has not been completed."

Slightly broader, more philosophical and historical tones were adopted in a *Pravda* article of March 17, "It Is Impossible to Wait," by Vladimir Nevskii, who later played a leading role in the Bolshevik seizure of power. Noting the role of the soldiers in the February Revolution, he pointed out that the army would not be under arms in Petrograd forever, and that since "reaction never sleeps," it was necessary to go beyond a simple militia and form a "national guard from the workers." He cited especially the lessons of the French revolutions of 1789 and 1848, asserting that the destruction of the working class in the "June Days" of 1848 resulted from allowing the national guard to fall into the hands of the bourgeoisie. If such an outcome was to be avoided in Russia, then the arming of the people and the creation of a national guard from among the workers must be undertaken immediately. If this were done, then there would be no need to fear the eventual removal of the revolutionary garrison from Petrograd. Nevskii made clear that he favored the creation of a special "workers' guard" and called on the Soviet to organize one. *Pravda* carried the demand for a new type of militia a step further the next day with the article "The Armed People" by Vladimir Bonch-Bruevich, who also played an important role in organizing the armed forces used in October. Like Nevskii, Bonch-Bruevich discussed the historical examples of armed groups in revolutionary situations, and noted especially the creation in 1905 in Finland of a Red Guard. He called for the creation of a *"Red Guard of the Proletariat"* (emphasis in original, and apparently the first printed use of the term "red guard" in 1917) created by workers and trained by revolutionary soldiers. The emphasis was upon a permanent, disciplined, democratic, class-based organization. He asked for a wide discussion of this and quick action.

The Bolshevik spokesmen were able to use not only their own press but also the newspaper of the Petrograd Soviet, *Izvestiia*, to expound their views. The Petrograd Soviet, as we have seen, lacked a clear-cut position on the militia. Although there were frequent references to the militia in *Izvestiia*, they concerned the workaday problems of organization without any attention to broader principles. *Izvestiia* at this time was so disorganized that it can hardly be considered the mouthpiece for any official position. Rather, it reflected a variety of viewpoints, mainly the personal views of its editors, most of whom were radical Social Democrats without clear party affiliation. One result was that its major article on the militia question was an unsigned essay by Vladimir Nevskii on March 19. Similar in tone to his earlier *Pravda* article, it held up the specter of the June Days in France and the danger that would be posed when the revolutionary army was removed from Petrograd. It also called for arming the people in a "national guard, a genuine people's, that is, workers' army." * The militia was not adequate to the task; a workers' army was, in the words of the article title, "a press-

* The use of the term *narodnyi* created a useful double meaning for Nevskii in his two articles but a problem for the historian; in this context it seems best to translate it as "national," to keep the parallel with France that Nevskii intended, but usually throughout this study it is translated as "people's," as in "people's militia," which is more in keeping with the connotation that seems most commonly intended. Positive identification of Nevskii as the author is given by Malakhovskii, "Kak sozdavalas'," pp. 40, 46, although he miscites the title.

ing need." Nevskii was able to repeat and amplify his ideas in a March 29 article, written in response to letters to the editor about his earlier article.

The Bolsheviks, then, almost immediately after February began to call for organizing a permanent, autonomous, revolutionary, class-oriented armed force. Both Nevskii and Bonch-Bruevich laid heavy stress on wide distribution of arms among the people as the only means to defend freedom. Clearly implied was the concept of an armed force to be used in a future class conflict. These issues were discussed also in Party meetings. The Red Guard and arming the people turned up regularly on the agenda of the Petersburg Committee at the end of March and beginning of April.[31] An authoritative statement in favor of armed workers' units came in a resolution by the Russian Bureau of the Central Committee on March 22 that called for both the arming of all the people and the formation of a "workers' Red Guard."[32] Thus even before the return of Lenin, the Bolsheviks were already groping their way toward the notion of "arming the people" and of a special proletarian force to advance the revolution. Their activity, however, was limited mainly to discussion and articles: as an organization they did, or could do, little to further the actual formation of worker armed units. The Bolshevik Military Organization* recognized that arming and organizing workers' units was one of its functions, but in fact it concentrated entirely on the military garrison.[33]

Wholly different was the attitude revealed by the Menshevik Party's newspaper, *Rabochaia gazeta*. In an article on March 8 it stated that the militia question was one of the most important facing the revolution, but one that was misunderstood by many people who mixed up under this title two different things. If by militia was understood the "*armed people*" (emphasis in original), a body that would replace the army and defend the revolution from any efforts on the part of the old regime to restore itself, then this was an erroneous concept. Creation of such a militia at present, during the war, was impossible and unneeded, for the "armed people" already

---

* The Bolsheviks' Military Organization was created by the Petersburg Committee in March and placed under the Central Committee in April. Its primary purpose was to conduct agitation and organizational activities among the soldiers and sailors of the garrison, but it did give some attention to the workers' militias and Red Guards.

existed in the form of the revolutionary army. A militia understood as a citizens' police or guard was a wholly different matter, *Rabochaia gazeta* asserted, and in fact the organization of such a citizens' guard to maintain order was a pressing task. It should be democratic in nature and have the trust of the people, and it should preferably be elected by the citizens of the local area. This article failed to address points that were raised in the *Pravda* article of the same date and in subsequent Bolshevik writings: that a "workers' guard" was needed because one could not depend upon the continued existence of the revolutionary army, and that the organization of the City Militia was not satisfactory. The whole mood of impending social conflict that underlay the Bolshevik articles was not present in the Menshevik one. The difference in attitudes was underlined by the striking absence of further commentary on the militia question in *Rabochaia gazeta* for the rest of the month; when passing references to the militia were made in connection with, say, matters of local political organization, the newspaper simply treated the militia question as if it were settled. Even more striking was the almost total silence of the Socialist Revolutionary newspaper, *Delo naroda*. It began publication only on March 15, but for the rest of the month it did not run a single major article or editorial on the militia. Its most extensive reference was a four-line item on March 29 about the efforts of the city government to work out a decree on the militia.

The nonsocialist parties, as might be expected, took a very different view of the militia question. The Constitutional Democrats (Kadets) remained the only significant nonsocialist party in Russia after February, and their major statement on the militia was an article in *Rech'*, the party newspaper, by N. A. Lenskii on March 14. The article stressed the need for a regularized City Militia to take up fundamental police functions and to replace the "motley" volunteer militia then existing. Lenskii noted that the volunteer groups were slowly melting away and approved of this as a sign that life was returning to its normal channels. Nonetheless, this development underlined the need to establish a regular municipal police force that would not only maintain public order—which he conceded the volunteer militias had done fairly well—but also perform administrative tasks (registration, certification, and so on), criminal investigations, and prosecutions. This new militia, the article argued, must be under the direction of the city authorities and have a chief appointed by the City Duma. Warning against "misunderstood democratic ideas," Lenskii pointed out that the kind of militia being proposed was in some ways even more advanced than the English police! So much for those who would find the proposal "insufficiently radical." The main theme of his approach was normalization. He stressed the need for a nonpolitical, Western-style police, however termed, shorn of the odious features of the old police. Lenskii's article was reinforced by regular reporting in *Rech'* on the progress of city officials in setting up the new City Militia, including the listing of district militia office addresses and phone numbers. However, the paper generally ignored the whole phenomenon of workers' and factory militias, as if these were temporary aberrations that could be expected to go away now that life was returning to normal. The mood of general goodwill that pervaded the first weeks of the Revolution made this attitude a not unreasonable one; nevertheless, it was erroneous. Instead, the mood in the working-class districts, as we will see, was one of determination not only to maintain the independence of their own militias, but to strengthen their organization.

Overall, the political parties played but a small role in the formation of militias—either city or workers'—during the first month of the Revolution. Later they would have an impact, especially through the actions of district and factory leaders, but at the beginning the parties were still too disorganized to play much of a role. Moreover, the workers' urge to obtain arms and to form their own organizations was too strong, and their understanding of party programs and sense of party identification too weak, for the parties to take the lead. Still, the attitudes revealed in the first month accurately reflected the positions the parties would take throughout 1917, which in turn determined their success or failure in winning the support of the armed workers. For the workers, their localism was a source of strength because it bound them so closely at the factory to worker concerns, but it was also a source of weakness in defending themselves against attacks on their existence or in mobilizing their potential strength. It is not surprising, then, that some militia leaders soon turned to the problem of forming district and city organizational structures, and that this remained a major issue throughout 1917.

4

The Emergence of the Red Guard

"If we had a Red Guard, then they would take us seriously."
— *Unnamed speaker at the April 23*
Red Guard organizational meeting

During late March and April, an effort was being made among the armed workers' bands to create some sort of general, citywide leadership outside the framework provided by the City Militia administration. A new term was emerging, too—"Red Guard." Its meaning was neither precise nor consistent, but it did imply a more aggressive, politicized, disciplined force, totally separate from the City Militia administration. The term smacked of more strident class conflict and suggested a group dedicated to carrying forward the Revolution by arms. These two developments reinforced each other and resulted in late April in a major effort to establish a unified Red Guard in Petrograd.

From the first week of the Revolution there had been efforts to provide some sort of central leadership for the multitude of workers' armed units that were coming into being. As the City Militia consolidated itself, the sense of a need for better organization of the workers' militia became more urgent. The first attempt was the meeting on March 7 of representatives of workers' militia organizations from six districts. The delegates considered it necessary to strengthen the workers' militia, as distinct from the City Militia, and proposed that the Petrogradskii district militia commissariat coordinate the activities of all workers' commissariats.[1] This reflected the success of Peshekhonov and Shakh in establishing a comparatively centralized organization on the Petrograd side, a success they were certainly proud of and willing to hold up as a model—as they did in mid-March by inviting "comrade representatives of the militia section of other districts" who wished to receive information on the organization of the Petrogradskii district militia to come to the commissariat.[2] There were other, local efforts of more modest scale. Vyborg's first subdistrict militia commissariat, where the energetic Botsvadze worked, on April 4 discussed appealing to other districts to send representatives to a meeting on the question of unity; a few days later, the first subdistrict decided to unite with the second Vyborg subdistrict for common work and to organize a general meeting.[3] Nothing seems to have come of this, however.

Another half-hearted effort came from meetings of representatives of factory militias convened by the Petrograd Soviet, probably by the Executive Committee's department for militia organization, which was formed in mid-March. At the first meeting on March 16 the representatives discussed arms, pay, and a set of regulations for all workers' militias, but little headway was made on a citywide organization. Indeed, that seems not to have been a central concern: one report suggests that the emphasis was on the workers' militia cooperating with the City Militia. There were only five districts represented, and the meeting ended with a decision to convene regular meetings at which all factory militia commissariats would be represented.[4] Apparently there were efforts to hold such meetings, but little if anything came of them. The Petrograd Soviet, though concerned with the militia question, simply did not provide strong leadership. Aside from tending to deal only with the most pressing issues in the crush of events, the Soviet leaders were torn between their willingness to have the militia unified under the City Militia directorate and their sympathy with the workers' demand for their own autonomous armed units. As a result, the Soviet failed to take any particularly strong measures. This failure to act vigorously and to bring the armed workers' bands under the Soviet's direct organizational control had important long-term implications, for it meant that these armed bands would grow and develop without Soviet guidance and with a strong sense of independence that it would be almost impossible to counteract later.

The initiative for organization, therefore, devolved onto the district soviets, which could do little more than organize on the local level, if that. In some districts, such as Vasil'evskii Island, Peterhof, and Petrogradskii, the local soviets tried both to organize, discipline, and train workers' militias and to regulate their relations with the City Militia officials. In this respect it is interesting to note the claim advanced at the March 16 meeting of factory militia delegates that in all five of the districts represented a central organ had been formed to unify the factory militias of the district and that this organ maintained contact with the City Militia.[5] Though this claim may have been exaggerated, and certainly did not apply to all the districts of the city, it is worth examining more closely.

In three of the five districts the workers' militias had been relatively centralized from the beginning. One of the three was the Petrogradskii district, where the militia organized by Peshekhonov's commissariat provided a general direction and unity to armed bands drawn from many factories. Scattered references indicate a significant degree of centralized control; moreover, though individual patrols were often of homogeneous composition, the overall militia was socially mixed. The second was the Porokhovskii district, where the militia, as we have seen, was formed in the process of creating a district soviet, which presumably continued to exercise central authority over it. This task was simplified in that this thinly populated area had only a small number of factories, although they were large ones. In the third district, Peterhof, the giant Putilov works dominated the area, facilitating efforts by the district soviet (composed mostly of Putilovites) to establish some control over the workers' militias there. The district soviet had a militia commission as early as March 8. There also was a City Militia commissariat in the district, and the two apparently kept in close contact.

The organization of the militia in the fourth district represented, the sprawling Nevskii district to the south of the city center, is simply unknown in any detail, but it does not appear that central direction was ever established. In the fifth district, Vasil'evskii Island, the situation was different from any of those outlined above. As we saw in Chapter One, a number of independent militia units had sprung up on the island during the first few days of the Revolution. However, some unity was imposed following the formation of a district soviet in early March, for the soviet soon took an active role in the direction of the militia in most of the island. At the March 10 meeting of the soviet's executive committee, a report was heard from the militia commander on the constitution, organization, and functions of the militia. This report included references to the existence of a district militia council seemingly elected on a proportional basis from workers, soldiers, citizens, and students. That all was not well, however, is made clear, first, by the strong assertion of the need for better organization and, second, by the fact that at a meeting the next day it was noted that there was great chaos in the militia.[6] Moreover, the soviet and council did not direct all of the militia activities: on the eastern tip of the island, around the Bourse, the University, and other public buildings, the separate militia organized by Drozdov and directed by a residents' committee still was conducting patrols. It eventually became part of the City Militia (indeed, it probably already was by March 16) and took directions from the City Duma militia officials. This part of the island was apparently never under the unified workers' militia organization and control.

Though some district-level organization existed in a few places, this should not be overestimated. District-level leadership remained fairly weak, and it was usually a question of a little or none at all. On a citywide level there was even less authority or structure. The efforts in March failed not only to create an all-city organization for the workers' militia, but even to convene a broad-based meeting. Nevertheless, the urge for better organization was still present among the workers and their lower-level leaders, despite their early lack of success and the inactivity—indeed, lack of interest—of the Petrograd Soviet leadership. This fundamental urge led to new efforts from below in April to convene an all-city conference and to set up a general headquarters and regulations for the workers' armed groups. This was connected with the emergence of the term Red Guard and with a turn from social concerns such as public order toward more political and revolutionary issues.

The term "Red Guard" was first used in 1917 in Vladimir Bonch-Bruevich's *Pravda* article on March 18, as we have noted already. Leaving out the usual references to the need for a militia to maintain order and security, he stressed the importance of a workers' army for defense against counterrevolution and the preservation of the people's freedom. It is particularly interesting to note that Bonch-Bruevich mixed into the article two very different notions: first, the formation of a disciplined military organization, and second, a general arming of the people, the creation of "a huge army of proletariat." General arming of the population and discipline probably were mutually exclusive, although Bonch-Bruevich may well have had vague notions of the entire proletariat being well-armed and disciplined; that would not have been entirely out of keeping with some Bolshevik attitudes.

After its use by Bonch-Bruevich, the term "Red Guard" came into increasingly frequent use, especially by the Bolsheviks. The two notions of a general arming of the people and the formation of a Red Guard as a defense against counterrevolution were embodied in a resolution about the Provisional Government adopted by the Russian Bureau of the Bolshevik Central Committee on March 22 and presented to the All-Russian Conference of (Bolshevik) Party Workers on March 29. The Red Guard idea surfaced several times in the discussion of the Bolshevik attitude toward the Provisional Government. Though the Bureau's resolution spoke of a Red Guard as necessary for defense against counterrevolution, others argued that it was not the best means. V. V. Voitinskii argued that not the formation of a Red Guard, but the strengthening of the army's adherence to the Revolution and the fulfillment of socialist programs was the best guarantee against counterrevolution. P. I. Starostin from Irkutsk echoed that sentiment, adding that such measures as forming Red Guards might alienate the army, since they might be understood as signifying a lack of faith in the soldiers, and that Red Guard units would be of no value anyway if the army was not with them. This view apparently had some impact, for the much revised resolution on the Provisional Government that was passed omitted the reference to a Red Guard and to arming the people, merely declaring the need to unite around the Soviet as the means to defend against counterrevolution and to broaden the Revolution.[7] The term "Red Guard" turns up in numerous other Bolshevik documents of late March and early April: in the agenda of the Petersburg Committee for March 27 and April 13; in the minutes of the Vyborg district Bolshevik committee session of March 31; in the minutes of the Petrogradskii district Bolshevik committee session of April 6; and in the records of the Moscow district Bolshevik conference of April 13.[8]

Just when the first armed band calling itself "Red Guard" came into existence is difficult to date. The revolutionary committee in the nearby suburb of Sestroretsk, where the Sestroretsk Arms Factory was a stronghold of radicalism throughout 1917, resolved on March 21 to organize a "workers' militia (Red Guard)"—the first use of the term after Bonch-Bruevich's article.[9] Apparently there were some Red Guard units already in existence by April 11, when the Vasil'evskii Island Soviet decided to allocate space for "a club of the Red Guard," for its minutes refer to the Red Guard as an existing organization. The existence of another Red Guard is confirmed by an April 11 decision of the first Vyborg subdistrict militia commissariat to remove militia verification cards from people entering the Red Guard.[10] This would suggest that there was a clear distinction between the Red Guard and the militia—at least in areas such as this where the militia had close ties to the City Militia even though composed of workers—and that the Red Guard was considered to have a different purpose. It also shows that guardsmen were sometimes drawn from among the militiamen, presumably those of more radical temperament. The term comes up also in numerous factory resolutions from this period that refer to or call for formation of Red Guard units. The Old Parviainen Factory on the Vyborg side passed a list of strongly antigovernment and antibourgeois resolutions on April 13, including a call "to organize a Red Guard and to arm all the people." A very similar set of demands was issued by the workers of the nearby Russian Renault Automobile Factory on March 16, including the identical demand "to organize a Red Guard and to arm all the people."[11] The similarities in the two sets of resolutions suggest either that both were inspired by the same source—the most likely common source being local Vyborg Bolsheviks—or that one factory was influenced by the other's resolution. The call for a Red Guard cropped up elsewhere, too, as time passed: a meeting of workers at the Skorokhod Shoe Factory in the Narva district on April 22 passed a resolution for organizing a "people's Red Guard" of 1,000;[12] and the Peterhof District Soviet issued a call to arms on April 26 in which it urged workers to join the Red Guard, the "vanguard of the proletariat," for which it also provided a local leadership structure.[13] The formation of such units apparently progressed rapidly in the second half of April, even if one assumes that actual organization ran well behind the resolutions.

The two trends toward the creation of a central organization of workers' armed units and the emergence of the term and concept of a Red Guard were brought together in the convening of a citywide Red Guard conference in late April. This represented a merging of the workers' sense of a need for their own armed force with a felt need for unity and leadership to give direction, cohesion, and legitimacy to their activities. Indeed, the initiative for the conference came not from the Soviet or any important political leaders, but from the militiamen and workers and their local leaders, specifically the Fighting *Druzhina* of Printers, one of the best organized workers' armed bands. It is perhaps not accidental that, being trade-union-based, it was the only workers' armed unit to have a citywide rather than a factory or district structure. The leading role in organizing the conference was taken by N. Rostov, a Menshevik printer just returned from exile, who was invited by the Printers' Union to work with its *Druzhina* and specifically to help with all-city organization of workers' militiamen. The printers felt that the poorly organized nature of the various armed bands was responsible for the growing demoralization—even vandalism—in their ranks, created a competition for arms, and caused an uncertainty about responsibilities that could lead to armed clashes. Rostov, therefore, was charged with the task of forming a committee to begin work on this problem. Opinion was sampled in the districts in April, including meetings of militiamen, and this confirmed that there was considerable interest in such an endeavor and even some other, faltering efforts in this direction. Rostov emphasizes that the initiative in forming a citywide organization was coming from the *druzhiniki* and militiamen themselves and that the soviets (city and district) and the political parties played a very minor role; help from the latter was only occasional and had an amateurish, tinkering character.[14] The thrust for organization, both local and citywide, was from below, not from the major political leaders.

The first meeting was held on April 17 in the City Duma building, and was attended by representatives from 22 factories in five districts, plus representatives elected by subdistricts in the Petrogradskii district. The major industrial districts were represented: Vyborg, Petrogradskii, Vasil'evskii Island, Peterhof. The delegates decided that they should try to organize a Red Guard in all factories and that it should be composed only of people recommended by one of the socialist parties. Nonetheless, they stressed that the Red Guard was not a party organization and remained separate from all parties. This reflected the peculiar relationship between the armed workers' movements and the political parties. On the one hand, the parties were always considered important, and membership in one was verification of a person's political reliability. Yet on the other hand, the party role in organization was minimal until later, nearer October, and there was a strong sense of the appropriateness of being nonparty (although socialist). The contradiction was partially covered up by the active role of local party figures. Although this and some other issues were discussed, the conference participants felt they did not have sufficient representation—owing to inadequate publicity—to go ahead with organizational matters and so decided to elect a temporary commission of five members to organize a larger meeting of representatives from more factories. The three Mensheviks and two Bolsheviks chosen met the next day, April 18, but business was apparently limited mainly to charging Rostov with drawing up draft regulations and setting a date for the larger conference, April 23.[15]

Before the next conference could meet, the disorders called the "April Crisis" intervened and caused its postponement. A conflict had been developing for some time between the Provisional Government, especially Foreign Minister Paul Miliukov, and the Soviet leadership over the question of Russia's role in the war. Miliukov had taken the position that the Revolution had not changed Russia's foreign policy objectives and that continuation of the war until final victory, in close association with the Allies, was essential. The Soviet leaders, especially Irakli Tsereteli and Victor Chernov, pressed for a revision of Russia's foreign policy in the direction of a negotiated peace, the first step of which was a revision of war aims along the lines of the formula "peace without annexations or indemnities, self-determination of peoples." This formula enjoyed great popularity, for it combined the widespread yearning for an end to the war and its attendant miseries with the still strong sense of the need to defend the country against an occupying foe. Finally Miliukov was forced to send a document embodying these sentiments to the Allies, but he sent along an accompanying note that effectively negated the document and the Soviet's formula. This note, when published on April 18, touched off an uproar. Demonstrators demanding the removal of Miliukov surged through the streets and clashed with smaller groups demonstrating in his support. Many feared civil war.[16]

The April Crisis and attendant demonstrations had a major impact upon the efforts to organize the Red Guard. It was the first major internecine confrontation of the Revolution. Workers' militia detachments took part in many of the demonstrations against Mili-ukov during the tumultuous days of April 20–22, although they were outnumbered in terms of arms by the soldiers who also dem-onstrated against the government. For the workers' militia and armed bands it was their first opportunity to show their strength. Armed workers commonly marched at the head of processions; often each factory contingent or column in a larger demonstration was headed by its own armed detachment. In the great demonstra-tion of April 22, which moved the length of Nevskii Prospect, armed groups were prominent: at the head marched a detachment of soldiers, with officers; then came an armed workers' detach-ment; and between the columns marched other workers' militia units. Considering the number of armed people on the streets and the passions aroused, it is surprising how little shooting and how few casualties there were, the most significant incident being a con-fused firing on Nevskii Prospect on April 21, in which armed work-ers' detachments were involved.[17] Nonetheless, the demonstrations and the disorderly firing convinced some workers' leaders of the need for more and better armed groups, and for better organization and discipline within the units. Rostov's account of one confronta-tion underlines the situation. A somewhat disorganized demonstra-tion originated in the Narva district, where Rostov was working as a Menshevik organizer at the Treugol'nik Rubber Factory. The pro-cession of Treugol'nik, Putilov, and other workers started for the center of town, with *druzhiniki* and militiamen—some armed—at their head. When they ran into a confrontation at Nevskii Prospect, militiamen were among the first to lose their heads and run, firing indiscriminately. The mood of the marchers on returning home included discouragement, bewilderment, and a feeling that ill-disciplined militiamen had been the cause of the clash. Rostov claims that the event converted many to the conclusion that the militia needed to be better organized.[18] For the rank and file of workers it underscored the importance of arms: at the Diuflon-Konstantinovich Electrical Machine Factory, for example, workers during the April Days appeared at work with arms, and when asked why, replied "just in case."[19]

The recent demonstrations provided the backdrop for discus-sions on April 23, when instead of the general meeting (postponed because of the April Crisis disruptions), a smaller meeting of the temporary commission and 42 factory delegates met to discuss the regulations drawn up by Rostov and the whole problem of a workers' armed force. Rostov used as a basis for the regulations those of the Printers' *Druzhina*, the earliest existing such document from 1917. He also drew upon the experiences of Kock's Finnish Red Guard of 1905, borrowing that name for the workers' armed organization and entitling his handiwork the "Draft Regulations for the Petrograd Red Guard worked out by the temporary commission for the organization of the Red Guard." The regulations stated that the "Red Guard exists for the protection of the achievements of the Revolution and for struggle with counterrevolutionary attempts." The first point read in part, "in its activities the Red Guard works in close unity with the Soviet of Workers' and Soldiers' Deputies"— the expression "close unity" being an amendment after Bolshevik objections, for Rostov's draft had made the Red Guard a department of the Soviet. Point two also caused debate, eventually resulting in a definition of membership as open to "workers and peasants recommended by socialist parties." Rostov had originally proposed that only party members be allowed to join, and this opening up to nonmembers probably reflected a victory of the outlook of the factory delegates as against that of the organizing committee members, all five of whom were party members. Both changes had the effect of emphasizing local autonomy and reducing control by the Soviet and the political parties. The rest of the document concerned itself with the organizational structure of the Red Guard, and with discipline.[20]

The delegates were terribly concerned with the events of the preceding few days, and the minutes of the meeting make clear that the speakers felt the recent disorders underscored the need for a strong Red Guard. One speaker stated that "if we had a Red Guard, then they would take us seriously. . . . At the head of districts [demonstrations] will go armed guardsmen and then they will not tear up the red flag."[21] This mood was reflected in the proclamation "To All Workers of Petrograd," passed by the meeting, which summarized the purpose of the Red Guard:

Defending the interest of the proletariat, the Red Guard at the same time protects the interests of the entire democracy and by the fact of its existence is a threat to any counterrevolutionary attempts from any source. Only the armed working class can be the actual defenders of the freedom

we have fought for. . . . The business of the Revolution is not yet finished.
. . . The Red Guard, as the true sentry of the Revolution, will be its defense
in the hour of need.

The proclamation ended by urging the workers to send delegates to
the all-city meeting and to organize themselves into a Red Guard.[22]
This appeal, drafted by Rostov, was distributed around the city in a
printing of 10,000 copies.*

The period between the meeting of April 23 and the opening of
the general conference on the Red Guard on April 28 was hectic,
confused, and very important for the development of the Revolution. The Provisional Government was in the midst of its first major
internal political crisis, which stretched from the publication of
Miliukov's note on April 18 through the collapse of the ministry on
May 2 to the formation on May 5 of a coalition ministry that included the leaders of the Petrograd Soviet. This crisis consumed
most of the energy of the Soviet. On another level, the demonstrations of April 18–21 and the general political tension helped stimulate interest in forming armed workers' bands and using them. The
Nevskii Mechanical Shoe Factory passed a resolution calling for the
Soviet to transfer power to the proletariat and peasantry and immediately to arm all workers. On April 26 the Peterhof District Soviet
not only appealed to workers to join the Red Guard as a "strong
battle organization that must be the bulwark of the revolutionary
working class," but also set up an organizational structure and membership requirements. These belligerent developments occurred in a
soviet still dominated by Menshevik and SR leaders and is an example of the divergence between the district and the city leaders of the
two parties. Further underscoring this divergence is a resolution
from the Skorokhod Shoe Factory, where a meeting of workers on
April 22 resolved to ask the Petrograd Soviet for 500 rifles and 500
revolvers to arm a Red Guard of 1,000 to be formed at the factory.[23]
This request indicates a complete misunderstanding of the attitude
of the Soviet leaders, who were anxious to avoid creating such

---

* An interesting insight into the way things were done in those days is Rostov's
casual comment that the appeal was not distributed in the Narva and Nevskii districts because the car carrying the broadsides crashed before getting there. Something of the fragility, indeed the chancy character, of historical knowledge is illustrated by Rostov's additional comment that only one copy of this document out of
the 10,000 has survived—in the Museum of the Revolution. There is no explanation
for why it was not printed in the papers—or even if it was sent to them.

armed groups. The gap between the Soviet leaders and the facto-ries—even those with Menshevik or SR leadership—was enor-mous, and on such an emotional issue as arms it could only lead to quick estrangement.

One decision of the April 23 meeting was to select factory dele-gates to the Red Guard conference—one for each 1,000 workers—as well as representatives from the various workers' *druzhiny*. Elec-tions accordingly took place at the Treugol'nik Factory on April 24, at the Putilov Factory on the 25th, and at other factories during the period between the 25th and the 27th. In all, 82 factories sent 156 delegates, most apparently members of worker armed units. In ad-dition there were 26 members of socialist parties and worker orga-nizations.[24] The election of factory delegates probably further stim-ulated worker interest in forming Red Guard detachments.

Just as the preparations for the conference on April 28 were being completed, the organizers began to receive indications that the leadership of the Petrograd Soviet opposed the conference and the entire Red Guard project. Rostov had been questioned by the Menshevik central committee (Organizational Committee RSDRP) about the project, and although he and the other Mensheviks were not forbidden to continue their work, disquiet about the guards was communicated. Rostov also claimed that his awareness of mis-givings on the part of the Soviet leadership had resulted in his ton-ing down the appeal issued April 23.[25] Then on the morning of the 28th, *Izvestiia* published an editorial on the Red Guards denounc-ing them as "unnecessary and harmful" from a "proletarian point of view." This editorial, though unsigned, was written by Fedor Dan and thus represented the attitude of the innermost leadership of the Soviet and of the Menshevik Party. Referring to the con-ference scheduled for that day and the draft regulations (which were published in the same issue), the editorial acknowledged the natural anxiety of workers over the fate of the Revolution and their concern to have arms in their own hands. However, it argued, here the example of the French Revolution misled, for the nature of ar-mies and weaponry had changed, as had the role of both armed crowds and armies—especially the role of revolutionary soldiers in Russia. The important concern now, Dan argued, was the unity of the workers and the soldiers, a unity that would be damaged by the formation of a Red Guard, which would allow enemies of the Revolution to tell the soldiers that the workers were being armed against them. The article went on to hint at possible confrontations between confused soldiers and "passionate" young workers. The workers must contribute to the Revolution not through possession of a few ineffective revolvers and other arms, the article argued, but through the political education and organization of the soldiers. The theme of unity of workers and soldiers was seconded by the theme of general revolutionary unity under the leadership of the Petrograd Soviet. The editorial noted that the draft regulations, by providing not for subordination of the Red Guard to the Soviet but only for "close unity" between the two, in fact promoted the Red Guard's independence from the Soviet and the consequent disorganization of the revolutionary movement and of its political unity. Thus the Red Guard might, under harmful influences, not only fail to act in accordance with the Soviet and the rest of the revolutionary democracy, but even act against them.

The *Izvestiia* editorial caused great consternation among the Red Guard conference organizers. The Mensheviks and SRs among them were put in a terrible position, since the views expressed implicitly represented their parties' positions—for the old disorder at *Izvestiia* had long since been replaced by the firm control of the Soviet Executive Committee under the leadership of Irakli Tsereteli and the dominance of the Mensheviks and SRs. Moreover, the entire scheme assumed a close working relationship with the Petrograd Soviet. The Menshevik and SR organizers finally decided to push on, feeling on the one hand that any attempt to stop the conference at this point would be rejected by the workers and capitalized on by the Bolsheviks, and on the other that they were representing the true sentiments of the mass of workers better than their party leaders and might later be able to bring the latter around.[26] They did not realize the extent of the gap opening between the worker masses and the socialist intelligentsia leaders of the Soviet.

The conference finally opened on the afternoon of the 28th. The sponsors were hard-pressed to reconcile their project with the *Izvestiia* editorial. In the report on the work of the organizing committee, Rostov lamely argued that the *Izvestiia* editorial did not represent an *official* Soviet position, for the matter had not yet been officially discussed in the Executive Committee. He argued that the Red Guard was very much necessary to protect against counter-

revolution and that better organization and discipline were necessary to prevent disorganized and even disgraceful behavior, such as
had sometimes taken place during the April demonstrations. Rostov rejected the *Izvestiia* argument of possible conflict between the
army and the Red Guard. Another speaker pointed out, in an argument that found frequent expression among advocates of workers'
armed bands, that just such a force was needed because the revolutionary army would be disbanded when the war ended (presumably
shortly), and then the Red Guard would be the chief defender of the
revolutionary freedoms and the interests of the workers. Some soldiers present supported this argument, claiming that they welcomed the Red Guard's formation.[27]

In the stormy debates of the conference the authority of the Executive Committee of the Petrograd Soviet became a key issue. A representative of the Executive Committee, Iudin, a Menshevik, spoke
out strongly against the guards. He stressed that their formation
would cause tension with the soldiers and urged the workers to devote their energies to educational activities and the organization of
trade unions. Only then could they be armed. "I must tell you
frankly," Iudin stated, "that our workers are in ignorance. One can
hold a gun strongly in one's hands only when one has become
strong in the head." This brought forth a storm of denunciation,
including calls to throw him out. Only after a strong counterpro-
test, including threats by a considerable number to leave the hall,
was Iudin allowed to continue speaking. Some other speakers opposed the Red Guard, apparently supporting the Executive Committee view, but most, especially guardsmen, objected heatedly to
the Soviet position. They exhibited a sense of bewilderment and of
having been betrayed, for they were able to point out that the representatives of the Soviet earlier had passed out arms to the workers.
On no account, they insisted, would they give up their arms voluntarily. There was even a threat to take measures to see to it that the
next day's edition of *Izvestiia*, which Iudin had said would carry
the official statement of the Executive Committee against the Red
Guard, did not appear. Finally the meeting resolved to ask the Executive Committee to reconsider its position and decided to send a
delegation to talk to the Soviet leaders.[28]

The conference leaders pressed their case with the Soviet leadership to no avail. The deputation from the conference met with a few

members of the Executive Committee, including Fedor Dan and B. O. Bogdanov, two prominent Mensheviks, later that day. In a heated and rather unpleasant exchange, the Executive Committee members argued that the Red Guard was a Bolshevik movement, whereas Rostov and the others tried to convince them that it was a genuine workers' movement that should not be left to the Bolsheviks by default. Neither side could persuade the other. The organizers presented their case at a full Executive Committee meeting the next day, but were again unsuccessful, although apparently they left with some hopes that they might have won. In fact the Executive Committee's Bureau proposed a resolution that the "comrades from the Red Guard . . . take no kind of organizational and no kind of agitational steps." [29] This was not published in the newspapers, but *Izvestiia* ran a new editorial on April 30 reaffirming the position of the editorial of April 28 and announcing that it expressed the view of the Bureau of the Executive Committee. In a rather confused discussion of what useful functions armed workers could play, *Izvestiia* made clear that rather than special and independent workers' guard units, the Soviet leaders preferred extensive worker involvement in the regular City Militia. At no place did the editorial speak approvingly of workers' militias or Red Guards, and it specifically disapproved of "the independent existence of an armed workers' *druzhina*." The position of the Soviet leadership was underscored by an editorial against the Red Guard in *Rabochaia gazeta* on April 29 and by a resolution passed on May 1 by the Menshevik faction of the Soviet condemning the idea of a self-created Red Guard (published May 5 in *Rabochaia gazeta*). The resolution held up the specter of worker-soldier antagonism and urged workers to channel their efforts toward close relations with the revolutionary army and toward democratizing the "people's militia" by the addition of more workers. Shortly afterward Rostov was ordered by the Menshevik Party leaders to drop his activities on the Red Guard commission. Rostov and the other two Mensheviks on the commission bowed to party pressure and quit, thus leaving the field to the Bolsheviks. [30]

The motives of the Soviet and Menshevik leaders in opposing the Red Guard movement are a little perplexing until one looks at their general position on order and their fear of anarchism and of Lenin. The only significant rationale given in either of the *Izvestiia* editorials was the danger to unity with the soldiers. This argument was to be used frequently during 1917 by opponents of armed workers' organizations, and the basis for it probably lay in the memory of 1905, especially the recollection that although many army units had mutinied or proved unreliable, the old regime had found enough reliable units to overwhelm the workers. The crushing of the Moscow workers' uprising was an especially vivid memory. Therefore, a rupture of soldier-worker unity was to be avoided at all costs. Still, the argument does not seem particularly convincing. Although there were instances of soldiers opposing such workers' units, normally because of the shortage of arms, they usually did not and in fact most often aided them. Soldiers at the April 28 conference expressed their approval of the formation of the Red Guard. There may have been some soldiers who so valued their status as guardians of the Revolution that they resented any other group pretending to it, but there is little evidence that such an attitude was widespread or strong, and in fact the few manifestations of it disappeared by the end of April. Indeed, the constant harping that if the soldiers were alienated from the workers then they could be used by counterrevolutionaries probably had the opposite effect from that intended, increasing the workers' feeling of a need to form armed units. In fact, it was fairly common for the workers to express a lack of confidence in the ability of the soldiers to defend the Revolution over the long term, and hence arguments for reliance on the soldiers were not likely to be persuasive—especially to those most inclined to join armed bands to protect their interests.

Much more likely as the real reason for the Executive Committee's hostility to the Red Guard were two largely unspoken but interrelated worries of the Committee. One was a general concern for public order (so apparent in many of its activities), a striving to avoid demonstrations and confrontations (especially as the April Crisis had just shown how unruly and uncontrollable the crowds could be), and a desire for a certain regularity, even normalcy, in civic affairs. This had already been formulated in the support for creation of a unified City Militia under the control of the city officials. The April 30 editorial in *Izvestiia* praised this approach. For men like Rostov the lesson of the April demonstrations was the need for better organization; for the Soviet leaders it was the danger in the very existence of armed worker bands. The Soviet leaders remained sufficiently revolutionary and sufficiently afraid of counter-revolution not to want the workers disarmed, but they wanted them integrated into the general militia, where they would be better disciplined and where their spontaneity would be controlled. Fear of a fundamental anarchism among the "dark masses" was basic to the intelligentsia leaders.

The other concern, closely related, was a fear that the Red Guard was Bolshevik-oriented or at least could be manipulated by the Bolsheviks. It was already apparent that the term "Red Guard" connoted a more radical, aggressive force than did "workers' militia" or *druzhina*, and it was obvious that the Bolsheviks were active in the Red Guard movement. This fear was expressed in the conversations of Dan and Bogdanov with the conference delegates. Apparently the Soviet leaders hoped that by preventing the citywide organization of the Red Guard they could thereby deprive the Bolsheviks of one of their sources of support. What they did, of course, was remove the more moderate leadership from the Red Guard movement, leaving it to the Bolsheviks. They did not comprehend—perhaps could not from the perspective of the times—that the formation of the Red Guard could not be stopped by such actions and would continue, resulting in a less well organized but also more radical body. However, one must be cautious in condemning their actions with the help of hindsight—after all, the workers' militias had shown signs of decreasing in numbers in late March and early April and for all they knew would continue to do so. Still, their position on the Red Guard was an early example of a broader attitude of distrust about where spontaneous activity by the masses might lead and of an insensitivity to worker concerns and fears that would result four months later in their loss of control of the Petrograd Soviet. Indeed, their suspicion of the Bolsheviks coupled with distrust of the masses came out very clearly in the editorial condemning the Red Guard published in *Rabochaia gazeta* on April 29. It charged the "Leninists" with having organized the Red Guard for unspecified dark motives. Moreover, it claimed, the Leninists knew their calls for a general arming of the people were empty phrases that could only lead to bad results by alienating the soldiers. Unfortunately, it sighed, "as always in such situations, the workers, revolutionary-minded but insufficiently politically educated, follow revolutionary slogans rather than the voice of reason."

The workers did indeed chase after "revolutionary slogans," or, more accurately, their interests as they saw them. For example, an assembly of 800 workers of the shipbuilding factories on Vasil'ev-skii Island heard a report on April 30 from their deputy to the Red Guard conference and then passed a resolution on the importance of organizing a Red Guard "as the single and true base for defense of the class interests of the revolutionary democracy and for struggle with counterrevolution."[31] An even more stinging rebuke to the Petrograd Soviet leaders came from the Bolshevik-dominated Vyborg District Soviet, which on April 29 approved regulations for a new armed force that would reorganize the militia into a "workers' guard" (rather than "Red Guard") with the goals of (1) struggle with the counterrevolution, (2) armed defense of the working class, and (3) defense of the life and safety of all citizens. Membership was limited to workers who were members of a socialist party or a trade union, or who were elected at factory shop meetings.[32] This resolution, not dissimilar in spirit to Rostov's regulations, reflected the newer idea of a more militantly class-oriented armed force, but it still maintained some ties to the older basic militia concept—and financing was to come from the city administration police fund. This project had been under discussion by the Vyborg District Soviet for some time, but its adoption the day after the collapse of the Red Guard conference reflects the determination to push ahead with formation of more militant, strictly worker armed bands, even if only on the local level. The Vyborg regulations became, by default, the main model for Red Guard organizations. They were to be used as such by many worker groups across Russia in the following months.

The adoption of the Vyborg statutes had another ominous implication for the Petrograd Soviet leaders. A. G. Shliapnikov claimed in a May 5 *Pravda* article that the Vyborg workers' guard project had the support of the Mensheviks and SRs of the district soviet as well as of the Bolsheviks. If so, this meant that they were breaking from the party leaders in the Petrograd Soviet, perhaps because of grass-roots pressure but perhaps also because these local leaders often were more radical. The implications went far beyond the issue of the Red Guard.

The Bolshevik press fanned the Red Guard issue after the collapse of the city conference. An article entitled "About a Red

Guard," by Gavriil Zabrodin, identified as a soldier in the 1st Special Engineering Battalion, appeared in *Pravda* on May 2. Zabrodin argued that the fate of the Red Guard was of extreme importance at the present critical moment. Looking to the experience of 1905, he argued that the workers must form a guard while the revolutionary army still stood. After the army is demobilized, he asked, who will have arms, who can guarantee the safety of the workers and the Revolution? If one remembered the lessons of 1905, he insisted, then it was clear that only by possessing arms and being trained in their use could the workers guarantee their freedom. Shliapnikov (writing under his pen name Belenin) picked up the argument in *Pravda* three days later. He also pointed out that the Petrograd garrison would melt away at the end of the war. This would leave only "professional police-militiamen, estranged from daily working life," a development the workers would not tolerate. He chastised the editors of *Izvestiia* and the organizers of the Red Guard conference for not realizing the importance of organizing the guards on a broad basis around the district soviets. Therefore, he recommended that the other soviets follow the example of the Vyborg District Soviet and take the initiative in organizing such guards in order to prevent the growth of uncontrolled, irresponsible armed bands. Despite Shliapnikov's strictures, however, the Bolshevik leaders themselves were doing very little: the Petrograd City Bolshevik Conference (April 4–22) had the Red Guards on the agenda and dropped discussion of them for lack of time; and the Seventh (April) All-Russian Bolshevik Conference (April 24–29) did not discuss them either. This is in sharp contrast to what is found in protocols of the district soviets and in factory resolutions.

Despite the efforts of men such as Rostov, the actions of the Vyborg District Soviet, criticism from the Bolsheviks, and the protests and actions of the workers themselves, the attempt to create a unified Red Guard with a common form and set of regulations died because of the hostility of the Menshevik-SR leaders of the Petrograd Soviet. On the surface the latter had been successful: there was no effective immediate opposition to their position and, as one early Bolshevik writer on the Red Guard pointed out, the death of the Red Guard project after the Mensheviks left it underscored the fact that the Bolshevik Petersburg Committee was not strong enough and aggressive enough to seize control of the conference and continue its work.[33] Yet the Bolsheviks were the beneficiaries of the failure of the conference in the long run, for by default the field was left to them to develop over a period of time. More important, the failure to perceive the significance of spontaneous, broadly supported local organizations—and, even more, the inability to cope with them—was one of the most important reasons for the failure of the moderate socialists in 1917. Their attitude toward the April 28 conference on the Red Guard is one of the clearest—and earliest—examples of that outlook that was to cost them so dearly among their working-class supporters. The impulse toward a more class-oriented, disciplined, aggressive armed workers' force was a fundamental urge among the workers in 1917, emerging time and again as one of their most deeply felt needs. One could debate whether they should have arms, or whether they could use them effectively, but this missed the essential point: they felt that they must have them. This was an article of faith and of self-assertion. No party could afford to ignore this. The Menshevik and SR leadership in essence tried to do so. Individual Mensheviks or SRs might participate, but that could do little for the overall prestige of their parties. Only the Bolsheviks made arming the workers an integral part of their party posture, and only they "legitimized" the workers' desire for arms. The Menshevik and SR leaders of the Petrograd Soviet—and of many other cities—would have done well to have pondered one sentence in Shliapnikov's article of May 5: "No kind of essay, no kind of resolution, can force the revolutionary workers and people to refrain from arming themselves." This proved all too true in the following months.

5

"Insignificant Fellows" Organize

"In May 1917, at the Peterhof district Bolshevik committee
. . . (long before Party decisions and directives on this
question), three insignificant fellows set up a table in the entry with a sign saying 'sign up here for the Workers guard,'
and seated themselves at the table with pencils in hand."

—*Evgenii Trifonov*

The failure of the April Red Guard conference did not end efforts to
create district and citywide Red Guard organizations, nor did it diminish the workers' sense of a need for arms. Moreover, because
government officials and factory managers were attempting to undermine, destroy, or at least reduce the importance of the workers'
armed bands, conflicts arose that combined with the general political and economic developments of the summer to push the armed
workers toward a more radical stance and to make them think of
the workers' *druzhiny* less as an order-keeping militia and more as
a workers' guard to be used in confrontations between the proletariat and the bourgeoisie. Indeed, the attempts to form a new
type of workers' armed organization are not understandable from
the perspective of workers' initiative alone. They were also responses, both to specific measures of the government and employers and to broad political and economic currents—the June offensive, the July Uprising, the worsening economic condition of the
workers, the resurgence of political activity on the right after the
July Uprising, and the generally less optimistic mood that prevailed
from July on, with its concomitant atmosphere of impending social
and political confrontations. May to August was a period of transition in the Revolution: the optimism and expectation of rapid solutions to old problems that characterized the first two months had
evaporated, but the intense excitement and apprehensions of Sep-

tember and October had not yet fully emerged. It was in this transition period that the workers struggled to keep alive their armed bands and to organize them better.

At first, in early May, the problem was to defend the workers' armed bands against government and employer efforts to reduce or destroy them. The City Militia administration undertook to create a more orderly police force, which involved not only extension of its control over autonomous worker militia commissariats but also a purging of the militia membership lists. Simultaneously, factory managements tried to end the requirement—forced on them by workers during the February Revolution—to pay the salary of workers serving in the various militias. This put a double pressure on the armed workers and threatened both the existence of organized worker armed bands and the legal possession of arms by workers generally.

The conflict between the workers and the City Militia officials over pay and control came to a head on May 1 with the City Duma's adoption of a new law on the militia. The law provided for a sharp reduction in the City Militia's size, from about 20,000 to 6,000 members (the size of the old city police), and a fixed salary of 150 rubles a month for beginning militiamen (a figure well below prevailing skilled-worker rates) to be paid by the city.[1] This new law, to become effective June 1, particularly threatened the workers' militias, for it struck at their very foundation: the ability of workers to be paid for militia work—usually temporary—by their employer and still keep their factory job. Workers now were faced with having to decide whether to leave the militia or to leave their job. The latter choice, by cutting them off from their fellows, was undesirable for psychological reasons. For many, especially skilled workers, it also represented a drastic pay cut. From the point of view of the factory committees and district soviets representing the industrial workers, the new law raised the specter of the loss of their own armed forces at just the moment when increasing industrial conflict made such support more important than ever. Industrial workers were determined to have greater control over their own lives, especially in the factory, and saw the workers' militias and Red Guard as essential to that. Moreover, they were extremely distrustful of the City Duma, which they saw as representing the interests of the upper classes, including the factory management.

The partial democratizations of the City Duma since February had not erased that distrust. To have it acquire a monopoly of nonmilitary means of coercion simply was not acceptable. The result was a sharp struggle between the workers' militias and worker organizations on the one hand and the city officials and factory management on the other over the new militia law.

The new law sparked protests from various sources. A May 19 meeting of "representatives of militiamen and workers' organizations of 18 districts of Petrograd" protested the enforcement of the law by the Council of the Militia, charging that the latter was not elected from "the broad masses of Petrograd." Therefore, they continued, they would resist it in every way. The workers of the Sliusarenko Aviation Factory passed a resolution condemning the new law as counterrevolutionary. The soviet of the First City District on June 3 condemned the reorganization of the militia by a body not democratically elected.[2] The militiamen of Vasil'evskii Island's fourth subdistrict and of Liteinyi's fourth subdistrict both passed an identical resolution asking the All-Russian Congress of Soviets* to countermand the project and sanction instead another set of instructions passed by a citywide conference of militiamen and factory representatives on June 3.[3] I. M. Liapin, active since March in the workers' militia of the Cartridge Factory and the Liteinyi district, claims that he wrote this resolution.[4]

At the same time that the City Duma was moving to regularize the City Militia and, in effect, to destroy any independent or autonomous workers' militia, efforts from the factory managements to end the payment of salary to worker-militiamen by the factory were bringing pressures to bear that worked toward the same result. If

---

* The All-Russian Congress of Soviets, June 3–24, was organized by the Petrograd Soviet leaders to provide themselves with a national base. Composed of delegates from local soviets around the country, the Congress overwhelmingly approved the general policies of the Menshevik-SR leadership of the Petrograd Soviet. The Congress created a Central Executive Committee (as against the Executive Committee of the Petrograd Soviet) to act in its name until a Second Congress could convene. This Committee, though its geographic base was broadened by the inclusion of some of the provincial delegates, echoed the political position of the Petrograd Soviet and was headed by the same Tsereteli-led Menshevik-SR bloc that made up the leadership of the Soviet. The existence of two executive committees became of major importance in September, when the Bolsheviks captured the Petrograd Soviet and its Executive Committee while the Mensheviks and SRs continued in control of the Central Executive Committee. The Second Congress coincided with and played a role in the Bolshevik Revolution in October.

successful, these efforts would destroy the economic base of any autonomous workers' militia and separate from the factory and their fellows any workers wishing to remain in the militia. Moreover, worker participation in the City Militia would be effectively discouraged, for its pay was considerably less than a skilled worker received. This effect was well recognized by the factory management, as a March 22 document from the Society of Manufacturers (*Obshchestvo Zavodchikov i Fabrikantov*) shows.[5]

At first most factories had grudgingly accepted the obligation to pay worker-militiamen, on the basis of assurances from the Society of Manufacturers that this was temporary and that on April 1 the city administration would take over the responsibility for pay.[6] However, this transfer arrangement fell through as workers continued to insist on receiving pay from the factories, despite managers' efforts to end the system. District branches of the Society of Manufacturers and individual factories besieged the headquarters of the Society in March with requests for clarification and direction; they got assurances that they were not obligated to pay for militia service after April 1—assurances that did factory managers little good.[7] Meanwhile, the Society of Manufacturers appealed to the City Militia officials to explain to worker militiamen that pay for their services was a responsibility of the city, not of factories.[8] Sometimes individual factories made the same appeal directly to city officials, or even to the Provisional Government's Ministry of Labor.[9] The stalemate continued through the spring and into summer. On May 23 the Society of Manufacturers asked the commander of the City Militia, Dmitrii Kryzhanovskii, about worker demands for pay during militia service; the next day members of the Society heard a report that Kryzhanovskii said the continued existence of the factory militias was inadmissible under the reorganization of the militia to take effect on June 1, but that he was unwilling to give them a written statement to this effect. Nonetheless, they resolved to try to enforce this position. On June 6 the All-Russian Society of Leatherworking Manufacturers sent an appeal to the Ministry of the Interior asking its support for their position of categorical refusal to pay the factory militias, noting that at the larger factories the workers were choosing a group of militiamen to study shooting and other duties for one month, then another group for another month, and so on, so that eventually all workers would have such training. This, they observed gravely, created some uncertainty about the purpose of the workers' militia, which perhaps was political, and in any case certainly did not meet the needs of factory production. The Provisional Government's Main Administration for the Militia responded to their letter by agreeing that indeed the factory had no responsibility for paying militiamen either inside or outside the factory. Kryzhanovskii also sent out an official circular on June 19 to the same effect. However, it was very difficult for the Provisional Government or city officials to enforce their interpretations of the law in the face of worker determination to the contrary.[10] It must be noted, however, that although most factory managements opposed paying the workers, some did support the idea on the grounds that it was not a large fiscal burden and that the factory militias took their job seriously and did it well.[11] Most, however, considered the militias an unwarranted intrusion and financial burden and continued to try to get rid both of the obligation to pay the militiamen and of the militias as entities.

The efforts of management brought forth counterpressures, sometimes violent. The issue erupted as early as May 8, when worker-militiamen at the Nevskii Mechanical Shoe Factory demanded pay for time lost during the April Crisis. During the long negotiations that followed, the factory management declared both that they had no responsibility to pay and that there was no money available. Three workers, including the militia commander, Gusev, then checked with the fiscal office and found that there was money, though it was being held for another purpose. They threatened to take it by force, and the management gave in and paid.[12] In their efforts the worker-militiamen were supported by factory committees and often by general meetings of the workers. The Leather Workers' Union at the N. M. Brusnitsyn Leather Factory supported the worker-militiamen in their demand to be paid by the factory.[13] At the Osipov Leather Factory things took a more violent turn on June 16 when the management refused to pay for worker-militiamen. The militiamen arrested the factory management and called a general meeting of the workers. When the director, G. P. Kochurnikov, refused to attend, they brought him by force. The meeting gave the militiamen full support. Despite pleas from the Ministry of the Interior and the Petrograd Soviet, the workers remained adamant and the administration of the factory gave in.[14]

Similar if less violent events took place at other factories, and insistence that factories pay worker-militiamen at their work rate is a frequent theme in the records of factory committees.[15] Success by the workers in one factory sometimes sparked similar demands at others nearby: for example, when the Petrograd Metallurgical Factory gave in and paid militiamen the rates they demanded, two neighboring factories complained that they had to follow suit in response to worker pressure and demanded sanctions against the Metallurgical Factory for violating the policy of the Society of Manufacturers. The workers also received support for their stand from some of the district soviets. The Peterhof District Soviet on June 5 ordered that militiamen continue to be paid at their work rate by the factory administration until the question was resolved by an all-city conference of militiamen.[16] On June 13 it sent two deputies to investigate a reported refusal by the Putilov management to continue payments.

The pressures from the City Militia officials, the government, and factory managements had a double effect: they did contribute to bringing the workers' militias under closer city control in some instances and in reducing worker participation in the City Militia, but they also reinforced the fears of the workers about the survival of worker-controlled armed units, encouraged movement toward more militant groups outside the pale of official recognition, and drove home the need to form larger, district- or citywide structures in order to protect themselves. The new militancy and organizations were more important in the long run than a temporary drop in numbers. Several sources testify to the psychological impact of these efforts by the City Militia and the factory management, and to their effect in driving some workers toward formation of completely independent Red Guard units. Zigfrid Kel'son, who was working in the City Militia administration, claims that one of the main sources of the new Red Guards was the militiamen mustered out during the drive to regulate the militia at this time. A. R. Vasil'ev, who was active in the workers' militia, is emphatic that the pressure from the city and the workers' refusal to submit and to turn in their arms was an important step in strengthening among the workers' armed bands a sense of being a special group with special functions. Another militia commander, Vasilii Vinogradov, states that the crises of late spring and summer were important both in radicalizing the workers and in reviving interest in worker armed bands. I. M. Liapin states explicitly that conflict with City Militia officials in July led him and others to quit the militia commissariat and undertake to build a completely independent force at their factory.[17] These acts of defiance in turn helped to shape among the armed workers a feeling of unity and of being a revolutionary organization in opposition to "authority" broadly defined. This mood was apparent even among those who retained some sort of loose ties with the city administration, such as the Vasil'evskii Island second subdistrict militia commissariat (workers' militia), which, according to the report of a City Militia inspector in June, "presents itself not as a democratic but as an armed class organization that, in the opinion of the militiamen, must safeguard both ordinary residents and capitalists but is exclusively in the hands of the workers as the revolutionary majority of the population." [18]

The attacks on the workers' militias, and the workers' responses, were closely related to larger economic, social, and political disputes in Russia in 1917, the broad outlines of which are familiar and need not be traced in detail here. However, a brief description, with special reference to the role of the armed worker movement, will be helpful in making more understandable worker insistence on maintaining these forces. The economic problems were many. Establishing a minimum wage for all workers was a serious source of dispute, as were salaries in general, both in individual factories and in whole industries. This conflict led to strikes, especially in smaller factories and by unskilled workers in the large metallurgical factories. Tensions were high over these issues even where strikes did not result. One sticking point was the size of raises: although the shortening of the work day led to sizable hourly wage increases, the smaller number of hours being worked often meant no actual increase in total pay. The manufacturers argued they could afford no more, whereas the workers pressed for "new" raises, an actual increase in total pay. In fact, it seems that real wages did rise slightly faster than inflation from February to June, but they lost ground again thereafter. Another source of dispute was who would bear the burden caused by increasing factory downtime. The Society of Manufacturers estimated that during the summer 40 percent of work time in the Petrograd region was lost because of raw material or fuel shortages. This created both hardships and disputes: should workers be paid for such time?[19] During the spring and summer a steady stream of reports flowed into the Ministry of Trade and Industry recounting problems of labor unrest over pay, supply shortages, factory closings or fears thereof, and other difficulties.[20]

Aside from industrial economic disputes, general living conditions declined. As we noted in the first chapter, living conditions in Petrograd—and in other cities—deteriorated during the war. The process continued during 1917, and if anything accelerated as many public services and the flow of food and other materials were disrupted and became increasingly unreliable. Perhaps the situation is best summarized in the graphic words of a June 29 article in *Vestnik gorodskogo samoupravleniia (Herald of City Self-Government)*: "it is simply impossible to describe what is now to be observed in the quarters of the city poor. . . . The population swims in mud and filth, insects are everywhere, and so on."[21] These living conditions not only spawned discontent, they helped bring forth new kinds of socioeconomic demands by the workers in their dealings with management: demands for paid vacation, for factory-maintained sanatoriums and rest houses, and for summer camps outside the city for children. These and other similar demands reflected the workers' determination to use their newfound power to obtain a better life for themselves and their families.

Besides economic issues, other developments kept tensions high and, with them, the sense of a need for armed worker units. One important example was the vigorous campaign in the nonsocialist press in the spring that questioned worker patriotism in seeking higher wages and shorter working hours. For the workers this was the more dangerous in that it was cast in terms of comparison with the soldiers' sacrifices. Indeed, during the spring soldier delegations from the front visited the factories to study this question. Though the final result was that the soldiers declared their satisfaction with the workers and often supported their demands, the whole episode—and continuing criticism in the conservative press—led to worker fears of losing the economic and other gains of the Revolution. For the workers, the attacks on their institutions and the resistance to their demands threatened their newly acquired sense of gaining some control over their lives. Their own armed force—coupled with the frequently stated vision of the workers' militia as the initial step toward and nucleus of a future all-people's militia based on universal, rotating service—was a key element in that control. Even when they did not have any precise idea of its function, the workers felt the factory armed band to be important: A. Bodrov, from the Okhta Factory, recalled that the workers there debated the exact purpose of the Red Guard without coming to a conclusion but nevertheless felt one was necessary.[22]

The significance of worker armed bands becomes even more obvious when seen against the backdrop of broader organizational efforts by the workers. A wide range of worker institutions came into being after February, and worker (or at least socialist) presence in other institutions was greatly enhanced or initiated—in the City Duma and the district *dumy*, in food and supply commissions, in conciliation commissions for settling industrial disputes,* and so on. This was seen by manufacturers, as William Rosenberg has so well put it, "as part of a huge and frightening process of working-class consolidation, a perspective reinforced by Social Democratic rhetoric, and a vision which itself soon became an important ideological factor in the broader process of Russian social polarization."[23] Manufacturers therefore began to take steps to resist worker demands, while the workers pressed the harder. In such a situation the presence of armed units acquired renewed significance. For the factory management and the government, city or state, armed worker units responsive or subordinate to factory committees, district soviets, or even simply radical appeals (Bolshevik or anarchist in particular) took on very menacing implications, especially given the absence of reliable coercive and police forces at their disposal. Moreover, for manufacturers the pill was the more bitter to swallow because they were forced to subsidize the workers' guards by paying their salaries.

From the workers' perspective, however, these armed forces were of vital importance in defending and extending both their new economic gains and their new political influence. Therefore the mass of workers readily backed the demands of the activists who formed them. This support ranged from the sweeping statement in the June 3 resolution of the first Petrograd Conference of Factory Com-

---

* One of the main features of industrial relations after February was the establishment of "conciliation commissions—what we would call mediation or arbitration boards—to hear disputes over pay, working conditions, and other issues between workers and management. At first they worked fairly well, although this varied by locality.

mittees that the measures necessary for preventing economic disaster "demand the introduction of a workers' militia," to the day-to-day backing given by district soviets and factory committees. An example of the latter was the agreement reached at the Admiralty Shipbuilding Factory between the factory committee and the management on June 5 that, pending clarification at the forthcoming city conference, the worker-militiamen would continue in their functions and would continue to draw their full work pay from the factory.[24] Moreover, the Red Guard units were showing in practice how effective they could be in protecting worker interests and in backing factory committees in disputes with management. At the Osipov Leather Factory on April 24, the factory committee decreed that no hides were to be sent from the factory without its permission and used the workers' militiamen to guard the carts of hides that had been intercepted earlier that day.[25] At the Metallurgical Factory on the Vyborg side, the workers' demand for a pay increase went to a conciliation commission and a compromise settlement was reached. On May 5, however, the factory Red Guard unit presented the factory management with the prepared text of an agreement fully satisfying all the workers' demands and ignoring the commission's recommendations. Threatening to use their arms, the guards demanded compliance within 24 hours. The demands were met.[26] It was this kind of action by the Red Guards that gave them a particularly bad reputation among the nonsocialists and some of the moderate socialists, but that probably boosted their prestige among the workers. Moreover, it illustrates the close connection between the workers' frustration in achieving their objectives and the growth of Red Guard units, for it appears that this Red Guard was formed at the time of the salary dispute. Though undoubtedly there were workers who disapproved of the armed bands, they must have been few, and they find no expression in the resolutions and other materials of the time. Moreover, they failed to have an impact on the development of the Revolution.

Given all these issues and the attacks on the integrity of armed worker bands, it is hardly surprising that the summer saw new and repeated efforts to form a broader Red Guard organization. There were some efforts at districtwide organizations, although little is known of them. In May various armed detachments in the area around the Putilov Factory held a meeting at the "Zhar-ptitsa" movie theater and formed a district Red Guard.[27] A prominent

member of the Bolsheviks' Military Organization, Vladimir Nevskii, addressed this meeting and, judging from his earlier editorials,
probably encouraged it in its aim. More important were the renewed efforts to form a citywide organization, the first of which
came in late May. A. R. Vasil'ev, one of the participants, ties it directly to the efforts of the city officials to disarm the workers in the
process of reorganizing the militia. He is vague on who initiated the
conference, attributing it to an awareness of need among "the most
advanced part of the workers' militia," which in turn led to formation of an "initiative group," of which he was a member. As Vasil'ev
normally is quick to attribute actions to Bolshevik influence, the absence of such a note here suggests that the initiative came from a
broad spectrum among the militiamen rather than from any party
group. He does mention, however, that political exiles—who had
entered the militia in significant numbers—played a role.[28] They
probably gave a more dynamic and confident leadership to this
rather diffuse movement. This would fit the pattern of the April Red
Guard conference, which returning exiles such as Rostov played a
significant role in organizing.

The initiative group organized several meetings of militiamen.
Meetings on May 19 and 25 protested the reorganization of the
City Militia, especially the reregistration of militiamen, and called
upon the workers to defend their organizations.[29] On May 27 the
group convened an all-city conference of militiamen at the Durnovo
Villa, the former summer home of a tsarist general, whose use by
anarchists and other radical groups for meetings of all kinds had
already made it notorious. The conference billed itself as the "Conference of Petrograd People's Militia." Why the term "people's" was
used is not clear, for though it had been widely used during the February Revolution, it had since largely fallen into disuse. Perhaps it
was an effort to devise a new term to encompass the variety of militias, guards, *druzhiny*, and other groupings that existed. It also
could be interpreted as a direct challenge to Dmitrii Kryzhanovskii,
the commander of the City Militia, who on May 23 had ordered
the disarming of militiamen who had the initials "NM" (People's
Militia) on their armband rather than "GM" (City Militia).[30] The
location of the meeting and the topics discussed suggest that this
was mainly a meeting of worker militiamen. When the conference
opened on May 27, the deputy commander of the City Militia,

N. V. Ivanov, an SR, spoke to defend the militia project of the city administration. The conference nonetheless rejected the project as "an attempt by the ruling classes to foist a form of militia organization favorable to themselves upon the population of Petrograd." The conference also criticized Kryzhanovskii for trying to establish "under the title of militia a police of the West European type, everywhere hateful to the majority of the people, especially the poorer classes." Ironically, the West European type of police was often held up as a model by the City Militia administration. In contradistinction to a professional police, the conference called for militia service to be a general civic obligation for all adults, including women. During the period of transition to a general arming of the people, a militia was to be formed composed of workers, "as the best-organized part of the population." The factory administration would be required to pay workers while on militia service. The conference also resolved that the admission and dismissal of militiamen was the prerogative of the militia commissariats and the district soviets. Reversing the review process found in the City Militia project, they proposed that by June 10 all militiamen in the city should have the recommendation of a factory committee, trade union, or political party.[31]

The results of the conference were discussed in some workers' meetings, for after such conferences delegates commonly reported to factory or other meetings. The soviet for the First City District discussed the militia on June 3, and its own resolution on reorganizing the militia stated that it should be in line with the resolution of the conference. A meeting of workers' militiamen of the fourth (harbor) subdistrict on Vasil'evskii Island resolved not to recognize the authority of Kryzhanovskii and proposed that the commission elected at the May 27 conference take upon itself the functions of a council of the workers' militia. When a second all-city conference opened on June 3, this proposal was accepted and the commission was renamed the "Council of the Petrograd People's Militia" (as distinct from the city's "Council of the Militia," which advised Kryzhanovskii).[32]

It is instructive to compare the composition of the Council of the Petrograd People's Militia with that of the organizing group for the April Red Guard conference. The latter had been composed of three Mensheviks and two Bolsheviks and hoped to work closely with the Petrograd Soviet leadership. The opposition of the Soviet to the project doomed it. The new Council had a very different composition and, apparently, no ties to the Petrograd Soviet. One of its members, A. R. Vasil'ev, says it had eleven members, seven of them Bolsheviks; however, Startsev states that only five are known to have been Bolsheviks. F. P. Neliubin, the chairman, whom Vasil'ev calls a Bolshevik, Startsev identifies as being formally nonparty but in fact an anarchist. The others, one of whom Startsev identifies as a Left SR,* appear to have been distinctly leftist. Vasil'ev states that the Bolshevik Central Committee supported the activities of the Council, and he even claims that Lenin encouraged its formation—but he is not very reliable on such matters. However, the Council probably is the "meeting of the militia that is being re-organized" referred to in the minutes of the Bolshevik Petersburg Committee meeting on May 30 and to which was delegated I. A. Rakh'ia as a participant, and this would suggest some formal support from that quarter.³³ In any case the Council had a clearly radical, especially Bolshevik, orientation.

Despite participation by some Bolsheviks, the Party's support seems to have been vague and generalized. The Party routinely and consistently encouraged arming the workers and opposed the City Militia on the grounds that it was an attempt to recreate the old type of police. *Pravda* in May devoted a number of articles to the militia issue, and an authoritative statement was provided in the Bolshevik municipal program published in *Pravda* on May 7. These articles stressed the formation of a militia based on the principle of universal service, with every citizen of both sexes serving a period in the militia, which would replace the army. An article on May 5

---

* The First World War split the socialist parties of Russia—and all of Europe—into two broad camps. Those supporting the war effort generally were dubbed "Defensists," whereas those opposing it were variously called "Internationalists," "Defeatists," and "Zimmerwaldists." In 1917, the Menshevik party was dominated by a compromise view called "Revolutionary Defensism" or "Zimmerwald Defensism" advocated by Tsereteli. This position soon became associated also with support of coalition with nonsocialists in the Provisional Government. The more ardent supporters of these views came to be termed "defensist Mensheviks" or "Menshevik-Defensists," whereas their critics on the left wing of the party gradually became known as "Menshevik-Internationalists." The counterparts of the latter in the Socialist Revolutionary Party similarly emerged by the fall of 1917 as the "Left SRs." The defensist majority of the SRs did not develop a specific term of identification, but occasionally the term "Right SR" was used for a person of strong defensist and pro–Provisional Government stance.

suggested that all adults devote two weeks a year to the militia. A *Pravda* editorial on May 27 stated that "we are for a general armed people. If Miliukov [the Kadet leader] also wants a *Berdanka* [a brand of rifle], let one be given to him also." This emphasis upon arming all the people and universal service was in keeping with the pronouncements of Lenin in his various writings on the militia since the Revolution, both in Switzerland and after his return to Russia. His first five writings after hearing of the Revolution include references to arming the proletariat or the entire people. His first published statement on his return, the "April Theses," called for arming the whole people, as did his draft for a party program, on April 10, which specified everyone between the ages of 15 and 65.[34] What is striking is that Lenin—and other top Party leaders— had little to say about the armed workers' bands that already existed. There is practically no evidence, especially in his own writings as against what others later reported him as having said, of Lenin's vision, if any, of the role they were to play in the Revolution and in the creation of his new society, or even in leading to the process of "arming all the people."[35]

Active support by the Bolsheviks came not from the top but from the second level of leaders (such as Nevskii) and especially the third level (such as Vasil'ev), activists who were far ahead of the central leaders on such issues. It manifested itself in the kind of local initiative and self-formation of units described by Evgenii Trifonov in the epigraph to this chapter. Trifonov stresses that this was "before Party decisions or directives on this matter."[36] This lower level of Bolshevik leaders seems to have had more appreciation of the potential long-run as well as short-run role of the workers' guards than did the higher Party levels.

In discussing political support for arming the workers, one should not overlook entirely the role of the anarchists. Alexander Rabinowitch has shown clearly the role they played in stimulating discontent among workers and soldiers in June.[37] Aside from Neliubin's probable anarchist affiliation, we know that in some places the workers' militia headquarters were quartered in the same building as an anarchist organization—the Durnovo Villa in the Vyborg district was not only an anarchist stronghold but also headquarters for the Metallurgical Factory militia and Vyborg's first subdistrict militia commissariat. On Vasil'evskii Island, the second subdistrict

workers' militia commissariat shared a building with the local anarchist club, which must have resulted in some influence of the one
on the other. Certainly anarchist attitudes and slogans were highly
sympathetic to the workers' acquiring arms. Moreover, anarchist
participation in efforts to form independent workers' armed units
continued beyond the work of the Council, as we will see later in
this chapter.

The Council of the Petrograd People's Militia, with whatever
amount of support from the Bolsheviks and anarchists—and certainly with none from the Menshevik and SR leaders in the Petrograd Soviet—pushed ahead. The Council set itself up in the offices
of the Metallurgical Factory militia in one wing of the Durnovo
Villa and remained there until it was disbanded in the aftermath of
the July Uprising. On June 5 it sent a letter to the mayor of Petrograd declaring that the City Duma's plan for militia reorganization
was unacceptable,[38] and on the same day it sent a delegation to
present the resolution of the second all-city conference to Kryzhanovskii. The matter of regular work pay by the factories to workers'
militiamen was especially pressed, for without this not even the existing workers' militias could survive—much less the kind of universal militia service envisioned in the conference resolution. The
delegation insisted that Kryzhanovskii retract his circular instruct-
ing factory managers to cease paying salaries to workers on militia
service, but he refused to do so. Then three members were sent to
the Petrograd Soviet with a request that they guarantee pay to
workers' militias. This was not successful either. Finally the frustrated Council sent armed groups to the City Duma and the City
Militia administration demanding that Kryzhanovskii be handed
over; they were not successful, and at least one group was disarmed
and sent back.[39]

The Council of the Petrograd People's Militia found itself not
only frustrated in its efforts to pressure the City Militia officials but
soon on the defensive against them. The nonsocialist press was de-
voting a great deal of space to complaints about the general lawlessness in the city and the lack of safety for person or property, usually
tying these complaints to demands for better organization of the
City Militia. The City Militia administration, under constant criticism for not doing enough fast enough, pressed ahead with the task
of building a new police force, even publishing a description of

the new uniforms.[40] More threatening to the workers' militias and the Council of the Petrograd People's Militia, however, was the general review of the militia begun at the end of May and continued through June, which included a special commission to examine district and subdistrict commissariats. This accompanied efforts to enforce the new City Militia rules and to reduce the size of the militia, which as we have seen struck especially at the workers. The Council's problems were compounded by the "Durnovo Villa affair," which erupted on June 19, when the Provisional Government, fed up with the activities of the anarchists, used troops to take the building and arrested those found in it. The best the Council could do was to call a meeting of representatives of the workers' militias for June 21, which vigorously denounced the government and the measures Kryzhanovskii had been taking against the workers' militias.[41] The protests were futile, however, and the Council was forced to seek new quarters.

While the Council of the Petrograd People's Militia was trying to unify the workers' armed bands, provide leadership for them, and struggle with city officials, the general political situation was deteriorating. A series of events in June pitted the Menshevik-SR leaders of the Petrograd Soviet—who since May 5 were also the dominant members of the Provisional Government—against the Bolsheviks, the anarchists, and the more impatient and radical workers and soldiers. The government's effort to launch an offensive at the front was the prime cause of the confrontation. This ill-conceived offensive—a result of pressure from the Allies and the Russian military leadership combined with a desperate hope on the part of the Provisional Government and Petrograd Soviet leaders that a successful offensive would shore up their prestige at home and lend weight to their peace efforts abroad—met with widespread resistance among the garrison troops and the war-weary populace, especially the workers.[42] A measure of the opposition to any offensive was the success the Bolsheviks seemed to be having in organizing a giant antiwar and antigovernment demonstration for June 10. The alarmed Petrograd Soviet leaders forced the cancellation of the demonstration at the last minute but had to promise that they would sponsor a demonstration on June 18.[43] Conceived as a way to channel soldier and worker restiveness into a controlled demonstration, the June 18 demonstration in fact became a major expression of discontent with the policies of the Menshevik-SR leaders of the Petrograd Soviet and Provisional Government. The banners carried by the columns of marchers far more often condemned the policies of the moderates and called for an end to the war and to political coalition with the "bourgeois-capitalist ministers" than they supported official policies. A few of these columns were accompanied by armed workers' *druzhiny*, despite Petrograd Soviet appeals for an unarmed demonstration. Nonetheless, the Soviet and government leaders pressed ahead with the offensive, which began on June 18 and was announced officially on the 19th. Nonsocialist, Menshevik, and SR papers hailed it; the Bolsheviks denounced it, as did many factory resolutions. Moreover, many troops, both at the front and in rear garrisons, refused to participate or did so only under coercion. The offensive itself, after initial successes, soon faltered and became a rout by the first week in July.

Nor was the offensive the only source of conflict. The debate on the offensive may for a time have overshadowed other sources of discontent, but it did not make them go away and in the long run probably exacerbated them. The question of land distribution remained a major source of dissatisfaction, as did demands by the "over-forties" to be demobilized, concerns about the provisioning of Petrograd and other cities, and the emergence of separatist movements in some of the national minority regions, especially the Ukraine. Overall there was a general sense of disorder and insecurity that led *Rabochaia gazeta*, the Menshevik newspaper, to end its analysis of the June 18 demonstration with a ringing denunciation of the recent appearance of "grievous and even terrifying signs of the beginning of a breakdown." It went on to cite reports of "lynchings, savage arbitrary dealings with those holding different views, the wanton tearing down of placards bearing slogans of confidence in the Government, . . . drunken pogroms, [and] mass rapes of women and girls." [44] The optimism and sense of common purpose following the overthrow of the tsar, which helped keep social, economic, and political tensions in check in the early months of the Revolution, were rapidly dissipating by June and being replaced by a feeling of imminent conflict.

These many dissatisfactions increasingly found expression in the demand for "Soviet power." On the surface this meant that the Petrograd Soviet or All-Russian Congress of Soviets should simply replace the Provisional Government; presumably something similar would happen throughout the rest of the country. For the workers, soldiers, and peasants who shouted support for this slogan, it represented more an article of faith and a demand that the entire system be changed than any clear understanding of how such a change would solve the tremendous problems facing Russia or make any real improvement in their own wretched condition. Soviet power not only meant replacing the Provisional Government with its "ten capitalist ministers" by the Soviet, it also meant replacing capitalism and the privileged orders of society by socialism and worker dominance in the city and peasant control of the land. Again, the existence of armed worker bands was essential both in carrying out such a transformation and in guaranteeing its perpetuation after the war ended and the soldiers went home. These ideas were not well articulated, but they seem to have been well understood and deeply felt.

These pent-up frustrations burst loose with the tumultuous disorders usually called the "July Days" or the "July Uprising." The beginnings of the uprising usually are traced to the activities of the 1st Machine Gun Regiment and its resistance to being sent to the front. Worker discontent played a major role also, however, and it is unclear who led whom out. The mood in working-class quarters was tense, and anarchist agitators as well as Bolsheviks and others were active there as well as in the barracks. An illuminating small crisis took place on June 20. Twenty-five militiamen from the Rozenkrants Factory, where anarchist influence was high, appeared at the Moscow Guard Regiment led by V. Iu. Gessen and asked if the soldiers were ready to come out with them. Although the regimental committee was cautious, the soldiers were in a hot mood. The Vyborg district Bolshevik committee was informed and M. Ia. Latsis was sent to the regiment; he succeeded only with difficulty in convincing the soldiers not to go out in demonstration without a call from the Bolshevik leader. Before Latsis got back the Rozenkrants militiamen turned up at the Machine Gun Regiment. By the time Bolshevik and Soviet spokesmen arrived, the regiment was ready to go out.[45]

The intermingling of workers and soldiers continued. Workers were present at some of the soldiers' meetings on July 1 and 2, most notably workers from the New Lessner Factory at the meeting organized by the machine gunners on July 2. On July 3 there were spontaneous strikes at some factories, especially in Vyborg, where excitement was particularly high (and where the machine gunners were quartered). By that afternoon many Vyborg workers were to be found mingling with the machine gunners at the latter's barracks, demanding arms and helping them mount machine guns on automobiles. The contagion quickly spread to the nearby Petrogradskii and Vasil'evskii Island districts, and jumped across the city to the huge Putilov works. The actual demonstrations began at the factories at about the same time as at the machine gun barracks, if not earlier. Between 6 and 7 P.M., the workers of New Lessner formed into a column, headed by their Red Guard, and started down Sampsonievskii Prospect, the main thoroughfare of the Vyborg district. At about the same time workers of the New Parviainen, Old Lessner, Old Parviainen, Nobel, and Barankovskii factories, all Vyborg metalworking factories, also formed columns, including their own worker armed detachments, and marched out. News of this encouraged the machine gunners, and they came out into the street at about 7 P.M. The other factories and many military units of the garrison followed suit.[46] This chronology suggests that the role of the workers in leading the demonstrators into the streets was considerably greater than usually thought (most accounts concentrate on the activities of the troops).

The Vyborg workers and soldiers made their way either to the Kshesinskaia Palace (Bolshevik headquarters) in search of leaders or directly to the Tauride Palace (Petrograd Soviet) on the opposite side of the Neva River. News of their movement excited other districts. Around 11 P.M., after long meetings and guarded by their own armed detachments, the Putilov workers formed columns and started for the Tauride Palace, picking up workers from smaller factories en route. During the evening columns of soldiers and workers from the main factories of Vasil'evskii Island formed and also moved toward the Tauride Palace. There were numerous confrontations and shootings as these demonstrations moved into the city center and ran into hostile citizens and military units.[47] By about midnight, tens of thousands of workers and soldiers had assembled at the Tauride Palace. There they listened to speeches and angrily demanded the transfer of all power to the Soviet. Faced with the intransigent refusal of the Menshevik-SR leadership of the Soviet, tired, and frustrated, they finally broke up between 3 and 4 A.M. on the 4th, amid promises to return.

During the night the Bolshevik leaders in Petrograd tried to assess the situation and decide what to do. Officially the Bolsheviks had tried to prevent the demonstrations, but many leaders at the factory, regiment, and district level had encouraged them, as had Bolshevik slogans, in fact.[48] Their dilemma was compounded by the absence of Lenin, who was resting outside the city. At the Kshesinskaia Palace on the evening of July 3, the Bolshevik Petersburg Committee Executive Commission and Military Organization debated what to do and received delegations of machine gunners and Vyborg workers. Faced with the angry crowds, they finally gave their blessing to a march to the Tauride Palace, thus giving a sort of sanction and direction to the demonstrations. This was reinforced by a resolution of the Second City Conference of Bolsheviks late on the 3d recommending that the workers and soldiers press their demands in the streets. With these actions the Bolsheviks committed themselves to the uprising and the Military Organization began to prepare the next day's actions. The Bolshevik Central Committee and Lenin still hung back, even after the latter's return in mid-morning on the 4th, but the uprising rumbled on of its own momentum, the Bolsheviks providing hesitant—and ineffectual—leadership.

On the morning of the 4th, despite appeals from the Soviet leaders to the contrary, new demonstrations were organized, especially in the Vyborg district. The demonstrators were buoyed by news of support from the nearby towns, and especially from the Kronstadt sailors, and some began to move toward Nevskii Prospect and the Tauride Palace while others moved first toward the Kshesinskaia Palace. It appears that almost all the major factories of Petrograd participated, most with armed worker detachments as guards. From the Putilov Factory a militia of 2,000 led a column of 30,000 through the Narvskii Gate toward the city center. At the Skorokhod Shoe Factory, located in the same section of town, a large column set off about noon, guarded by 45 Red Guards and 50 worker-militiamen.[49] Often the workers marched with troops, as on Vasil'evskii Island, where the workers joined rebellious soldiers and Kronstadt sailors in the demonstrations. The demonstrations continued through the afternoon and evening as successive waves of demonstrators arrived at the Tauride Palace only to be frustrated by the obstinate refusal of the Soviet leaders to take power. The Provisional Government in the Winter Palace was virtually ignored. As the Soviet leaders debated through the evening their hand was strengthened as a result of at least three factors coming together: news that troops from the front were en route to support the Soviet; the release of documents about Bolshevik ties with Germany, which brought as yet neutral regiments out in support of the Soviet, and general disillusionment and frustration on the part of the demonstrators after two days in which they had controlled the city but seemed no closer to obtaining their objectives.[50]

What role did the armed workers' bands play, and what impact did their experiences have on their future development? Znamenskii estimates that between 40,000 and 60,000 soldiers and between 300,000 and 350,000 workers participated in the demonstrations.[51] Descriptive accounts of the July Days and general estimates of the number of arms held by workers suggest that at least several thousand of the workers were armed. V. I. Startsev has identified 48 factories whose militias or Red Guards participated in the July Days with their own factory demonstrations. He also cites the militias controlled by various subdistrict workers' militia commissariats as participating, and notes that at least one, the second Vasil'evskii Island, was involved in a firefight with Cossacks on Liteinyi Prospect, one of the central city's main thoroughfares.[52] Armed workers, then, played a significant role as part of organized armed detachments marching in factory demonstrations, as freely operating armed militia, and as individuals. In some instances they seized buildings; the Red Guard of the Kebke Canvas Factory occupied the offices of the conservative newspaper *Russkoe slovo* and held it for a few days.[53] Clearly, armed workers, as units or as individuals, *did* take to the streets in support of their demands. Moreover, there were no "neutral" or wavering units, as there were among the soldiers, who could shift to support of the government and tip the balance of power; this lesson was remembered in October.

Despite the workers' readiness to take to the streets, there was little if any broader—city or district—leadership or coordination of their efforts. The Council of the Petrograd People's Militia had scheduled the opening of the third all-city conference of militiamen for July 3. The conference did open, but it was interrupted by the demonstrations started by the machine gunners and Vyborg workers. At this point the Council decided to support the demonstrations and to form a "committee of movement," the chairman of which was Iustin Zhuk and the vice-chairman Fedor Neliubin, the chairman of the Council. It is worth noting that Zhuk definitely and Neliubin probably were anarchists, and it is striking that an anarchist leader who was not on the Council became head of the new committee whereas the Council chief became only vice-chairman. This suggests that anarchists at the city conference may have taken the leading role at the moment of crisis, the Bolsheviks following along. Apparently the committee played an active role in the July Days, sending members of the Council to factories to encourage worker-militiamen to join the demonstrations; several members in their later writings referred to themselves as having been leaders of armed demonstrations. Startsev draws the conclusion, based on this information and allowing for exaggeration, that the Council took a much more active role than has been realized heretofore, that a re-evaluation of the role of the working class, especially the armed workers, in the July Days is necessary, and that perhaps the sudden rebellion of the machine gunners has been overemphasized.[54] He may be correct. The role of such groups as the Council of the Petrograd People's Militia has traditionally been overlooked, as has the extent of organized armed worker bands at the factory level. The size of the turnout of armed workers certainly underscores the potential of an effective citywide Red Guard structure if it were successfully created.

The participation of workers' militia and Red Guard units in the July Uprising led in its immediate aftermath to demoralization and, inevitably, to attempts to suppress them. The demoralization is difficult to evaluate in precise terms, but there are references to it in the memoirs of former guardsmen. V. Iu. Gessen notes, for example, that at the Kebke Factory worker-militiamen abandoned their units and returned to work after the July Days, although they went back to the militia two or three weeks later.[55] In addition to the demoralization, the independent workers' militia and Red Guards were threatened by attacks from both the government and factory managements. The Provisional Government tried to disarm the workers beginning with the last stages of the July Uprising, when troops reoccupying buildings taken by the workers and soldiers disarmed any workers found on the premises. During the following days special units were used to mount searches in factories, Bolshevik organization headquarters, and workers' militia commissariats, the main purpose being to seize arms held by the workers. These drives were not especially successful, in that they did not yield large numbers of arms. Drawing upon archival materials, Startsev estimated that between July 6 and 11 about 295 rifles, 18 machine guns, and a few other items were seized on the Vyborg side, which would have been only a tiny part of the actual armaments.[56] One Red Guard member reported that at the Military-Medical Supply Factory the weapons were hidden and the list of guardsmen destroyed.[57] The purging of the worker-militiamen and the collection of arms went together, as witnessed by events in the Liteinyi district. The district had a mixed population, mostly nonproletarian but including some factory workers, especially in the fourth subdistrict. I. M. Liapin, a leader of the fourth subdistrict militia, learned that the militia was to be purged of workers. Before this could be done, he and other worker-militiamen carried the subdistrict militia's arms to the Petrograd Cartridge Factory, where they worked. Liapin was summoned to the district *duma* and ordered to return the weapons. However, he went "armed from head to foot, including a bomb," and was accompanied by armed workers; thus despite denunciations by the *duma* members, no arms were returned.[58] Even assuming a certain exaggeration in the telling, this kind of confrontation between the more radical workers and the forces of order must not have been too uncommon.

The workers got support from some of their elected organizations in their efforts to keep arms—if not from the Petrograd Soviet. When the government issued a formal order for the turning in of all weapons held by civilians, to be completed by July 16, various organizations joined in resisting. Several of the district soviets discussed the issue and were unanimously hostile. Some accepted, reluctantly, the principle of turning over arms, but did nothing to implement the order. Some, such as the Vyborg District Soviet and the fourth Narva subdistrict soviet, evaded endorsing the measure, even though it had the sanction of the Petrograd Soviet. The Interdistrict Conference of Soviets, a body formed to coordinate the activities of the district soviets, on July 17 flatly refused to go along with the collection of arms from the workers. Some factories, such as the giant Putilov Factory and the Franko-Russkii Factory, passed resolutions condemning the government's efforts to disarm the workers. Others, such as the Baltic and Admiralty factory committees, agreed under pressure to provide lists or give an accounting of the arms they held but refused to deliver them up—a tactic frequently used to assure soldiers that they were not keeping arms needed at the front. A conference was held at the Putilov Factory in late July to discuss how to prevent confiscation. Not only did the government's efforts fail to yield many weapons, but there was a countermovement, for some military units threatened with disarmament or disbanding because of their involvement in the July Days handed over arms to the workers.[59]

At the same time, there were renewed attempts to exclude workers from the City Militia and to reorganize some district commissariats, replacing autonomous workers' militia commissariats with commissariats subordinate to and staffed by officials appointed by the City Militia. On July 5 the new commander of the City Militia, N. V. Ivanov, ordered the removal of militiamen who had failed to perform their duties during the July Days. On the basis of this order some worker-militiamen were purged: in the second Narva subdistrict, for example, 60 were removed, and at the Baltic Factory on Vasil'evskii Island all were dismissed on July 11 without warning. Simultaneously, various workers' militia headquarters were raided by troops and their leaders arrested or expelled. The first Vyborg subdistrict commissariat was raided on July 8 and again on July 9, and a new commissar, L. L. Ruma, an SR, was appointed. Startsev cites further raids during this period on the workers' militia commissariats in the following districts and subdistricts: the Petrogradskii district; the first Petrogradskii subdistrict; the second Vyborg subdistrict; and the second and fourth Vasil'evskii Island subdistricts. The commissar and ten militiamen were arrested at the second Vasil'evskii Island subdistrict headquarters.[60] The Provisional Government further roiled the waters when it finally got around to publishing, on July 14, a general militia law for the cities of Petrograd, Moscow, Kiev, and Odessa that provided for considerable centralization of authority at the City Duma level. Although the law did not have any discernible impact on actual City Militia operations or structure—much less on those of the workers' militias or the Red Guard—it stirred up fears among the workers and provoked numerous denunciations. Even the Petrograd Soviet, which was generally cooperative with the government on matters of law enforcement, denounced the law as undemocratic and smacking too much of the old police.[61] Coming at the time it did, the law, though ineffectual, probably encouraged the City Militia administration and factory employers and certainly increased the workers' fears of being disarmed.

These government measures also undermined the already shaky influence of the moderate socialist leaders of the Petrograd Soviet among the workers. Despite the Soviet's denunciation of the July 14 general militia law, its publication in fact occurred when the most influential member of the Soviet leadership, Irakli Tsereteli, was temporarily minister of the interior. Although the law had long been in preparation, it is clear that its publication at this time was a part of the measures the government and Soviet leaders were taking to restore order and suppress unruly groups—especially armed ones—in the aftermath of the July Days. Indeed, Tsereteli was readier than the majority of his colleagues to take measures against the Bolsheviks, and he clearly associated armed worker bands with the Bolsheviks. His conviction about the connection of Bolsheviks to the Red Guard and of the latter to political disturbances is clearly expressed in his memoirs, for in writing of this period he states that these measures were "necessary to disarm the Red Guard, created by the Bolsheviks for experiments" such as the July Days. Tsereteli attached special importance to the collection of arms; he later recalled that he appointed as Petrograd *gradonachal'nik* (city governor) E. F. Rogovskii, an SR and acquaintance from their days of political exile in Siberia, and that Rogovskii reported to him each evening about the measures being taken to disarm "Bolshevik groups."[62] Given the attitude of the moderate socialist leaders and their interest in collecting arms, it is hardly surprising that those workers who felt that possession of arms was important became completely alienated from them after midsummer. Nor is it surprising that future direction and leadership of these workers, to the extent it came from the political parties, was almost entirely Bolshevik or anarchist.

The measures of the government against the armed workers were seconded by renewed efforts on the part of factory owners and managers in July to free themselves of the militia. These were a continuation of earlier attempts, taking advantage of the seemingly more favorable circumstances after the July Uprising. The Osipov Leather Factory, where the management had persistently opposed the workers' militia, on July 8 sent a letter to the Society of Manufacturers stating that, since armed bands in the city were being liquidated, it was time to raise the matter of ridding the factories of "Red Guard members who call themselves militiamen." A meeting of representatives of factory owners on Vasil'evskii Island took up this question on July 11. Some argued that, in light of the participation of factory militiamen in the July Uprising, it was impossible any longer to have faith in them or to continue to support them with salary. A spokesman for the Simens-Shukkert Factory reported that requests by the militiamen to be taken back into the work force had been refused. The meeting resolved to ask the Society of Manufacturers to raise with the proper authorities the matter of the full liquidation of workers' militias. At the Skorokhod Factory in the Narva district, the managers complained of the cost of the workers' militia and charged that instead of keeping order it supported the workers in disputes and had taken part in the July Uprising. They, too, called for the Society of Manufacturers to take steps to disperse the workers' militia. The management of the Nobel Factory reported to a meeting of factory owners in the Vyborg district on July 24 that it had refused a demand from the workers that a militia be continued there until the Constituent Assembly met. The Provisional Government responded to these complaints in circulars stating that no payments to workers' militias by factories were necessary and that such payments were in fact contrary to existing law.[63] The efforts of the factory managers thus met with some temporary success. At the Obukhov Steel Factory the administration successfully refused to pay wages to workers in the militia, and after August 4 worker-militiamen left their militia posts. Some worker-militiamen from the Peterhof and Narva districts decided at a meeting on July 10 to quit the militias and return to the factories because of the refusal of the managements to pay them while on militia duty.[64]

More typically, however, the administrations were unsuccessful in their stand against the worker armed bands and the government could do very little to help them. On July 7, the directors of the large Skorokhod Factory told the factory committee that they would no longer pay the members of the factory workers' militia; the workers retaliated by seizing the commercial director and holding him until he ordered immediate payment of the militiamen. The factory management then appealed to the Society of Manufacturers for help, but the appeal was unsuccessful and the militia survived. To ensure continued payment, the factory committee ordered the shop masters to fill in the work records of all militiamen as if they were working their regular jobs. Workers from some shops of the huge Franko-Russkii shipbuilding works on July 22 resolved that as "in all revolutions counterrevolution began with efforts to disarm the revolutionary workers," the Central Executive Committee of the All-Russian Congress of Soviets must immediately countermand the Provisional Government's order to disarm the workers. The Vyborg District Soviet went further and itself ordered the Russian Renault Factory to continue paying the factory militia there.

Faced with worker resistance on the militia question, the manufacturers began to retreat. After numerous reports of failure in efforts to disarm the militias, the Vyborg district branch of the Society of Manufacturers decided that the disarming of the workers was the business of the military officials who decreed it and not of the factory administrations, adding that liquidation of the factory militias was possible only with the cooperation of central workers' organizations. What the manufacturers did not realize was that even the help of the latter, which meant especially the Petrograd Soviet, would not do the job but would only speed the alienation of the workers from those organizations. They were closer to the truth when they stated that the workers viewed efforts by owners to liquidate the factory militias as efforts to destroy workers' organizations, and that the workers were ready to resist being disarmed by all means possible. The trend was well summed up by the management of the Russian Renault Factory in its attempt to justify to the Society of Manufacturers why, in violation of the latter's order, it was again paying workers for time spent in the militia: not only was it a matter of worker insistence, but other factories were doing so—a list was given—and the management had decided that the best way to avoid conflict was to give in.[65] Some factory managers still supported the workers' militia: at the large Pipe Factory, in response to a war ministry order and a demand from the district *duma* for action against the workers' militia, the factory director stated that without the help of the factory militia he could not guarantee factory security and discipline.[66] This view, however, was the exception.

The various attacks upon the workers' armed bands and other worker gains of the Revolution seem only to have strengthened in the working class the sense of a need to be armed and organized for defense against a hostile "them." The possession of arms, as we have noted earlier, was extremely important to the workers psychologically—quite aside from any clear plan of action for their use. The attacks on the workers' militias were viewed, therefore, as proof of management and government hostility toward the workers in general. Indeed, the factory management attack on paying the militia was seen as part of a larger effort to roll back worker influence in the factory, an influence that had developed since February. The workers resisted this rollback in general and efforts to destroy their militia units in particular. The existence of armed worker units, as many instances had shown already, could play a decisive role in the outcome of worker-management conflicts. An awareness of this was reflected at the July 17 Putilov factory committee discussion of the militia, where one Comrade Safronov argued the need for the factory to pay the salaries of the worker-militiamen (who were threatening to quit if they had to accept the city pay rate of 150 rubles a month) and to use them to replace the Cossacks who had been guarding the factory since the end of the July Days.[67] The psychological and physical advantages of having a workers' militia rather than Cossacks as the main armed force in the factory and its environs were obvious.

The repressive measures against the armed workers and the temporary demoralization were part of what has traditionally been viewed as a swing to the right politically following the July Uprising. This period, from July 5 to the Kornilov Revolt on August 27, saw a resurgence of political activity on the right as conservatives took heart from the Bolshevik defeat and tried to reassert themselves. Indeed, the period after February had been abnormal in the almost complete absence of activity by the traditionally conservative political elements; the Kadets, who were moderate liberals basically, had been forced into the uncomfortable role of representing the right wing of the political spectrum. Accompanying the re-emergence of the conservatives was an apprehensiveness among the socialist political leaders that their own influence had diminished, and this was symbolized by the departure from the Provisional Government of several of the most influential Soviet leaders. The extent of the rightward trend, however, was much exaggerated by contemporaries: the turn right was both briefer and shallower than the intelligentsia politicians believed. Even before July ended, the soldier and worker masses resumed their leftward trend, turning toward ever more radical political positions in response both to ongoing problems such as the economy and to new attacks upon their gains since February. This is graphically illustrated by the Bolshevik successes in the district soviets in Petrograd in late July and August.[68] It is ironic, therefore, that the political elite's exaggerated perception of a conservative swing, which both right-wing and left-wing papers proclaimed, helped alarm the workers and strengthen their resolve to defend their armed units against efforts to disband them.

The attacks on the workers' armed bands after the July Days disrupted efforts to build a broader organization, for the Council of the Petrograd People's Militia was broken up when its headquarters was raided, and some members were arrested and others were forced to go into hiding. This, however, proved only a temporary setback. By the second half of July, the workers' militias not only were reasserting themselves as individual units once more but were turning again to the matter of forming broader organizations. The militiamen of Vyborg by that time had already taken steps to organize a districtwide structure: at some point not too late in July, Vladimir Malakhovskii says that a decision was made to convene a district conference of representatives from Red Guard units. The organizers appear to have been mainly Bolsheviks, for in addition to Malakhovskii they included N. P. Vishnevetskii from the Bolshevik Military Organization and S. Potapov, a Bolshevik who in October became a member of the General Staff of the Petrograd Red Guard. A staff of 11 was selected, including Malakhovskii. It adopted a new set of regulations to replace the inoperative ones passed in April, and used a military type of structure and terminology. There is no evidence that this staff and regulations ever became really functional, although the staff may have provided guidance for some of the Red Guard units existing or being formed. Malakhovskii's comment that no copy of the regulations has survived suggests that they were not widely circulated. He claims, however, that they were used in writing the regulations adopted by the all-city Red Guard conference in October.[69] There probably were other efforts at developing district-level organizations during this period—M. G. Fleer refers to such efforts in the Narva and Nevskii districts[70]—but little is known about them.

The most ambitious new project for organization of the armed workers' bands was the attempt in August to create a citywide Red Guard structure and staff. We know a great deal about this effort thanks to the preservation of records, minutes of meetings, and resolutions by Valentin Trifonov, a Bolshevik and one of the leaders of it. These materials were presented by his widow in 1956 to support his political rehabilitation (he was among those "subjected to groundless repression and destroyed" in the Stalin era) and provide an invaluable insight into the mentality of the Red Guard organizers, their goals, and their relations to the political parties.[71] Indeed, one of the most important contributions of these records is that they clarify the role of the Bolshevik leadership in organizing the Red Guard. Comments made at the meetings, especially the first one, a conference of representatives of workers' armed bands from 12–13 districts in Petrograd on August 2, clearly suggest that the initiative came from local Red Guard leaders, mostly Bolsheviks, and that the higher Bolshevik centers—the Central Committee and the Petersburg Committee—had no role. Valentin Trifonov commented at this conference that the "Bolsheviks have not so far occupied themselves with [the] question" of the wider organization of the armed strength of the proletariat and the formation of a city center. Other speakers, clearly Bolsheviks, seconded this: one from the Vyborg district said that it "is time for the Bolshevik organizations to wake up." Moreover, when the Petersburg Committee was asked between August 5 and 8 to send a representative to help with the task of organizing the Red Guard, it refused. Thus the organizers were left on their own, and one can safely assume local initiative.

The initial conference on August 2 began with a report by Valentin Trifonov, who warned of the coming struggle for power to determine whether the proletariat or the bourgeoisie would rule. The army was demoralized, he declared, and would play a role only if "cemented" by workers' armed *druzhiny*. Therefore, it was necessary to organize the armed strength of the proletariat and create a city center. He concluded by proposing that the issue be brought before the district Bolshevik Party committees and that efforts be made to arouse either the Central Committee or the Petersburg Committee about the need for immediate work on this problem. His proposals were seconded by a speaker from the Porokhovskii district, who emphasized also the workers' demand for arms and organization. The main discord in the meeting was an exchange between Trifonov and the delegate from nearby Shlissel'burg, an anarchist not otherwise identified in the record but probably Iustin Zhuk, who was active in the Red Guard there. The anarchist argued that it was time to lay aside all order-keeping functions and that the Red Guard ought "to prepare itself for the destruction of the existing order, for the expropriation of property, and for executions." For this he was rebuked by Trifonov. What apparently excited the meeting most, however, was a report on the numbers of armed, organized workers in the 12 or 13 districts represented: 14,600, including 3,500 in Vyborg and 2,500 on Vasil'evskii Island. This number, even if somewhat exaggerated, was impressive. The meeting of August 2 ended with approval of Trifonov's proposal to establish a five-man organizing group (*piaterka*) that would make contact with the district Bolshevik committees and soviets and try to set up district conferences of representatives of socialist parties to establish Red Guard centers at that level. The *piaterka* was to take measures to insure that these centers were Bolshevik-controlled, and (perhaps in view of the fate of the Red Guard organizers in April) was to confer with the Bolshevik faction of the Petrograd Soviet and with the Petersburg Committee to guarantee if not the support then at least the neutrality of the Petrograd Soviet.

The *piaterka* consisted of Valentin Trifonov, his brother Evgenii, Vladimir Pavlov, A. Kokrev, and Iustin Zhuk (always identified in the records simply as "the anarchist" or as the representative from Shlissel'burg). The Trifonov brothers, Pavlov, and Kokrev were Bolsheviks. They were soon joined by a sixth member, A. A. Iurkin, also a Bolshevik.* These men now undertook to provide leadership for a new effort to organize the armed workers' bands into an effec-

---

* We have more biographical data on the *piaterka* members than on any other group of Red Guard leaders. They will be examined in some detail in Chapter Eight, when we look at the social and political composition of the Red Guard leaders.

tive armed force. The *piaterka* met at least six times between August 3 and 20. Its discussions and the regulations it drafted give a good insight into the objectives of and the obstacles facing the would-be organizers. The first meeting was concerned with general tactical problems in organizing. First was the problem of a name. Valentin Trifonov suggested—and this was to be accepted—that they call the organization the "workers' guard" so as to keep the verbal association with the "workers' militia" and not needlessly offend potential members who might dislike "Red Guard." The *piaterka* members agreed on the importance of maintaining Bolshevik control of the district centers: they must not escape "our direction," must be staffed with "our people." Still, they were anxious to draw in supporters from other parties who were not hostile to the idea of arming the workers. There was also much concern with the problem of obtaining arms. For example, one member reported the location of a cache of arms belonging to the Officers' Union and two members were charged to investigate. At the next meeting they reported a successful raid, carried out with the help of Vasil'evskii Island workers' guardsmen, that resulted in the seizure of a stock of 420 rifles, 870 revolvers, and eight machine guns, plus cartridges. These already had been distributed to workers. V. Trifonov reported that he did not expect any fuss to be made about this seizure, since the arms had probably belonged to a counterrevolutionary group. The same members also carried out a successful raid on a railway depot, seizing 3,600 rifles. These two operations alone, then, netted a hefty store of arms to add to existing armaments of the guards. Moreover, it suggests the seriousness with which these men—and the workers carrying out the seizures—took their task and the prospect of a coming confrontation.

The regulations for the workers' guards were presented for discussion at the August 20 *piaterka* meeting. They show well the trend of thought of the organizers. They provided for a "Workers' Guard" composed of workers recommended by a socialist party, trade union, or factory committee. The point of organization was the factory or shop, with the basic unit a *desiatok* of 13 people. Then it progressed in a pyramid structure through a series of four steps to reach a battalion composed of 480 riflemen plus special units to handle such things as explosives or machine guns. The battalions together formed the district detachment (*otriad*). The command staff at each level was to be elected, and members were subject to strict discipline. Breaches of discipline would result not only in expulsion but also in general worker ostracism. The organizational scheme provided for district *komendatury* and a Central Komendatura composed of one representative from each district *komendatura* and one representative each from the Petrograd Soviet, the Interdistrict Conference of Soviets, and the trade union and factory committee central councils. Thus the guardsmen themselves would have clear control. The regulations were concerned more with establishing a structure than with defining the purpose of the workers' guards. The opening statement described them as "an organization of the armed strength of the proletariat for struggle against counterrevolution and for defense of the Revolution." Article 13 provided for the workers' guard to undertake safeguarding of streets and buildings in times of trouble with permission of the Central Komendatura. Put the other way, this reflected the notion that this organization was not normally to be concerned with patrol and security provisions. A clearer picture of the *piaterka*'s thinking about the purposes of the organization probably is that found in Valentin Trifonov's opening comments about preparation for the coming struggle for power between the proletariat and the bourgeoisie.

The *piaterka* members accepted Trifonov's draft organization with minor changes and made plans to convene a conference of district representatives on August 28 to approve the regulations and set up the staff. Before they could do so, however, the crisis precipitated by General Kornilov's move on Petrograd intervened—giving a major impetus to the creation of Red Guards and other workers' armed units as well as changing the political arena within which they could be organized.

1. Militia of the Mining Institute with policemen arrested during the February Revolution. Photo courtesy of the Hoover Institution Archives.

2. Militiamen and soldiers patrolling Petrograd by car in the aftermath of the February Revolution. Photo courtesy of the Hoover Institution Archives.

3. "Militiamen and soldiers in Petrograd in the February Revolution."
From *Proletarskaia revoliutsiia v obrazakh i kartinakh*.

4. Red Guards of the New Parviainen Factory. From *Velikii Oktiabr'*.

ШТАБ КРАСНОЙ ГВАРДИИ
ОБУХОВСКОГО ЗАВОДА
в 1917 г.

5. Obukhov Factory Red Guard staff (bottom); Red Guards of the
Vulkan Factory (top). From *Velikii Oktiabr'*.

6. Central Staff of the Petrograd Red Guard, October 1917. From top to bottom: E. A. Trifonov, K. N. Orlov, Il'ia [Konstantin] Iurenev, V. A. Trifonov, V. N. Pavlov, A. A. Iurkin. Lower right: Red Guards of the Petrogradskii district. Upper left: Sestroretsk Arms Factory. From *Velikii Oktiabr'*.

7. Red Guards and soldiers on patrol outside Smolny. Photo courtesy of TsGAKFD SSSR.

8. Red Guards on the steps of Smolny. From *Proletarskaia revoliutsiia v obrazakh i kartinakh*.

9. Iustin Zhuk, the anarchist member of the *piaterka*. From *Krasnyi Petrograd, 1919*.

10. A Red Guard patrol keeping warm, October 1917. From Nenarokov, p. 191.

11. A detachment of Putilov Factory Red Guards with their armored car. From *Al'bom revoliutsionnoi Rossii.*

12. Enlistment of volunteers for the Red Army. From *Al'bom revoliutsionnoi Rossii.*

13. Members of the Putilov Red Guard after the battle at Toroshino Station, Pskov Province, February 15, 1918. From *Velikii Oktiabr'*.

14. Bourgeoisie at forced work (note armed guards in the background). From *Proletarskaia revoliutsiia v obrazakh i kartinakh*.

6

The Growth and Development of the Red Guard: Fall 1917

"In the dangerous and crucial moment that we are now living through one pressing need stands before the working class—to arm itself.

"We must, comrades, create a strong bastion for freedom and the Revolution that will threaten the bourgeoisie—a workers' Red Guard."

—Appeal to workers issued by the Vyborg district
Red Guard staff in early October

The entire question of the militia and Red Guard units changed almost overnight with the so-called "Kornilov Affair." General Lavr Kornilov, the supreme commander of the army and something of a popular war hero, became the rallying point during the revival of conservative political activity in July and August for those thinking in terms of some type of counterrevolutionary coup to weaken the political influence of the left and, in broad terms, to "restore order." Both Kornilov and Kerensky, who had become premier in July, were trying in their own way to restore order, and each hoped to use the other in doing so. Kerensky seems to have had ill-formed notions of using Kornilov as a counterweight to the influence of the left as represented by the Petrograd Soviet. Kornilov had even vaguer notions of what he meant by restoring order, but they pointed inevitably toward a military coup and the suppression of the Soviet. The differences slowly became apparent to them, and then garbled messages between them provided the spark to set aflame the smoldering mistrust. Receiving from Kornilov what appeared to be a demand for dictatorial authority on August 26, Kerensky responded by dismissing Kornilov from his post. The general, thunderstruck at what he considered his betrayal by Kerensky, refused to step down and launched what can only be termed an attempted military coup by sending troops against Petrograd. The actions of Kornilov provided the long-anticipated "man on horseback," the military counter-revolution the left had feared since February and against whose danger the Bolsheviks had warned constantly. It galvanized the political left, and especially the Petrograd workers, to action.[1]

The workers responded to the Kornilov advance by a massive rallying to the armed defense of the capital. On the evening of August 27, the Soviet Central Executive Committee formed a "Committee for the People's Struggle Against Counterrevolution" to direct the resistance to Kornilov. At its first meeting, on August 28, this committee reversed the Soviet's attitude on workers' armed bands and resolved "to recognize as desirable the arming of separate groups of workers for the security of workers' sections and factories under the closest direction of the district soviets and under the supervision of the committee,"[2] with the main responsibility for the actual organization and direction of the armed workers resting with the district soviets and the Interdistrict Conference of Soviets. The Interdistrict Conference responded by placing itself in charge of coordinating the efforts of the district soviets to organize a workers' militia and to provide political direction for it. It also decided to organize special detachments to stop "counterrevolutionary agitators."[3] On August 28 it set up an organizational scheme that called for a command structure in each district and a chain of command from the district to the Interdistrict Conference and through it to the committee for the people's struggle against counterrevolution. On August 29 it issued an "Instruction" on the organization of a unified workers' militia in each district, each with a central *komendatura*, to maintain order and suppress counterrevolutionary activity.[4] This seems to have been followed in some districts, but generally the effort to channel formation of workers' *druzhiny* inside this structure was unsuccessful—the urge to self-assertion remained too strong, and the workers formed *druzhiny* at the factory level in only loose coordination with such organizations.

The district soviets responded swiftly to the crisis and the role outlined for them, assisting in formation of armed workers' bands. The Peterhof District Soviet on August 28 ordered the creation of a "Red Guard of fighting *druzhiny*" of workers. Only those recommended by a factory committee or party organization were to be admitted and armed. A directing "revolutionary center" was created composed of representatives from the Peterhof District Soviet, the factories in the area, and the political parties (Bolsheviks, Mensheviks, SRs, and anarchists). Special meetings were held at factories where workers were encouraged to sign up. The Soviet also undertook to keep close watch on the district City Militia commander, a Cossack it considered unreliable. The efforts in this district were especially important because it included the Narva Gate, which Kornilov's troops would most likely use to enter the city. The Peterhof District Soviet followed up these actions by choosing a *komendatura* of the Red Guard, consisting of S. M. Korchagin, a Bolshevik, Comrade Safronov, an SR, and a Comrade Vukolov, otherwise unidentified.[5] Similar steps were taken in other districts. A "revolutionary center for struggle against counterrevolution" was formed by the Petrogradskii District Soviet, with Ia. I. Kramer, a Menshevik-Internationalist member of the soviet, as commandant of the workers' militia there. The soviet of the Second City District on August 29 named I. F. Shchelokov, a man without party affiliation, commander of the workers' militia. In the fourth Narva subdistrict a "committee for struggle against counterrevolution" and a Red Guard *komendatura* were organized on August 28, the former undertaking to direct the arming of the workers, the election of militia commanders, the establishment of first aid and refreshment stations, and the control of road traffic, the latter, with five members, forming a staff composed of the commanders of the guards in the larger factories. In the First City District, the soviet requested factories to provide lists of people willing to perform various tasks such as trench digging, and devoted considerable attention to strengthening the security of the component districts and to acting against local counterrevolutionary elements. It was particularly concerned with getting rid of "unreliable" militia commissars appointed by the district duma and replacing them with its own representatives to all commissariats. On Vasil'evskii Island, a meeting of factory committees and the district soviet on the morning of August 29 undertook to direct the forming of fighting detachments. The other district soviets were similarly active.[6] The efforts of the district soviets were seconded by the Central Council of Factory Committees, which met frequently during the Kornilov Crisis and issued an appeal for factories to organize defenses and militias.

In some districts, such as Vasil'evskii Island, the factory committees worked on a district level to encourage formation of workers' armed *druzhiny*.[7] The primary organization, however, took place at the factory level. The factories responded enthusiastically to the call to defend the Revolution against Kornilov. Workers gathered at the factories to pass resolutions on arming the workers and forming or enlarging Red Guard Units. From August 28 on, factory after factory held mass meetings denouncing Kornilov and calling for formation of fighting *druzhiny*, workers' militias, or Red Guards. Some factories envisioned broader organization—for example, a meeting of workers of the Obukhov Steel Factory on August 28 called for the creation of an elected workers' militia throughout Petrograd—but most simply undertook to form or expand workers' detachments, with little regard to details or broader organizational issues. At the New Langenzipen Factory (a machine works), the resolution specified "the organization of a fighting workers' self-governing *druzhina*." The Skorokhod Shoe Factory increased its Red Guard from 230 to 592, and the workers demanded boots for the new guardsmen from the factory's administration. The workers of the Simens-Shukkert Factory resolved to organize both fighting *druzhiny* and a special *druzhina* to assist the sappers in the defense of Petrograd through trench and fortification work. Dozens of other resolutions poured out of the factories during and immediately after the Kornilov Affair for arming the workers and forming Red Guard or other fighting detachments.[8] Most called for armed detachments, presumably for guard and fighting purposes, but some specifically called for support units to do work ranging from trench digging to medical aid. No doubt the calls from the Petrograd Soviet, the Interdistrict Conference of Soviets, the political parties, and other organizations helped stimulate creation of Red Guard and other worker armed units. However, both the factory meetings calling for the formation of such units and the actual formation or mobilization of them seem to have occurred independently of those "higher" organs and often before their actions were known. As was the case earlier, the role of the socialist parties was limited mainly to the work and initiative of their lower-level members at the factory—or sometimes district—level.

The actual role of the various Red Guard bands and *druzhiny* in opposing Kornilov is difficult to assess. The Kornilov putsch collapsed from a combination of factors—disorganization, obstruction by the railway workers, defection of its troops—before fighting could occur. Nonetheless, some worker armed units prepared to resist Kornilov on the outskirts of the city. Trenches and strongpoints were prepared. One memoirist states that the Peterhof workers' militia *komendatura* sent units to the "front." This probably refers to the approximately 800 armed Putilov workers, plus trench diggers, that M. L. Lur'e cites as having been sent to meet Kornilov. He also refers to a "hundred," that is, a unit of approximately that size, being sent from the Moscow Gate district. A. Chechkovskii mentions Red Guard units from the Vasil'evskii Island, Nevskii, Moscow Gate, Narva, and Peterhof districts serving along with the soldiers placed to oppose Kornilov.[9] It is doubtful that these armed workers played any major role in the collapse of Kornilov, although their actions may have helped stiffen the resistance of the Kerensky government and weaken what little enthusiasm Kornilov's troops had for the venture.

The main significance of the Kornilov Affair for the Red Guard units was not their role in the defeat of Kornilov, but the effect of the mobilization that called them into being or strengthened them upon the psychology of the workers themselves. After the affair, arming the workers became a much more pressing concern than at any time since the February Revolution. Moreover, the mood changed and became more businesslike, even grim, as the workers anticipated a hard and perhaps bloody struggle. This was in marked contrast to the optimistic mood of February, when workers, students, ordinary citizens, and soldiers, intoxicated by liberty, had careered around the city in trucks brandishing arms they did not really expect to use. Now workers drilled and took shooting practice after work, while their spokesmen talked of class war. Yet, paradoxically, one senses that the Kornilov Affair provided a certain feeling of relief: the dragon had reared its head, so now they could get on with the long-dreaded—but also long-awaited—political and social confrontation. Ordinary workers would have been hard-pressed to articulate these sentiments, much less translate them into a political framework, but this was the mood that was in the air. It is perhaps not stretching it too far to suggest that this temper was a sort of mirror image of the one that had come to prevail among the Kadet and liberal leaders after the July Days and that continued in altered form after Kornilov.[10]

The new attitude was reflected first of all in the workers' responses to government efforts to halt their organization after the collapse of Kornilov's attack. Initially, the Provisional Government—which at that point really was simply Kerensky—uncertain of its ability to halt Kornilov, had turned to the Petrograd workers for support. But once Kornilov's drive had collapsed, Kerensky, worried about the implications of the existence of large numbers of armed and aroused workers, attempted to stop the formation of irregular armed bands, i.e., the various workers' *druzhiny* and guards. On September 2 he issued an "Order to the Army and Fleet," point 6 of which could be construed as applying to the workers' armed groups. It ordered an immediate stop to the formation of volunteer detachments "under the pretext of struggle against counterrevolutionary activities." The Interdistrict Conference of Soviets responded that same day by ordering the organizing and arming of workers' militias to continue on the grounds that Kerensky's order applied only to the army and to groups forming on the "pretext" of struggle with counterrevolution: their struggle was real and no pretext![11] The government continued its efforts against the workers' groups, however, and again met the resistance of the Interdistrict Conference. On September 5 the government decreed the dissolution of the committee for the people's struggle against counterrevolution and its local branches, claiming they were no longer needed. On the same day N. I. Pal'chinskii, the governor-general of Petrograd, ordered the securing of all military stores and the registration of all firearms.[12] Pal'chinskii's order was generally ignored, and the Interdistrict Conference openly challenged the government's right to dissolve organizations set up by "competent revolutionary institutions" and declared that the revolutionary organizations for struggle against counterrevolution it had set up were not dissolved. The Interdistrict Conference was taking a very aggressive posture in general at this point, for it not only was challenging the government on the militia question but simultaneously was challenging the leaders of the Petrograd Soviet and demanding their replacement.[13]

Nor were the workers inclined to cease formation of militia units, which they continued to do steadily into September. Their attitude was well reflected in a resolution of the Petrograd Metallurgical Factory on September 1 arguing that the Kornilov Affair neither was the first nor would be the last attempt to take away the gains of the Revolution and that the immediate formation and arming of workers' battalions was therefore essential because it was impossible to be certain that the soldiers, under military discipline, might not fall under the sway of counterrevolutionary officers.[14] The resolution reflects a widespread attitude of the time. The workers deeply felt the need for arms, and they did not entirely trust the soldiers to defend what they increasingly viewed as "their" revolution. The Bolshevik newspaper *Rabochii* (successor to *Pravda*, which was suppressed after the July Days) fed this sentiment. On August 30 it editorialized that "It is clear that for armed offensive against counterrevolution the soldiers alone are not enough—it is necessary to arm the workers." Opposing the armed strength of the workers to that of the bourgeoisie is "the first, urgent task." Even if some of this was rhetoric, the article nonetheless reflects a mood that was growing stronger among the working class. Factory managers continued to complain about the disruptive activities of guardsmen and the problems of paying them, as shown for example in a letter from the Society of Manufacturers to Kerensky on September 30,[15] but to no avail.

This more militant attitude fed not only upon the political crisis but upon the worsening economic situation. A brief sketch of the latter will help explain the workers' fears and how those fears led to support of the Red Guards. First, whatever economic gains the workers had made in the spring were wiped out from July onward as real wages fell sharply—a combined result of rocketing prices, management resistance to additional significant salary increases, and increasing shutdowns of factories. An important factor in the mood of late 1917, certainly, was the sharp increase in prices coupled with the growing scarcity of food and other supplies. Petrograd stood at the end of a long and increasingly tenuous supply line, a fact that manifested itself in every kind of shortage. Food was especially critical. On August 10 there was only enough bread reserve for two days. Although the food situation improved in September, it remained erratic, and in mid-October incoming bread supplies again fell dramatically below daily demands. Delivery of meat, fish, butter, vegetables, and other foodstuffs lagged dangerously behind previous consumption levels. By October only about one-tenth of the prewar milk supply was arriving. More and more basic items joined bread and sugar on the list of rationed goods—and sometimes were not available at all. The black market flourished. Horses died in the city at the rate of 120–30 a day for lack of forage, adding to the problem of moving goods in the city. Government attempts to fix prices and set monopolies seemed only to compound the problem. The specter of hunger was real, especially for the lower classes of the city, who were least able to take advantage of the black market.[16]

The shutting down of factories became a major problem. Temporary shutdowns or below-capacity operation caused by the shortage of raw materials or supplies became common, and some shutdowns were permanent. The press and records of the time are filled with examples and with threats of closings for these reasons. The Putilov works, the largest factory in Petrograd with around 30,000 workers, is an example. From August on there were various reports either that the factory might be forced to lay off large numbers of workers because of lack of supplies, or that there were only enough supplies on hand, especially coal, for a day or two of production. Then on October 9 it happened: General N. F. Drozdov, the director, reported that the factory had completely run out of coal and that as a result 13 shops were completely closed and six would operate at partial capacity.[17] On October 10 the Putilov factory committee worriedly discussed the supply problem and its implications. One speaker asked whether the fact that the factory was receiving one-third less fuel than it needed to operate meant that one-third of the work force would be laid off.[18] In some factories makeshift arrangements were made—as at the Baranovskii Factory, where after the administration threatened major layoffs the factory committee developed a system of reduced workweeks so that everyone could be kept on.[19] Increasing labor strife also closed factories. Although stoppages caused by labor disputes were not as significant in Petrograd as in some other cities (Kharkov, for example, as we will see later), they were on the rise and by their nature especially exacerbated class tensions. Newspaper reports, gossip, and alarmist statements from management (often true, but often exaggerated with the intent to force workers into line on wages or other issues of dispute) created an air of uncertainty and fear that fed class antagonisms and reinforced worker demands for soviet power and worker control. What if the workers had known that both the ministry of trade in August and the Petrograd Council of Trade Unions in September came to the same conclusion: by winter, if not before, half of Petrograd's industries probably would close down?[20]

Ironically, it appears that fear of unemployment rather than actual unemployment was the real problem in the fall. Various high unemployment figures exist and are often cited, but as Z. V. Stepanov points out, they represent aggregates over a period of time, not the number unemployed at any given time, and most unemployed workers readily found new employment. The metalworkers, three-quarters of the work force, had an unemployment rate of 2–3 percent at the beginning of October and the textile workers virtually zero. Other groups had similarly small unemployment rates. Stepanov estimates a total of 6,000–8,000 unemployed in mid-October,[21] or only about 2 percent. The real offender was fear brought on by *under*employment because of temporary shutdowns or slowdowns combining with all the other problems of the fall of 1917. In February and March there had been massive shutdowns of factories, but workers viewed them as temporary and leading ultimately to improvement in their own situation. Now, in the fall, each closing or threat thereof also carried the menace that it could be permanent, that the factory might not reopen. Workers feared also that factories would be moved from Petrograd to the provinces, as was extensively discussed.

Public disorder, events at the front, the wildest rumors—all combined to cause great apprehension and fear that the gains of the Revolution might be lost, including that modicum of control over their lives the workers had acquired since February. The economic and political concerns increasingly merged, for without economic security they could not protect, much less extend, their political gains. In such a complex situation, racked by forces they only poorly understood and had negligible control over, the workers increasingly saw "soviet power" as the only way out, a sort of panacea. Little wonder, then, that maintaining and strengthening their worker armed forces took on greater urgency and that these units grew steadily in size and organization in September and October. The efforts to better arm and organize the Red Guard were visible expressions of worker fears and growing social polarization.

Now for the first time the Bolshevik Party took a prominent role in efforts to organize the Red Guard through its central organs as well as through local leaders, giving a more markedly—but not exclusively—Bolshevik cast to the movement. The major Bolshevik organizations had generally encouraged, but otherwise given little attention to, the workers' militias throughout 1917. After the Kornilov Affair, the Military Organization, which had devoted most of its time to the soldiers, began to give more attention to the workers. On September 6 it issued a detailed document on "workers' *druzhiny*" in its newspaper, *Soldat*. This provided for a system of *druzhiny* organized at the factory and brought together in district-level detachments. The command staff at each level and subdivision was to be elected, but leaders were subject to removal by "democratic organizations." No provision was made for a citywide organization, however. Instead, reflecting the concern of the time, most of the document was given over to detailed instructions on how to train the *druzhiniki* in the use of arms. An accompanying article entitled "What Each Red Guard Must Remember" devoted itself to telling the guardsman his duty[22] and gives some insight into the thinking of the Bolshevik leaders, or at least those in the Military Organization. The ultimate goal of arming all the people, a consistent theme in Bolshevik writings since February, was emphasized repeatedly, as was the voluntary nature of service and the electoral, and hence democratic, nature of the command organization. Also insisted upon was the importance of the Red Guard as a defense against "capitalist oppression." Most striking, however, is the obvious distrust of the army that pervades the document, especially since it came from people who had been concentrating on work among the garrison. Apparently the refusal of the troops to support Kornilov had not convinced the authors of their reliability. Twice they refer to the oppression of the masses by a standing army in service of the bourgeoisie, and in the penultimate paragraph they stress the role of the Red Guard in showing the feasibility of abolishing the standing army. This is more striking yet when other passages referring to arming the people are added in. The whole represents a strong statement of the need to create a mass armed workers' guard as the first step toward arming all the people and abolishing the army.

Distrust of the soldiers was expressed in other Bolshevik articles during this period. On August 30 *Rabochii* warned that the soldiers alone were not an adequate defense against counterrevolution; the armed workers were essential to this task. Even more emphatic was a very long article in the September 21 issue of *Soldat* signed by "V. N."—perhaps Vladimir Nevskii, one of the Military Organization leaders. The author argued that a Red Guard and an armed people were essential because the army had, for one reason or another, not maintained its revolutionary fervor. It is quite clear that at least some of the Bolshevik leaders believed the soldiers were not a reliable revolutionary force and felt that a truly proletarian armed force was essential. The attempt by Kornilov to stage a military coup probably stimulated this distrust; soldier resistance to Kornilov, however, seems not to have reassured the Bolshevik leaders. When added to the frequent expressions of such distrust found in factory resolutions, as we saw earlier, these Party doubts suggest that uncertainty about the soldiers' reliability and feelings of a need for strong worker Red Guards were very widespread.

The various Bolshevik organizations continued to devote considerable attention to the Red Guard throughout September—aside from the question of the soldiers' reliability. *Soldat* published a number of articles on the Red Guard, especially emphasizing the importance of arms and training for the guardsmen and the role of the Military Organization in that training. On September 19 it concluded an article entitled "About the Workers' *Druzhiny*" with an appeal for the Petrograd workers to organize their armed strength as an inspiration for other cities and to show that arming the workers and peasants was not an "idle invention of the Bolsheviks" but a necessary, deeply felt need of the people. Yet the Military Organization, despite its vigorous statements, limited itself primarily to assisting in the training of guardsmen, not in their organization. (This is detailed in the next chapter.) The other central Bolshevik organizations seem to have been even less active. A long discussion at the September 24 meeting of the Petersburg Committee reflected a sense of need to strengthen the Red Guard but also revealed the absence of any program, direction, or leadership to do so.[23] The Petersburg Committee did submit a resolution on the Red Guard to the Bolshevik Third All-City Conference on October 7, which approved it. The resolution, however, merely stated the importance of the Red Guard and the general arming of all the people, called on the Party organizations to give more attention to this issue, and expressed hope that the Petrograd Soviet would take up the organizing of a Red Guard.[24] The Central Committee seems to have given it even less attention, although the declaration of the Bolshevik fac-

tion at the Democratic Conference* on September 18, approved by
the Central Committee, did include "general arming of the population and organization of the Red Guard."[25] Party organizations on
the district level were more active: one author, compiling a list of
issues with which the local Party organizations were most concerned in September and October, lists the Red Guard as the second
of nine items.[26]

Despite the verbal support of the Bolsheviks, the actual task of
organizing still was left primarily to the guardsmen themselves and
to local Party leaders. Renewed discussion about a citywide organization began in September as a response to the attempts to define—
and limit—the role of the workers' armed bands. These discussions
also underscored the gulf separating the moderate socialists and
government figures from the armed workers. One of the last acts of
the Soviet's Committee for the People's Struggle Against Counterrevolution was the issuance on September 5 of "Regulations of the
Workers' Militia," which provided for a militia of limited functions: to perform guard and patrol duty in factories, workers' districts, and other such areas not patrolled by the City Militia, and to
provide general backup support for the City Militia. The total number of worker-militiamen was fixed at 8,000.[27] This limited role was
hardly in keeping with the attitude of many workers about their
function, a fact that became abundantly clear when a newly formed
committee on the workers' militia met on September 9 and 13. This
committee, provided for in the "Regulations" of September 5, was
composed of two representatives each from the Central Executive
Committee, the Executive Committee of the Petrograd Soviet, the
Central Council of Factory Committees, the Petrograd Council of
Trade Unions, and the Interdistrict Conference, and of one each
from the staff of the Petrograd Military District, the City Duma, the
City Militia, and the Provisional Government.[28] As might be expected from such a body, at its first meeting on September 9 it gen-

---

* The Democratic Conference was a conference "of all the democratic organizations of Russia" organized by the Menshevik-SR Soviet leaders. It represented
basically the socialists, especially moderates. Running from September 14 to 19, it
grappled with the political chaos that followed the Kornilov Affair, and especially
debated whether or not to continue the socialist-nonsocialist coalition in the Provisional Government. It failed to reach a workable program and only underlined the
disarray of the moderate socialists and the disintegration of the old Tsereteli-led
Menshevik-SR bloc.

erally reaffirmed the limited functions suggested by the September 5 "Regulations." The second meeting, on September 13, took a very different position.

When the committee reconvened on September 13, a group of Red Guards attended in addition to the regular members. K. Koval'skii, the Provisional Government representative, described these guardsmen as "12 commandants and 12 commissars of the workers' militia" from the workers' districts of Petrograd, and called the majority at the meeting "Bolshevik," a term he uses loosely but that does indicate the generally left position of the meeting. His report provides our main record of the meeting.[29] According to Koval'skii, the workers' militia representatives firmly rejected the committee's scheme for "a workers' militia with the characteristics of a reserve for the City Militia," insisting instead on "a workers' (red) guard." The meeting was dominated by these workers' militia representatives, who probably were seconded by some of the other participants, such as the representatives of the Interdistrict Conference and the Central Council of Factory Committees. They then proceeded to draft a new set of rules, proposing the creation of a "Central Komendatura," the staff of which would be composed of five representatives of the workers' militia and of representatives of the Interdistrict Conference, the Petrograd Soviet, the trade unions, the factory committees, and the City Duma. They decided to begin immediate training and to demand 7,000 rifles from the Petrograd Soviet. These actions brought objections from the two government representatives, Koval'skii and P. P. Gonek, who represented the army command. They denied the need for and legitimacy of such a guard, an objection which revealed that they were thinking in terms of maintaining domestic order and did not fully appreciate the class and political attitudes involved. They then stated their intent to withdraw from the work of the meeting, which elicited from the workers' representatives the rejoinder that they had not expected to meet government officials there anyway. After considerable debate, the meeting passed a resolution declaring that "the meeting of commanders of the workers' militia looks on the militia as a *workers' guard*, whose task is to struggle against counterrevolution and to defend the gains of the Revolution."[30]

The use of the term "Central Komendatura" and the composition envisioned for it both suggest that some of the workers' leaders at the September 13 meeting either were from the *piaterka* or had been influenced by it, raising some intriguing questions about continuity from one Red Guard organization to another. The resolution passed at the September 13 meeting does not assert any continuity, organizationally or in personnel, but Pinezhskii claims that this meeting merely reaffirmed the Central Komendatura established "at the end of August or beginning of September"—i.e., by the *piaterka*—and cites the authority of Valentin Trifonov, one of its members.[31] Indeed, there is indirect evidence that some of the *piaterka* members were at the meeting. The Interdistrict Conference of Soviets at its September 11 meeting resolved to send Vladimir Pavlov to the next session of the committee on the workers' militia "for further working out and implementation" of the project he had presented;[32] since Pavlov was one of the *piaterka*, this may mean that the ideas and structure of the *piaterka* influenced the new Central Komendatura[33] and that its members were active at the September 13 meeting. It appears that by this time there had emerged a core of Red Guard activists who were providing some continuity of leadership, especially in organizing a citywide center.

Tracing the work of the Central Komendatura after this meeting is extremely difficult; despite its potential importance as a leadership core for the various Red Guard units, little is known about it. Pinezhskii claims that it drew up regulations providing for district *komendatury*, each to consist of five men—the commandant of the Red Guard in the district and four representatives of the guardsmen. The district *komendatury* were responsible for organizing, training, and supplying the units in their district. They acted on their own responsibility but were subordinate to the Central Komendatura and to the political supervision of the district soviet. Pinezhskii acknowledges, however, that except in the Vyborg district these *komendatury* were "weak" and the Central Komendatura "no stronger." The latter, wishing to avoid difficulties with the Menshevik-SR–dominated Soviet, was "cooped up" in the Interdistrict Conference of Soviets until after the Bolshevik victory in the Petrograd Soviet was consolidated toward the end of September.[34] Indeed, one can assume—and Pinezhskii and Malakhovskii suggest—that the Central Komendatura did little during September and early October toward translating its organizing efforts into a meaningful Red Guard structure for the city.

Despite the attempts to create a city structure before and after Kornilov, and despite their importance for later developments, the really concrete organizational achievements in September and early October were found not at the city but at the factory and district levels. Only after considerable progress had been made in the districts would endeavors to create a city structure succeed—on the very eve of the October Revolution. At the factories, efforts were directed not so much at the formation of new units as at the enrollment of new members, their training, and the development of a command structure. The Red Guard increased from 120 to 200 at the Rechkin Factory, and from 85 to 145 at the tram park. At the Wireless Telegraph Factory the Red Guard grew to 150, divided into three detachments, each with its own commander and under the overall command of the secretary of the factory committee, himself an SR. The factory committee of the Metallurgical Factory encouraged intensive training of new enrollees in early October and supplied instructors for it. At the huge Obukhov Steel Factory, the Red Guard is claimed to have swelled to 2,000, again with the chairman of the factory committee as commander.[35] The role of the factory committees in the organization and command of the Red Guard is particularly striking.

The new degree of organization and determination is shown by the rules for their workers' militia produced by some factories during this period. One set of such rules, at the Admiralty Shipbuilding Factory, was for a workers' militia of the older type; that is, its main purpose was maintaining security in the factory and the surrounding area. It was to work with the City Militia but remain independent of it. The rules provided for three detachments of militiamen: the first, composed of 60 men, protected the factory; the second, of 50 men, carried out militia functions in the area and was to be paid by the City Militia; the third, of 100–200 men, was a reserve intended to help safeguard the workers' interests and combat counterrevolution. Members of the third group remained at their regular jobs and came out only if needed. Each of the three detachments was led by its own elected "elder" and subcommanders, and an overall commander was elected as well.[36] The mild, almost traditional nature of these rules might be compared with the more radical and belligerent "Temporary Regulations of the Red Guard of the Simens-Shukkert Factory," written in late September. The members of the Red Guard must remember, the regulations stated, that they are the defenders of the people's democratic interests, ready at any time of day or night to rise to the defense of the Revolution, disregarding all personal interests or fears. The document puts considerable emphasis upon training and discipline, returning several times to the need for discipline and listing provisions for punishment in the event of infractions. It also conveys a strong sense of impending crisis, making provisions for mobilization, for obtaining automobiles during a crisis, and for succession to command if the commander is killed. There is an injunction to guardsmen to remember their duty "in a fighting situation."[37] This document was for a fighting Red Guard, and it makes no allusions to or provisions for factory guard duty or general militia functions.

Particularly striking about the activities of late September and early October is the success in going beyond factory-level organization to the development of districtwide organizations and command staffs. On these a city structure could be built; more important, where they were well established they could provide an important leadership element in a crisis—as they would in the October Revolution. The best documented and perhaps the earliest such organization was that set up by a district conference of Red Guards in Vyborg on October 7. The efforts here were especially significant because of the importance of the Vyborg workers and their radicalism in any workers' movement. In Vyborg, despite early efforts and the active role of the district soviet in the affairs of the workers' militia and Red Guard, no central directing organization had been firmly established. Therefore, between September 20 and 22, the district soviet again made an effort to set one up when it appointed a commission for organization of fighting *druzhiny*. This commission immediately undertook to work out draft regulations and to organize a district conference.[38] The conference organized by the commission included representatives of 22 factories plus one delegate each from the Bolshevik Party, the Union of Socialist Youth, the district soviet, and the Central Komendatura. The opening speakers on October 7 stressed the importance of direction by the district soviet and unity among all the existing but separate Red Guard cells. The greatest debate was caused by the report of N. P. Vishnevetskii, a member of the Bolshevik Military Organization, on the election of a district staff of the Red Guard and on the draft regulations. The main bone of contention was whether the Military Organization ought to have the right to be represented on the district staff. Ia. A. Sodman, a nonparty member of the Vyborg District Soviet executive committee, proposed either to deny the Military Organization specifically the right to be represented or to permit all socialist political parties to be represented. Vishnevetskii and Malakhovskii, both members of the Military Organization, argued against removing the Military Organization, stressing the important role it had played and still could play in providing instructors and other support. Moreover, since all the instructors were from the Military Organization, its representatives would speak not for a party but for the instructors. Inclusion of representatives of all parties was opposed by some speakers on the grounds that it would make the staff too unwieldy, especially at the factory level. Sodman's insistence upon the importance of including all parties in order to get their support was unsuccessful, and his amendment was voted down. Then a staff was elected: N. P. Vishnevetskii, Vladimir Malakhovskii, Zakharov, Abramov, Stepanov, and Slavinskii. The first two are known to have been Bolsheviks, and the last four are further unidentified. Nonetheless, the structure, plus the traditionally Bolshevik orientation of the Vyborg district, assured Party dominance.

The "regulations" of the Vyborg Red Guard are probably the most complete such document to this point, especially on the problems of broader, districtwide organization, yet they are also a curious amalgam of earlier regulations. Of the 14 points in Part 1, "Goals and Tasks of the Red Guard, Duty of Members," seven are from the Military Organization's September 6 article in *Soldat* ("What Each Red Guard Must Remember") and six are from the Simens-Shukkert Factory regulations; the fourteenth simply states that members are to receive an identifying card. The clauses taken from the *Soldat* article repeat its stress on the Red Guard as defender of the Revolution and the oppressed, and as leader in the arming of all the people. The Red Guard's voluntary, elective, and democratic nature is highlighted. The clauses taken from the Simens-Shukkert regulations are more specific, dealing mainly with admission, attendance, discipline, care of weapons, and command. Given that the Simens-Shukkert Factory was on Vasil'evskii Island, the borrowings raise some tantalizing questions and suggest the possible interrelatedness of the various efforts to organize the Red Guard. Unfortunately, no connection between any of the members of the Vyborg commission and the Simens-Shukkert Factory can be documented. In the light of their difference from the Military Organization's September 6 statements and other documents, the Simens-Shukkert regulations appear to have been worked out locally and independently from other sources, but it is possible that local Bolsheviks brought them to the attention of the Military Organization or to Malakhovskii or some other member of the Vyborg commission as the latter began work on its own regulations.

After Part 1, the Vyborg regulations become more original and deal with details of organization. They provide for each factory to have a factory Red Guard committee responsible for general direction, including preparedness. This committee was to consist of at least five men, including the factory detachment commander, three guardsmen, and one representative of the factory committee. The factory Red Guard committee was to organize Red Guard units where none existed, strengthen weak ones, oversee preparedness, provide instructors, and organize special detachments, such as machine gun units or medical units. The district staff was to be composed of 3 – 5 representatives from the district soviet, 4 – 6 from the guardsmen themselves, 2 from the Military Organization, and 2 from the command staff. In turn, it recognized the authority of the General Staff of the Petrograd Red Guard, which, in turn, "while retaining full internal autonomy," was subordinate to the Petrograd Soviet. Thus was provided a full structure of authority from the factory through the district to the city level. A citywide organization did not exist in any meaningful sense, aside from the shadowy Central Komendatura and an inactive department in the Petrograd Soviet, but the conference did call for a city Red Guard conference (which in fact did finally convene on October 22). Finally, the regulations specified that they were obligatory for all factories in the Vyborg district. There is no clear evidence concerning the extent to which this provision was enforced—or enforceable.

The Vyborg conference, then, managed to establish a district organization, at least on paper. Moreover, the district staff immediately set to work. A lengthy flyer was issued in 100,000 copies invoking the memories of the Kornilov Days and calling on the workers to join the Red Guard: "In the dangerous and crucial mo-

ment that we are now living through one pressing need stands before the working class—to arm itself. We must, comrades, create a
strong bastion for freedom and the revolution that will threaten the
bourgeoisie—a workers' Red Guard." [39] Other broadsides followed,
and orders to factories. One reminded the workers of the importance of the Red Guard and appealed for financial aid. Another on
October 16 urged those who did not have a copy of the regulations
to get one, asked factory committees for financial help, and reminded the committees of a forthcoming district conference of Red
Guards on October 20.[40] In addition to issuing these communications, general and specific, the staff undertook to establish closer
ties with the factories, provide instructors, obtain arms, and otherwise strengthen and improve the fighting ability of the Red Guard.[41]
Overall, the Vyborg Red Guard staff clearly was the most active
and effective district organization thus far created. In addition, its
members apparently played an active role in organizing the citywide Red Guard conference later in October, and its regulations
were one source for the city conference's regulations.

The Vyborg conference was not an isolated instance. A joint conference of the Narva and Peterhof districts at about the same time
also adopted a set of regulations and established a staff. The precise
date remains unclear, but it was probably about October 7 or a
little later.[42] The Narva-Peterhof regulations are generally dissimilar
to those adopted across the city in Vyborg and show no sign of influence or borrowing. They state that the "Workers' Red Guard is
an organization of the armed strength of the proletariat," members
of which must be workers "who recognize the [need for] class struggle in the name of the liberation of labor" and who are recommended by a socialist party, trade union, or factory committee. The
Red Guard's tasks were the maintenance of revolutionary order and
the defense of the rights and freedom of the working class. Although the regulations provided for protecting streets and public
places—unlike the Vyborg ones—this was to be at times of crisis
rather than routinely, as in earlier workers' militia arrangements.
The regulations spoke also of "fighting operations" and gave extensive space to the need for discipline and to provisions for disciplinary measures. Organizationally, the Narva-Peterhof regulations
have one unique feature: they provide for a rotation cycle of 10
days of active full-time duty and training followed by 30 days in

reserve. The structure otherwise falls within the general pattern: a series of building-block steps from the smallest group (60 "bayonets," 15 active in any 10-day period and 45 in reserve) up to the battalion (240 active plus 720 reserve). All commanders were elected. The district Red Guard was directed by a council composed of six representatives of the guardsmen plus three of the district soviet. Important issues—such as the election of the general commander—were to be decided by a joint meeting of the council and the elected commanders. Thus the organization was basically self-formed and self-directed—more so than in Vyborg—although the district soviet had some voice in its affairs. The desire for a broader city structure was reflected here as in the Vyborg regulations by a final section about an as yet nonexistent city center with general responsibility for the Red Guard, which suggests that this aspiration was so generally held that it independently made its way into both documents.

Similar efforts took place in other districts. In Petrogradskii the local soviet gave considerable attention to the organization of "workers' guards" in the district. On September 22 the district soviet executive committee approved "draft regulations of the workers' guard,"[43] but no copy of these has survived. According to S. I. Tsukerman, a participant, the district soviet retained direct control and named the commander, Ia. I. Kramer, a Menshevik-Internationalist he describes as "thoroughly sickened" with his party but not yet broken away from it.[44] Various references indicate that in Petrogradskii the district guards structure was created by the soviet rather than by a conference of guardsmen, which fits with the fact that the district had a tradition of greater centralized or soviet authority over local workers' militias dating back to the February Revolution. Other districts, including the most important workers' districts, also appear to have set up districtwide Red Guard organizations of some type during October.[45] The organization, extent, and effectiveness of these units certainly varied, but at least district structures now existed. The next task, then, was the creation of a city structure.

The building of a meaningful city Red Guard structure was assisted by the Bolshevik capture of the Petrograd Soviet. The Bolsheviks, temporarily weakened after the July Uprising, quickly recovered and in late July and August again began to make major gains among both workers and soldiers—gains that were reflected in electoral victories resulting in the capture of factory and garrison committees, district soviets, and other worker organizations. As a result, Menshevik and SR deputies were gradually replaced by Bolshevik supporters in the ongoing reelection of deputies to the Petrograd Soviet. Then on September 9, the Petrograd Soviet adopted a Bolshevik-sponsored resolution that was in effect a vote of no confidence in the old leadership, which promptly resigned from the Soviet presidium. The Soviet leadership was restructured under Bolshevik control, and on September 25 the shift of power was completed when Leon Trotsky replaced Nikolai Chkheidze as chairman of the Soviet. However, the old Menshevik and SR leaders still controlled the Central Executive Committee of the All-Russian Congress of Soviets, elected in June. Thus during the next month the two executive committees stood in opposition to each other, until the Second All-Russian Congress of Soviets assembled in the midst of the October Revolution.

With the Bolshevik victory in the Petrograd Soviet, the Red Guard leaders looked to the Soviet for assistance rather than the opposition they had previously experienced. A new Soviet Department for the Workers' Guard was set up, with Konstantin Iurenev as head. Iurenev undertook a series of informal meetings with Red Guard leaders such as Vladimir Pavlov, Valentin and Evgenii Trifonov, and A. A. Iurkin (all from the old *piaterka*), and A. K. Skorokhodov, a Bolshevik activist in the Petrogradskii district who was chairman of the district soviet, a Red Guard commander, and a representative to the Interdistrict Conference of Soviets. Out of these conversations came, according to Pinezhskii, a decision to retain and strengthen the Central Komendatura because it was already functioning and known in the districts. The Department continued to exist, however, giving the Red Guard movement the legitimacy and authority of the Petrograd Soviet. This revitalized Central Komendatura was located at the Smolny Institute, the Soviet headquarters. It included Konstantin Iurenev (chairman), Valentin Trifonov, Vladimir Pavlov, Evgenii Trifonov, A. K. Skorokhodov, and A. A. Iurkin, the first three of whom formed its bureau, which took care of daily business. The Komendatura as a whole met at least once a week.

The Komendatura now set about the tasks of supervising the organization and training of Red Guard units, procuring arms, and preparing for a general, citywide Red Guard conference. To facilitate these tasks, toward mid-October it set up a general section—a chancellery, in effect—and an arms section to oversee the acquisition and distribution of arms. There was also an informally established section for ties with the districts, which used a system of messengers rather than relying on the telephones.[46] In preparing the citywide Red Guard conference and drafting regulations applicable to all units in the city, the Central Komendatura worked closely with the Petrograd Soviet Department for the Workers' Guard. The bureau of the Central Komendatura worked on the problem of a set of regulations during the early part of October, drawing upon both the Vyborg and the Narva-Peterhof regulations, and possibly those of the *piaterka* and the Moscow Gate district, plus the earlier *Pravda* articles of the Military Organization.[47] On October 13 the Department published a statement that it was working on a set of regulations and that a general city meeting of the Red Guard was planned for the second half of October.[48] On October 16 Iurenev made a report to the Executive Committee of the Petrograd Soviet about the work of the Department, and the Executive Committee responded with a resolution stating that organization of the Red Guards, who were to defend the revolution from counterrevolution, was an "urgent task of the moment" under its full responsibility. Circulars were sent out shortly afterward announcing a conference on October 22 to discuss the "regulations" and general affairs of the guard. Workers were urged to elect deputies at general district meetings of the workers' guards, at a ratio of one representative for each 200 guardsmen. Some such meetings are known to have taken place, such as that on October 20 in the Vyborg district.[49]

If minutes of the meeting of the city conference on October 22 were kept, they did not survive. Nor are there any newspaper accounts—which is not surprising, since the conference was followed almost immediately by the October Revolution, which preempted the news from such meetings. Therefore, we are dependent upon the remembrances of participants, particularly E. Pinezhskii and to a lesser extent Vladimir Malakhovskii.[50] The meeting opened on the evening of October 22 at the building of the Liteinyi District Soviet, which was centrally located but just across the Neva from the Vyborg district. About 100 Red Guard delegates participated (which if the formula of 1:200 was adhered to meant they represented 20,000 guardsmen), and there was a distinct Bolshevik or Bolshevik-oriented majority. According to Pinezhskii, the work progressed in a nervous political atmosphere, with an awareness of impending crisis. The gathering confrontation between the Petrograd Soviet and the government over control of the garrison; the meetings that day to mark the "Day of the Petrograd Soviet"; the arrival of deputies to the Second All-Russian Congress of Soviets; rumors of a planned Bolshevik seizure of power—all provided sufficient reason for excitement. The first items on the agenda proceeded smoothly: a report from the Central Komendatura about its work, reports from the districts, a report on the situation at the current moment. The presentation of the draft regulations, by Valentin Trifonov, aroused more debate, particularly on the matter of terminology. The Vyborg delegates insisted upon the more military-sounding terms they had used instead of the proposed wording, which sometimes used nonmilitary terms, arguing for example in favor of the term General Staff rather than Central Komendatura for the central command group. Opposition to the Vyborg position was based on a reluctance to carry tsarist military terms into the new proletarian fighting force. The nonmilitary terms carried the day except in the case of the central command, where the term General Staff (*Glavnyi shtab*) was adopted. After long consideration, point by point, the regulations were adopted on the morning of October 23, only a day before the October Revolution began.

The regulations themselves do not differ much from earlier ones in their general characteristics, and in fact drew upon some of them. There are passages that are identical to or barely changed from passages in the Narva-Peterhof, Vyborg, and *piaterka* regulations. Like them, they defined the task of the "workers' Red Guard" as the organization of the armed strength of the proletariat for struggle against counterrevolution and defense of the revolution, they limited membership to workers recommended by a socialist party, factory committee, or trade union, and they laid heavy stress upon the need for discipline and made provisions for punishment by comradely judgment of those who violated discipline. They placed the Red Guard at the disposal of the Petrograd Soviet, directly subordinate to the General Staff, which was composed of one representative from each of the districts, plus one each from the Petrograd Soviet Executive Committee, the military section of the

Central Executive Committee, the Interdistrict Conference of Soviets, the Central Council of Factory Committees, and the Petrograd Council of Trade Unions. The General Staff was to be responsible for directing the organization and general activity of the district staffs and was to have a smaller bureau to provide daily direction and aid to the Red Guard, including instructors. In each district there was to be a duplication of the city structure: general subordination to the district soviet and immediate subordination to the district staff, which was to be responsible for the activities of the Red Guard in the district. The basic unit of organization was the factory, where the guards were responsible to the factory committee. The basic fighting unit was the *desiatok*, "ten," which, curiously, had 13 members; four "tens" made up a *vzvod*, three *vzvoda* a *druzhina*, and three *druzhiny* a battalion. With attached special elements, such as machine gun, artillery, and communications units, a battalion could thus number 500–600 men. All the battalions of a district made up the district detachment (*otriad*). All command staffs were to be elected.[51]

The city conference, then, on the very eve of the October Revolution finally put together a citywide structure for the Red Guard. Obviously there was not time in a single day to put into effect the full organizational structure outlined at the conference, but at least a General Staff now existed that could—and did—play a role in mobilizing the armed workers in the October Revolution and its aftermath. Moreover, as the leadership was largely composed of those who had taken an active role since August (the bureau of the General Staff consisting of Valentin Trifonov, Vladimir Pavlov, A. A. Iurkin, S. Potapov, and Konstantin Iurenev, who was also president of the General Staff),[52] it had experience with the problems and techniques of mobilizing various worker detachments. Though the Red Guard was still far from the kind of organization needed to prepare for a seizure of power, it was one that could, for the first time in 1917, give a reasonable amount of coordinated support once a crisis or a revolution began. That was what would happen in the October Revolution. However, before turning to the role of the Red Guard in that event, we need to look more closely at its numbers, arms, training, and social and political characteristics. This will be the focus of the next two chapters.

7

The Red Guards: Size, Arms, Training, Medical Units

> "All day we instructed changing groups of workers' detachments, shouting ourselves hoarse, like noncoms in reserve regiments."
> — *Vladimir Malakhovskii*

There are a number of related problems about the workers' militias and Red Guards to which we have made only scattered references to this point, including such questions as their size, armament, training, and possession of special medical units. We will focus on the militias and Red Guards as they were in September and October, on the eve of the Bolshevik Revolution, but with backward glances at the earlier period.

The size of the Petrograd workers' armed bands clearly increased in the second half of 1917, but it fluctuated with the ebb and flow of revolutionary crises. For example, the Kornilov Affair saw a dramatic new surge of enrollments, but many workers who signed up for the assorted *druzhiny* at the end of August probably never went beyond that step or else dropped out after the end of the crisis. Still, the new mood in the capital kept many in, and the efforts to organize them better led also to more exact, though still woefully inadequate, records. On September 5, *Izvestiia* published an estimate by the Central Council of Factory Committees of 25,000 workers' militiamen at that time, a figure used by many writers afterward. This represented the great surge of enrollments during the Kornilov period. After the crisis passed, the number dropped off. Pinezhskii cites only 10,000–12,000 in late September, and Startsev seems to accept this as generally accurate, though he rejects the earlier *Izvestiia* figure as inflated. Instead, using figures for a group of factories in the Vyborg district, Startsev projects a figure for the entire city of 13,000–15,000 militiamen at the beginning of September.[1] My own feeling is that this figure is too conservative.

To begin with, the sources used by Startsev are not especially impressive—the Left SR newspaper *Znamia truda*, and a statement by N. A. Baturnov, a Bolshevik instructor in the Vyborg district. From them he deduces a Vyborg militia or Red Guard of 3,200–3,500.* Calculating that Vyborg supplied roughly one-fourth of the Red Guards, he arrives at the above figure of 13,000–15,000. Using the same one-fourth calculation (although it may overstate the Vyborg role, about which the Bolsheviks were best informed) and the more reliable figures produced at the Vyborg Red Guard conference on October 7, we get considerably larger figures. Of 43 factories represented at the conference, 27 responded to a questionnaire that they had 4,084 guardsmen.[2] If we assume that the 16 that did not respond had fewer militiamen than the others, just to be cautious, we would still have a conservative figure of over 5,000 in Vyborg. Multiplying this by Startsev's factor of four, we get 20,000 for early October. Some figures, however, deviate widely from this in both directions. Vladimir Pavlov, a member of the Central Komendatura, though he claimed a ridiculously low figure of 4,000 armed Red Guards at a meeting of the Bolshevik Petersburg Committee on September 24, stated that there were another 40,000 men waiting for arms. Evgenii Trifonov, another leader of the Komendatura, cites the figure of 35,000–40,000 Red Guards for this time in his memoirs.[3] Though these figures seem too high, they cannot be ignored, for these two men were deeply involved in Red Guard organization.

Part of the problem of estimating size is that different sources use different criteria for inclusion in the Red Guard. Some contemporary authors apparently adopted very strict criteria, counting only people enrolled in certain recognized Red Guard units. Others counted any kind of organized armed workers' unit, whatever it called itself, whereas still others appear to have counted armed workers in general. An illustration of the problem is provided by the Pipe Factory on Vasil'evskii Island. The Red Guard unit there provided training not only to its own active members but to other

---

* Although all workers' militias were not consolidated into units named Red Guards, I use the term Red Guard from this point on in referring to all workers' armed bands, whatever they may have called themselves.

workers as well. As a result, there existed a cadre of 700 well-trained Red Guards plus about 2,000 other workers with some training.[4] Depending upon the criteria used, different sources might calculate 700 or 2,700 for this factory. Different counting methods, then, have produced wide variation in the estimates of size, and this variation has obviously affected estimates of the importance of the Red Guard. Moreover, other workers who were armed but not part of an official unit represented a significant destabilizing factor in 1917 even if they were difficult to mobilize for offensive actions.

What figure can we safely use, then? Startsev, who tends to be restrictive rather than inclusive, estimates about 20,000 Red Guards on the eve of the October Revolution.[5] In the welter of conflicting estimates this seems a cautious minimum figure. There probably were more, perhaps 25,000–30,000, but we will use his conservative figure in order not to inflate inadvertently the role and importance of the Red Guard and armed workers' detachments in this and subsequent chapters.

How well armed were these workers? Some accounts suggest that they were poorly armed—in quantity and quality—with many guardsmen not having weapons, whereas others suggest a plenitude of arms, including machine guns. Obviously, adequate arms were important to their ability to be perceived as a significant force by other political or social groups, as well as to their ability to be one in time of crisis. The evidence suggests, paradoxically, that there were ample arms available to the workers but that they often still felt inadequately equipped, and that the political party leaders never understod this and systematically underestimated the available arms.

The Petrograd workers, individually or through the workers' militia, acquired a large but difficult to quantify stock of arms in the period up to the July Days. We know that considerable quantities of arms fell into their hands during and immediately after the February Revolution—arms taken from police stations and railway depots, and handed over by soldiers. M. P. Tsinis, a workers' militia and Red Guard activist from February to October, claims that in the Vyborg district workers were fairly well armed, especially with weapons provided by the Moscow Guard Regiment and the machine gun regiments.[6] There are virtually no reliable overall figures, but from all the accounts we can assume that by July 1 there were upwards of 20,000 rifles, plus revolvers, including the 1,200 new rifles sent from the Sestroretsk Factory on February 28.[7] This is admittedly a rather arbitrary figure, but one more likely to be low than high; indeed, as we shall soon see, it may be far too low. The various accounts of the February Revolution are filled with stories of acquiring arms, but most cannot be quantified. Some accounts, however, do give figures, and they suggest a total much larger than commonly assumed. A report to the Petrograd Soviet on March 10 spoke of 1,800 guns in worker hands in the Petrogradskii district alone.[8] V. A. Tsybul'skii reports the claim of a Bolshevik at the New Parviainen Factory, D. E. Solov'ev, that he transported 5,000 rifles from Sestroretsk to Vyborg district factories before July.[9] V. N. Kaiurov speaks of obtaining 10,000 rifles and revolvers in the Vyborg district alone.[10] We might be disposed to discount this last figure as loosely exaggerated were it not for figures of comparable size from much more reliable sources: Zigfrid Kel'son and General Lavr Kornilov, the latter then commander of the Petrograd Military District. Kel'son, who worked in the City Militia administration, reports that on March 31 Kornilov demanded the return to military stores of 40,000 rifles and 30,000 revolvers given out during the February Revolution.[11] The possibility that this figure has a basis in reality is enhanced by the fact that it is also used by I. I. Mints in his history of the Revolution, citing a Soviet archive source.[12] In addition, G. I. Zlokazov, in his study of the Petrograd Soviet using the archive collection of the Soviet Executive Committee, notes that the Soviet's Military Commission gave out 24,000 rifles, plus cartridges, to the masses between March 2 and 4.[13] We should also recall the earlier comment of Kel'son that most of the arms distributed by the City Militia authorities during the first days went to the workers' districts—half to Vyborg alone.[14] Thus it is possible that our figure should read well over 50,000–60,000 rifles, plus other arms, by July 1. For purposes of estimating the arms available by October, however, let us use the cautious figure of 20,000 rifles by summer.

After the July Days, the government made an effort to collect arms held by the populace, but as we have seen this was largely unsuccessful. Indeed, the acquisition of arms, by individuals and groups, continued even before the Kornilov Affair stimulated a new drive to acquire them. On August 12 the *piaterka* raided a building in Petrograd and secured 420 rifles and 870 revolvers from "coun-terrevolutionaries." Four days later it secured a shipment of 3,600 rifles from Sestroretsk, which were distributed in the working-class districts.[15] Once the Kornilov Affair began, of course, the workers received large numbers of arms. Between August 29 and 31 Sestro-retsk sent 1,680 rifles to the Petrograd Soviet for distribution and another 928 directly to factories in Petrograd and its environs. Moreover, some factories obtained arms on their own from various sources. The Putilov Factory Red Guard, acting with the mandate of its district revolutionary committee, got arms from the Peter-Paul Fortress and from friendly troops, especially from the depot of the Novocherkask Regiment. One worker recalls going with a con-voy of three trucks to bring arms from the Novocherkask depot. Indeed, S. M. Korchagin, the Narva-Peterhof district Red Guard commander, says that there were about 11,000 rifles there (includ-ing those at the Putilov Factory) by mid-October and that every fifth Putilovite had a rifle or revolver.[16] Other factories were busily obtaining arms also. On October 5 the Skorokhod Shoe Factory workers forced the management to agree to a proposal from Sestro-retsk that they provide 6,000 pairs of shoes in exchange for arms. They received a supply adequate not only for their own factory Red Guard but also for distribution to some other factories.[17] In addi-tion to rifles, efforts were made to acquire machine guns, hand gre-nades, and other explosives and arms. During the Kornilov Days, a barge loaded with explosives and grenades was sent to Petrograd by the Shlissel'burg workers; after the Petrograd Soviet leaders refused to accept it, Vyborg Red Guard members unloaded it and dis-tributed its contents.[18]

This process continued up to the October Revolution. The Petro-grad Soviet, now Bolshevik-dominated, began to play a more active role in obtaining arms. It got 5,000 rifles from Sestroretsk in mid-October, and another 400 on October 17. On October 18 the Putilov Factory got weapons from the Okhta arsenal, including ma-chine guns. The factory committee of the Baltic Shipbuilding Fac-tory sent workers to the Izhorskii Arms Factory south of the city for weapons. The Menshevik-SR–led Central Executive Committee tried to forbid the acquisition of weapons from arsenals and facto-ries by a decree on October 18, but this was unsuccessful. Indeed, on October 22 the Bolshevik-dominated Military Revolutionary

Committee sent its own commissars to all arsenals, thus ensuring the distribution of arms to desired worker and army units.[19] Throughout this period factories asked for and got a steady supply of cartridges from the Petrograd Cartridge Factory. Sometimes a humorous note creeps into the process, as when a Red Guard leader named Egorov from the Obukhov Steel Factory, returning there from the Peter-Paul Fortress with a truckload of arms on October 22 or 23, was stopped by an anarchist named Piler, who demanded at gunpoint half of the arms. Egorov, in the truck's cab, drew his own pistol, and the two men faced each other with drawn weapons until Egorov's driver slowly began to edge away. Piler chased them down the street shouting, and Egorov yelled back: "I got these through organized means; organize and you can get some too." [20]

How many arms did the workers have in October? Working with the figures given so far, we have at least 24,000 acquired before the Kornilov Affair, another 10,000 during it, and at least that amount again in September and October, or about 44,000. And yet these figures are based on very fragmentary reports from only part of the factories, reports that also reveal that factories often got their own arms without working through higher bodies. Hence the figure probably is quite low. Moreover, this calculation leaves out most of the 40,000 rifles in the Kel'son/Kornilov/Mints accounts and the 24,000 mentioned by Zlokazov, which would push our estimate toward 100,000. Working from another direction, we have S. M. Korchagin's figure (based on information supplied by the district *komendatura*) of 11,000 rifles in the Peterhof–Narva Gate region alone in mid-October.[21] Since this district accounted for about 10 percent of the city's industrial work force, if the rest of the city were comparably armed we would again have some 100,000 rifles. Or, from Korchagin's assertion of a rifle or pistol for every fifth Putilov worker,[22] we can calculate that an industrial work force of about 350,000 would have 70,000 weapons among them. In addition, many more arms went to the Red Guard on October 24–25, especially from the Peter-Paul Fortress.[23]

The above figures have concentrated on rifles, the most important weapon in the circumstances. However, we should note also that many Red Guard units had machine guns, which must have increased their confidence—and their ability to menace opponents—considerably. Some even had artillery: one detachment at the Petrograd Metallurgical Factory had six three-inch field pieces.[24] Although it is doubtful that the Red Guards were well trained in the use of artillery, it must have had considerable psychological impact on both them and their rivals. Some factory units had grenades and other explosives, and revolvers were so plentiful that almost everyone who wanted one could get one.

The scattered testimony, then, suggests a huge flow of arms. Yet paradoxically, Red Guard and Bolshevik leaders consistently complained about the small supply of weapons and armed workers. For example, Vladimir Pavlov, a member of the Central Komendatura, not only gave a meeting of the Bolshevik Petersburg Committee on September 24 a ridiculously small estimate of the number of armed Red Guards, as we have seen, but also cited lack of arms as a reason why some guards had quit since the Kornilov enrollments.[25] How does one explain such a discrepancy? One explanation is given by Pinezhskii: local commanders "pleaded poor" in their reports in order to underline their requests for more arms.[26] A second involves the fact that discussions sometimes centered around just those Red Guard units affiliated with the Central Komendatura, which would exclude a large number of unregistered workers' militias, factory militias, and *druzhiny*. The most important, however, is that organizing and arming basically was a local or factory affair. The state of central organization and information was so poor that there was no comprehensive knowledge of what was going on throughout the city. Even those meetings of the Bolshevik Petersburg Committee that tried to get an overall view by means of reports from the districts—e.g., the meetings of September 24 and October 15—got only the general impressions of people who themselves had only a vague knowledge of this matter.[27] Moreover, workers guarded their arms jealously from *any* higher authority's efforts to control or regulate them. The repeated Provisional Government and Petrograd Soviet efforts to regulate possession of arms had created a wariness that probably led the workers to block outside knowledge of how many arms they had and how they were distributed. And as they rarely if ever felt they had enough arms, they could honestly continue to appeal for more. One suspects that bodies such as the Petrograd Soviet, the Military Revolutionary Committee, and the Petersburg Committee heard only the complaints and requests for arms, never the cases of factories such as Skorokhod that had so many weapons they could give some to other factories.

When all is said and done, we simply do not have accurate arms figures, and one can calculate widely divergent totals. What comes through clearly, whatever the figures, are three points. First, the Petrograd workers, contrary to traditional statements about their shortage of arms, were in fact very well armed: our most conservative estimate would provide a rifle for one in every 11 or 12 members of the total work force—men, women, and youths—or about one in every five adult male workers. And this does not include revolvers and machine guns. Second, there clearly were many more arms than recorded guardsmen (indeed, some of the low estimates of arms may have resulted from only counting the number of guardsmen). Many arms must have been in the hands either of factory militias uncounted by the Central Komendatura or of individual workers. Third, the distribution of weapons was uneven. The next logical question, therefore, is how well were those who had arms trained in their use?

Training of workers in the use of arms began soon after the February Revolution. Until September—that is, until after the Kornilov Affair—such training seems to have been sporadic and strictly at local initiative. M. P. Tsinis, an army deserter and Bolshevik activist, claims that he began to train Aivaz Factory workers in the use of arms shortly after the February Revolution.[28] On June 6 the All-Russian Society of Leatherworking Manufacturers sent an appeal to the ministry of the interior complaining, among other things, that the workers were choosing groups of militiamen to study shooting and other matters for a month at a time, so that eventually all the workers would have training in the use of arms.[29] M. L. Lur'e cites the manuscript memoir of one Red Guard commander who claimed that after the July Days he began to train his unit in the basics of street fighting: advancing in groups, forming a skirmish line, firing around corners, and so on. This training included the use of a machine gun.[30] An interesting factor during this period is mentioned by Chechkovskii—the long summer "white nights."[31] Training, after all, had to be done either in the evening after work or on Sunday, and so the long days were of great help. Still, at the time of the Kornilov Affair very little had been accomplished in the way of training. The events of late August, however, and the new mood of a coming political and social confrontation they engendered made training more imperative than it had ever seemed before.

One major problem was getting competent instructors. At first many workers' militia units had tried to use those workers who had military experience—for example, M. P. Tsinis, although his career was perhaps exceptional. Tsinis deserted from a training unit near Petrograd, where he was a noncommissioned officer, just before the February Revolution. He made his way to the capital, participated in the Revolution, and shortly thereafter embarked on a career as a workers' militia activist. He served as an instructor in the Aivaz Factory in the Vyborg district, where he also found work. After the July Days he was marked for arrest and had to move about, landing a job in the Optical Factory in the Rozhdestvenskii district. He continued to work as an instructor in both districts, and one of the things he particularly undertook to impart was the importance of being familiar with strategic points in the city and how to seize them.[32] Men such as Tsinis were not common, but some factories were fortunate in having active-duty soldiers to draw upon. I. P. Leiberov calculates that there were 1,143 workers returned from the army working in Petrograd factories on January 1, 1917.[33] More came back after the February Revolution. For instance, the Admiralty Shipbuilding Factory got back a few hundred workers who had earlier been drafted as punishment for strike activity, and the Peterhof District Soviet ordered 1,000 positions held open at the Putilov Factory for returning draftees from the February 1916 strike.[34] Others came back singly or in small groups and certainly increased the number of militia instructors available.* Their value was lessened, however, by the fact that most had been low-ranking soldiers or had served in technical positions or army shops and knew little of the use of arms, much less how to train others; Tsinis was an exception in this respect. Sometimes factories were able to get active-duty soldiers from a nearby unit as instructors, but this was a hit-or-miss operation.

When the Bolsheviks and other organizations began to take

---

* Absorption of returning workers into the factory was often coupled with efforts to purge the factory of people suspected of having gone to work there in order to obtain military deferments, especially people of middle-class or prosperous peasant background. At the Putilov Factory a special commission was set up to investigate these people. Similar actions took place elsewhere. The reasons for expulsion included "has own house," "son of a *pomeshchik*," and "owns a shop."

greater interest in the Red Guard after Kornilov, the situation improved, for in the case of the Bolsheviks their Military Organization undertook to provide instructors for the Red Guard. For example, Vladimir Malakhovskii, one of the early writers on the Red Guard, was assigned in September by the Military Organization to work as an instructor at the New Lessner Factory in the Vyborg district.[35] He had been expelled from the army for Bolshevik agitation after the July Days and his career, if at all typical, suggests that efforts to cleanse the army of troublemakers and Bolsheviks after July may have had the unintended effect of providing experienced instructors and leaders for the Red Guard. During the Kornilov Affair, the Military Organization, in agreement with the Central Komendatura, began to organize a cadre of instructors,[36] and in early September it set up a special ten-day course to train instructors in their task. How frequently this course was given is not clear, but Chechkovskii cites the names of several instructors from the Moscow Gate district who took it, and people also came from other cities to take it.[37] The district soviets and *komendatury* also helped provide instructors. Indeed, Pinezhskii states that the latter played a more important role in providing instructors than did the Military Organization, getting them from military units in the district and from former soldiers in the factories. Malakhovskii indirectly substantiates this by denigrating the role of the Military Organization. In fact, we should not overemphasize the role of outside instructors, for most instructors came from inside the armed detachment or factory. Indeed, in some instances the factories even forced management to pay the salaries not only of the worker-militiamen, but also of the militia instructors![38] Here, as in almost everything about the Red Guard, local initiative was primary.

The actual training, of course, varied tremendously from unit to unit. It took place on the factory grounds, in nearby vacant lots or parks, and sometimes in the streets, especially dead-end streets or lanes leading to the factory. Finding a place for shooting practice was difficult. Sometimes the factory could be used, but more often it took place at the shooting range of a nearby friendly regiment or in the countryside outside Petrograd. At first training was irregular, but by September a routine had been established in many factories. The Putilov Red Guard, for example, trained 3–5 times a week. At the Baltic Factory, training was carried out in a nearby alley for

2–3 hours after work. A report from the Erikson Telephone and Electromechanical Factory in late September states that their fighting detachment trained on Thursdays and Fridays, from 5 P.M. until 7 P.M., under the direction of three unpaid worker-instructors.[39] At the Shell Casing Factory, a regular three-times-a-week training schedule was established in September.[40] There is one interesting report by two instructors from the Bolshevik Military Organization at the New Parviainen Factory, Konstantin Lifonov and Lavrentii Kupriianov. On September 18 they drilled 23 workers from 2 to 4 P.M., and a second shift of 53 from 4 to 6 P.M., on the manual of arms. On September 20 they again drilled two shifts, this time on the loading and firing of arms.[41] On Vasil'evskii Island, the Red Guard of the Pipe Factory and nearby factories gathered on Malyi Prospect after work, turning it into an armed camp. Interestingly enough, here not only the guardsmen but other workers as well were trained—a situation that apparently was not uncommon, for I. G. Gavrilov refers to it also in the Vyborg district.[42] Though training centered primarily around the use of rifles, sometimes it included the use of machine guns, as at the Aivaz Factory, where the instructors were soldiers of the First Machine Gun Regiment.[43]

Training in the use of arms became a feature of factory life in September and October. M. L. Lur'e quotes a guardsman of the Franko-Russkii Factory as describing his factory as being turned into an armed camp in September: "The turners were at their workbenches with cartridge pouches over their shoulders, rifles standing at the benches. In the locksmith shop, rifles stood in the corners, and the locksmith also had cartridges over his shoulder." An hour before work ended, the unit commander would come and tell the men where to go for training that evening.[44] Even allowing for poetic license, we get a clear sense of the psychological mood among many workers. Training certainly was aided by the work stoppages and strikes that became increasingly frequent as the year wore on. Vasil'ev describes how the woodworkers took advantage of their strike in early October to turn a shop into a Red Guard camp, using their workbenches to clean arms.[45] Strikes, especially prolonged ones (as the woodworkers' strike was), gave the workers free time for training and heightened the sense of its importance. A good description of what must have been a fairly typical scene at these training sessions is given by Malakhovskii. "In these clearings [in

the Vyborg district] we maneuvered our ranks, deployed formations, charged, marched, and practiced the use of arms. Everyone
was in full swing. All day we instructed changing groups of workers' detachments, shouting ourselves hoarse, like noncoms in reserve regiments."[46]

What kind of fighting material did this training turn out? The
ability to use arms effectively must have varied immensely from unit
to unit, and even from person to person within units. In some instances former soldiers made up a considerable portion of a unit—
35 of 76 active Red Guards at the Erikson Factory,[47] for example—
but there are no figures for soldiers in the Petrograd Red Guard as a
whole. They probably were a considerably smaller proportion than
in the Erikson Factory, though. Where the guardsmen had good instructors, they made rapid progress: at the New Lessner Factory,
under the instruction of Lieutenant Solov'ev, a disciplined, well-
organized unit was created.[48] Podvoiskii states that the instructors
reported back to the Military Organization favorably about the
workers' determination and progress in training.[49] Certainly, these
Red Guards were not capable of facing up to disciplined regular
troops, and many disparaging comments were made about their appearance, especially by foreigners and members of the upper and
middle classes. However, disciplined troops did not exist in Petrograd and its environs, as the Kornilov Affair had shown and the October Revolution would reemphasize. In fact, the workers in October tended to show considerably greater determination than the
soldiers. To the extent that they acquired even a smattering of training, they had increased confidence and were more willing—and
able—to use arms to obtain their objectives. In the actual situation
in Petrograd by October, they represented a significant force. In
any confrontation, their morale and determination would prove
more important than formal training or theoretical fighting ability.
Trotsky underscored this point when he recalled that during the
October Revolution weapons proved critical mostly as an "external
sign of power," and that most of the key points in the city were
seized by armed groups facing down their opponents rather than
shooting.[50] Almost all of the participant accounts clearly support
his observation.

Although very little actual fighting was to take place in October,
that was not known beforehand. Thus it is important to take note

of the formation of medical aid units within or attached to Red Guard detachments, for these testify to the seriousness with which many guardsmen took the possibility of fighting, and of casualties. The frequent references to medical units and first aid training suggest that the Red Guard organizers felt them to be important. Major crises stimulated their organization, as they did the organization of the Red Guards in general. The Kornilov Days, as might be expected, spurred the formation of medical units, and most of them date to this period or later.[51] Nonetheless, some units date from much earlier. L. Ganichev recounts that a medical aid unit formed among women workers of the Military-Medical Supply Factory aided wounded workers during the July Days. With adequate supplies at the factory to draw upon, and perhaps the stimulus of their place of work, this unit was especially active. Its members sometimes accompanied the factory Red Guard when it went out on patrol before the October Days, and they also organized training in first aid for women workers and aided in the establishment of medical units in other factories of the Petrogradskii district.[52]

The history of the Vyborg Red Guard provides us with our only extensive account of the development of medical units before the October Revolution. Malakhovskii, one of the Red Guard staff members in the district, recalls in his memoirs that the staff tried to set up a central medical aid apparatus shortly before the October Revolution in response to an initiative not from the staff or the soviet but from below: some Bolshevik women medical students proposed to the Bolshevik district committee that they organize a course of first aid study among women workers.[53] They were sometimes able to get assistance from qualified instructors, such as Professor V. I. Voriarchek of the Military-Medical Academy, who in October gave lectures on administering first aid to those wounded by gunfire.[54] The Vyborg Red Guard apparently did get a rudimentary first aid structure formed before the October Revolution, under the direction first of one of the medical students, T. A. Fortunatova, and then of one A. F. Kornev, for it fielded some medical detachments during the October Revolution and immediately afterward. Malakhovskii's brief account also provides some detail about the kinds of people who worked in the medical units. They were mostly women, and included medical students, hospital attendants, nurses, "Sisters of Mercy" (a volunteer group doing medical aid

work during the war), and factory workers. There were a few doctor's assistants but almost no doctors; Malakhovskii says there
were no doctors at all in the Vyborg organization. Such male members as there were served mostly as drivers of autos used as ambulances and as doctor's assistants. The medical units were active in
giving aid to the injured in the October Revolution, but their most
important role lay in the future, as the nucleus for Red Cross and
medical units on the Bolshevik side in the Civil War. At this point
they served to symbolize the seriousness with which many took the
prospect of armed confrontation.

The medical units, like the Red Guards generally, were primarily
factory-oriented and self-created. Normally they were formed as an
auxiliary detachment of the local Red Guard unit. In most cases
they seem to have been formed from and by women factory workers, although in some instances leadership was provided by medical
students, the factory committee, or Red Guard leaders. There was
even less district- or citywide organization here than among the
Red Guard generally. In late September the Vyborg District Soviet's
commission on fighting *druzhiny* took a new interest in the medical detachments, and in a questionnaire sent to factories and Red
Guard commanders about their units asked if each local Red Guard
had one, and if so of what size, training, supplies, and ability to set
up dressing stations and provide transport.[55] This would suggest
that the district soviet not only took the matter seriously but was
concerned to strengthen and enlarge these units. There appears to
have been some sort of districtwide organization or direction by
district Red Guard staffs also in the Rozhdestvenskii, Nevskii, and
Petrogradskii districts.[56] The distribution of medical detachments
among districts and factories was very uneven; some did not have
any, whereas in at least two factories the medical detachments outnumbered the Red Guards, reflecting the fact that women formed
the bulk of the workers there. Estimates of total size are very im-
precise, but the medical units may have numbered around 3,000
members by October.[57]

This discussion of the medical units provides a good point of departure for some comments on the role of women in the Red Guard
generally. Women made up one-third of the Petrograd industrial
work force in 1917 and in many factories, including large ones,
were in the majority.[58] They were also naturally interested in the

course of the Revolution, and some took an active role in it. In factories where women were a big part of the work force—as for example the Treugol'nik Rubber Factory, two-thirds of whose workers were women—some even served in regular militia and Red Guard units.[59] Women in fighting units were not common, however, and most detachments did not contain any. The most common form of active involvement in the Red Guards for women was through the medical detachments, though some other opportunities arose in auxiliary services such as clerical work or food and drink service.

By the eve of the October Revolution, then, a large, well-armed, and partially trained Red Guard had come into existence. Though its exact size and its fighting ability are subject to argument, its significance as a force that could play a major role in determining the outcome of the Russian Revolution is not, especially given the chaos in Russia and the notorious volatility of the Petrograd garrison. Before turning to its role in the October Revolution, however, let us look next at the Red Guard's social and political characteristics.

8

The Social and Political
Characteristics of the Red Guards

"Despite different world outlooks and levels of political development, the ranks of the Red Guard were united by the simple and understandable slogans put forward by the Bolsheviks."
—*I. M. Liapin*

Who joined the Red Guards and other volunteer armed bands? It is only with difficulty and an often frustrating imprecision that we can gather any information that tells us more about the social and political characteristics of the people who composed the Red Guards and workers' militias. Here we are probing an area that the various writers on the Red Guard or the Revolution in general have rarely discussed. Much of our information is accordingly drawn from chance references in memoirs and the early literature, though there is also an important recent Soviet source, Startsev's *Ocherki po istorii petrogradskoi Krasnoi gvardii*. Between 1930 and 1935, the Leningrad city government established a Commission for the Affairs of Former Red Guards and Red Partisans that undertook to register former guardsmen. As part of the verification process, people were asked for data about their activities and were required to fill out a special questionnaire. From the resulting materials, held in Soviet archives, Startsev set up a statistical base of approximately 3,700 former Petrograd Red Guard members and has drawn valuable statistical profiles that we will examine in the following pages.[1]

Despite the suggestions in some of the general Soviet writings on the Revolution that those who took up arms voluntarily and joined armed bands were experienced proletarians, veterans of earlier political and even armed confrontations, logic suggests—and most memoir and other early accounts confirm—that armed band members were disproportionately younger workers. Pinezhskii refers to the Red Guard as being made up mostly of younger workers. M. D. Rozanov comments that his detachment at the Obukhov Steel Factory was composed mostly of young workers. I. M. Liapin, a Red Guard commander and one of the best sources on the attitudes and traits of the guardsmen, strongly stresses their relative youth: most, he says, were 17–24 years of age, "youths who had not yet mastered theory, but felt inside" what must be done. Other memoirs make similar points. Another indication of the youth orientation is reflected in the actions of the Socialist Union of Young Workers, a generally radical and Bolshevik-influenced organization that functioned partly to get young workers into the Red Guard.[2]

Somewhat more precise data on age are given by Startsev. From a statistical base of 3,557 Red Guard members in ten districts of Petrograd at the beginning of October for whom age was known, he computes a percent distribution as follows:

under 18	18–20	21–22	23–25	26–30	31–40	41–50	over 50
7.87%	20.16%	10.51%	14.54%	21.08%	21.26%	4.10%	0.48%

Startsev further refines this by making an allowance for statistical error resulting from population movement and differential mortality. Many young workers drawn from the villages during the war years and having only tenuous ties to the city would have left during the factory shutdowns of 1917–21 and not returned, and many in the two oldest age groups would have died from natural causes between 1917 and 1930. Accordingly, he works out the following age distribution:[3]

under 18	18–20	21–22	23–25	26–30	31–40	41–50	over 50
8.22%	20.81%	10.47%	14.32%	20.53%	20.93%	4.22%	0.50%

Startsev also tries to compare the ages of Red Guard members to the ages of the general work force. For the latter he has to go to prewar census figures, which hinder the comparison, but his results suggest that younger men joined the Red Guard in larger proportions than older men, i.e., that the ratio of Red Guard members to workers overall was higher in the younger age brackets than in the older ones.[4] And if younger men took up arms and joined the Red

Guard more readily than their older comrades in 1917, this suggests that young workers were a primary source of unrest and violence. Interestingly enough, this fits with one of the conclusions reached by Leopold Haimson in his study of urban unrest and the radicalization of the industrial work force in 1912–14: that "green youths" were especially activist and radical at this lower level of revolutionary turmoil.[5] We should be cautious about placing too much emphasis on these youths' "greenness," however, for people joined the work force much younger then. The average age for joining the work force was 15,[6] and so by 18 or 19 the young worker might already have a strong identification with the factory and a list of grievances acquired firsthand. Thus the considerable enrollment of workers under the age of 21 in the Red Guards does not necessarily mean that such guardsmen did not have factory experience and a strong class identity.

One problem in discussing age this way—or any other similar trait—is that we are talking about general characteristics, composite profiles. In fact, any given factory Red Guard might deviate from the norm considerably. M. L. Lur'e cites figures on five metalworking factories that emphasize this (see Table 1). Striking differences exist between, say, the Baltic Factory and the Nail Factory for workers to age 20, and a surprisingly high proportion of the Red Guard at the Military Horseshoe Factory was over 35. Presumably the variations were influenced by the age distribution at the factories, which would in turn reflect a multitude of factors, including what the plant produced and how skilled a work force was required. It is also noteworthy that the two factories with the smallest percentage of the youngest workers—Baltic and Pipe—were the largest of the five.

The issue of age leads us to the related issue of marital status. Common sense suggests that workers without family responsibilities—unmarried workers or married workers without children, and especially the former—would have been most likely to run the risks inherent in bearing arms. There are some indications that this was the case. Z. V. Stepanov, in his study of Petrograd workers in 1917, notes that 45 percent of the male metalworkers aged 21–30 did not have families.[7] We can assume that the figure would be even larger for those under 21, so that probably over half of those 30 and under were without family obligations. This age group made

TABLE I
*Percentage of Red Guards by Age
at Five Metalworking Factories, 1917*

Factory	To age 20	20–25	25–30	30–35	35–40	40 and over
Baltic Factory	7.7%	24.7%	36.4%	23.5%	1.2%	6.5%
Pipe Factory	9.4	29.2	40.6	16.6	4.2	—
Simens-Gal'ske Factory	16.0	20.0	26.0	24.0	8.0	6.0
Military Horseshoe Factory	14.3	14.3	28.6	14.3	21.4	7.1
Nail Factory	30.0	37.5	17.5	10.0	5.0	—

SOURCE: M. L. Lur'e, *Petrogradskaia Krasnaia gvardiia*, p. 28.
NOTE: Age groups overlap in Lur'e.

up three-quarters of the Red Guards by Startsev's calculations. Stepanov's figures apply only to metalworkers, but there is no reason to assume that their family patterns were greatly different from those of other industrial workers of Petrograd; moreover, three-fourths of the Red Guards were metalworkers. A picture emerges of a Red Guard made up disproportionately of younger workers without family obligations. Also, younger and single workers were more likely than older and married workers to live in barracks or other communal dwellings at or near the factory, and this probably facilitated their recruitment into the Red Guard.

Closely related to age and marital status in determining the composition and outlook of the Red Guards are social and geographic origins and the length of time spent in Petrograd. Were the guardsmen drawn more heavily from natives of the capital or from recent migrants from the countryside and other towns? Were they long-time factory workers or recent peasant migrants? We saw in an earlier chapter that Petrograd's industrial work force grew from 242,000 before the war to 392,800 in January 1917.[8] Since some prewar workers were drafted into the army and replaced, about half the 1917 work force was new since the beginning of the war. Haimson argues that one important ingredient in the growing industrial unrest of 1912–14 was the influx into the work force of new labor recruits from the villages who added old peasant grievances to their newly acquired urban dissatisfactions,[9] and we might expect that trend of 1912–14 to have been heightened in 1914–17. Do we then find an unusually high proportion of recent migrants among the Red Guard in 1917?

Startsev's figures show a slightly larger percentage of Petrograders in the Red Guard than in the work force generally, but there are some serious problems with his figures that leave the matter inconclusive. Moreover, he does not really address the question of how long those guardsmen who gave village or small-town birthplaces (a clear majority) had been in the city industrial work force and thus proletarianized.[10] Hence the statistical data on the Red Guard do not shed much light on our question. However, it is perhaps significant that memoirs and contemporary literature on the Red Guard do not mention peasant origin or recent arrival as factors in enrollment. On the contrary, they suggest that a generalized discontent and hostility against the privileged orders—whether landowners, factory owners, factory managers, or even skilled workers in positions of authority, such as foremen—were more important in the decision to join workers' armed bands. If urban or rural origin was a factor in joining the Red Guard, it is not reflected in the records. Rather, what does come through from scattered references (and it is hardly surprising) is that the members of workers' armed bands were more radical than the bulk of their factory comrades: one incident that reflects this is Liapin's description of his failure to get the Petrograd Cartridge Factory workers to endorse a resolution calling for the dropping of charges against Lenin and other Bolsheviks after the July Days, a resolution that the fourth Liteinyi subdistrict workers' militia—drawn extensively from the Cartridge Factory—had just passed.[11]

When we look at the composition of the Red Guard by vocation, we find a profile that is hardly surprising but that is nonetheless different from other cities. Of 3,663 guardsmen for whom Startsev had data, 95.9 percent listed themselves as workers in 1917. Of the remaining 4.1 percent, almost two-thirds were soldiers. The rest were chiefly salaried employees. The percentage of workerguardsmen is higher in Petrograd than in any other city that has been studied, including Moscow, as we will see later. Among the Petrograd Red Guards, approximately three-fourths were metalworkers—about the same proportion metalworkers were in the adult male work force overall. Thus the common assertion that the metalworkers were especially militant does not appear to be borne out in terms of their providing a significantly larger share of members to the Red Guard. Among guardsmen from other industries and trades, chemical workers led with 7 percent.[12] It appears also that some of those listed as soldiers were in fact often former workers who had been drafted and then sent back to work in factories. For example, on October 19 at the Putilov Factory, 260 soldiers of the Taruntinskii Regiment working there joined its Red Guard as a group. They formed their own detachment, with elected commanders, within the larger Putilov Red Guard organization.[13]

One final social characteristic worth examining is nationality. We know that there were many non-Russian workers in Petrograd in 1917, particularly those evacuated from Poland and the Baltic region with their factories. By 1918, 5.8 percent of the Petrograd workers spoke Polish as their native language, 2.6 percent Latvian or Lithuanian, and 2.3 percent Finnish.[14] Non-Russians were thus not a large portion of the work force, but there were enough of them to play some role, especially when concentrated in a given factory. M. P. Tsinis records that in the October Revolution he was with a Red Guard unit from two factories (Optical and Russko-Baltic Motor) whose workers were mostly from Riga. The commander, like Tsinis, had a Latvian name—Guzis—and one presumes that most of the men in the unit also were Latvians.[15] There are other examples of Baltic and Polish guardsmen and factories, but nothing to indicate that they played a role out of proportion to their numbers overall. Yet in Saratov and Kharkov, as we will see, evacuated Baltic workers played a significant role in the Red Guard, both in numbers and in militancy. Looking at nationality questions from a different angle, there is some evidence of tension between Russians and minority nationalities and that factory militias—probably composed of Russians—were used to repress the minority. Chinese workers seem to have had particular difficulties, and reports of unrest among them and clashes with other workers appeared in the press periodically. In late September at Kenig Factory, conflict flared up between Chinese workers on the one hand and Russian workers and the factory administration on the other. The ostensible cause was argument over some sacks of flour, but unemployment among Russians was an underlying cause. A protest demonstration by Chinese workers was put down by the factory militia.[16]

We have made references throughout to the attitude of the political parties toward the workers' militia and Red Guard, but what of the political attitudes and affiliations of the guardsmen? Scattered references in memoirs and other early accounts support two basic impressions: that the armed workers' bands were predominantly nonparty, and that Bolshevik influence increased as time passed. Almost all writers, especially the memoirists, stress the nonparty orientation of the majority of rank-and-file members, although they also claim a general Bolshevik influence or direction. Most writers also acknowledge the participation of members of other socialist parties, which is underscored by the few contemporary references. For example, the response of the Moskovsko-Narva region Bolshevik committee to a Military Organization questionnaire in September stated that the workers' guards were nonparty.[17] All of the various "regulations" for workers' militias and Red Guards between February and October specified recommendation by a party, factory committee, or other worker organization for admission, but none required party membership, much less membership in a given party. Indeed, as late as September 8 the Bolshevik newspaper *Soldat*, in an editorial on arming the workers, felt it necessary to stress that party membership was not essential for membership in the Red Guard, that it was irrelevant to which revolutionary party a worker belonged, and that the Red Guard leaders should be responsible to nonparty organizations such as the district soviets. It should be stressed that nonparty did not mean a complete absence of political orientation: a socialist outlook was assumed, even if only in the most general and vague way, as was hostility to the Kadets and other liberal, conservative, or nonsocialist parties.

Startsev gives some statistics on party affiliation, but they must be used with great caution. Working with a base of 3,663 former guardsmen, he finds 40.4 percent of the rank and file and 55.8 percent of the command staffs listed as Bolsheviks in 1917, 2.5–3.0 percent listed as Mensheviks and SRs, and the rest nonparty. These figures overstate the Bolshevik membership, as Startsev acknowledges, and understate the Menshevik and SR. For one thing, the figures include those who joined in November and December, and the October Revolution probably changed the political complexion of the Red Guard considerably. First, I suspect that a large number of Bolsheviks joined the Red Guard after October, rallying to the defense of Soviet power. Second, there probably was a drop in Menshevik and SR members, especially in command positions. And third, there probably was an influx into the Bolshevik Party of guardsmen who previously had not been members. Indeed, the records of the Commission do not indicate whether a guardsman joined the Party before or after joining the Red Guards; of the 1,603 former guardsmen who were Bolsheviks, only 258 had joined the Party before the February Revolution. Moreover, there probably is a further statistical bias in that many former Mensheviks and SRs may simply have registered with the Commission as nonparty or even declined to register at all. The benefits of registration were not all that large, and even if the great terror of the 1930's was only beginning during the registration period, there had been sufficient purging of former Mensheviks and SRs to lead many to avoid anything that would draw attention to their former affiliation. Indeed, Startsev acknowledges that "almost all who indicated their sojourn in other, non-Bolshevik parties subsequently entered the Bolshevik Party in 1918–19 and, as a result, were required to report that." [18] Others probably chose to ignore that part of their history.

That considerable numbers of Menshevik and SR workers belonged is borne out by memoir references. Menshevik and SR party leaders were hostile to the Red Guards, but their rank-and-file members apparently joined in significant numbers. At the Military-Medical Supply Factory, Menshevik workers not only retained their ties to the workers' armed bands after the July Days but helped to hide arms when the Provisional Government and the Petrograd Soviet ordered their surrender. Similarly, A. R. Vasil'ev stresses that when the Wireless Telegraph Factory organized a Red Guard in response to Kornilov's attack, it was done with the full support of the factory committee chairman, Kankul'kin, a Menshevik, and of the secretary, Alekseev, an SR who also became the unit commander. Moreover, the assistant commander was F. F. Poplavskii, who joined the Bolsheviks only in 1919. The detachment included Bolsheviks, Mensheviks and SRs, among whom, he says, "with only a few exceptions, there were not any party arguments." [19] However, the negative attitude of the Menshevik and SR Party leaders probably took a toll, leading some party members to avoid joining or to withdraw from their local armed units, and creating in others the tension of divided loyalties when they attached great importance to their *druzhiny* or Red Guards. N. Rostov (Kogan), a leader in the April Red Guard conference who had been censured by the Menshevik leadership and ordered to cease his involvement in the Red Guard movement (see above, Chapter Four), turned up immediately after the October Revolution as a member of the committee directing the Fighting *Druzhina* of Printers. Others, less strongly attached to the Menshevik or SR party, switched their allegiance, as a group of SR workers at the Putilov Factory did on September 25 by publicly announcing their adherence to the Bolsheviks.[20] There are other such examples, and the whole drift of the elections to factory committees, soviets, and other bodies shows the defection.

On the opposite side of the coin, the support the Bolshevik Party gave the various armed groups, especially after Kornilov, must have swelled the numbers of those who were both Red Guards and Bolsheviks. In some instances Party members joined the Red Guards as a matter of Party policy. Pinezhskii states that this was required of Party members,[21] and some memoirists state that they were expected to do so as a part of their Party membership obligations—although obviously not everyone was so required. Often, however, it was a matter of workers who were members of armed detachments joining the Bolsheviks, the party whose support for the Red Guard paralleled their own sense of its importance. For example, Pavel Skuratov joined the fighting detachment at the Putilov Factory during the February Revolution but entered the Bolshevik Party only in April.[22] Similarly, I. M. Liapin was active in the workers' militia of the Cartridge Factory from February but joined the Party in April.[23] Liapin claims, reasonably enough, that the "simple and understandable slogans" put forward by the Bolshevik Party enabled guardsmen of diverse political outlooks and levels to be united,[24] and those "simple slogans" probably brought many guardsmen into the Party. In some instances the local Bolshevik organization—factory or district—made a special effort to gain control of local workers' militias, as in the Obukhov Factory and district,[25] and this must have had as a side effect the enrollment of militiamen in the Party.

The local Red Guard leaders and commanders were drawn from all socialist parties and from nonparty elements, but they seem to have been more party-oriented than the rank and file. This is not especially surprising, for one would expect political activists to rise to positions of leadership and also to be registered party members. However, this is not to deny that Bolshevik activists did tend to play a major role. Most later writers—virtually all Bolsheviks—do stress that Bolsheviks dominated the command positions. Liapin, for example, who acknowledges the role played by Mensheviks and SRs, states that in the First City District the Bolsheviks were only a small part of the Red Guard membership but controlled "all" of the command positions.[26] Startsev's statistics, as we have seen, show a larger Bolshevik membership among commanders and staff than among the rank and file. It is probable that Bolsheviks did occupy command positions out of proportion to their numbers—perhaps even most of them—by virtue of their energy and the commitment of the Bolshevik Party to support of the Red Guard. In this respect it is worth noting that the trend of leadership among those trying to organize a citywide structure was increasingly Bolshevik: the leadership in April was very much mixed; the *piaterka* in August was with one (anarchist) exception all Bolshevik; and the leadership of the Central Staff in October was virtually all Bolshevik and had closer ties to the Bolshevik leadership than did earlier groups. A similar trend occurred, as we will see below, in Saratov and Kharkov.

Nonetheless, many Red Guard leaders were Mensheviks, SRs, or members of other parties or of no party. This is well illustrated by the shift of leadership at the Pipe Factory: in the late spring a defensist Menshevik, F. Galakhov, was replaced as head of the factory militia by Aleksei Maksimov, who was more leftist but still a Menshevik and apparently still a defensist; later A. E. Remizov was commander of the Red Guard there, and though his party affiliation (if any) is unclear, he was not a Bolshevik. In October the Wireless Telegraph Factory Red Guard was commanded by an SR, Alekseev, who was also secretary of the factory committee and, on October 23, elected a member of the Petrogradskii district Red Guard *komendatura*. I. N. Stodolin-Sheikman was a leader in the Petrogradskii district Red Guard staff, but he joined the Bolshevik Party only in November.[27] Often factory or district Red Guard rules provided that the leadership staff include representatives of various organizations, including appropriate political parties. One example was that of the Peterhof District Soviet, which on August 28 set up a directing center for the Red Guard consisting of 18 persons repre-

senting different organizations, including the Bolsheviks, the Mensheviks, the SRs, the Anarchist Federation, and a fifth party not
identified.[28] Among the instructions that the factory committee of
the Arsenal of Peter the Great gave to the "socialist center" in
organizing a fighting *druzhina* was to "maintain a nonparty principle."[29] The variety of party affiliation reflects the extent to which
the Red Guard, and armed workers in general, were oriented more
toward the notion of "Soviet power" than toward support of the
Bolsheviks as a party.

The mention of anarchists in the Peterhof Red Guard center
brings us to the one other political element that must be considered.
Despite being split into several groupings, the anarchists seem to
have had a considerable impact on the armed workers' movement.
They were hostile to the existing order in general, and many were
inclined to violence. They carried influence in the factories among
exactly those more impatient and aggressive elements who could
also be expected to join the Red Guard. Moreover, the local anarchist headquarters was often to be found in the same building as the
local workers' militia commissariat or Red Guard staff headquarters—the Durnovo Villa, for example—which must have led to
close contact. The great weakness of the anarchists, of course, was
their inability to provide broader leadership and direction; but
given the intensely local orientation of the Red Guards and many
other worker organizations, this may actually have increased their
role. Paul Avrich quantifies their influence on the local level nicely:
"Typically, a large enterprise might have elected [to its factory committee in the early fall] a dozen Bolsheviks, two anarchists, and perhaps a few Mensheviks and SRs."[30] Anarchists played a major role
in the leadership of the Council of the Petrograd People's Militia in
June, and the anarchist Iustin Zhuk was one of the *piaterka* and the
leader of the Shlissel'burg Factory Red Guard. Anarchists also crop
up in district soviet records as having the right to be represented in
the district Red Guard staff or supervisory center. Moreover, at
least four anarchists—I. S. Bleikhman, G. Bogatskii, V. S. Shatov,
and E. Iarchuk—were members of the Military Revolutionary
Committee in October. Evidence is more spotty at the factory level,
where party affiliations tend for the most part not to be specified.
One suspects, given everything known about the anarchists and
about the Red Guard, that many who joined factory units were in-

spired by anarchist appeals and that local anarchists were active in the formation and leadership of units. There were even some anarchist armed detachments: at the Russian Renault Factory there was an anarchist "Black Guard" as well as a Red Guard, and the two later merged.[31]

While discussing party features of the workers' militias and Red Guards, we must discuss also the existence of separate party *druzhiny*, that is, purely party armed bands. These are mentioned only in passing here and there in the literature, and did not play a particularly important role. They appear to have existed mostly in the southern districts of the city, especially in the Peterhof, Narva, and Obukhov districts. We find references to them for all socialist parties except the Mensheviks. Most references are to the Peterhof-Narva region, particularly the Putilov Factory. In the fall, there were in this area SR, anarcho-communist, and Bolshevik *druzhiny*. There was also a Bolshevik *druzhina* of 43 members in the Obukhov district. (The Obukhov Factory was a staunch SR stronghold, and this may have led the Bolshevik district committee there to form its own small armed force.) Startsev refers to Left SR *druzhiny* at three other factories about September 1. Although not large, these party fighting organizations were sufficiently significant that representatives from them were to be included in the proposed Military Revolutionary Committee of the Petrograd Soviet approved by the Soviet Executive Committee on October 12.[32] Their main function was to protect party offices and guard party meetings and rallies rather than serve as the nucleus for any major armed force.

Closely related to the political orientation of the Red Guard leadership is the role of activist local leaders in tying together a number of local organizations, including both Red Guard and party groups. We have numerous indications of the extent to which a single activist was able not only to spread his personal influence through involvement in several organizations but to coordinate activities and bring the point of view or interests of one to bear upon the others. A small political cadre could play a major role in this way. Indeed, some of the lines of influence we have seen in the discussion of the various regulations in September–October and in the adoption of identical resolutions on the Red Guard in widely separated factories can be explained only by assuming extensive contact among activists and leaders at this tertiary level. Vladimir Malakhovskii is

emphatic not only that the major Bolshevik organizations—the
Central Committee, the Petersburg Committee, and the Military
Organization—failed to provide leadership, but that "comrades,
working together and in neighboring factories, formed a compact
group, making up a core around which" the Red Guards of an area
could unite.[33] Supporting each other, transmitting information, and
making a network of local leadership not dependent on direction or
help from above, they established a framework of horizontal linkages that has largely been overlooked in the historical literature.
Writers have tried to trace the vertical linkages from top party leaders to lower levels in order to shed light on the problems of mass
mobilization,[34] but the horizontal linkages have been ignored. The
activities of A. V. Vasil'ev, for example, linked various parts of the
city. He arrived in Petrograd on April 4, apparently from political
exile. In the course of the next few months he became a member of
both the Red Guard of the Wireless Telegraph Factory and the local
soviet in the Petrogradskii district (where he worked), while also
being active in the Okhta district (where he lived) as a member of
the Bolshevik district committee and of the local woodworkers'
strike committee. In May and June he was a member of the Council
of the Petrograd People's Militia. He participated in the July Uprising and went into hiding afterward. In the October Revolution he
led his factory Red Guard unit to the siege of the Winter Palace.[35]
He and people like him must have played a major role in transmitting information from one place to another and from one type of
organization—factory committee, *druzhina*, local party committee—to another. For the most part these contacts seem to have
evolved naturally, but sometimes party leaders consciously pushed
them: at the time of the October Revolution, for instance, M. P.
Tsinis was charged with maintaining communications among the
Red Guards of the Rozhdestvenskii district (where he worked), the
Vasil'evskii district (where he lived), and the Petrogradskii district.
His extensive personal ties with the Vyborg district—where he had
worked at the Aivaz Factory before July and been a Red Guard
commander—could also have been put to good use.[36]

More common than the interdistrict activity that one finds with
Tsinis and Vasil'ev, however, was activity in several organizations in
a single district. V. P. Vinogradov, who joined the Bolsheviks in
1915 at the age of 20, became in 1917 a member of the Vyborg
district Bolshevik committee, a deputy from Vyborg to the Petro-

grad Soviet, and an organizer of his factory's Red Guard.[37] N. V. Barychev, a veteran of the barricade fighting in Moscow in 1905, worked at the Ekval' Factory in the Lesnoi district on the edge of Vyborg. After February he became chairman of the factory committee, was elected deputy to the Petrograd Soviet, participated in trade union affairs, and was elected to the district *duma*. In May he was also elected to the Central Council of Factory Committees. He was involved throughout with the Red Guard and was a member of the Vyborg district Red Guard staff. He had a long history of involvement in Social Democratic groups and was active in Bolshevik Party organizations at the factory level.[38] Yet another such activist was P. V. Mikhailov, a Bolshevik since 1907 who in 1917 worked at the Petrograd Artillery Factory, where he participated first in an armed workers' unit during the February Revolution and later in the factory Red Guard. He was elected to the district and city soviets and to the factory committee, and he was also active in Bolshevik Party organizations.[39]

Though most such activists known to us were Bolsheviks (the sources available naturally document their activities to a far greater extent than those of members of other parties), some examples of Mensheviks and SRs exist. We have already mentioned N. Rostov, who returned from exile in April, went to work with the Printers' Union and their Fighting *Druzhina*, and worked on the organizing committee for the April Red Guard conference. He also worked as a Menshevik organizer at the Treugol'nik Factory (and at others also, apparently). Another example is Ia. I. Kramer, a Menshevik-Internationalist who was a deputy to the Petrograd Soviet, a leading figure in and secretary of the Petrogradskii District Soviet Executive Committee, the district Red Guard commander, and a participant in the October Revolution. Kramer joined the Bolshevik Party in 1919.[40] A. R. Vasil'ev refers in his memoirs to one Alekseev, an SR at the Wireless Telegraph Factory who was secretary of the factory committee, commander of its Red Guard, and (from October 23) a member of the Vyborg district Red Guard staff.[41] If he was like most Bolshevik activists, he may well have held party and other posts as well. And certainly there were similar activists among the nonparty guardsmen. These persons underscore the linkages that existed and demonstrate the extent to which Red Guard leaders were integrated into the larger network of worker organizations.

Another way of looking at the character of the Red Guard leadership is to study all the members of one particular group. However, the necessary information is usually not available. For example, the names of the members of the Council of the Petrograd People's Militia are known, as are the party affiliations of some, but for most members no biographical data are available. In sharp contrast is the *piaterka*. Some biographical information exists for all six members, and we have fairly extensive data for five. A brief look at these men will be informative.[42]

As noted earlier, Iustin Zhuk was an anarchist, and Valentin Trifonov, his brother Evgenii Trifonov, Vladimir Pavlov, A. Kokorev, and A. A. Iurkin (who joined them as the sixth member) were Bolsheviks. The Trifonov brothers were of Don Cossack origin, but had been sent to craft school as boys when their father died. They entered industrial work young and joined the Social Democratic Party in 1904 while still in their teens. In 1905 they participated in barricade fighting in Rostov-on-the-Don, for which they were exiled to Siberia. After years of arrests, escapes, hiding, and illegal activities, Valentin arrived in Petrograd in 1914. In February 1917 he was working there and took an active role in the Revolution. He was apparently reasonably well known in Bolshevik circles, for he was appointed Soviet commissar to Vasil'evskii Island during the February Revolution and soon became secretary of the Bolshevik faction in the Petrograd Soviet, a post he held until June. Shortly after his Party service ended, he became involved in the Red Guard movement—perhaps through the influence of his brother, who arrived in Petrograd in April and became first a member and then a unit commander of the Putilov Factory Red Guard.

Vladimir Pavlov, a metalworker at the Russian Renault Automobile Factory, joined the Bolshevik Party in 1911 at the age of 19. He was arrested for political activities and exiled from Petrograd in 1914, and did not return until shortly after the February Revolution. Nonetheless, he quickly immersed himself in both Party work (as a member of the Petersburg Committee) and Red Guard activity (as an organizer, commander, and instructor in the Vyborg and Porokhovskii districts). Of A. Kokorev all we know is that he was a worker at the Lorents Electromechanical Factory, where he was chosen as commander of the factory militia after the February Revolution. A. A. Iurkin left his peasant village at 13 in search of work in Moscow, where in time he became a skilled metalworker. Involved in a series of strikes and other activities, he was blacklisted in Moscow and forced to move to Petrograd in 1915. He joined the Party that same year. After the February Revolution he was elected to the Vyborg District Soviet, and he later was a member of the Interdistrict Conference of Soviets, the New Lessner Factory militia, and the Vyborg district Red Guard staff.

Iustin Zhuk was an "anarchist-communist" from the Ukraine who achieved notoriety as early as 1908, when at the age of 21 he capped an already tumultuous career by attempting to blow up some police—and himself. He spent a decade in the Shlissel'burg Prison on the outskirts of Petrograd, from which he was released after the February Revolution. He became the unchallenged leader of the workers of the important Shlissel'burg Explosives Factory and a Red Guard organizer. He was so successful at acquiring scarce supplies that he got the reputation of a miracle worker, and legends soon began to circulate about him. After his death, Lenin wrote to Grigorii Zinoviev: "They say that Zhuk . . . made sugar from sawdust? Is this true? If true, it is absolutely essential *to find his assistants* in order to continue the business. *It is of gigantic importance.*"[43] That Lenin spoke seriously suggests the immensity of Zhuk's reputation—and the desperation of the Bolsheviks in October 1919. The legend probably grew in part out of the fact that as a youth Zhuk had worked in a sugar factory.*

We have to be very careful about treating the *piaterka* members as typical—they operated at a slightly higher political level and had more connections to the upper layers of the Bolshevik Party than most. Still, these men—the most prominent Red Guard leaders of 1917—drew their support from the factories where they worked and the district Red Guard and party organizations they belonged to. With the exception of Valentin Trifonov, each entered even

---

* Of the *piaterka* members, Zhuk was killed and Kokorev paralyzed in the Civil War, and Pavlov died in an accident in 1925 in the Soviet Union. Valentin Trifonov held a number of government, diplomatic, and military posts and was purged in 1937, apparently as part of the purge of the military. Evgenii Trifonov also held various government positions and was a writer associated with the famous "Smithy" group in the 1920's under the pen name Brazhnev. Turned down as a volunteer for service in the Spanish Civil War, he died in December 1937 from a heart attack, having already been expelled from the Party (and his brother having been purged). Iurkin, who rose to important Party positions, including the Central Control Commission, was purged in 1935.

the Petrograd leadership or the Military-Revolutionary Committee from these bases. Their long careers as activists propelled them into prominence among their fellows in 1917, and I suspect that many of the lesser Red Guard leaders of 1917 had similar backgrounds; the biographies in the two volumes of *Geroi Oktiabria 1917* tend to bear that out, as do various other accounts, especially memoirs, that give biographical data. Indeed, one is struck by how often the factory committee chairman or the head of a special factory or district soviet committee in charge of the militia was appointed commander of the factory or district armed detachment. Many local leaders, of course, were simply detachment commanders or local staff members, without other positions, but it seems clear that many of them held other positions in the factory committees, district party committees, soviets, trade unions, other workers' organizations. These kinds of people must have played an important role in transmitting ideas and information on the Red Guard from one place to another, and from an earlier organization to a later one. Quite possibly they provided a certain degree of coordination and encouragement among Red Guard units and between the Red Guards and other local worker and party organizations. They provided leadership and linkage in a way that is only poorly recorded in the historical sources but that played a key role in both the entire revolutionary process of 1917 and the October Revolution.[44]

9

The October Revolution

"The Red Guard was brought to fighting readiness earlier than the regiments. It occupied the most important strategic points. It took over the defense of Smolny. In the districts it undertook the guarding of factories and public buildings."

—Nikolai Podvoskii

"In the light that streamed out of all the Winter Palace windows, I could see that the first two or three hundred men were Red Guards with only a few scattered soldiers. Over the barricade of firewood we clambered, and leaping down inside gave a triumphant shout. . . ."

—John Reed

Tensions in Petrograd—and throughout the country—built up steadily through the month of October. Increasingly these tensions were tied to rumors of a possible Bolshevik attempt to seize power. Many of these speculations focused on the actions that would be taken by the forthcoming Second All-Russian Congress of Soviets, scheduled to convene on October 20 and then postponed to the 25th. The Bolsheviks expected to have the largest block of delegates and to be able, with the support of other groups, especially the Left SRs, to form a majority that could declare the transfer of political authority from the Provisional Government to the Congress. The idea of "soviet power," the transfer of all political authority to the soviets of workers', soldiers', and peasants' deputies, grew steadily in popularity throughout 1917 and became the rallying cry of the discontented masses. It also meant the creation of an all-socialist government; after the Kornilov Affair, what little favor the idea of coalition with the nonsocialists had found among the masses evaporated, leaving only the socialist intelligentsia of the disintegrating Menshevik and SR parties to champion it. The workers and soldiers wanted "soviet power," a government for them, a government of socialist party leaders. The Red Guards were among the more militant exponents of this idea.

It was against this background that the series of crises occurred leading to the October Revolution. One of the first was the dramatic Bolshevik walkout from the Preparliament on October 7. The Preparliament (officially, the Provisional Council of the Russian Republic) was a body formed by the Provisional Government with the help of moderate socialists to provide some sort of forum for debating issues and to shore up support for government policies. Its 550 members represented a broad political spectrum, but it was strongly weighted in favor of the moderate socialists. At its opening session, Trotsky violently denounced the "council of counterrevolutionary connivance" and "the government of the betrayal of the people," called for the transfer of all power to the soviets, and led the Bolsheviks out of the hall.[1] Trotsky's speech and the Bolshevik walkout caused intense debate in the newspapers and in the streets about Bolshevik plans.

Other problems and rumors kept tensions alive. Strikes and factory closings not only created economic hardship and contributed to the increasing breakdown of the economy but also increased social tensions. A nationwide railway strike from September 23 to 27, though short-lived, had a tremendous psychological impact on an already nervous capital. The ongoing agrarian crisis, with its peasant disorders resulting from failure to redistribute the land, agitated the urban population as well as the peasantry. An important source of worry, certainly, was the sharp increase in prices and the scarcity of foodstuffs and other supplies. Petrograd, which stood at the end of a long and increasingly tenuous supply line, began to suffer every kind of shortage, from bread to electricity. The food problem was especially difficult. At an economic conference on October 15 the speakers painted a bleak picture of a city with only three to four days of food reserves.[2] Both management and government officials warned of forthcoming factory shutdowns—involving perhaps half the factories of the city—because of inadequate supplies of fuel and raw materials. From the borderlands came news of nationalist movements demanding autonomy or even independence. The newspaper regularly reported pogroms, robberies, assaults, and other violence against which the government was powerless. The litany of problems was well summed up by *Volia naroda*, the newspaper of the right wing of the SRs and thus a very moderate socialist paper, on September 20:

> An open revolt flares up in Tashkent, and the Government sends armies and bullets to suppress it.
> A meeting in Orel. Armies are sent there.
> In Rostov the town hall is dynamited.
> In Tambovsk *guberniia* there are agrarian pogroms; experimental fields are destroyed, also pedigreed cattle, etc.
> In Novgorod-Volynsk *uezd* zemstvo storehouses are looted.
> Grain reserve stores in Perm' *guberniia* are looted.
> Gangs of robbers appear on the roads in Pskov *guberniia*.
> In the Caucasus there is slaughter in a number of places.
> Along the Volga, near Kamyshin, soldiers loot trains.
> In Finland the army and the fleet disassociate themselves completely from the Provisional Government.
> Russia is threatened by a railway employees' strike . . .
> Unbridled, merciless anarchy is growing. Any cause is used.
> Events of colossal importance take place throughout the country. The Russian state collapses. Whole regions secede . . .
> How much further can one go. . . .[3]

Looming above and behind all of these problems remained the war, its stresses on the entire country, and the presence of unruly garrisons. It was in response to both the pressures of the war and the problems posed by the Petrograd garrison that the government announced plans in October to send much—perhaps half—of the garrison to the front to bolster the sagging Russian defenses. In August the Germans had occupied Riga, thus threatening both the land and the sea approaches to Petrograd. Then in the first week of October they seized three important islands guarding the approach to the Gulf of Finland. This news caused great excitement and the exchange of bitter recriminations among political and military groups. It also fueled a rumor that the government might abandon Petrograd. In response to the German landings, Kerensky and the Provisional Government decided to shift some of the Petrograd garrison troops to the Northern Front, a decision based in part on real military concerns. Nonetheless, it must have seemed an excellent excuse to get some of the unruly troops out of the city and, perhaps, to replace them with more reliable ones withdrawn from the front for rest. But as word of the impending transfer spread it caused angry denunciations of the government among the Petrograd garrison, providing the Bolsheviks with a golden opportunity to increase their influence there and, even more critically, to undermine the authority of the government and the military command—essential to any seizure of power.

A number of meetings and demonstrations in mid-October kept the populace apprehensive. The Northern Regional Congress, a gathering of delegates from military and other local soviets in northwestern Russia, was a focus of intense concern before and during its meetings on October 11–13. Strongly radical in outlook, the Congress denounced the Provisional Government and was viewed by some as a potential vehicle for a Bolshevik seizure of power.[4] Another point of heightened tension came as October 22, the planned "Day of the Petrograd Soviet," approached. This was to be a day of meetings and demonstrations both to raise funds and to consolidate support for the Soviet. There was fear of armed conflict, for the Union of Cossack Military Forces had announced plans for a procession that same day in memory of the 105th anniversary of the liberation of Moscow from Napoleon. But at the last moment the Cossack procession was canceled. Still, rumors spread that "counterrevolutionaries" would attempt something on that day, and some Red Guard units were ordered to be on the alert.[5] The arrival of delegates to the Second All-Russian Congress of Soviets, scheduled to open on October 20, added to the confusion, too, especially given repeated Bolshevik assertions that the Menshevik-SR leaders of the Central Executive Committee might try to prevent the Congress from opening. Adding to all the rest were the efforts to convene the citywide conference of the Red Guard on October 22–23 and to form a city Red Guard organization, however imperfect.

The mood in the factory districts seems to have been especially tense. Despite some after-the-fact romanticization and exaggeration, numerous recollections by guardsmen and some contemporary sources give us a clear sense of the increasing scale of military preparations and the growing feeling that the moment of confrontation was near. The assumption seems to have been more that they were preparing to defend against counterrevolution or any attempt to prevent transfer of power to the Congress of Soviets than that they were planning for an armed assault to seize power. As early as October 21 the Vyborg district Red Guard staff ordered the Petrograd Cartridge Factory—and presumably others, as the order does not name the factory but seems a general one—to put its Red Guard on full alert for the entire day of October 22, the "Day of the Petrograd Soviet," because of the possibility of a counter-revolutionary offensive.[6] On October 23 the Vyborg Red Guard staff, which was especially active and well organized, sent a secret order to all units to hold themselves in full fighting readiness and to stay at the factories.[7] Preparedness seems to have been fairly widespread. Memoir and quasi-memoir accounts suggest that some units went on the alert in response to orders whether specific or vague, but that others acted on their own. A worker at the Vulkan Factory, F. A. Ugarov, wrote that "after the 'Day of the Soviet' the mood of the workers was intensified. . . . An order from the staff of the Red Guard was received to prepare the Red Guard for action. The bolts of rifles clicked. In the yard of the factory they fitted the trucks with sheet armor and mounted machine guns. The factory ceased to be a factory and became an armed camp."[8] Another worker, N. Dmitriev, recalls that in the last days before the Revolution some armed workers did not leave the factory but slept there, with their arms, turning the factory cafeteria into a barracks. At the Old Lessner Factory the Red Guard was on full-time duty for some days before the Revolution. Lur'e refers to Red Guards at factories such as the New Lessner and Erikson going on "barracks status" on the 23d. This may or may not have been in response to orders from the newly created city staff of the Red Guards, which Lur'e says decided on the 23d, immediately after its creation, to hold the Red Guards in a state of preparedness, under arms.[9] At the same time there was a renewed scramble for arms and ammunition to equip units. Despite the obvious German threat, there seems to have been little thought of using the Red Guards to protect the capital against a German attack; the focus was almost entirely internal.

Rumors of a Bolshevik seizure of power and of possible government countermeasures circulated through the city in the press, in conversations, and in meetings. Just what the Bolsheviks were intending in mid-October has been the subject of a great deal of confusion. The traditional view among historians, Soviet and Western, was that a unified Bolshevik Party under Lenin's leadership carefully planned and executed the seizure of power on the eve of the Second All-Russian Congress of Soviets. This view has been questioned, especially by Western scholars, who have come to see a Bolshevik Party responding to government challenges as much as it was consciously shaping policy. Even more significant, as Alexander Rabinowitch has clearly and carefully delineated, the Bolshevik Party was suffering from major internal disagreements over what to do. In brief, following Rabinowitch,[10] it seems clear that the Bolsheviks were determined to make a bid to seize power but that there was little agreement beyond that. At one extreme stood Lenin, arguing vigorously from his hideout just outside Petrograd for the need for an armed uprising before the Congress of Soviets. At the other stood a wing represented by Grigorii Zinoviev and Lev Kamenev that wished to proceed cautiously, that insisted on a *soviet* government composed of members of all socialist parties rather than a Bolshevik government, and that wanted to work through the Second All-Russian Congress of Soviets if there was to be any transfer of power. The other Party leaders sought some sort of intermediate position in the fluid and uncertain situation. Gradually Bolshevik policy, if it can be so termed, moved toward a kind of watchful maneuvering to undercut the government's authority, especially in the garrison, while preparing either to seize power or to arrange and defend its transfer to the Congress of Soviets, as conditions permitted. To this end the Bolsheviks began feverish activity to bolster their strength and to gain effective control of the garrison—or at least to deprive the government of control over it.

Throughout the records of the October meetings of the main Bolshevik organizations—the Central Committee, the Petersburg Committee, and the Military Organization—there runs a constant theme: the need to assess their sources of support. Two major conclusions were drawn from these assessments, one that proved correct and one quite wrong. Over and over again we find repeated the notion that the workers and soldiers would come out to defend the Petrograd Soviet and "soviet power," but not at the call of the Bolshevik Party. This led Trotsky and others to conclude accurately that any seizure of power before the Congress could come only in response to government or "counterrevolutionary" moves. The other repeated notion was of the weakness or unpreparedness of the Party's potential nonmilitary supporters, especially Red Guard units. The October 15 meeting of the Petersburg Committee arrived at this dual conclusion and accepted an absurdly low estimate of the number of guardsmen and arms in the districts,[11] and other Bolshevik meetings of the period show similar underestimates. Without a citywide Red Guard structure, and hence any effective direct control over these factory-based units, the Bolsheviks repeatedly underestimated them. The Bolshevik leaders simply had little concept of the extent to which worker discontent had been translated into armed forces. This error grew in part out of the nature of the Red Guards and their local, spontaneous, grass-roots origin and structure. The Party leaders' misunderstanding of what role the Red Guard could—and would—play was reinforced by their preoccupation with the garrison and their struggle for control of it.

The instrument used in the struggle for the garrison was the Military Revolutionary Committee (MRC).[12] Although Bolshevik-dominated, the MRC was an agency of the Petrograd Soviet and had its origins in the struggle to prevent the garrison from being sent to the front. Only slowly did the Bolshevik leaders recognize its potential in planning a seizure of power; indeed, not until October 20 did it hold its first organizational meeting. The MRC, as a Soviet rather than a party body, and including as it did Left SRs as well as Bolsheviks in its leadership and anarchists and others in its membership, was the perfect vehicle to lead the struggle for control of the garrison on behalf of soviet power. This struggle quickly took form in a demand by the MRC on October 21 to the commander of the Petrograd Military District, General Polkovnikov, that only orders countersigned by the MRC be valid for the garrison. Polkovnikov, not surprisingly, rejected this. Although the MRC backed off from this position somewhat on the 23d, its demand, plus its efforts to send its own commissars to military units, already had undermined government control of the garrison, increased Soviet influence, and helped spur the government to take its ill-fated moves against the Bolsheviks on the 24th.

During the night of October 23–24, the Provisional Government decided to arrest a number of Bolsheviks on charges of carrying out antigovernment agitation, and to close two Bolshevik newspapers, *Soldat* and *Rabochii put'*.* Troops and military cadets from nearby garrisons were called to the city to defend the government. The raid

* *Rabochii put'* was a successor to *Pravda*, which was closed after the July Days, and to *Rabochii*.

on *Rabochii put'* was carried out before dawn on the morning of the 24th, and news of it and of the call for troops reached the Bolshevik leaders during the morning. The actions of the government precipitated the long-awaited confrontation and gave Lenin the opportunity for his ardently desired violent seizure of power *before* the Congress of Soviets convened. It turned October 24 into a day of mobilization of forces and of the first, confused skirmishes. The Red Guard played an active role.

The role of the MRC in mobilizing the Red Guard is not clear, and for the most part mobilization seems to have come on local initiative, reflecting the Red Guard's local autonomy and the weakness of central direction. Most of the eyewitness accounts of the events of October 24 and 25 suggest that MRC and other directives were important in mobilizing the soldiers, but only marginal for the Red Guard. Almost all *known* MRC orders are to military units; none is to a specific Red Guard detachment. On the 24th the MRC ordered the garrison units to hold themselves in a state of battle preparedness and to await orders,[13] but if any similar order was sent to mobilize the Red Guard it is not recorded. However, despite the fact that no such order may have been sent, at least some local Red Guard leaders interpreted the message to the garrison as including them. On October 24 the Vyborg District Soviet executive committee and the Vyborg Red Guard staff together sent a circular to all factory committees "in accordance with the telephonogram of the Petrograd Soviet . . . and the [Military] Revolutionary Committee" urging the immediate requisitioning of all automobiles and the preparation of ambulances and their supplies and staff.[14] Other than this there are only scattered and vague references in later accounts about orders received by the Red Guard from the MRC or the Petrograd Soviet.

There are considerably more references to the Red Guard acting on the local initiative of district or factory leaders. In some instances such actions may have been in response to verbal orders from higher authorities, and it seems that toward the end, on October 25, more instructions were received from Smolny as the Bolshevik leaders began to gain a better grip on events. Local initiative was paramount, however, especially in the early stages during the confused struggle for control of bridges and other key points before the balance of power swung clearly to the insurgents. Indeed, the workers hardly needed central direction in this: their long history of clashes with the police had taught them about the importance of holding key locations, and the events of 1917 had further sharpened that awareness. Some of the Red Guard leaders had included such strategic thinking in their training and preparation activities, and district leaders certainly were aware of such matters. The fact of local initiative is underscored not only by the many references to directives from district leaders, but by the accounts of some guardsmen. For example, a guardsman named Aleksandrov from the Arsenal Factory tells how on the evening of the 24th the factory Red Guard leadership gathered to discuss what actions to take.[15] The Red Guard at the large Pipe Factory on Vasil'evskii Island marched to Smolny on the afternoon of the 24th out of frustration with waiting around and a desire to see what was happening there.[16] Over and over the accounts, especially the earlier ones, paint a picture of local Red Guard and political leaders, tense and alerted by the events of the preceding days and the widespread discussions of impending revolution or counterrevolution, moving in response to the news and events of October 24 without need of instructions from above. What is striking, however, in contrast to February, is the absence of mass demonstrations; October witnessed the movements of organized armed detachments rather than massive turnouts of thousands or tens of thousands of workers.

Whether responding to directives or simply to the mood of the city and the events of the morning, Red Guard units throughout the capital mobilized on the 24th. Squabbles about doing patrol duty, when units would be relieved, food, and supplies disappeared. At the Military-Medical Supply Factory a general meeting enrolled a large group of new members into the existing Red Guard. The factory committee of the Arsenal Factory ordered the Red Guard to be at fighting preparedness, to protect the area around the factory, and to keep in contact with other "democratic organizations." The Red Guard at the huge Putilov works mobilized. On Vasil'evskii Island the whistle of the Pipe Factory blew the signal for the Red Guards of the district to mobilize. Those of the Baltic and Pipe factories gathered on the 16th Line (street), where the district *komendatura* was located, and were sent out on duty from there. A composite unit was formed from the Nobel, Bakumoil, and Sololin factories, and it received orders at 9 P.M. from the Petrograd Soviet to be on an alert status. Chechkovskii states that "all" the Red Guard units of the Moscow district went into fighting preparedness on the 23d and 24th. In the militant Vyborg district, which had the best-organized district Red Guard staff, units began to gather at staff headquarters on Sampsonievskii Prospect and from there were sent to Smolny or on various assignments.[17] Similar accounts are given for other factories and districts, as the many Red Guard units mobilized, drew in new members, and took up whatever posts or assignments fell to them, whether on their own initiative or on the order of the district soviet, district Red Guard staff, MRC, or other agency. Overall, the events of the 24th galvanized the already agitated workers and propelled their armed detachments into the confused struggle for control of the city during the night of October 24–25 that ultimately gave the Bolsheviks their Revolution.

How important a role the Red Guards played in the Bolshevik seizure of power on October 24–25 remains, by the nature of that confused event, undeterminable with any precision; the Revolution was much too chaotic, with groups of armed men groping—literally and figuratively—in the dark. Soldiers and workers often acted together, so that their respective roles cannot be completely disentangled. Still, some conclusions are possible. The garrison certainly outnumbered the Red Guards and other armed worker groups, but only a small proportion of the garrison—ill-disciplined and not disposed toward actual fighting—took part in the events of October 24–25. By contrast, it appears that virtually every Red Guard unit estimated to be in existence on the eve of the Revolution, plus many other armed workers, participated. Nikolai Podvoiskii, who as a leader of the Bolshevik Military Committee was primarily concerned with the garrison, later wrote that "the Red Guard was brought to fighting readiness earlier than the regiments. It occupied the most important strategic points. It took over the defense of Smolny. In the districts it undertook the guarding of factories and public buildings."[18]

Although one needs to be careful not to overstate the effect of the workers' involvement, since the *attitude* of the garrison was essential, the testimony of Podvoiskii and others suggests that the workers played a role greater than usually attributed to them by most Western historians. Not only did they provide actual armed support, patrolling large areas of the city and occupying many important positions, but they gave important moral support to the insurgent troops through their unequivocal commitment to a soviet government. There were no wavering units among them as among the soldiers, no detachments that a worried Bolshevik leadership in Smolny need fear might support the government. Much of the Bolshevik focus on the garrison stemmed, first, from a realization that they were the only potential source of armed support for the government and, second, from a fearful memory of the July Days, when wavering garrison units finally swung against the insurgents and helped doom the uprising. Though there undoubtedly were individual workers who did not support the actions of October 24–25, they were not the type who would be enrolled in the armed detachments or otherwise threaten the seizure of power that day, and the overwhelming mass of workers, and especially the Red Guards, did support the new Revolution. Indeed, the role of guardsmen even in situations where soldiers predominated numerically is illustrated by a comment of John Reed, observing the encirclement of the Winter Palace the evening of October 25, that the patrols of soldiers were "invariably" commanded by a Red Guard.[19] The traditional emphasis upon the garrison in historical accounts has reflected the Bolshevik leadership's worry over the soldiers, but seems thereby to have inadvertently downplayed the role of the workers in the actual seizure of power.

This overall assessment of the general role of the Red Guards in the October Revolution can be best illustrated by a look at some of their specific activities in the uprising. The Red Guards were active in the seizure of many of the more important points in the city—bridges, utilities, military schools, and railroad stations—as well as in guarding the factories, keeping public order and, finally, taking the Winter Palace. The first actions on the afternoon and night of the 24th involved especially securing bridges, railroad stations, utilities, and the safety of the Smolny Institute, the seat of the Soviet and the headquarters of the Bolshevik Party. During the early stages of the Revolution there had been considerable fear that the government might launch an attack on Smolny and seize the Bolshevik leaders—a not unreasonable fear if one assumed that the Provisional Government might really be determined to move against the Bolsheviks. Only a weak guard had previously been maintained at Smolny, and it was finally strengthened on the evening of the 24th when Red Guard detachments from Vyborg, Narva, and other districts relieved the soldiers who had been there. Additional Red Guard units arrived during the night, some responding to a summons from the MRC, others coming on their own. Startsev estimates that ultimately 2,000 Red Guards took up positions there.[20] Machine guns were mounted at the entrance, and the surrounding gardens swarmed with guardsmen and various other people. It is noteworthy that the guarding of the Bolshevik leaders and the Soviet itself was entrusted primarily to the Red Guards, not to soldiers, at this critical point.

One of the first, and certainly one of the most important, confrontations in the contest for the city was the struggle for control of the bridges across the Neva River from the Vyborg, Petrogradskii, and Vasil'evskii districts to the city center. By mid-afternoon on the 24th it became clear that the government hoped to control the bridges, raising them if necessary to block movement to the city center. The MRC earlier had ordered troops to patrol the bridges, but now the Red Guard moved to secure them. Units from Vyborg, especially from the Erikson Factory, succeeded in establishing control over the critical Liteinyi Bridge, but the government managed to raise the Nikolaevskii Bridge. Red Guards at one point forced its lowering, but in the early evening they were overwhelmed and disarmed by a detachment of cadets, who in turn were displaced with the aid of the sailors and guns of the *Aurora* around 3 A.M. on the 25th. The Troitskii Bridge, connecting the city with the Petrogradskii district, apparently was first controlled by soldiers but later, on the 25th, was held by Red Guards from the Rozenkrants and Military-Medical Supply factories. There are two different reports on the Sampsonievskii and Grenadierskii bridges connecting the Vyborg and Petrogradskii districts: one claims that the Grenadier Regiment seized the bridges and took the keys necessary to raise them to their barracks for safeguarding, whereas the other claims that the bridges were seized by guardsmen from the Old Parviainen and Russian Renault factories on the night of October 24–25. (It is possible that both occurred, but in which order we can only guess.) Red Guards and soldiers of the Chemical Battalion took the key from the Tuchkov Bridge between the Petrogradskii and Vasil'evskii districts. Thus the insurgents, after some confusion, managed to secure control of most of the bridges across the

Neva and between the Vasil'evskii, Petrogradskii, and Vyborg districts. (The Palace Bridge is rarely mentioned and apparently was not secured until late on the 25th, because it was subject to fire from government defenders in the Winter Palace.) Red Guard units played a major role in securing the bridges, which were critical in giving the large and militant population of the three districts on the right bank access to the leaders on the left.[21]

A second major set of strategic points were the railroad stations, which would be the assembly points for any troops responding to the efforts of the government to bring reliable units to the city. The earliest reported taking of a station is the claim of a commander of a Putilov Factory Red Guard detachment, M. I. Mukhtar-Londarskii, that his detachment occupied the important Baltic Station on the evening of the 24th. Another account reports that this station was taken around 2 A.M. on the 25th by insurgent troops.[22] Both versions are plausible, as important points frequently were "taken" by successive waves of troops or workers, who either bolstered or replaced their predecessors. The Nikolaevskii (Moscow) Station was taken by troops around 8 A.M. on the 25th; Red Guards from the Narva Gate area occupied the Warsaw Station; and the other main railroad station, the Finland Station, was occupied during the night by Vyborg Red Guards and soldiers of the Moscow Guard Regiment.[23] Thus the main entrances to the city were secured, even though the feared government troops never materialized.

Utilities and assorted other strategic positions were occupied on October 24 and 25 by workers and soldiers. The telephone and telegraph offices were secured in a series of actions on the night of the 24th and early morning of the 25th, but apparently this was almost entirely the work of soldiers and sailors—assisted eventually by technical specialists from the army to help staff the offices when the employees proved hostile to the Bolsheviks. Red Guards from nearby Sestroretsk arrived around midnight on the 24th and were charged with guarding the main water pumping and electric power stations.[24] Guardsmen from the Vyborg side occupied the Kresty Prison on the 25th, releasing among others some Bolsheviks held since the July Days. The Vyborg Red Guard also sent a detachment northwest to the suburb of Beloostrov to guard against counterrevolutionary troop movements from that direction.[25]

In addition to seizing key points, the Red Guards provided general public security functions. On October 25, about noon, the MRC sent a circular to the Interdistrict Conference of Soviets, which in turn transmitted it to the district soviets, asking that the latter take upon themselves all necessary measures for public safety in the city. The only force they would have had for this purpose was the Red Guard. In fact, Red Guards had undertaken such security functions long before this time. The Peterhof District Soviet formed a new military-administrative department, gave it charge of "all militias, Red Guards, workers' fighting *druzhiny*, and other armed groups found in the district," and made it responsible for public order. Similar arrangements were made by some other district soviets.[26] The City Militia seems to have continued to function for a while to provide public security, but it did not participate in the power struggle. Although in some instances the Red Guard and other worker armed groups simply replaced the regular militia, in most cases the City Militia continued to exist, supplemented by the guardsmen. The newspaper *Novaia zhizn'* for October 25 reported that on the previous day "at posts along with militiamen [were] found patrols of Red Guards," and that guardsmen were also protecting wine stores and various buildings. The City Militia commissar of Vyborg's first subdistrict reported that on the afternoon of the 25th guardsmen took up positions with the militiamen to help them as necessary.[27]

One other very important military operation, especially in light of the continued fear of the government's somehow finding armed support, was the disarming of cadets at the military schools and some training commands. The Red Guards seem to have played a central role in this. The cadets at the Nikolaevskii Cavalry School were first prevented from leaving the building, and later disarmed by the Red Guard of the Putilov Factory. Cadets of the Nikolaevskii Artillery School were disarmed by Vyborg Red Guard units, especially from the Metallurgical and Rozenkrants factories; cadets of the Konstantin Artillery School were disarmed by units from the Vyborg and Vasil'evskii districts; and cadets of the Vladimirskii Military School were disarmed by sailors and Red Guards from the Pipe Factory. What is notable in the many, usually cryptic, accounts is that the Red Guard seemed to have played the main role in disarming the cadets. Perhaps the MRC or district leaders, to the extent that they ordered these actions, felt it better to use workers rather than soldiers for fear that the latter might either fall prey to efforts to assert command authority or else (more likely) vent their hatred of officers upon the cadets.[28]

By midnight on October 24, when Lenin came out of hiding and appeared for the first time at the Smolny Institute, the balance of power had already shifted in favor of the Bolsheviks. Red Guards and troops loyal to the MRC and the Petrograd Soviet had already gained control of the most important strategic points in the city. When a cold gray day dawned on the 25th, the insurgents controlled almost the entire city, with the exception of the Winter Palace and its environs. The Bolsheviks at Smolny, encouraged by their own success and by the prodding of Lenin, proclaimed the transfer of political authority: at 10 A.M. on the 25th, the MRC sent out announcements that the Provisional Government had been overthrown and authority in the city assumed by itself on behalf of the Petrograd Soviet. Early in the afternoon, Trotsky made the same announcement at a meeting of the Petrograd Soviet.

Despite the proclamations, the last resistance had not been overcome and the Provisional Government still existed, however precariously. Lenin desperately wanted the Winter Palace taken before the opening of the Second All-Russian Congress of Soviets, scheduled for the evening. Despite their favorable position, it took the MRC until the early morning hours of the 26th to complete the task. The delay was a result of several factors: a consistent overestimation of the ability of the government to resist; the disorganization and unpreparedness of the MRC; the lack of a central command among the Red Guards and insurgent troops; and perhaps the desire to let the helplessness of the Provisional Government sink in so that its defenders might become demoralized and surrender, thus avoiding a bloodbath (as Podvoiskii later claimed). This last consideration was probably more real among those on the front lines of the besiegers than among the political leaders, who were fearful that delay might allow the government time to bring loyal troops from the front—which it was trying to do. In fact, as it turned out the taking of the Winter Palace was virtually bloodless: contemporary estimates range from zero to six deaths among the attackers and none among the defenders.

The mid-morning hours of the 25th saw a sort of lull in the siege around the Winter Palace. People came and went freely in the Palace Square area. Kerensky left at 11:30 A.M. in search of troops from the front. Some reinforcements arrived to bolster the government guard around noon, and throughout the afternoon the cadets making up the bulk of the government's support worked on barricades around the Palace entrances, while insurrectionary troops looked on from surrounding streets. By early afternoon the Palace defenders numbered about 2,700 troops. These were mostly from the various officer-training schools, but included also about 200 Cossacks, assorted officers and soldiers, and about 200 women of the recently formed Women's Shock Battalion.[29] These numbers dwindled during the evening, some cadets and the Cossacks leaving as whole units. During the early afternoon the MRC managed to complete a fairly definite encirclement, relying particularly on the Pavlovskii Regiment, whose barracks were nearby, to close off the area from the Neva around past the General Staff building to the Nevskii Prospect, and on sailors and soldiers of the Keksholm Regiment to close the gap from the Nevskii Prospect to the Neva on the downriver side. Across the river Bolshevik supporters in the Peter-Paul Fortress confronted the Palace, and downriver, at the Niko-laevskii Bridge, lay the cruiser *Aurora*. As the siege wore on, the troops, especially the Pavlovskii soldiers, who had been in position since early morning, were bolstered by the arrival of Red Guard detachments. Around 3 P.M., 400 Red Guards from the Petrogradskii district joined the Pavlovskii soldiers, and shortly afterward Red Guards from the Vyborg district plus more from the Petrogradskii district arrived, with medical units.[30]

The Red Guard reinforcements probably included the detachment described by A. Vasil'ev, a Bolshevik leader at the Wireless Telegraph Factory in the Petrogradskii district who had been active in the Red Guard movement since early summer. He gives an illuminating account of how his unit mobilized and got to the Winter Palace. In the early afternoon of the 25th, Vasil'ev was ordered by a member of the Petrogradskii district Red Guard staff to take charge of that portion of his Red Guard unit still at the factory and to bring it to the district soviet so that arms could be distributed to those without them. When he arrived at the factory, he found not only the guardsmen but both shifts of workers, in full force, wanting to join. Ten to twelve men had to be left to guard the factory, but since no one wanted to stay behind, Vasil'ev solved the problem by choosing those with the poorest shoes—a slushy snow was falling—to remain. En route to the soviet the detachment joined up with units from other factories, of which that from the Military-Medical Supply Factory was especially welcome because it included a medical unit. From the district soviet some detachments were sent to join the siege of the Winter Palace. Joining with still other Red Guard units, Vasil'ev's men forced their way across the Palace Bridge, suffering at least one casualty in the process, and finally took up their position with the forces encircling the Palace.[31]

For some of the besiegers, at least, the arrival of Red Guards was most welcome. Konstantin Eremeev, one of the MRC members on the spot and also commissar to the Preobrazhenskii Regiment, which was quartered near the Palace, recalled that during the early afternoon he had wished for the arrival of the Red Guard. This, he reported, would have made him feel on firmer ground, especially given the wavering attitude of the nearby Preobrazhenskii troops, most of whom had taken a "neutral" position.[32] Presumably the arrival of the Red Guards did encourage the leaders of the siege. Gradually the noose around the Palace was tightened as the nearby buildings were infiltrated and taken by soldiers and Red Guards. By the time the MRC managed to sound the signal for the attack— artillery from the Peter-Paul Fortress—besiegers were already filtering into the Palace, especially from the now virtually undefended Millionaia Street side, where the Palace came up against other buildings. One defender described the process. "As long as the groups of guardsmen were small, we disarmed them. . . . However, more and more Red Guards appeared, and also sailors and soldiers of the Pavlovskii Regiment. The disarming began to be reversed."[33] About the same time the besiegers from the Palace Square and Aleksander Garden sides began to move into the building. John Reed, the American journalist who managed to be in the crowd of soldiers and Red Guards who "stormed" the Palace, gives something of the flavor of the attack and a comment on the role of the Red Guard:

Voices began to give commands, and in the thick gloom we made out a dark mass moving forward, silent but for the shuffle of feet and the clinking of arms. We fell in with the first ranks.

Like a black river, filling all the street, without song or cheer we poured through the Red Arch, where the man just ahead of me said in a low voice: "Look out comrades! Don't trust them. They will fire, surely!" In the open we began to run, stooping low and bunching together, and jammed up suddenly behind the pedestal of the Alexander Column [center of the square].

. . .

After a few minutes huddling there, some hundreds of men, the army seemed reassured and, without any orders, suddenly began again to flow forward. By this time, in the light that streamed out of all the Winter Palace windows, I could see that the first two or three hundred men were Red Guards with only a few scattered soldiers. Over the barricade of firewood we clambered, and leaping down inside gave a triumphant shout as we stumbled on a heap of rifles thrown down by the yunkers [cadets] who had stood there.[34]

Finally, around 2 A.M. on the 26th, a group of insurgents found their way—they had gotten lost in the maze of rooms and corridors—to the room where the government ministers were waiting and arrested them. The ministers were then conveyed to the Peter-Paul Fortress. There were threats of mob action against them, but a reliable guard was provided—mostly Red Guards apparently—to get them past the hostile crowd of soldiers.[35]

———————◆———————

The storming of the Winter Palace, and even the entire seizure of power of October 24–25, were in some ways anticlimactic, strange though such a statement might seem. But the more I study the events of 1917 the more I am struck by the extent to which the critical developments of the year had already occurred by late October. The closer one looks, the more evident is the power vacuum that existed by that point. All the major leaders save the Bolsheviks had been popularly discredited, had proved unable to harness the powerful forces of spontaneity let loose by the February Revolution, and had failed to begin to solve the problems facing the country. By October they had either sunk into despair and resignation (Tsereteli, Miliukov, most of the military commanders) or lost contact with political reality (Kerensky). At the same time, groupings such as the Red Guard had already made the really decisive shift in attitude that the Revolution would be decided by arms and that they must therefore arm themselves and be prepared to use force against the new "old order" of the Provisional Government and its middle-class and intelligentsia supporters. Once these attitudes had developed, the outcome was already decided and the actual use of arms in October became in many ways anticlimactic. This is what makes it important, first, to understand the perseverance of large numbers of workers in acquiring arms, organizing themselves into fighting detachments, and preparing themselves to use those arms, and, second, to understand that this was done largely under the aegis of local leaders, with little assistance from the major political figures. Once done, it resulted in the formation of a critical mass of socially cohesive, politically determined armed workers who could and would support a radical revolution in the name of "soviet power." The armed workers were not as numerous as the garrison soldiers, nor could they have stood up against the garrison in conventional battle. Revolutions, however, are rarely conventional. Moreover, the same disintegration which insured that the garrison would not support the government also meant it could not be a reliable base for a seizure of power. The swing of the "neutral" army units in the July Days was vividly remembered in October. Even though not under firm Bolshevik control, the Red Guards did provide that dependable element of active support for a seizure of power in the name of the Soviet. This was their great significance in the October Revolution in Petrograd.

10
Saratov

"Well, this is real revolution!"
—*A Menshevik observing a Saratov Red Guard
demonstration, September 1917*

The citizens of Saratov had good reason to recognize "real revolution," for the area had a long-standing reputation as one of the most turbulent in the Russian Empire. During the Revolution of 1905, Saratov Province was one of the areas of greatest disturbance. Now, in September of 1917, that turbulence again manifested itself in a parade of Red Guards and armed workers. This demonstration had its origins in a decision of the city Red Guard staff to test the readiness of their organization by raising a false alarm. On a day in late September, after the workers had gone home from work, the warning signal was sounded at the railroad works. Within 45 minutes about 100 armed railwaymen had gathered, as well as another 200 who were unarmed. They all proceeded to the Soviet, where they found other railwaymen and workers from other factories already gathered. Upon being told that the alarm had been a test, the excited workers insisted on holding a demonstration and proceeded to parade their armed strength through the city.[1] The incident provided the Red Guard leaders a certain satisfaction that they could raise a force quickly; one imagines, however, that it had a rather disquieting effect upon the good burghers of Saratov. The incident also reflected the excitability and hardening political attitudes of the workers, for it was they—not their ostensible leaders—who insisted on the armed demonstration. This reflects the fact that in Saratov the impetus for forming armed workers' bands came very much from below, as in Petrograd, and that the Soviet and other leadership played a lesser role.

Saratov in 1917 was one of the more important provincial capitals of the Russian Empire, even though it had an unenviable but perhaps not entirely deserved reputation as a dusty, unattractive backwater. Lying on the west bank of the Volga River at the eastern end of the rich black-earth agricultural district, it was founded in the sixteenth century as a defensive outpost and became commercially important only in the nineteenth century, when it developed as a major food-processing center and transportation hub. During the last years of the nineteenth century and the early years of the twentieth it underwent significant growth, attaining a population of 242,425 in 1913. Population shifts during the war dramatically changed the social composition of the city: the draft took a third of the industrial work force as well as recruits from other parts of the population; between 50,000 and 75,000 displaced persons, especially Latvians and Poles, flooded into the city; the military garrison became a significant element, totaling approximately 70,000 soldiers in both January and October 1917; and new laborers from the countryside flowed in to replace drafted workers. The total population at the time of the Revolution was nearly 300,000, of whom nearly a third were refugees, garrison soldiers, and other new people who had moved to Saratov since 1913. As might be expected, these new people were a disruptive force in Saratov, compounding social problems by bringing pressure on available housing and other facilities. The working class, numbering about 80,000, made up slightly over half the non-military adult population in 1916. Of these about 25,000 could be called a true industrial proletariat, of whom about one-third were new since 1913 (mostly Baltic refugees), replacing an equal number who had been drafted. They lived and worked under the conditions of poor housing, long hours, and low pay familiar to Russian industry at that time, compounded by the strains created by the war.[2]

The social and economic development of Saratov in the late nineteenth and early twentieth centuries was accompanied by a political evolution similar to that taking place throughout Russia at the time. The city during this period had a sizable local intelligentsia that mirrored the national arguments about reform and revolution. Because of the rich populist tradition in the province, Saratov became one of the national centers of the Socialist Revolutionary Party. In the 1890's a Social Democratic movement developed, and it engaged in the factional and ideological battles of the national movement, including the Bolshevik-Menshevik disputes. A reform-oriented liberal movement also existed, with a moderate wing based in the gentry and a more radical wing drawing on the professions, just as elsewhere. After 1905, the Kadet and other liberal parties emerged. The Revolution of 1905 in Saratov witnessed numerous strikes and bloody clashes between workers and the police and troops, the formation of a Workers' Soviet, and the creation of a united SD and SR fighting detachment of about 300 workers. This legacy of both a soviet and workers' armed bands was important for 1917.[3]

News of the February Revolution in Petrograd reached Saratov early on March 1. Governor S. D. Tverskoi held up the earliest tele-grams about disturbances in Petrograd, but by noon the news began to leak out. The streets quickly filled with crowds of people seeking more information. A meeting of the City Duma was held at 5 P.M. and was open to the public. Governor Tverskoi, who attended at the Duma members' request, asked their help in keeping public or-der. Uncertain what to do, the representatives called for an enlarged meeting of the Duma that evening to which would be invited mem-bers of various public organizations such as the war industries com-mittee, cooperatives, and merchants' organizations. Some radicals and workers who were at the afternoon session decided that before the evening one they would gather at "Maiak," a workers' cultural club and the main meeting place during the war for socialist leaders and workers, to discuss what course of action to follow. At the club, people from trade unions, workers' medical fund offices, and other worker organizations chose some representatives to attend the eve-ning meeting of the Duma.[4] At the enlarged meeting of the City Duma that evening the divisions that would soon rack the Revolu-tion appeared immediately. Deputy Mayor A. A. Iakovlev opened the meeting by reading a telegram from the President of the State Duma, M. V. Rodzianko, and proposed a telegram of greetings and support to Rodzianko and the Duma. M. I. Vasil'ev-Iuzhin, a local Bolshevik leader, then rose to speak about the need to greet all those responsible for the Revolution, especially the Petrograd pro-letariat and soldiers. A spokesman for the university students, N. N. Miasoedov, an SR, supported Vasil'ev's proposal. This brought a protest from some of the more moderate members. In the midst of quarrels, it was tentatively agreed to elect a local committee to manage municipal affairs, but further action was postponed until the next day. A manifesto was drafted calling upon the population to remain calm and to support the new government in Petrograd, and finally around 1 A.M. on March 2 the exhausted participants went home, agreeing to resume at 9 P.M. that evening.[5] What is striking about this meeting, aside from the fact that it revealed future lines of disagreement, is that it did so very little. No firm steps were taken to secure political power in the city, and it was not until the next day, with the Revolution already secured in Petrograd, that the Duma finally took more decisive actions, including deciding what to do with the police and the armed bands that had sprung up. Even the radical leaders held off a full day, until the evening of March 2, before forming a soviet.

Just how the Saratov Soviet was established is unclear, but it seems likely that a committee was formed early on March 2 by local Social Democrats, perhaps at a meeting at "Maiak," which sent out the call for a soviet to the factories.[6] That evening, in the basement of the Duma building, in a small, poorly lighted, dusty room hung with old portraits of the tsars, 58 representatives from 29 enterprises, plus a few intelligentsia socialists, assembled as the Saratov Soviet. Amid comings and goings and periodic interruptions as Soviet leaders went out to address the garrison soldiers who kept arriving at the Duma building (the parallel with the scene at the Tauride Palace in Petrograd is striking), the basic tasks of organization were carried out: V. P. Miliutin was elected chairman, with M. I. Vasil'ev-Iuzhin and I. A. Skvortsov, a Menshevik worker from the Bering Metalworking Factory, as vice-chairmen; an Executive Committee of four Bolsheviks, three Mensheviks, and one SR was chosen; and it was decided to send five representatives to what became the Public City Executive Committee.* The Soviet members discussed the political situation and the organization of factory committees, and issued a call for the workers to strike the next day

---

* *Obshchestvennyi gorodskoi ispol'nitel'nyi komitet.* Originally composed of 15 members—five chosen by the Soviet, five by the old City Duma, and five by various public organizations—the Public City Executive Committee functioned as the provisional government for Saratov until a new and more democratically based Duma was elected in the summer. Thus it was a sort of "coalition government" long before one was formed in Petrograd in May.

and join a planned parade of soldiers. None of the early accounts of this meeting mentions any call for the workers to form fighting detachments, or even to arm themselves, and apparently no such call was issued.[7]

The workers, however, were already arming themselves and undertaking to disarm and arrest police and other government officials, quite aside from any directives or lack thereof from the Soviet or other new authorities. A report by officials of the old government states that during the night of March 1–2 and continuing through the 2d there was spontaneous arming among the workers and creation of detachments.[8] The various memoirs and other accounts concur. At first these groupings were for self-defense, but from the 2d the workers, together with students and soldiers, took more aggressive action in disarming police and arresting officials, including Governor Tverskoi, who was arrested at 5 A.M. on March 3. A meeting of workers and students at the university organized groups to arrest officials and police and to free political prisoners from prison, which was done on the morning of the 3d, though in fact most of the arrests seem to have been made by soldiers, especially machine gunners under the leadership of V. Sokolov. The large Titanik Metalworking Factory at a general meeting on the night of March 2 authorized a workers' militia on the grounds that the creation of "a strong, durable people's militia, well trained," was one of the most important steps to be taken in solving the country's problems. It is indicative of how popular action outstripped nominal leaders that when, at 1 A.M. on the 3d, the new Public City Executive Committee met and debated whether to arrest former government officials and police, the issue was in fact being preempted by spontaneous popular action. Some arrested officials were even being shut up in one part of the Duma building while the debate was going on in another part.[9]

The formation of militias among the workers continued. E. D. Rumiantsev, drawing on archives in Saratov, cites numerous examples of meetings at factories during the period March 2–4 at which, among other things, a militia was formed or authorized. A general meeting at the Saratov railroad shops on March 3 decided to form a militia and opened enrollment for joining; six days later a list of members was sent to the Soviet.[10] At the large Zhest Metalworking Factory the factory committee authorized a militia on

March 3. At the Saratov railway depot and station 109 men signed up for a militia on March 4, and the same day 54 of 124 workers at the Merkurii Factory joined the militia.[11] The initial thrust to arm and organize continued, with the Saratov *Izvestiia* reporting several factory meetings during the first two weeks of the Revolution that passed resolutions including a call for workers to form a militia or arm themselves.[12] Between 300 and 500 workers is the best estimate of the number of organized armed worker-militiamen for the first week.[13] This growth, it is worth stressing, took place with little or no help or guidance from the Soviet or Public City Executive Committee.

Though the workers were in the long run the most important component in the volunteer armed bands, two other sources of significant armed force surfaced in March. One was students, whether from the university or from other higher institutions, and the other was soldiers from the garrison. The students in Saratov played a more important role during the first days than in Petrograd, their numbers in armed bands being about the same as those of the workers during the first week of March.[14] Student involvement in armed bands soon declined, however, as it did in Petrograd, ceasing to be important after mid-March. As for the soldiers, the Revolution in Saratov did not involve the immediate and complete breakdown of traditional military relationships that it did in Petrograd, but soldiers did participate in the disturbances nonetheless and helped patrol the streets and secure the Revolution. During the night of March 2 3 soldiers arrested some unpopular officers, participated in the arrest of police, and joined in a march to the Duma building. At the same time that the Soviet was being formed, the soldiers were electing a Temporary Military Committee. An attempt to abolish it by the new Public City Executive Committee on March 3 failed, and the soldiers went on to elect a permanent Military Committee. Reflecting the nature of the Revolution in Saratov, they provided for extensive officer involvement: one-third of the representatives were to be from the officers, elected separately from the soldiers. The Military Committee became the primary directing force for the soldiers and, dominated by SR-oriented officers, provided some soldiers for patrol duty in the city.[15] Although on March 6 the Saratov Soviet was transformed into a Soviet of Workers' and Soldiers' Deputies, the Military Committee retained a separate existence as the dominant force in the garrison until late spring, only merging into the soldiers' section of the Soviet in June.

Despite all this activity, one does not sense in the Saratov accounts as intense a feeling of urgency about arms—the massive movement toward them or sense of need of them to make and protect a revolution—as one finds in Petrograd. Rather, the arms were necessary primarily to protect the city against lawlessness and only secondarily to arrest local officials and secure the Revolution. Though uncertainty about the success of the Revolution prevailed momentarily—one participant states that some of the professional revolutionaries on their way to the first meeting of the Soviet wondered if they might have 1905 all over again [16]—it was never so intense as in the capital and was shorter lived. It took only a day from receipt of the first news of the Revolution in Petrograd to word of its complete success there. Thus Saratov never knew the feeling of being a besieged revolutionary headquarters and the fear of counterrevolutionary military action that gripped both the Petrograd Soviet and the State Duma leaders at times. As a result, the need to arm against those feelings and fears was not so keenly felt. Also, in Saratov there were not the days of strikes and turmoil before the Revolution that had helped heighten the sense of a need for arms, nor was the breakdown of government so graphic, the patterns of life so deeply shaken and sharply broken. These differences may help explain the seemingly less intense concern for forming workers' armed bands. In any case, the euphoria that accompanied the collapse of the autocracy was less tempered by initial fears than in the capital. The same comments, as we will see, apply to Kharkov as well.

The different context of the Revolution in Saratov and resulting different psychology may help explain the path of development of the militia there. The formation of a city militia certainly proceeded more easily and successfully than in Petrograd, and the workers' militias were at first weaker and less independent than their Petrograd counterparts. The Saratov Soviet cooperated with the Public City Executive Committee on the militia question, although the two bodies pursued separate if parallel paths from about March 5 to March 9. On March 6 the Soviet adopted "Regulations on the Militia of the Saratov Soviet of Workers' Deputies" proposed by V. K. Medvedev. This provided for a two-part militia drawn from the workers. One part was a militia for the defense of the city, the population, and essential services; it was intended to replace the former police. The other part was a "militia *druzhina*" for safeguarding the factories. All militiamen were to be registered and approved by the factory committees, and those guarding the city were to be paid no less than the former police and to be armed with revolvers. The "Regulations" established a structure of city and district command, although they do not make entirely clear whether the top command staff was responsible to the Soviet or who appointed them. Duty lasted for two weeks, so apparently the Soviet envisioned a steady turnover that would, among other things, give a large number of workers experience as militiamen. The militia for defense of the factories would be set up by the factory committees and be headed by a commander chosen by them. This service was to be unpaid unless the members were called up for city duty.[17]

However, the Public City Executive Committee was busy also and on the 5th announced the organization of district militia directorates, named a number of attorneys and army officers as directors, appointed A. A. Minkh as overall militia commander, and established a special commission for the organization of the militia. The Soviet apparently accepted the Public City Executive Committee's initiative, for two representatives of the Soviet entered the special commission. Indeed, on March 9 Medvedev reported to the Soviet that the Public City Executive Committee had accepted the Soviet's militia plan with only a few changes, mainly that convalescent soldiers be included. Apparently the Soviet soon decided to turn responsibility for the militia over to the local "government" authorities—on March 5 the Public City Executive Committee declared itself the local organ of the Provisional Government—and to retain only a supervisory "control" function, as for example when it discussed in mid-March the matter of verifying the right to hold arms.[18] Quite possibly this transfer of responsibility was intended from the beginning, that is, from the time the "Regulations" were introduced in the Soviet on the 6th. This may explain one of the peculiarities of the Soviet "Regulations": the failure to specify who appointed the commander and other staff.

City officials pushed ahead rapidly with their plans. On March 10 Minkh reported to the Public City Executive Committee that a militia was being set up with a core of officers and soldiers wounded in the war and unable to resume regular military duties. The role of workers in the militia continued to be an issue, however, and was discussed at Public City Executive Committee meetings. The "Regulations" of the City Militia, ultimately adopted on March 24, did provide for 20 worker-militiamen in each district, with special status. They were allowed to choose their own senior militiamen and to have a voice in their assignments, they would be part-time, and they would be paid for time on duty. Thus they were able to retain their factory ties and had their own separate existence, but they were subordinated to City Militia officials. The official transfer of authority to city officials took place between March 11 and 15, with Medvedev giving up his position as commander of the workers' militia on March 14.[19]

There was some worker opposition to these developments, but it was fairly weak and certainly ineffective. There were factory resolutions opposing the arrangement and demanding the arming of the workers, such as at the Zhest Factory on March 18.[20] A meeting at the Titanik Factory resolved to organize a factory militia,[21] but whether this was in protest against the City Militia or merely the kind of local factory guard provided for both by the Soviet "Regulations" and by the Public City Executive Committee "Regulations" is not clear from the brief newspaper report. However, it does appear that some factories did turn toward emphasizing the factory militias, that is, those under the supervision of the factory committees and officially limited to factory security functions. The railway workers set up such a factory militia on March 15, i.e., after the new provisions for the City Militia had gone into effect limiting the role of workers' militias in patrolling the city.[22]

There was some opposition inside the Soviet, too. As early as March 3 one Comrade Kaplan, a Menshevik, insisted that the militia must be composed of workers and argued—unsuccessfully—against either cooperating with the Public City Executive Committee or including soldiers, students, and others in the militia. On a different level, the Oblast [Regional] Congress of Soviets, meeting in Saratov on March 22, called for transferring the organization of the militia to the Soviet,[23] but nothing came of this. In any case, by the second half of March the initiative had passed to the Public City Executive Committee and worker interest in the militia issue had dropped off, with the workers' militias becoming inactive at most factories.[24] Such a slackening of worker interest following the Soviet transfer of authority to the city officials seems quite natural. More important, it reflects a general lessening of interest in the militia once the Revolution was completed, a development we have seen in Petrograd as well. A similar falling off of interest, it should be noted, affected other organizations after the excitement of "February" subsided.

By late March, the political situation in Saratov was settling into a pattern similar to that in most cities. The more moderate socialists of the Menshevik and SR parties increasingly dominated the Soviet (their control was not complete until May), and the early leading role of the Bolshevik intelligentsia gradually diminished, as did that of nonparty deputies. Party lines gradually hardened. In the workers' section of the Soviet on March 25 there were 28 Bolsheviks, 16 Mensheviks, 6 SRs, 5 Popular Socialists, and 193 nonparty members.[25] The soldiers' section was smaller, with 144 members on March 30, and no party breakdown available. Later data suggest that it was mostly SR or nonparty. Both a continued shift toward party alignment and a drop in Bolshevik strength relative to that of other parties is shown by the figures for the new Soviet elected between May 25 and June 1. Now the workers' section had 85–90 Bolsheviks, 65–70 Mensheviks, and 44–46 SRs.[26] The new soldiers' section was larger than the workers' section, reflecting an arrangement worked out in May whereby the Military Committee of the garrison abolished itself in return for a reorganization of the Soviet that gave the soldiers' section a much larger representation than before—indeed, a majority. In the new soldiers' section the SRs had 260, the Mensheviks 90, and the Bolsheviks 50.[27] The result, of course, was a great increase in SR influence in the Soviet. The election for the new Soviet Executive Committee, held June 24, resulted in a committee of 13 SRs, 9 Bolsheviks, and 8 Mensheviks.[28] By June, no sources mention nonparty deputies in the new Soviet, suggesting that they ceased to be a significant factor. Most probably the election and voting processes forced them to take on some party identity, however tenuous.

The shifting party fortunes were accompanied by the emergence of political alliance patterns similar to Petrograd's. Both the records of the Soviet and the memoirs of the leaders of the Bolshevik minority show that by late spring the same split between the mod-

erate socialists and the Bolsheviks was taking place and that a
Menshevik-SR alliance was forming; moreover, the Menshevik-SR
leadership pretty much followed the positions of the central leaders
in Petrograd on major questions such as the war, agrarian reform,
foreign policy, and coalition governments. Despite policy disagreements, however, there seems to have been a fairly good working and
personal relationship among the various Saratov party leaders, including the Bolsheviks, at least into the summer.[29] As late as April
there was an attempt to unify the Mensheviks and Bolsheviks, and
on April 29 there was a meeting of all socialist parties to discuss
revolutionary strategy, with the proposal that such meetings continue. On May 27 the Mensheviks, Bolsheviks, and SRs put out a
joint statement, published in the Saratov *Izvestiia*, that all three
parties had the same goal of establishing socialism, differing only
on tactics, and that arguments among them should be considered
"comradely arguments within the fraternal socialist family."[30] Even
as late as June 3 the Bolsheviks and Mensheviks presented a common list in the voting for the Workers' Section Executive Committee, although some Bolsheviks objected.[31] Indeed, one of the Bolshevik leaders later, in 1922, wrote of D. K. Chertkov, a Menshevik
who for a time was chairman of the Soviet, that he was "a fine
orator and very intelligent person."[32] Among the Bolsheviks, V. P.
Antonov-Saratovskii especially seems to have enjoyed general respect and good relations with the non-Bolsheviks, whereas M. I.
Vasil'ev-Iuzhin was more partisan, strident, and less well liked outside the Party. It is worth noting also that the Bolsheviks were relatively strong in Saratov as compared to Petrograd, not only in their
early domination of the Soviet but also in that even afterward they
continued to have a large bloc in the Soviet, and were the largest
single party in the workers' section.

The general political structure for the summer in the Soviet is reflected also in the July election for the City Duma. There, a Menshevik–SR–Jewish Bund bloc got 73 seats, the Bolsheviks 13, the
Kadets 13 (on a slightly smaller vote than the Bolsheviks), and others 13.[33] Thus the City Duma was firmly controlled by the same
moderate socialist, Menshevik-SR bloc that controlled the Soviet—
a situation analogous to that in Petrograd and most other cities that
held Duma elections. This Menshevik-SR leadership recognized as
the legitimate political powers in Saratov first the Public City Exec-

utive Committee and then the City Duma, in both of which they
participated, plus the Provincial Commissar of the Provisional Government. Their own position was that of a spokesman for the "democracy" and a watchdog, even though they were the *real* power in
Saratov. There was, then, a local version of the *dvoevlastie* in Petrograd, but with the very important difference that the local government was much more clearly controlled by the same socialists who
led the Soviet, whereas in the Provisional Government the socialist
leaders of the Petrograd Soviet were influential but not clearly in
control.* This political situation lasted until the end of August, until the aftermath of the Kornilov Affair.

At the same time that this evolution was going on, and perhaps
in part because of it, the role of the workers in the general City Militia and Soviet interest in it declined. Worker participation in the
City Militia dropped sharply: from 400–500 in March to 120 by
April 1, 35 by May 1, 20 by July 22, and 9 by September 1.[34] This
remarkable worker withdrawal was much greater than in Petrograd. One partial explanation is that in Saratov there were no separate districts where semiautonomous workers' militia commissariats continued to perform regular militia functions. Workers' and
factory militia detachments in Saratov quickly came to be entirely
divorced from the City Militia structure. Moreover, the Soviet
seems to have taken little interest in militia affairs, judging from its
own records—an abdication that went much further than in Petrograd and most other cities. This lack of concern about building up a
workers' armed force in the spring is a little surprising given the
fact that, despite the adding of a soldiers' section to the Soviet, until
May the Military Committee of the garrison still claimed—and
with some reason—to be the chief authority for the garrison. This
meant that the Soviet leaders had even less control over the local

---

*Donald J. Raleigh, in an unpublished paper presented at a meeting of the
AAASS, has argued persuasively for caution in using the concept of *dvoevlastie* in
Saratov on the grounds that neither the Public City Executive Committee nor the
City Duma elected in the summer had real power, both being even weaker in relation
to the Soviet than the Provisional Government was to the Soviet in Petrograd, and
both being dominated by the same men who controlled the Soviet. His point is well
taken, not only for Saratov but for many cities in the provinces. Still, there were two
centers claiming political authority, even if composed largely of the same people, and
in September and October new life was breathed into the City Duma, so *dvoevlastie*
remains a useful concept.

means of coercion than in most cities. Perhaps their lack of concern reflected the fact that SRs dominated the Military Committee, as they were coming to dominate the city government. It almost certainly mirrors the general majority socialist (Menshevik and SR) lack of concern with arming the workers and sense that this was the bourgeois stage of the Revolution.

Nonetheless, an undercurrent kept alive the notion of a workers' militia, or at least of arming the workers. The Soviet and party newspapers raised the question from time to time. An editorial in the Saratov *Izvestiia* on March 19, when general responsibility for and control over the militia were being turned over to the Public City Executive Committee, stressed the general Social Democratic theories of arming the people. In tones reminiscent of those in some Petrograd newspapers of the time, the editorial pointed out that the minimum program of the Social Democratic party demanded replacing the standing army by a general arming of all the people. This was put in rather broad terms, and the editorial acknowledged that it was not expected to be fulfilled immediately. It was more a statement of a general position, a justification for workers having arms rather than a call to arms. An article in the Saratov Bolshevik newspaper, *Sotsial-Demokrat*, on May 21 was not much more explicit. Reacting to a speech by the City Militia commander, Dmitrii Chegodaev, against the idea of a union being formed by militiamen, it repeated the doctrinal position of arming all the people and stressed the need for general militia training of the entire population. The same ideas were repeated in an editorial of June 2 in response to a speech by the SR leader Victor Chernov in Petrograd against the idea of arming all the people, but in this instance the writer did go a little further and called for the immediate arming of the workers of the main cities as the first step toward the general arming of all the people. Again, however, the editorial did not propose specific steps.

Despite the general lassitude on the part of the Saratov Soviet and the parties, there is evidence that some workers did retain an interest in the formation of their own armed bands and that this interest grew through the summer. The reasons for the workers' continued interest are not hard to find when one looks at their general situation in the spring and summer of 1917, and especially at the economic situation. The euphoria of February, with its high expectations, quickly evaporated under the impact of harsh economic reality, giving way to frustration and hostility. As early as April lay-offs began because of supply shortages. The greatest problem was caused by the slowdown of grain shipments from the countryside, a result both of peasants withholding grain from the market and of transportation problems. Layoffs followed in the flour mills—Sara-tov was a major food-processing center—and in some other plants processing agricultural products. Moreover, the slowdown gave rise to the threat of food shortages; and indeed, in June rationing cards were distributed for bread, and rations were reduced August 1. The specter of hunger hovered over the city and exacerbated tensions. Moreover, strikes—mainly over wages but also over other issues such as the length of the work day, medical facilities, and night work—became serious by May and grew in significance as the sum-mer progressed. The economic problems were reflected in a rise in crimes such as thefts and assaults, and in vigilante measures in re-sponse. Both had a disquieting effect on the public. In addition to economic problems, political issues came more to the fore in work-ers' resolutions and hence, one assumes, in their worries about the future. In May and June resolutions against the government and the war began to appear, coupled with calls for the transfer of all power to the soviets. These increased steadily thereafter. Hostility to the propertied elements, especially in the person of the factory and mill owners and managers, became more visible.[35]

Given these developments, we can hardly be surprised to find that worker interest in maintaining separate, independent factory militias or workers' *druzhiny* continued and grew. Such bodies were established at many factories, under the direction and au-thority of the factory committees. Some developed out of those workers' militias formed in March that survived the militia take-over by the Public City Executive Committee, others derived from the special factory militias provided for when the City Militia was set up, and still others grew up totally on their own outside any offi-cial structure. All were concerned primarily with protection of the factories and of worker interests in them. Generally the militiamen demanded and got work-rate pay while serving, although in the summer, in Saratov as in Petrograd, there was an effort by the own-ers to get rid of this obligation and even of the factory militias al-together. Most of those that survived were poorly armed, although the workers' militias of the railroad shops, Levkovich Tobacco Factory, and Zhest Factory were exceptions.[36] Resolutions from factories on the workers' militia are scarce for this period but do surface. At the Titanik Factory in early May, a general meeting resolved that the organization of a strong workers' *druzhina* was essential not only for them but for all factories, that *druzhiniki* should be paid at least work rate by the management, and that these sentiments should be sent along to the Soviet.[37] A notable characteristic of this factory, one of the largest in Saratov, was that it had been evacuated with its work force from Riga and most of the workers were Latvians. Interest in forming an armed force during this period comes also from another factory evacuated from Latvia, the huge Zhest Factory. There, on June 15, a general workers' meeting with both Bolshevik and Menshevik spokesmen present discussed the question of a "Red Guard"—apparently the first use of this term in Saratov. The meeting decided to work one holiday to get the financial means to support a Red Guard.[38] Both factories passed resolutions against the Provisional Government during this same period—Titanik on May 12 and Zhest on May 19[39]—and both had relatively large and well-organized *druzhiny* throughout 1917.

Are there any special implications in the fact that our clearest data for interest in the *druzhiny* for this period come from two factories manned by people uprooted by the war and without strong local ties? One might expect that their experiences may have made these people more susceptible to radicalization, especially along lines such as formation of armed forces. At the same time, the Baltic factories before the war generally were more politicized than those of the Volga, both factories were metalworking plants, and the metalworkers generally played a leading role in such matters. Moreover, in Kharkov, as we will see in the next chapter, the relationship between evacuated Latvian factories and the early creation of significant armed bands seems even greater. The longer and stronger political tradition of the Latvians was probably reinforced by the experience of dislocation, leading them to a strong and early interest in forming armed bands. In Saratov there also was a significant but much smaller Polish contingent, with about 1,000 Polish workers involved in an active Polish Socialist Party. However, the Poles were not grouped in a major evacuated factory and do not play as important a role in the Red Guard as do the Latvians.

Armed workers' detachments, then, continued to exist in Saratov during the spring and summer, even though they were small and weak. Their survival was the result of local, factory-level organization and the determination of small groups of workers, despite Soviet and city indifference or even hostility. There was, for example, in Saratov as elsewhere an effort to get the workers and others to turn in arms in the aftermath of the July Days in Petrograd. This was endorsed by the Soviet Executive Committee, and was specifically aimed at past and present militiamen.[40] There is no indication that it was any less unsuccessful in Saratov than elsewhere. Still, it would be a grave mistake to overestimate the size or strength of these armed workers' groups. Their overall condition was well summed up by a report at the Guberniia [Provincial] Congress of Soviets in May: "Saratov workers' militia—affairs disorganized. Factory militia is weak, affairs not right."[41]

In Saratov as in many other places the revolt of General Kornilov, news of which arrived the night of August 27–28, stimulated the organization of workers' militias, *druzhiny*, and Red Guard units. Interestingly enough, however, the Saratov Soviet seems not to have been galvanized into rapid and vigorous action during the Kornilov Days, and in particular not to have been especially concerned to form armed worker bands. On August 29 a meeting of the Executive Committee of the Soviet raised the question of the organization of a workers' *druzhina*, but the matter was not resolved and instead was sent to a commission to be worked out and presented at the next meeting.[42] The following morning the Executive Committee discussed what measures to take in connection with the Kornilov Affair, but the arming of the workers was not among them. The meeting was dominated by factional strife and lacked a sense of great urgency, although a "Committee to Save the Revolution," to include City Duma members, was approved.[43] Not until August 31 did the Soviet, in a Bolshevik-sponsored resolution, include in a list of measures to counter Kornilov, " . . . first of all to arm all workers, to form factory druzhiny."[44] That it came so late and was the last point in a 12-point resolution belies the "first of all." This would suggest that the Soviet leaders, including perhaps the Bolsheviks, did not feel that there was a great urgency to forming workers' detachments. One reason may well have been that they did not have an identified military threat which had to be met immediately, although they did receive a call from the Tsaritsyn Soviet for help against a possible move by General A. M. Kaledin and his Cossacks in support of Kornilov. The thesis that the lack of an immediate armed threat was a factor in Saratov is supported by the fact that in nearby Tsaritsyn, closer to Kaledin's troops, a Red Guard was set up quickly. In Saratov, by contrast, the only mobilization of forces occurred in response to an order from Petrograd to aid Tsaritsyn— it amounted to sending a volunteer detachment composed mostly of soldiers.[45] Earlier leftist turbulence in Tsaritsyn (the so-called "Tsaritsyn Republic") may also have contributed to the reluctance of the Saratov Soviet to arm the mass of workers.[46] The Kornilov Days in Saratov passed mainly in factional arguments among political parties and disputes over whether to organize through the Soviet or the City Duma. Though the inaction was in part a result of these factional disputes, they were a luxury made possible by the absence of immediate danger to Saratov.

The workers themselves did not seem at first to have responded much more energetically than the Soviet. We know that at the railroad shops on August 30 the workers passed a resolution on Kornilov in which they demanded the immediate arming of all the workers in a factory militia.[47] On the same day, the reelection of the "Local Executive Committee of Workers' Deputies of the Saratov Railroad Shops" resulted in an overwhelming Bolshevik majority— 14 of 16 instead of the former 8 of 17.[48] This is the first clear expression in Saratov of the disastrous loss of support that the Kornilov Affair caused the moderate socialists and the rapid increase in Bolshevik influence (although Bolshevik influence may already have been on the rise in shops in August). Evidence for other factories for August 30–31 is lacking, but there was a flurry of activity in early September. It is quite possible that the workers responded to Kornilov by forming armed detachments but, like the political leaders in the Soviet, did not feel the strong sense of immediacy, of a need to rush to arms at once upon receipt of the news of the revolt.

If there was not the immediate urgency one finds in Petrograd, the workers did exhibit in September and early October a growing feeling of the need for arms. Quite probably fears and frustrations produced by the shock of counterrevolution combined with their own steadily deteriorating economic situation to enforce a conviction that they needed arms not only for protection but also to advance their economic and political interests. The economic problems of the summer, mentioned earlier, continued in the fall. There were numerous strikes and layoffs. In September a newly formed union of flour mill owners announced its intention to dismiss all 1,500 workers on October 1. The angry mood of Saratov workers was underscored by the railroad workers: they joined the national railroad strike of September 26–27, but refused to end it along with the rest, ignoring the orders of Vikzhel (the All-Russian Executive Committee of Railroad Workers). The threat of hunger continued to hover over the city. Indeed, in October the city was without grain for one or two days on several occasions. The widespread peasant disorders in the area could not but affect the mood of Saratov, because of both its food implications and the close ties many workers still had with the villages. Moreover, agitation by extremists—both anarchists and Black Hundreds* seem to have been vocal in Saratov—added to the uncertainty as rumors of potential pogroms and attacks by criminal gangs circulated. The mood among the soldiers of the garrison exacerbated tensions: as winter approached they demanded to be moved from their inadequate barracks and quartered in civilian housing, which already was scarce. More important, many citizens feared the implications of moving the increasingly unruly soldiers closer into the city.[49] In all, the political and social situation was tense, and for workers there was the overriding reality that their standard of living had visibly declined and their presumed new political power had neither prevented that nor guaranteed them against counterrevolution and physical danger.

The situation was ripe, then, for formation of armed workers' bands, and they came quickly in September and October. Four hundred workers of the Bushkov Factory on September 2 passed a resolution demanding the arming of all the workers and the formation of a factory militia. This resolution was similar to that passed by the railroad shop workers on August 30. On September 6 the Zhest Factory workers discussed the question of organizing a fighting

---

* The Black Hundreds was the name of a reactionary and anti-Semitic organization founded in 1905 to fight revolutionaries and Jews. In 1917 it was active in fomenting antirevolutionary and anti-Jewish disturbances, although its influence and activities were greatly exaggerated at the time, since many disturbances of uncertain origin or purpose were ascribed to it.

druzhina, demanded the arming of all the workers, and assigned 3,000 rubles for the purchase of arms. On the 7th the Zhest factory committee reported to the Soviet that it had created a detachment of 150 men and requested aid in getting arms. After hearing a report by their Soviet deputy, the workers of the Levkovich Tobacco Factory decided on September 9 to organize a Red Guard. A Red Guard was organized at this time also at the Bering Factory; according to its organizer, it numbered 300, but that number probably was not reached until later, closer to the October Revolution. Red Guard detachments were also formed at other factories during late September and October, including some organized by trade unions, such as that of the dockhands and river transport workers, which had about 100 members. In some instances factory managers still tried to prevent the formation of armed units, as at the Saratov State Stables, but they were unsuccessful when faced with pressure from the workers or the Soviet.[50]

The most important of all these *druzhiny* was that formed at the Saratov railway shops. Workers' militias and *druzhiny* had existed there since the time of the February Revolution. After the Bolshevik capture of the railroad shops' "local executive committee" on August 30, the new chairman, Ivan Erasov, recently returned from exile, devoted a great deal of energy to building a well-trained Red Guard. According to a report in the Menshevik newspaper *Proletarii povolzh'ia,* a Red Guard was formed there in mid-September and undertook to train members in the use of arms under the direction of instructors with military experience. The growth of the Red Guard received a boost at the October 3 general meeting of workers at the shops when speakers stressing the importance of the Red Guard encouraged enrollment and a new commander, A. A. Fedorov, was elected. Considerable effort was made to obtain competent instructors. The two most important instructors seem to have been V. N. Krasichkov and Dmitrii Serov, the former a soldier recently returned from the front who was assigned to this task by the Bolshevik party organization in Saratov. Extensive training was necessary because many workers had never before handled rifles. The railroad Red Guard also took up the guarding of railway stores and strategic positions, alongside or in place of the soldiers previously assigned to those tasks. The detachment grew from about 100 in late September to about 700 by the time of the October Revolution.[51]

There are no exact figures for the total size of the Red Guards during this period, but there are several credible estimates. A figure of 600 guardsmen was given by *Sotsial-Demokrat* on September 28. The same day P. A. Lebedev, in his report to the Soviet, estimated that there would be 600 by the first of October.[52] (This is possibly the source of *Sotsial-Demokrat's* estimate.) We know that the Red Guards grew rapidly during October—sevenfold at the railroad shops alone. V. K. Medvedev gives a figure of 2,500 for October 25, and E. D. Rumiantsev estimates about 2,600 for October 27.[53] Allowing for a considerable enrollment during the course of October 25–27, after receipt of the first news of the Revolution in Petrograd, we can reasonably speculate on a figure of well over 2,000 on the eve of the Revolution, swelling to about 3,000 by the time of the armed confrontation on October 28–29.

Red Guard and radical political leaders turned also to the matter of organizing the emerging Red Guard. On September 3 the Soviet Executive Committee, still under the influence of the recent Kornilov Affair, discussed draft regulations for a workers' *druzhina*. These provided for a *druzhina* of workers and employees, completely subordinate to the Soviet, which would choose the commander. Enrollment would be through the factory on the recommendation of the factory committee, trade union, workers' medical fund office, or party committee. Military training would be provided by instructors named by the military section. Two days later the Executive Committee resolved to send the draft to the full Soviet, although it appears to have been slightly altered to give the factory committees more responsibility as the focus of recruitment of *druzhiniki*.[54] The question was presented to the Soviet on September 7. P. A. Lebedev, one of the leading Bolsheviks, introduced it, with references to socialist party programs calling for the abolition of standing armies and their replacement by a general arming of the people. Both he and M. I. Vasil'ev-Iuzhin warned of the danger of counterrevolution, especially from the Cossacks. Vasil'ev-Iuzhin stressed the importance of training, stating that the *druzhiniki* must train for 2–3 hours a day. The *druzhina* project was approved unanimously, with seven abstentions, and a commission was set up to implement it.[55] One interesting sidelight of the debate on the Red Guard (*druzhina* and Red Guard were used interchangeably) is that there was some opposition from the soldiers to arming the workers when they themselves did not have adequate arms. This led to provisions for the use of soldiers' arms to train the workers, but not the turning over of those arms.[56] The Soviet commission on organizing a workers' *druzhina* immediately began work, for about September 9–10 it sent a request to the various factory committees asking that they send lists of *druzhiniki* to them, including name, age, address, and military liability, and announced a meeting of all factory organizers of Red Guard units.[57]

More Soviet support for organizing the Red Guard came in late September as a result of the reelection of Soviet deputies and the subsequent reorganization of the Soviet leadership. When the elections were completed and the new Soviet held its first meeting on September 21, the Bolsheviks had a clear majority: 320 of a total of 533 seats. The Bolshevik delegates were split fairly evenly between the workers' and soldiers' sections. The Mensheviks dropped to 76 seats, not only a loss in both sections, but virtual elimination in the soldiers' section, where they now had only 4. The SRs dropped to 103, 60 of whom were in the soldiers' section. The total membership was rounded out by a group of 34 nonparty delegates in the workers' section. These figures show a dramatic upsurge of Bolshevik support, especially among the soldiers. The Bolshevik triumph was registered in the new Executive Committee: 18 Bolsheviks, 8 SRs, and 4 Mensheviks. The Bolshevik leaders now took over the top positions: V. P. Antonov-Saratovskii as chairman, and M. I. Vasil'ev-Iuzhin and P. A. Lebedev as two of the three assistant chairmen. (The third assistant chairman was an SR, Lieutenant Pontriagin.)[58] The Mensheviks and SRs in response henceforth concentrated greater effort on the City Duma, which they still dominated after the summer elections. Their efforts to breathe new life into that body helped set the stage for armed confrontation during the October Revolution.

By the end of September, when Lebedev made a new report to the Soviet, the organization of *druzhiny* and Red Guards had progressed to the point where a central staff was in existence and operating. This staff consisted of three representatives from the Soviet, one each from the factory committee and trade union organizations, and the commanders of the *druzhina* detachments. The chairman at first was Lebedev, but because of his heavy work load this task was passed to Ivan Erasov. Both were Bolsheviks. The assistant chairman was an SR officer, Plemiannikov, whose military training was deemed valuable and who later became the city Red Guard commander for a time. One activity of the new Red Guard staff was to draw up a new set of regulations for the guard, and for that purpose it organized a meeting of Red Guard detachment commanders in October. On October 22 the staff held a citywide conference of Red Guard units to approve the new rules, which were modeled on a set received from Petrograd. Although the Soviet sources are not explicit in identifying which Petrograd regulations were used, the passages quoted by A. V. Afanas'ev can only have come from the regulations adopted by the Petrograd city conference on the Red Guard during the morning hours of October 23.[59] The Saratov Red Guard organizers, therefore, must have had a draft of the Petrograd regulations prepared by the Petrograd conference organizers before the conference that actually approved them in Petrograd. Indeed, they passed it a few hours earlier. Once more, this suggests the influence of Petrograd as a model for the provinces and the existence of various undocumented lines of communication of information—in this instance probably through the Bolshevik Party.

One of the main problems in assessing the role of Saratov's various armed workers' *druzhiny* in the Revolution, quite aside from determining their numbers and organization, is evaluating how well they were armed and able to use their weapons, and hence what influence they could assert on events. As in Petrograd, the workers felt that they did not have enough arms; but that was a general feeling everywhere, no matter how many arms they had. However, in Saratov the Red Guards probably were not very well armed. The Zhest factory committee reported that the factory's *druzhina* of 150 could be increased to 1,000 with enough weapons.[60] The railroad workers, in connection with a strike of other workers in late September, asked for rifles from the military section of the Soviet so that they could provide protection for the striking workers. This request was turned down on the grounds that the military section had neither the arms nor the right to give them out. When the request was discussed again on September 28, in connection with a report on workers' *druzhiny* by Lebedev, the Soviet Executive Committee decided to request the military section to provide at least 50 rifles for training purposes.[61] At the very end of September, with great difficulty, about 50 rifles were obtained for the railwaymen. Some other arms—not numerous, probably—were obtained individually by workers from soldiers.[62] Thus, at the end of September it would appear that the various *druzhiny* were fairly poorly equipped, although we have virtually no hard information on how many rifles and other arms they actually had. A few hundred rifles—held since February or obtained in one way or another since then—would probably be a generous figure for the opening of October.

Given the shortage of arms and the failure to obtain more through the military section, where SR influence was still strong despite the nominal Bolshevik majority (and, perhaps even more important, where continuing soldier distrust of turning arms over to other groups was evident), the Soviet leaders looked elsewhere. On October 2 the Executive Committee of the Saratov Soviet sent a letter, signed by V. P. Antonov-Saratovskii, to the Moscow Soviet stating that sufficient weapons could not be acquired locally and asking that the Moscow Soviet provide 1,000 rifles and revolvers, for which the Saratov Soviet was willing to pay if necessary. The request was unsuccessful, the reply from Moscow stating that there was no Red Guard there and that there were not enough arms for the troops of the garrison. This response suggests that the letter fell into the hands of either a Menshevik or an SR—most probably an SR leader from the soldiers' section, since the remark about not having enough arms for the soldiers reflects a common attitude among the latter. Still trying to obtain weapons, on October 12 the Saratov Bolshevik Committee sent A. I. Anan'ev to the Bolshevik Central Committee in Petrograd with a request that they help him obtain arms for the Saratov Red Guard. What luck Anan'ev had in Petrograd is unclear, but his mission had no impact on events in Saratov, for he returned there only on October 30, after the Revolution. Ironically, at the same time that the Saratov Soviet was attempting unsuccessfully to get weapons it was being besieged with requests not only from factories within the city but from other cities along the Volga which, in their own search for arms, appealed to Saratov as a district center.[63]

Where the Soviet failed, local initiative sometimes worked—at least for the railway workers. Shortly before the October Revolution they managed to seize from two wagons in the railway yards enough arms to outfit their *druzhina*. V. K. Medvedev mentions that at the time of the Revolution the railwaymen had 700 rifles and two artillery pieces hidden away.[64] Since other sources indicate 700 guardsmen there at the time of the Revolution, we can assume that each member was armed. Overall, it appears that on the eve of the Revolution the Saratov Red Guard and *druzhiniki* had considerable numbers of arms, but that they were unevenly distributed among detachments and insufficient for all guardsmen in the city. Saratov workers and Red Guards were less well armed than those in Petrograd and Kharkov.

Political tensions in Saratov strained toward the breaking point as October wore on. The national debate over the transfer of all power to the soviets at the upcoming Second All-Russian Congress of Soviets and the possibility of a Bolshevik seizure of power had their local versions in Saratov, with all the uncertainties and insecurities those questions involved. These debates took on special significance for Saratov because the Bolsheviks not only controlled the Soviet but even more than in Petrograd were the preeminent political force in the city. The political crisis was heightened by the effort of the Mensheviks to bolster their own position by reviving the City Duma as a locus of political authority after their defeat in the Soviet in September, and by the decision of the SRs on October 18 to withdraw from the work of the Soviet's executive organs. Further controversy was stirred by decrees of the Soviet Executive Committee on October 20 designed to insure its control over key functions such as food distribution and to prepare to deal with any disorders in the city.[65] Although these Soviet measures appear to have been defensive rather than offensive, they further unsettled the political atmosphere and, added to the rumors and discussions of a major political upheaval in Petrograd, aggravated the tensions caused by the various economic and social problems we have discussed.

Word of the Bolshevik Revolution in Petrograd first reached Saratov shortly after midnight on Wednesday, October 25, in the form of a telegram to D. A. Torpuridze, the local commissar of the Provisional Government and a Menshevik. Torpuridze convened a meeting of the city and provincial administrators at noon on the 25th to discuss the news. They decided, on the proposal of the Menshevik and SR members, to find out the intentions of the local Bolsheviks. At 6 P.M., a conference of Bolshevik, Menshevik, and SR leaders convened, at which the Bolsheviks were asked to dissociate themselves from the Petrograd actions. Although the Bolshevik leaders had only a hazy picture of what was going on there, M. I. Vasil'ev-Iuzhin refused and declared Bolshevik support for the central leaders. This was reaffirmed at a Bolshevik Party meeting immediately afterward.[66] Following their unsuccessful meeting with the Bolsheviks, the Mensheviks and SRs returned to the Duma building to form a "Committee to Save the Revolution." The leading role in this and later events on the Duma side seems to have been played by the Menshevik leader D. K. Chertkov. For their part, the Bolsheviks spent the evening deciding upon a course of action and securing support. Antonov-Saratovskii met with both the Bolshevik members of the military section of the Soviet and the railway Red Guards. The stage was set for the forthcoming struggle for the city.

The first part of October 26 was relatively quiet, as both sides tried to assess the situation and pull together their support, and as the Bolsheviks maneuvered to get a Soviet resolution of "all power to the soviets." Any Bolshevik plan to seize power was threatened when a group of socialist officers who had been playing a leading role in the Soviet military section, including both SRs and Bolsheviks, approached the Soviet leaders with a proposal to set up a special military committee, headed by themselves, to provide a "neutral" leadership to keep order and protect the Revolution. This met strong opposition from the Bolshevik Soviet leaders, who nonetheless did agree to a special military committee to include officers of various political opinions, with the specification that this committee be under the direction of the Soviet. This potential check on the Bolshevik leaders soon collapsed, however, when the Soviet plenum met that evening and gave thunderous approval to the seizure of power under the slogan of "all power to the soviets." Vasil'ev-Iuzhin opened the Soviet meeting on the evening of the 26th with a report on events in Petrograd and then turned to the matter of electing the special military committee. Some of the officers proposed by the officer group were rejected, however, and the rest of the officers, including the Bolsheviks, then pulled out; as a result, the proposal for a special military committee died. Some of the officers made their way to the Duma to join in the defense against a Bolshevik takeover being organized there.

A formal declaration of Soviet power in Saratov now became the critical issue as the meeting went on through the night (it ended at 4 A.M. on the 27th). D. K. Chertkov and some other Menshevik leaders arrived during the night and tried to convince the Soviet that new telegrams showed that Kerensky was retaking Petrograd, but they failed. Antonov-Saratovskii proposed that all power be taken by the Soviet and received a vigorous assent from the huge crowd jammed into the Soviet hall. At this point the Mensheviks and SRs walked out, leaving the Bolsheviks in unchallenged control of a Soviet meeting completely filled with advocates of seizing power. The Executive Committee met immediately after the plenum and took a number of steps toward implementing the declaration of power. Among other measures, the Committee decided to replace the Provisional Government's provincial commissar with the Bolshevik P. A. Lebedev, to take by armed force the post and telegraph, to close anti-Soviet newspapers, to issue a decree on land distribution, and to announce its assumption of power.

During the 27th both sides moved to consolidate their armed support. Both the Soviet and the Duma committee issued proclamations asserting their sole authority in the city. The proclamation of the Duma called for volunteers to come to its aid in defending the government, the revolution, and the forthcoming Constituent Assembly. During the morning the Soviet learned of the Duma's appointment of a military staff and efforts toward building up an armed force of military cadets, officers, and volunteers at the Duma building. The same morning D. A. Torpuridze telegraphed to Cossack detachments in the area asking them to proceed to Saratov to the aid of the Duma, but the detachments never arrived. The Bolsheviks also moved that morning to organize their own armed support. Word had gone to the factories on the 26th—from whom it is not clear—to start mobilizing their *druzhiny* and Red Guards. During the morning of the 27th a conference of Red Guards was held and A. A. Fedorov was named commander of all the Red Guards in the city. The same morning the Soviet named Captain P. K. Shcherbakov commander of the garrison in an effort to establish reliable control over it. Curiously enough, according to Vasil'ev-Iuzhin, Shcherbakov was not known to the Bolshevik leaders but taken on the recommendation of Bolshevik soldiers. Finding a new Bolshevik to name as commander had become necessary after the leading Bolshevik officer in the garrison disgraced himself by joining the would-be "neutral committee." Following Shcherbakov's appointment, a "military council" composed of Shcherbakov, Vasil'ev-Iuzhin, and Antonov-Saratovskii was set up. The council spent the afternoon and evening securing the support of the troops, especially the large artillery component, which wavered for some time before coming to full support of the Soviet. The movement of armed men on both sides alerted the citizens to the prospect of fighting in the streets.

On the morning of October 28 the two sides faced off at last when the Soviet ordered that the Duma building, which by then had been well barricaded, be surrounded. This took considerable time, but it was accomplished by 4 P.M. by a force of about 3,000 soldiers and Red Guards. Neither side, however, wanted to start firing. The outnumbered Duma defenders, surrounded and their hope of Cossack help fading, sent a deputation to the Soviet to negotiate terms of surrender. At 6 P.M. the Soviet in turn sent representatives into the Duma building to complete the surrender arrangements. Hardly had the Soviet group left the Duma building after completing the negotiations, however, when firing broke out. Most Soviet histories not surprisingly claim that it was begun by military cadet supporters of the Duma manning a machine gun in a nearby church belfry and that Soviet supporters simply responded. However, Lebedev, who was in the midst of it, states that no one knows who fired first or why. Despite a freezing rain, shooting continued during the long cold night, joined by sporadic artillery fire from batteries that had taken up position on a hill overlooking the Duma building. Finally, around 6 A.M. on the 29th the Duma supporters capitulated. At 8 Vasil'ev-Iuzhin led out the Duma defenders and turned them over to the Red Guard for protection from threats of summary action by the soldiers and for convoy to Soviet headquarters, the guardsmen being considered better disciplined and more likely to obey orders to protect the prisoners. The Bolsheviks now held control of Saratov. Miraculously, the night of firing, including artillery bombardment, had led to only minor casualties: 1 killed and 8 wounded on the Duma side; 2 killed and 10 wounded on the Soviet side. The barricades were quickly destroyed, especially the part composed of boxes of quinces, the hungry besiegers literally eating the barricades away.

———————◆———————

When we look at the role of armed workers in Saratov in comparison to elsewhere, especially Petrograd, certain features stand out. One of the most important, of course, is the fact that Saratov had a model in Petrograd—and to a lesser degree Moscow—and was partially dependent upon what took place there. In February the radical leaders in Saratov seemed to focus their attention on the question of whether there would be local resistance to the Revolution they were learning of over the wire from Petrograd. This seems to have affected their feeling about the need for a local armed workers' force. The workers themselves seem to have had much the same attitude. In October, by contrast, although the Revolution in Saratov was sparked by Petrograd, both sides seem to have felt that their actions would be the determining factor in its success in Saratov (although the rapid and complete Bolshevik victory in Petrograd may have discouraged the outnumbered Duma defenders from persisting) and would contribute to its overall fate. Moreover, the activities of Red Guards in Petrograd and Moscow are explicitly cited as influencing their development in Saratov.

A striking feature about Saratov is the role of the factory committees. The local Soviet made them directly responsible for organizing and maintaining factory militias, *druzhiny*, and Red Guards, in contrast to Petrograd, where the factory committees' role was not institutionalized by the Soviet even though important in fact. This difference may help explain why so much of the activity of the workers' militias during the summer and early fall in Saratov was directed toward local factory concerns, such as workers' control and protection during strikes. The workers' militias were concerned with those functions also in Petrograd, but the relative importance of such activity was not so great there, where the militias had a much more active sense of playing a role in the overall fate of the Revolution and a much greater police role.

In Saratov as in Petrograd the city officials organized a City Militia as a substitute for the old police. In Saratov this was done with a measure of cooperation from the Soviet, and the City Militia gained a much greater monopoly of local police functions than in Petrograd. One does not find situations parallel to those in Petrograd where independent or autonomous workers' militias provided the police protection for certain workers' districts where the City Militia did not even penetrate. In Saratov, as elsewhere, this City Militia evaporated during the October Revolution, did not play a role as defender of the old order, and was replaced by patrols of Red Guards and soldiers.

Two other special features marked Saratov. First, there was a strong feeling among workers and radical leaders that the soldiers could not be relied upon.[67] It is difficult to assess the reasons for this; it involved perhaps the fact that the garrison troops had not played a major role in the February Revolution, perhaps the memory of their role in crushing the 1905 revolt in Saratov, perhaps the long existence of the Military Committee, and almost certainly the greater influence the officers retained in the garrison in Saratov. This distrust seems to have heightened interest in a workers' armed force, especially in the fall. Certainly the Bolshevik leaders felt that the garrison soldiers were volatile and unreliable, were very susceptible to anarchist propaganda, and were inadequately led by their own Party personnel there, who were less important and less reliable men than their counterparts in Petrograd or Kharkov. As a result, the Red Guards became much more important to the workers and to the Bolsheviks, and the garrison less so (although the Bolsheviks understood the importance of neutralizing the garrison lest it prove a source of support for their rivals).

Second, like Kharkov but unlike Petrograd, there was a great deal of unemployment in Saratov throughout 1917, and this was complicated by strikes in the fall that took many more workers out of the factories. The strikes coincided with the period of rapid growth of *druzhiny*, so we may assume that both the free time thus made available to the workers and the heightened sense of confrontation resulting from industrial conflict encouraged the growth of these armed bands. The connection is the more striking in that whereas the Red Guards were relatively slow in developing in Saratov in comparison with Kharkov, once the strikes began they grew rapidly in both cities.

How important were the Saratov workers' *druzhiny*, militias, and Red Guards in the October Revolution? This is very difficult to estimate, much less to compare. The various armed workers' forces gathered at the factories on October 26 and 27, where they were supplemented by new recruits and sent off to the Duma or other points. Representative is the account of one guardsman that at the shoe factory where he worked on the 26th the workers began to arm and organize themselves. At the gate of the factory there was a small shoemaker's cabin, in which stood a blond artilleryman giving out arms and quick instructions on their use. The workers then went to the Leatherworkers' Union and from there to the Soviet Ex-

ecutive Committee building to await their orders.[68] The gradual un-
folding of events from the 25th to the 28th allowed the workers
considerable time to organize and to respond. It is striking that neither contemporary records nor later Soviet historians cite a call
from the Soviet or one of its bodies to the workers to arm themselves. Indeed, among the points in an appeal of the Soviet Executive Committee to the population on the morning of the 27th was
one calling on the workers to remain at their jobs unless summoned
by the Soviet.[69] This would suggest that the workers were responding of their own volition as they learned of events, or else that the
decision of somebody—the military council, Red Guard staff, who-
ever—to summon them was made off the record and sent orally. In
a small city with a relatively small worker population—about
25,000–30,000 industrial workers—that could readily be done, especially as events unfolded over some days. It would seem in any
case that the workers responded with a considerable amount of
self-initiative. By the morning of the 27th large numbers had converged on the headquarters of the Soviet Executive Committee.

These Red Guards played several roles in the October Revolution
in Saratov. Some of them remained at the factories, where they
served both as guards and as reserves. Some were sent to seize control of various important points—banks, telephone exchanges, post
and telegraph offices, etc. They also disarmed the city militiamen
(police). Their most dramatic role was in the siege of the Duma
building. Although troops were sent first to take up the task of surrounding the building, Red Guard units were sent as well as the
28th wore on. They played an active role in the firing that continued through the freezing rain of the night of October 28–29.[70]
Despite their relative unfamiliarity with arms, they apparently held
their positions with determination. Lebedev relates that when firing
broke out on the evening of the 28th he suddenly found himself
standing alone in the street, the soldiers having disappeared some-
where. He hurried to a nearby building and found shelter with a
Red Guard detachment that had remained there under fire, returning the fire themselves.[71] P. K. Shcherbakov, a military man and the
new Bolshevik commander of the garrison, later stated that "it is
necessary to say that the Red Guard in the days of Great October
1917 had a great influence on the morale of the troops of the Saratov garrison."[72] His comments suggest that the workers' detach-

ments played an important role in stiffening morale during the
siege, as they did in Petrograd in the siege of the Winter Palace.
Moreover, their numbers probably were a factor of considerable
importance as well. The various accounts agree on a figure of about
3,000 besieging the Duma building (as against about 1,000 inside
by the 28th, many of whom were volunteers and probably no more
familiar with weapons than the Red Guards). As the garrison in Saratov amounted to nearly 70,000 soldiers, it is obvious that only a
very small fraction of the troops took an active role. There were
about 3,000 active Red Guards by the 28th. Some, of course, were
on guard duty at factories or elsewhere, but that would still leave a
large number available for action in the siege. Although we do not
have precise figures, it seems that roughly half or more of the besieging force were Red Guards. If, as some sources suggest, they
were determined and disciplined in contrast to the soldiers, then
their role in deciding the outcome of events must have been great
indeed, and relatively greater than that of their counterparts in
Petrograd.

11

Kharkov

"If one talks about the October Revolution in the usual sense of the term, in the sense of an immediate fight, then there was not such in Kharkov."

— *S. F. Buzdalin*

S. F. Buzdalin's characterization of the Revolution in Kharkov has strongly influenced later writers.[1] Though it is accurate if one puts the stress on "immediate," it has confused the question of the use of force, leading one Soviet historian to go so far as to say that "the transfer of power into the hands of the Soviets in Kharkov was done without an armed uprising."[2] In fact, there was a prolonged confrontation in which the mobilization of armed force was decisive, in which there was fighting and a dramatic showdown, and in which the Kharkov Red Guard played an important role. Indeed, Kharkov's "October" involved more deaths than Petrograd's or Saratov's. What is different is not the absence of force or of an armed uprising, but the protracted nature of the struggle for power, which lasted approximately a month and a half. Kharkov, then, represents the type of city where the Bolsheviks did not control the local soviet on the eve of the October Revolution and where the capture of power was delayed. The history of armed workers' bands in Kharkov—militias, *druzhiny*, Red Guards—shows both important differences from and striking similarities to the histories of similar bands in Saratov as well as Petrograd.

Kharkov in 1917 was one of the most important cities of the Russian Empire, competing with Kiev for leadership in the Ukraine even though it lacked the historical, political, and emotional significance of the latter city, as well as its large Ukrainian population. Founded in the middle of the seventeenth century, Kharkov originated as a military stronghold in the course of Muscovy's expansion in the Ukraine.[3] Gradually the frontier moved farther west and Kharkov was transformed into a regional agricultural market and administrative center. Because it was not located on important river routes, its broader commercial role was slower to develop, but gradually it became an important point on both east-west and north-south overland routes. By the late eighteenth century it hosted four important trade fairs annually, drawing customers not only from Russia but from abroad. These fairs continued into the twentieth century and are referred to in Baedeker's 1914 guidebook for the Russian Empire.

The second half of the nineteenth century saw a major transformation in Kharkov as a result of railroad-building programs and the development of South Russia's mining and metallurgical industries. Kharkov became a main railroad hub for South Russia and a major financial center: on the eve of the war in 1914, according to M. V. Kurman and I. V. Lebedinskii, banking capital in Kharkov disposed of 88 percent of all capital investment in the industries of South Russia. This reflected the fact that the industry of the Ukraine was concentrated in the Left Bank area, the center of which was Kharkov rather than Kiev. At the same time, by the end of the century Kharkov itself was being transformed into a major industrial center, especially of metalworking factories. The two most important factories before the war were the Gel'ferikh-Sade Factory (farm machinery), founded in 1879, and the Kharkov Locomotive Construction Factory (hereafter called by its Russian initials KhPZ), founded in 1897. The city also housed other factories, as well as railway shops to support the lines that ran through it. The growing economic importance of Kharkov was reflected in its population growth: from 35,000 to 244,700 in the 58 years from the end of the Crimean War in 1856 to the outbreak of the First World War in 1914.

The outbreak of war in 1914 had a dramatic effect upon Kharkov's population and industry. First, several factories were evacuated from Poland and the Baltic area to Kharkov, the most important being three Latvian factories: the General Electrical Company (hereafter VEK), the Leitner Factory (automobiles and bicycles), and the Gerliakh and Pul'st Factory (metalworking). These factories brought their workers with them, and they were to be among the most important sources of radical political activity in 1917—

including the forming of the Red Guard. They also introduced an important new ethnic factor into the city, 20,000 Latvians alone living in Kharkov in 1917. In all, 49,500 refugees, including workers and their families evacuated from the war zones, were living in Kharkov in 1916. As in Saratov they represented a major strain on housing and other resources, a strain made even greater by the flow of new workers to the factories and soldiers into the garrison. The population of Kharkov increased from 244,700 in 1914 to 382,000 in 1917, a 55.9 percent increase. This compared to a growth, during the same period, of 10.2 percent in Kiev, about 8 percent in Petrograd, and about 15–17 percent in Saratov. (Moscow lost 4.2 percent of its population.) Such an enormous increase would have caused severe social dislocations under the best of circumstances, and the war years and the methods of factory relocation were hardly the best of circumstances. Moreover, some of the 1914 population was drafted or left for other reasons, so that the figure of a 55.9 percent increase understates the population that had taken up residence only after July 1914.

Related to the growth and changing composition of the city population is another characteristic important for the study of the role of armed workers: the industrial working class in Kharkov significantly outnumbered the garrison in 1917, in contrast to both Petrograd and Saratov. The garrison numbered about 30,000 soldiers in February, including some posted in nearby towns. By October, however, the garrison had shrunk to less than 10,000. Estimates of the working class range from 35,000 to 90,000, the smaller figure representing only industrial workers in sizable industrial plants, the larger figure including all kinds of workers and laborers and even some small craftsmen. The industrial workers were employed in 150 different enterprises, about ten of which could be termed large, and three of which together employed about 14,000 workers (KhPZ, 7,000; Gel'ferikh-Sade, 3,500; and VEK, 3,500). This reverses the relationships found in Saratov, and indeed the Red Guard played a greater and the soldiers of the garrison a lesser role in Kharkov, even though the Bolsheviks had in the latter city a more reliable army unit—the 30th Infantry Reserve Regiment—than any they had in Saratov.

There is yet another characteristic of Kharkov that is difficult to pin down but important to discuss, namely the extent to which the

city was "Ukrainian" and the role Ukrainian nationalism played in
1917. Kharkov had long had a sense of being a major regional center, in both economic and political (including revolutionary) affairs,
for the "Left Bank Ukraine," the more easterly area of the Ukraine
that had longest been under Russian control. Kharkov was proud of
having the second-oldest university in the Russian Empire (founded
in 1805) and other higher educational facilities. In general, the political and economic leaders of the city, including the leaders of
1917, had an awareness of the importance of Kharkov as a regional
center and of the influence events there might exercise throughout
southern Russia, especially in the important mining and metallurgical settlements of the Donbas and Krivoi rog areas, and in the
Ukraine in general. Indeed, the first Ukrainian Congress of Soviets
would convene in Kharkov in December 1917 and declare a Ukrainian Soviet Republic. Kharkov after October played a large role in
efforts by the Bolsheviks to extend their control over the Ukraine.

   Yet Ukrainian nationalism does not seem to have been especially
strong in Kharkov, and only a minority of the population was
Ukrainian. Kharkov lay at the eastern edge of the Ukraine and had
been influenced and settled by Great Russians more than the western provinces had been. The census of 1897 showed that though
half the population of Kharkov had been born in Kharkov province
and two-thirds in the Ukraine, only 25 percent listed Ukrainian as
their native language (the census posed the question in terms of language, not nationality). The next census, in 1926, asked for nationality: 38.4 percent called themselves Ukrainians, whereas 37
percent were Russians, 19.4 percent Jews, and 5.2 percent "other."[4]
Moreover, the influx of non-Ukrainians, especially Great Russians,
was closely associated with industrialization at the end of the century, and Russian representation was especially strong among the
industrial workers. The addition of Latvian workers in 1915 weakened the representation of Ukrainians in the work force even more.
Similarly, government and business circles were disproportionately
Russian and non-Ukrainian. Thus, if one assumes Ukrainians were
about a third of the city's population, it appears that they were concentrated among the elements most difficult to mobilize politically
or else supported all-Russian parties such as the Bolsheviks. As
one writer with a Ukrainian nationalist orientation recently put it,
"some of the urban proletariat, lacking a fully developed national

consciousness, were more attracted by radical Bolshevik programs than by the Rada's [Ukrainian assembly's] hesitant approach to social problems."[5] Indeed, what election returns we have from 1917 indicate that Ukrainian nationalist parties fared badly. They drew poorly in the City Duma elections in the summer, and made only a negligible showing in the elections to the Constituent Assembly in November. Nonetheless, Ukrainian nationalism had some support and, as we will see, played a significant role in Kharkov's October.

The February Revolution in Kharkov, as elsewhere in Russia, followed soon after the receipt of news of the events in Petrograd. The local tsarist officials tried to suppress news of the Petrograd events, even succeeding as late as March 2 in closing the long-standing daily newspaper *Iuzhnyi krai* because it carried news of the Revolution in Petrograd. This was a last gasp of tsarist authority in the city, however, for the Revolution in Kharkov in fact was already well along by that time. Meetings in factories and elsewhere were held on February 28 and March 1. Early in the afternoon on March 1 there was a meeting of people from the socialist parties, worker medical fund offices, trade unions, and factories about how to develop the Revolution. A larger meeting with representatives from 20 factories convened at 6 P.M. and elected a temporary workers' committee to serve until a Soviet of Workers' Deputies could be formed. This meeting then adjourned so that representatives could be sent to the City Duma building to participate in the first meeting of the Public Committee (*Obshchestvennyi komitet*). This Committee was formed from representatives of various organizations, mainly from the professional and middle classes, but with worker representatives. At that meeting, running the night of March 1–2, the Public Committee declared that it was assuming government functions in the city. It also debated the question of a militia. Some speakers were against the arrest of the old officials and the formation of a new militia to replace the police. One Soviet historian quotes E. A. Moskov, an attorney, as speaking against the idea because of its lack of success in 1905. Nonetheless, a militia was decided upon and Moskov, who must not have been too opposed, was put in charge of it. As elsewhere in the Russian Empire, the revolutionary days in Kharkov appear to have been largely nonviolent and bloodless. The old chief of police even stayed on the job until he went to the Public Committee meeting at 4 A.M. on

March 3 to acknowledge its authority—only then was he told that
he had been replaced by Moskov.[6]

The Kharkov Soviet of Workers' Deputies held its first meeting
on the evening of March 2, making it one of the first organized in
the Ukraine. A local Menshevik metalworker, Laz'ko, was elected
chairman. The meeting, with 78 delegates from 43 organizations,
apparently concerned itself primarily with two matters: first, the
large demonstration planned (or shaping up without any plan) for
the next day, and second, the election of representatives to the Temporary Executive of the Public Committee. The sketchy accounts of
these early meetings do not mention the question of arming the
workers.[7] It would appear that this was not a pressing issue in Kharkov, where the Revolution met with no armed resistance. Not until
the evening of March 3 did the Soviet take up the militia question
in any formal manner. On that evening a resolution was passed "to
organize by factories a workers' armed militia for greater coordination of strength during mass demonstrations called by the Soviet."
It was decided also to work out an agreement with the Public Committee about the "technical details of the question."[8]

The belated activity of the Soviet leaders would suggest that they
had a less than urgent sense of the need to form a workers' guard to
protect the Revolution or to keep order. Rather, the Soviet leaders
seemed to have felt no need for any armed force to carry through
the Revolution coming over the wire from Petrograd. They had initially been concerned about the attitude of the troops, but doubts
on that score were pretty much resolved by the time of the first Soviet meeting on March 2. Any lingering doubts were removed by
the morning of the 3d, when the units of the garrison marched to
the City Duma building, with their officers, to declare their support
for the Revolution. The Soviet resolution on March 3 about organizing soldiers' committees and inviting their participation in the
Soviet was really only a recognition of general soldier support for
the Revolution.[9] There seems to have been an even greater acceptance than in Saratov of the notion that responsibility for order lay
with the civic authorities—in this case the Public Committee. Indeed, it appears that the old police, or at least parts of it, continued
to function to maintain public order in Kharkov through the first
week of the Revolution. This may help explain not only why the
Soviet showed so little sense of urgency, but also why the sources

about Kharkov are so vague on the matter of armed workers and students during the first days of the Revolution, in contrast to the extensive attention given to this issue in accounts of Saratov and most other cities.

How extensive or important were volunteer armed detachments in Kharkov? Was there the kind of spontaneous arming and self-organization one finds in Saratov? The answer seems to be that there was, and that it predated the forming of the Soviet. An account of the first days of the Revolution printed in the Kharkov *Izvestiia* suggests that the Soviet resolution on the militia of March 3 was prompted by an earlier one adopted at the Gel'ferikh-Sade Factory calling on the Soviet to organize a militia. The Gel'ferikh-Sade resolution also spoke of a factory workers' militia, functioning in contact with the City Militia, directed by the factory council (under the authority of the Soviet), but existing "on the principle of full internal self-direction." This suggests that a militia already existed at the Gel'ferikh-Sade Factory. The article also talks about student armed bands "for maintaining order and other functions" that were "completed" at meetings on the morning of March 3, and of student and worker bands wearing red emblems that began "gradually" taking over the task of maintaining public order.[10] P. Pavliuk, in his history of the Kharkov Red Guard, states that during meetings on February 29 (*sic*) the workers at the Shimanskii Factory (metalworking) seized the arms of 12 policemen present to equip the nucleus of a workers' *druzhina* formed that day. The *druzhina* got other arms from police and from a prison convoy that was at the factory and marched in the March 3 demonstration at the head of the Shimanskii workers. Similar events, he says, took place at other factories, notably the VEK and Gerliakh and Pul'st factories.[11] Although Pavliuk is not especially reliable, this fits with the kinds of actions workers took elsewhere and with the fact that worker representatives demanded formation of a workers' militia at the March 1 meeting of the Public Committee. These pieces of testimony suggest that there was considerable worker initiative and spontaneity in forming armed detachments during the February Revolution, before the establishment of a Soviet.

Toward the end of the first week of the Revolution the Soviet did begin to take some steps toward regularizing the workers' militias. On March 6 the Soviet presidium told Soviet members about progress in the organization of both factory and city militias, and about the Public Committee's acceptance of a scheme of organization of the militia proposed by the Soviet Executive Committee. On the 7th, all factories were informed of the need to choose a total of 500 worker-militiamen according to a formula set out by the Executive Committee—a formula that is unspecified but that presumably was designed to ensure worker representation in a City Militia. On March 8, the resolution on the militia that had been adopted March 3 at a meeting of workers of the Gel'ferikh-Sade Factory was accepted by the Soviet. It stated that the workers' militia must work in close contact with the City Militia, but that its organiza-tion was entrusted to the factory committees and that its main re-sponsibility was to the Soviet, from which it would receive direc-tions. At one of these meetings, apparently on March 7, three members of the Soviet were charged with preparing instructions for the workers' militia. At the March 10 meeting of the Soviet, one of the three, the Bolshevik leader P. A. Kin, reported on the militia and stressed not only that it had police functions, but that its main purpose was to liquidate any possible counterrevolutionary at-tempts.[12] Overall it appears that the Soviet supported the idea of armed workers, took an interest in the workers' militia, and tried to give some order and direction to it (although not terribly vigor-ously); but the Soviet also felt that the main responsibility for a mi-litia and for public safety lay with the city government—although it had to be watched. The posture of the Soviet on the militia, and on governmental authority in general, was similar to that in Petrograd and Saratov. The main burden of organizing the workers' militia in fact remained at the factory level, and the various detachments re-mained largely autonomous in the spring of 1917.

The exact party breakdown of the initial Soviet leadership is not clear, but Mensheviks dominated the Soviet of Workers' Deputies and SRs the Soviet of Soldiers' Deputies (formed soon after the for-mer). A clearer picture emerged on March 20 when a joint Soviet of Workers' and Soldiers' Deputies was established. The members of its Executive Committee included 14 Mensheviks (10 workers and 4 soldiers), 5 SRs (1 worker and 4 soldiers), and 2 Bolsheviks (both workers). Of the remaining members, one was a Popular Socialist and the other 7 were unaffiliated. Stepanovich, an SR soldier who had been a lawyer in civilian life, was chosen as the new chairman, although he was replaced in April by Svetlov, a Menshevik soldier who was an engineer by training.[13] This contrasts sharply with Saratov, where Bolsheviks played a much more significant role in the Soviet. However, the immediate result was the same in both cities: the Soviet acknowledged the Public Executive Committee as the de jure government agency, even though the Soviet itself held de facto power and took a major role in governing the city. Indeed, in both cities relative strength among initial leaders in the Soviet was probably more an accident of who was present in the city and of individual personalities than a reflection of conscious popular support or distinction among political parties, and did not at first make much difference in actions.

Though the Soviet leaders—and the Menshevik and SR party leadership—took only a slight interest in the workers' militias, the Bolsheviks took a more active interest. Indeed, their party organization pushed the issue earlier and more systematically than in Saratov or Petrograd. The Bolshevik organization was quite weak at the time of the Revolution, and many leaders made their appearance only on March 3—after being released from local prisons—or later. In addition, although distinct Bolshevik and Menshevik factions existed, there were continuing negotiations about unification that did not break down until May. This somewhat obscured party positions before that time. However, the Kharkov Bolsheviks soon began to push more vigorously on the workers' militia issue than the other parties. The first general meeting of members of the Kharkov Bolshevik Party organization on March 3 not only asserted the party line of a "general arming of the people," but charged the Kharkov Party committee to set up a "commission for organization of fighting *druzhiny*, both purely party and at factories."[14] This orientation toward party *druzhiny*—and by other parties than just the Bolsheviks—is one of the peculiarities of the Kharkov situation. In March and April the Bolsheviks repeatedly called for formation of armed workers' units through their newspaper, *Proletarii*. They were especially quick to pick up items from Petrograd dealing with arming the workers. On April 5 *Proletarii* published the March 22 resolution of the Bureau of the RSDRP(b) (the Bolshevik leadership in Petrograd) about the arming of the people and, especially, "the immediate creation of workers' Red Guards throughout the country." On April 16 it carried Vladimir Nevskii's article from *Pravda*

(Petrograd) of March 17 calling for creation of a Red Guard. And on May 3 it carried a letter from a worker demanding the formation of a workers' Red Guard.[15] Despite the firm sound of its editorial policy, however, the Kharkov Bolshevik committee appears to have been less decisive in action. Numerous accounts stress the lack of guidance for the various armed workers' detachments that existed in March and April. V. P. Miroshnichenko, a Bolshevik active in the Red Guard, states specifically that, despite the statements, until May there was no clear line in the Party committee about arming the workers. There were Party fighting *druzhiny* formed, he says, but this was done locally by factory Party members on their own initiative.[16]

Influence from Petrograd in May spurred the Kharkov Bolsheviks to greater action in forming the Red Guard. V. Surik (O. V. Emel'ianov), the chairman of the Kharkov Party Committee, and Aleksei Ivanov, a worker at the Shimanskii Factory and a local Party leader, attended the Seventh Party Conference in Petrograd on April 24–29 and were specifically charged to familiarize themselves with the organization of the Red Guard in Petrograd. On their return they reported on May 11 to a special Party meeting. Surik described the important role played by the Red Guard in the Revolution and the importance of organizing a Red Guard in Kharkov, and Ivanov delineated the organizational situation of the Red Guard in Petrograd.[17] Interestingly enough, their information seems to have come not from the work of the Bolshevik Seventh Conference, which said nothing specific about the Red Guard, but from two other important sources: the April 27–28 Petrograd Conference on the Red Guard (undercut by the Soviet leadership), and the regulations on the Red Guard adopted by the Vyborg District Soviet on April 30. Thus, it was in the midst of the greatest agitation about the formation of a Red Guard during the first half of the Revolution that the Kharkov delegates received their impressions. The Vyborg regulations especially seem to have had a strong impact, for Surik and Ivanov brought back a copy that was used in Kharkov for the Red Guard there.

The reports of Surik and Ivanov spurred the Kharkov Bolsheviks to push ahead with forming Red Guards. The Party meeting of May 11 ended by resolving, "first, to create a Red Guard in Kharkov under the immediate direction and supervision of the Kharkov

[Party] Committee; second, to place a set of regulations for the Red Guard before a general meeting of the Party for approval; third, to give the district committees of the RSDRP [Bolsheviks] responsibility for the organization of the Red Guard; and fourth, to charge the representatives of the Kharkov [Party] Committee in the Executive Committee of the Soviet of Workers' and Soldiers' Deputies to inform the latter about the existence at the factories of fighting *druzhiny* at the disposal of the Kharkov Committee of the RSDRP, and to propose to take immediate measures for the protection of these *druzhiny* from encroachment on the part of the City Militia."[18] This resolution is interesting and valuable for at least three different reasons: first, it is a firm verification of Bolshevik interest in forming a Red Guard, especially one under its own control; second, it gives a clear statement of the influence of events in Petrograd on Kharkov; and third, it suggests how very weak the factory or party *druzhiny* were at this time if the Bolsheviks had to appeal to the Soviet to protect them from the City Militia.

The Bolsheviks did not rest content with this resolution but pushed forward with a number of acts and meetings in May to bring such a Red Guard into being. The Party organization entrusted two members, Aleksei Ivanov (who had been one of the delegates to Petrograd) and V. R. Morgunov, with the task of supervising the formation of a Party fighting organization.[19] On May 14 there was a general meeting of Bolsheviks at which Ivanov reported again about the Petrograd trip and the need for a Red Guard.[20] It was apparently at this meeting that a decision was taken to create some sort of central staff, for one participant states that during it he was charged with making contact with all worker fighting organizations in the city and working out instructions for them.[21] On May 16 *Proletarii* devoted its lead editorial to the question. It stressed the importance of both arming the people and forming a Red Guard. Although there was some mingling of terms—and equating of "people's militia" with Red Guard—the editorial basically stressed the term Red Guard and the importance of its being well organized and disciplined. Also, it probably was the Bolsheviks who organized the meeting of representatives of fighting detachments held in the second half of May, on either the 17th or the 30th. Chaired by A. F. Paster, a Latvian Bolshevik leader from VEK, the meeting approved regulations for a Red Guard, probably the Vyborg ones brought from Petrograd by Ivanov and Surik.[22] Although this meeting did not result in the establishment of a functioning citywide organization, a district staff for the Red Guard was soon established in the Petinskii district of the city, the main industrial district. It had a staff of five, four known to be Bolsheviks (including Paster), and it was headquartered in the same building as the district Bolshevik committee.[23] The Bolsheviks, then, were pushing ahead vigorously. Indeed, though stimulated by Petrograd events, they were more interested in and active on the Red Guard issue than the Petrograd—or the Saratov—leaders, suggesting that they had a self-generated interest in forming Red Guard units.

Simultaneously with this Party activity, Red Guard or workers' *druzhina* detachments were being formed at some Kharkov factories, often at the initiative of the local factory committee. At the Gerliakh and Pul'st, Shimanskii, and Gel'ferikh-Sade factories, the factory committees had established special commissions for the organization of *druzhiny* or Red Guards in April.[24] At the huge VEK factory, some sort of militia or *druzhina* existed from March until the end of April or first part of May, when a factory fighting *druzhina* was authorized by the factory committee, with S. P. Simkin in charge of training (he had been a soldier). At first this unit drew only 50 volunteers, but by early summer it reached about 400, so that additional instructors were needed from the 30th Regiment.[25] VEK already was a Bolshevik stronghold and played a leading role in the development of the Red Guard. Fighting *druzhiny* detachments were formed also in late April or May at other factories, including Russko-Frantsuzskii, Ekonom, and Leitner, at the tram park, and at the shops of the Southern Railroad. The construction workers' union and the garment workers' union set up their own detachments, and there was even established in May a Latvian Cultural Center with its own fighting *druzhina*, under the direction of Silin, a Bolshevik.[26]

The work of organizing the Red Guard continued through the summer. By June the Bolsheviks had formed a Military Organization that provided some instructors for local Red Guard training activities and also got some arms for the Red Guard from the military units. The Bolsheviks were not alone in organizing fighting *druzhiny*, for by mid-July the SRs had begun to organize their own party fighting *druzhina*.[27] The formation of workers' armed detachments in the late summer was stimulated by the widespread labor strife that racked the city then, especially in August. The workers at VEK had been on strike since May, and their strike would continue until September and result in the arrest of the factory administration by the factory Red Guard. In mid-August there was a strike at KhPZ, during which the Bolsheviks managed to get a workers' meeting to pass a resolution calling for the creation of a Red Guard. The factory at that time had a Menshevik orientation and a *druzhina* limited to factory guard duties, however, and the Red Guard there was not actually organized until September. On August 24 labor unrest boiled over at the Gel'ferikh-Sade Factory as a result of the administration's announcement that it would close the factory on September 7, throwing upwards of 3,500 workers out. There were also strikes in smaller factories and workshops. One thousand garment workers went on strike under union leadership for four months in the late spring and summer.[28] This strike in turn contributed to the interest in forming armed detachments, for the garment workers' union maintained a strong *druzhina*, which was unusual for craft unions. Just as these events were coming to a head, however, the entire political situation was given a jolt here, as elsewhere, by the Kornilov Affair.

News of the revolt of General Kornilov reached Kharkov on August 28 and was announced at a meeting of the Soviet Executive Committee. A "Temporary Revolutionary Bureau" was set up immediately.[29] That same day a joint meeting of the executive committees of the Soviet of Workers' and Soldiers' Deputies and the Soviet of Peasants' Deputies was held, with the commander of the garrison, Colonel Kurilko, present. This meeting in turn created a United Revolutionary Committee that would assume all authority in the city; even orders by Colonel Kurilko would be under its supervision. The next day the subordination of the provincial commissar of the Provisional Government to this Revolutionary Committee was announced.[30] The exact composition of this committee is not known, but various references make clear that it was a creation of the Soviet. And since the Soviet was dominated by Mensheviks and SRs, one would presume that the Revolutionary Committee was also. Both the Soviet as a whole and the Revolutionary Committee moved quickly to oppose Kornilov and his supporters. The August 28 meeting of the Soviet passed a proposal to arm the workers, and the Soviet and the Revolutionary Committee quickly ordered the seizure of the railroads, post office, telephone exchange, and other key points. On the 29th the Soviet accepted a four-point proposal by Artem (F. A. Sergeev),* the Bolshevik leader, point two of which called for a reorganization of the militia and a general arming of the workers.[31] The Bolsheviks also acted on their own: a special evening edition of *Proletarii* on August 29 called for arming the workers, ending with "Long live the workers' Red Guard";[32] and a special meeting of the Bolshevik Committee the same day called on Party members to participate actively in the organization of fighting *druzhiny*.[33] Thus in Kharkov the Soviet and the parties moved much more quickly than in Saratov to call out the armed workers in response to news of Kornilov. Various memoirs imply that there was great agitation and that the event gave a tremendous boost to the forming of Red Guard units—which later events verify.

The Kornilov Affair galvanized political sentiments in Kharkov as elsewhere, stimulating class conflict and the feeling that the time was coming when a resort to arms would be necessary to settle the political, economic, and social issues before Russian society. This manifested itself in the growth of the Red Guard, which mushroomed in September, and in its improved organization and increased training. One of the most significant developments was a more extensive organizational framework. During the Kornilov Crisis a meeting of Red Guard representatives adopted a set of regulations for the Red Guard of the city. These regulations, published September 3, were virtually identical to the April Red Guard instructions adopted by the Vyborg District Soviet in Petrograd.[34] Apparently in the moment of crisis the representatives simply adopted or at least decided to publish the Vyborg regulations, which had been on hand since May. In the aftermath of the Kornilov Affair considerable strides were made in setting up district staffs for the

---

* Artem traced his Bolshevism back to 1903 and his Kharkov association to 1905. He had an active career as a second-level Party leader and activist until 1909, when to escape arrest he fled first to China and then to Australia, where he eventually became a naturalized citizen. The latter fact complicated his return to Russia, but he reached Kharkov in June 1917 and soon became the dominant Bolshevik figure there. In August he became a member of the Bolshevik Central Committee. See the biographical sketch in *Deiateli revoliutsionnogo dvizheniia v Rossii*, vol. 5, part 1, pp. 131–37.

Red Guard. The existing staff in the Petinskii district, the main industrial area, was strengthened and directed to provide leadership for the Red Guard units of several factories, including three very large ones—VEK, Gel'ferikh-Sade, and KhPZ. Staffs were organized in the three other districts of the city as well. These staffs were chosen at district conferences of the Red Guard on the principle of two representatives from the guardsmen and two from the command staff.[35] At the same time, many factories formed new directing bodies, the factory committees of the Red Guard. These were composed of representatives from the factory committee and from the guardsmen and headed by the factory Red Guard commander.[36] This trend was probably encouraged by the city conference of factory committees, held the first week of September, which adopted a resolution introduced by Artem in favor of organizing the Red Guard, and which endorsed a proposal by A. F. Paster to set up a commission to assist the process.[37] At the same time the size and number of factory detachments grew rapidly.

The post-Kornilov formation of Red Guards was encouraged by the continuing labor unrest that spilled over from the summer into the fall. At KhPZ, during a prolonged strike, the Bolsheviks made a major breakthrough in overcoming Menshevik resistance and starting a Red Guard. On September 1, at the last meeting before ending (temporarily) the strike, the workers voted to establish a Red Guard; about 200 enrolled immediately. There was also ongoing labor conflict at other factories. At Gel'ferikh-Sade, the workers seized control on September 7 and ran the factory themselves until October 5. At VEK the workers, using the Red Guard, arrested the factory directors on September 18 and held them for about 36 hours. Industrial conflict at KhPZ flared up again on September 20. This time the Red Guard played a major role, securing all entrances to the factory during a protest meeting and refusing to let the administration leave or the City Militia enter; the Guard may even have "arrested" the factory manager. On the same day workers at the Gerliakh and Pul'st Factory arrested their administration, which had threatened to close the factory because of labor and supply problems. The rash of arrests of factory managements at the three largest factories in Kharkov prompted the Provisional Government to send a special mediator to try to ease the labor conflicts, especially at VEK. There also were labor troubles at other factories through the late summer and early fall.[38] Such industrial strife could only have encouraged either the formation of Red Guard units or their growth where they already existed.

The Red Guard and other worker detachments got a chance to prove themselves—and probably got a strong shot of confidence—during "maneuvers" and disturbances in September. In the first part of September the local Red Guard leaders organized maneuvers at the city park under the direction of Artem, N. A. Rudnev, M. L. Rukhimovich, and N. A. Glagoev. The latter three were officers from the pro-Bolshevik 30th Infantry Reserve Regiment, and all but Glagoev were major figures of the Bolshevik leadership in Kharkov. The maneuvers showed that at least rudimentary training, discipline, and organization had been achieved.[39] This training was put to practical use later in the month during riots—Soviet sources invariably call them "pogroms"—in the city. The first and most serious was in mid-September, when soldiers of the Bogodukhovskii Regiment broke into wine stores and then into other shops. The city officials were unable to contain them. The Red Guards were called out, especially the units of the Petinskii district, and the soldiers were disarmed and order restored.[40] On September 27 new disorders broke out, this time caused by what a Stalin-era Soviet historian described as "anarchists" posting monarchist and anti-Semitic slogans (although it is difficult to understand why anarchists would post monarchist slogans). Again, the Red Guards were called out, and about 100 "pogromists" were arrested.[41] One suspects that these may have been in considerable part food riots, for there were rumors of impending food shortages, and food and supply stores were especially hard hit. The various accounts of the September disorders make clear that the Red Guards played the primary role in restoring order during these disturbances and that local military units played only a minor role. This suggests that local officials and party leaders had little confidence in the troops. What is puzzling is who requested the Red Guards to act. None of the accounts refers to the city officials or the Soviet in this connection, and most of the memoirs make no reference at all to who ordered the Red Guards out. Simkin refers to a central Red Guard staff, which hardly solves the problem, because despite resolutions no such body had been formed yet. In connection with the suppression of the "anarchist pogrom," P. Pavliuk and M. Ia. Onufrienko, two Soviet historians, attribute the order to the Kharkov Bolshevik Party organization, which is possible but must be taken with a grain of salt. S. P. Simkin, who is more reliable, does mention that the SR party *druzhina* also took part in suppressing the pogrom,[42] which casts further doubt on Bolshevik Party direction. Quite possibly local Red Guard leaders acted on their own, but we cannot be certain.

The role of the Bolsheviks and other parties in the organization of the Red Guard remains somewhat unclear. The major part seems to have been played by the Bolsheviks, although we must be cautious on this as our sources—almost entirely Bolshevik—have a built-in bias. Indeed, a modern Soviet historian, P. I. Garchev, acknowledges that on the eve of the October Revolution Left SRs, Menshevik-Internationalists, anarchists, and Ukrainian socialists all were joining the Red Guard in Kharkov and throughout the Ukraine.[43] Still, we do know that the Bolsheviks generally did play an especially active role in encouraging the formation of worker armed groups, and the Kharkov Bolsheviks seem to have been especially active and aggressive in doing so. In addition to the evidence mentioned earlier and the memoir accounts of the September disturbances, on September 16 *Proletarii* published an editorial stressing the need for the Red Guard and specifically warning against efforts to stir up friction between the soldiers and the Red Guard. The Bolshevik city conference, meeting September 17–20, expressed itself in favor of the immediate arming of the workers, and the Kharkov province Bolshevik conference on October 3 adopted a similar resolution.[44] Nor did interest in purely party fighting *druzhiny* lag: the City District Bolshevik Party organization on September 11 decided to organize a fighting *druzhina* responsible to the district Party committee.[45]

The position of the Soviet on the Red Guard after Kornilov was ambivalent, as was its political structure. A bloc of Mensheviks, SRs, and Ukrainian Social Democrats formed a majority. The Soviet had been reelected on the eve of the Kornilov Affair, so any rise in Bolshevik popularity stemming from those days was not yet registered in it. Although the Bolsheviks had increased their representation from 42 to between 110 and 120, they still had only about 30 percent. The SRs led with 130 to 150 deputies. When the new 40-member Executive Committee was chosen on August 25, on the basis of roughly proportional representation, the SRs led with 15, the Bolsheviks had 12, the Mensheviks 6, and the Ukrainian SDs 4 (there were also 2 nonparty deputies and an anarchist). Surprisingly, given the vote, P. A. Kin, a Bolshevik, was elected chairman.[46] Why a Bolshevik should be elected chairman is unclear. Perhaps Kin was some sort of compromise candidate, for in May he had been a leading advocate of Bolshevik-Menshevik unification. This may have been the case: V. R. Morgunov, writing in 1923, says that after the October Revolution in Petrograd and while there still was in Kharkov an SR-Menshevik-Ukrainian majority bloc, the Bolsheviks put forward Artem for the chairmanship but were subsequently forced to withdraw his name because of the objection to him as a "fanatical Bolshevik" and to substitute Kin as "more moderate and loyal." [47] Morgunov may have been confused on time and have been referring to the August election rather than the next one in November. In any case, Kin's election gave the Bolsheviks an influential position and the ability to get some things done through the Soviet—or its chairman—that had not been possible earlier. This is reflected in some of the conflicting Soviet statements and actions on the Red Guard. For example, on October 18 the Soviet newspaper, *Izvestiia iuga*, carried a lengthy article that reflected a very Menshevik view of the stages of revolution. It discussed at length the matter of how to create a proper City Militia in the present stage of the revolution and generally assumed the continued presence of a neutral police type of militia. No mention was made of any role for a special workers' force. Yet on September 20 the Soviet had elected a commission for the organization of fighting *druzhiny*,[48] and on October 5 and 11 the Executive Committee had resolved to start organizational work immediately. This commission of seven people was broadly based and included among its members A. F. Paster, the Latvian Bolshevik leader at VEK, and Dodonov, the local anarchist leader.[49] Kin's chairmanship may have been a factor in keeping the issue before the Soviet, for in the spring and summer he had been a leading advocate of the Red Guards, at a time when the Menshevik-SR majority had kept the Soviet from giving them much active support.

For Kharkov as elsewhere, any assessment of the growth of the Red Guards must include a look at the availability of arms. It was during September that the Kharkov workers for the first time received an adequate stock of arms. Until then they had been very short. Some weapons had been obtained during the February Revolution, and a few more were siphoned off from City Militia stocks during the spring or acquired from trains carrying broken rifles from the front to the Tula Arms Factory for repair. These broken Russian rifles—plus captured German and Austrian rifles—were made usable by repair and modification done by the workers in the metallurgical factories. Some other arms were obtained from soldiers of regiments in and around Kharkov. The situation was improved somewhat during the summer, when the 30th Regiment was sent to Kharkov from Tula. It was thoroughly Bolshevik and had been moved out of Tula in part because of that. In Kharkov it became not only a mainstay of Bolshevik support but a major source of both arms and instructors for the Red Guards.[50]

These varied means of finding weapons, however useful, could not provide an adequate number for any significant Red Guard force. Therefore the Red Guard leaders hit upon the idea of getting weapons directly from the Tula Arms Factory. The problem was that both the factory committee and the Tula Soviet were firmly Menshevik. Still, they decided to try, and two separate expeditions were mounted. The first took place in August, before the Kornilov Affair. One account specifies that several persons, led by A. F. Paster, went to Tula and brought back 400 new rifles, 40 machine guns, 100 boxes of cartridges, and 200 revolvers, which were kept for distribution at the shops of the Southern Railway and at VEK. Apparently old contacts of the 30th Regiment in Tula were instrumental in obtaining these arms.[51] The arms received in the second sortie to Tula were much more significant. Numerous memoirists refer to this expedition, but the most extensive account is given by one of the participants, I. A. Poliakov, a Menshevik at the time. He states that the main agency in setting this in motion was the Kharkov Oblast Committee of Soviets, which included many Donbas representatives who were especially concerned about getting arms, given their proximity to and distrust of the Cossacks. The Oblast Committee, evenly divided between Mensheviks and Bolsheviks, decided to send a delegation to Tula for arms. Officially this consisted of Poliakov and Nikolai Danilevskii, but to it were added M. A. Sapel'nikov and Paster, both Kharkov Bolsheviks. Using his position as a Menshevik and as secretary of the Oblast Committee, Poliakov got hold of two copies of the Soviet stamp; with these, plus the reputation of the Kharkov Soviet as being SR-Menshevik, and giving assurances that the arms would not fall into Bolshevik hands and that their distribution would be handled by Mensheviks, he succeeded in getting the approval first of the Tula Soviet and then of the arms factory committee to supply a large quantity of arms—about 5,000 rifles, 300 machine guns, and 5 wagons of cartridges. The four Kharkov delegates, aided by some Tula Bolsheviks, personally loaded the arms into railway wagons and set off for Kharkov. As they approached the city they received word that military cadets were being deployed to intercept them. Preparations were made to fight their way through, but the threat proved a false alarm and they reached Kharkov during the night. By morning the wagons had been transferred to the VEK branch line, and the weapons were soon added to the arsenal being built up there. Some apparently were sent on to the Donbas, but most were kept in Kharkov.[52] Thus, by the end of September the Kharkov Red Guard had a significant stock of rifles and machine guns.

Arms were important, but so was the ability to use them. In Kharkov as elsewhere, training in the use of weapons had to be done mostly after work. Various accounts refer to the *druzhiniki* gathering "daily" or 2–3 times a week at a nearby square or field to practice the use of arms. A concerted effort to train the workers seems to have begun rather earlier in Kharkov than elsewhere, in May. This may have been a part of the attempt of the local Bolsheviks to organize the Red Guard at that time to which we referred earlier, and seems especially to have focused on VEK. At first the detachments drew upon their own members who had military experience to train them, but later they obtained instructors, including officers, from the 30th Regiment. N. A. Rudnev, who was the most influential leader in the regiment (he was later elected commander) as well as one of the more important Bolshevik figures in the city, seems to have willingly sent instructors as needed.[53] An incident involving these 30th Regiment instructors provides a telling account of how seriously the workers took training: when instructors assigned to VEK complained that they lacked money (presumably for trolley fare) for the long trip to the factory and implied that they might not continue to come, the guardsmen collected money to pay them.[54]

From scattered references and from the activities of the Kharkov

Red Guards in the Kharkov "October Revolution," it would seem that they were probably somewhat better trained than most such units, not only in Saratov but perhaps even in Petrograd. One reason seems to be the longer period of training, another the greater stability of units, which were composed of men who joined fairly early and stayed in longer than was the case elsewhere. Moreover, the prolonged and extensive labor conflicts in Kharkov probably contributed both to a desire for training and to a psychological readiness to resort to arms. This outlook was reflected in the resolution of a meeting of construction workers on October 8, which called for forming a fighting *druzhina* because the "Russian revolution can end in the full triumph of the workers' interests only after a bloody battle with the defenders of capitalism."[55] Given the arms, training, and psychology that existed, the Red Guards and other armed workers' bands were in a position to play an extremely important role in the protracted "October Revolution" in Kharkov.

Before turning to those events, however, we need to look for a moment at Ukrainian nationalism. As we noted at the beginning of this chapter, this was not an especially strong force in Kharkov during most of 1917. The main expressions of and efforts toward Ukrainian autonomy (or independence) were centered farther west and south, especially in Kiev.* A Ukrainian Central Rada (Council) was proclaimed in Kiev on March 4, and local branches later developed in many areas, including Kharkov. These branches looked to the Rada in Kiev for leadership and inspiration. In June a General Secretariat—potentially a Ukrainian government—headed by V. V. Vinnichenko was established as an executive organ of the Central Rada. The Rada and the Provisional Government in Petrograd entered into prolonged negotiations, the latter resisting the Rada's demands for autonomy and effective self-governance for the Ukraine, the Rada steadily increasing the scope of its demands under the double stimulus of growing nationalism and the steadily deteriorating authority of the Provisional Government. The Rada itself was politically unstable, though dominated by Ukrainian SDs and Ukrainian SRs, both offshoots of the broader SD and SR movements, with nationalism often overriding their socialist element.

---

* It is perhaps reflective of this that most writings about the Revolution of 1917 in the Ukraine, and especially those that express strong nationalist sentiment, focus almost exclusively on Kiev, whereas Kharkov is rarely mentioned before December.

Their support came primarily from Ukrainian soldiers, peasants, and urban intelligentsia, although other Ukrainian nationalist parties drew backing from these same groups. Indeed, Ukrainian party politics were extremely fluid and confusing in 1917; the parties were new, their leaders usually inexperienced, their constituencies ill-defined, and their relationship to their Russian ideological comrades uncertain. Richard Pipes has succinctly summarized the June-October period as "a period of progressive disintegration of the Ukrainian national movement, marked by indecision, by internal quarrels, by unprincipled opportunism, and above all, by an ever widening gulf between the masses of the population and the politicians who aspired to represent them."[56] Yet nationalism remained a force and the Rada its main institutional expression.

The October Revolution in Petrograd confused the question of Ukrainian autonomy even further. At first the Central Rada and the Kiev Bolsheviks cooperated—although perhaps that is too strong a word—to defeat the local supporters of the Provisional Government. Further cooperation proved difficult, however. Most Bolsheviks expected a quick convening of an All-Ukrainian Congress of Soviets to elect a Ukrainian Central Executive Committee (the Petrograd pattern) that would govern the Ukraine in close cooperation with the new Soviet government in Petrograd. The Rada, however, declared itself the government for the Ukraine, though it left open the door to participation in a federal republic on the territory of the former Russian Empire. This set up a struggle between the Bolsheviks, banking on the city soviets (which were largely Russian), and the Rada, looking to the Ukrainian countryside. The Rada soon began to cooperate with non-Bolshevik Russians and to support the idea of a coalition of socialist parties to govern a new All-Russian Federation. Indeed, it explicitly refused to recognize Lenin's government. Relations worsened through November. When on December 4 a Ukrainian Congress of Soviets finally convened in Kiev, the Bolsheviks found themselves outnumbered by Ukrainians supporting the Rada. The Bolsheviks walked out and departed for Kharkov, which was already emerging as the focal point for Bolshevik efforts to control the Ukraine.[57] Although nationalism had not been terribly important in Kharkov up to October, the development of a Ukrainian national movement and the role of the Rada had an impact on the city, and this impact increased after the Bolshevik seizure of power in Petrograd. Indeed, only then did Ukrainian nationalism become a really serious issue in Kharkov.

News of the October Revolution in Petrograd was received in Kharkov late on the 25th. Although the Bolsheviks did not control the Soviet, Kin, the Soviet chairman, immediately summoned a number of Bolshevik leaders and undertook to proclaim soviet power in the city. The commander of the Ivanovskii district Red Guard, I. A. Korneev, was asked to send a detachment to guard the Executive Committee premises. Kin also summoned the other Red Guard commanders and the leaders of the Bolshevik Military Organization. Orders were given for the Red Guards and for the soldiers of the 30th Regiment to seize the railway stations, state bank, post office, telephone and telegraph exchange, and other strategic places in the city. They did so without opposition. On his own authority Kin also sent out telegrams to other Ukrainian cities stating that in Kharkov soviet power had been declared.[58] Soviet power was not so easily achieved, however, for the next morning, October 26, the Soviet refused to sanction the transfer of power into its own hands.

On the morning of October 26, a joint meeting of the executive committees of three bodies—the Kharkov Soviet of Workers' and Soldiers' Deputies, the Province (Gubernia) Soviet of Peasants' Deputies, and the Regional (Oblast) Soviet of the Donets and Krivoi rog basins—convened to study the events in Petrograd and decide on a course of action. A Bolshevik proposal to transfer power to the soviets was rejected. Instead, the assembled leaders decided to form a "Kharkov Province Military Revolutionary Committee" as the supreme governmental organ in the area. This Committee, of 56–60 members, included representatives from the three abovementioned Soviets (none of which was Bolshevik-controlled), the City Duma, the trade unions, the factory committees, the political parties, and Ukrainian organizations, most notably the Free Ukrainian Rada, the local affiliate of the Central Rada in Kiev. The Committee and its executive bureau of nine became the de facto governmental authority in Kharkov. Soviet historians generally brand the Committee as bourgeois-nationalist, but the resolution establishing it proclaimed it to be a union of the "revolutionary democracy," and in fact it appears to have been primarily a union of the various socialist parties. Its executive bureau consisted of two Bolsheviks, two left SRs, one Menshevik-Internationalist, two Ukrainian SDs, and two Ukrainian SRs. Thus it had both a distinctively left orientation and a strong Ukrainian component. The latter probably was a factor in its decision, after declaring itself the authority in Kharkov, to recognize the Ukrainian Central Rada in Kiev as one of the organizations to which it was responsible, along with the founding Soviets and the City Duma, and to establish ties with the Rada on October 27.[59] However, this latter action seems to have been the result not so much of strong support for the Central Rada as of a common desire on the part of the Ukrainian socialists and Russian Mensheviks and SRs to delay acceptance of the Bolshevik seizure of power in Petrograd. Indeed, the Military Revolutionary Committee does not appear to have made any real effort to change the political situation in Kharkov; rather, its formation was a temporizing move by local leaders that gave an illusion of responding to news from Petrograd while in fact waiting to see what would happen there and in Kiev.

The first armed confrontation in Kharkov followed efforts to support the Provisional Government. On October 27 local backers of the Provisional Government formed a "Committee for the Salvation of the Fatherland and Revolution" headed by V. I. Lebedev, an SR and former assistant navy minister in the Kerensky cabinet in July and August. This group issued leaflets calling for support of Kerensky, the failure of whose final effort to regain Petrograd was not yet known.[60] This introduced a new element of uncertainty into an already tense situation. Then the cadets of the military academy in nearby Chuguev decided to go to Moscow to aid the supporters of the Provisional Government there in their fight against the Bolsheviks. For this purpose they seized a train, emptying it of the wounded soldiers it was transporting. When efforts were made to stop them they seized control of the town of Chuguev, disarming the workers' militia there. It is not clear whether they were responding to the call of the Committee for the Salvation of the Fatherland or had any intention of intervening in Kharkov, but since they had to pass through the city en route to Moscow, the Kharkov socialist leaders feared the worst. When news reached Kharkov on October 30 of the actions of the cadets, the Military Revolutionary Committee set up a *semerka*, a special committee of seven, including three Bolsheviks, to deal with them. The *semerka* organized the Kharkov Red Guards and soldiers from the 30th Regiment and set up defensive positions at the edge of the city. Trenches were dug and, to guard against a night attack, a searchlight was mounted on the VEK factory smokestack. The cadets, who had started toward Kharkov, hesitated—they represented a sizable force of about 1,500, but they were fewer than the combined Red Guards and 30th Regiment troops. A delegation sent to negotiate with the cadets was arrested. A second group, including members of the City Duma, went out the next day and got the first delegation freed. The cadets then withdrew back to Chuguev. Some of them later were disarmed, and the others fled and eventually joined the White forces organizing to the south.[61] This face-off appears to have raised the spirits of the leftists while removing both the military cadets and the Committee for the Salvation of the Fatherland and Revolution as viable forces in the struggle for power in Kharkov, for the latter was associated in the public mind with the cadets regardless of whether or not it actually was. Also, by this time Kerensky's failure to regain Petrograd had become known, further undermining the position of any groups supporting the Provisional Government.

The composition of the Military Revolutionary Committee and the *semerka* underlines the extent to which affairs in Kharkov were being directed by a socialist coalition including but not dominated by Bolsheviks. At the end of October the Bolsheviks had not yet entirely separated themselves from the broader left grouping, but in November they began to do so in the process of pressing the Kharkov Soviet to take power officially. The immediate Bolshevik goal was to force a change in the policy of the Soviet or a change in its composition. On October 30 a plenary meeting of the Soviet rejected two Bolshevik proposals: to transfer power to the Soviet, and to subordinate the Military Revolutionary Committee to the Soviet. Following this defeat, the Bolsheviks responded at the meeting of November 3 with a proposal for reelecting Soviet deputies in those factories and units that expressed a desire to do so. The Bolsheviks, meanwhile, had already begun to agitate in the factories for such reelection, an appeal to this end having been published in the November 2 issue of *Donetskii proletarii* (as the Bolshevik paper was now titled). The new elections resulted in several Bolshevik victories, the most significant being their cracking of Menshevik control at the giant KhPZ factory, where they elected 19 of 28 delegates.

Though these gains probably do represent increased support for the Bolsheviks, they may also reflect in part the disillusionment and discouragement among Menshevik and SR supporters, for at KhPZ only 55 percent of the workers voted in the new election (by comparison, at VEK—long a Bolshevik stronghold—an election on November 7 showed 97 percent voting). Bolshevik success may have been in no small part a result of absenteeism caused by demoralization of their opponents' supporters.

Following their factory electoral victories, the Bolsheviks moved to gain control of the Soviet. When the regular weekly meeting of the Soviet plenum opened on November 10, the Bolsheviks introduced a resolution calling for recognition of the Soviet government in Petrograd and the transfer of power to the soviets in the Ukraine. After a stormy debate this passed by a vote of 120–75.[62] The smallness of the vote again raises the question of possible absenteeism of former opponents. Reelection of the Executive Committee on November 19–21 resulted in 19 Bolsheviks, 11 SRs, 4 Mensheviks, 4 Ukrainian Socialists (SDs?), and 2 nonparty. The more aggressively Leninist local Bolshevik leader, Artem, was elected chairman on November 24, replacing the more moderate Kin. Even so, complete control of the Executive Committee still eluded the Bolsheviks—lacking an absolute majority, they had to rely upon obtaining at least two votes from others. Moreover, they still had to give some reality to their resolution on soviet power, which apparently had not yet led to any real changes. In a series of forums in mid-November, the Bolshevik leaders spoke against the Rada and in favor of supporting the Soviet government in Petrograd and convening a Ukrainian Congress of Soviets, but with little success. Finally, at a plenary meeting of the Kharkov Soviet on November 24, the Bolsheviks, supported by some nonparty and leftist Ukrainian SD members, managed to pass a new resolution on relations with the Rada and the Petrograd Council of People's Commissars. In this resolution the authority of the Central Rada was rejected, political authority in Kharkov was declared to rest with the Kharkov Soviet, and supreme political authority in the "Russian Federal Republic" was recognized as resting with the Council of People's Commissars.[63] Soviet power had at last been declared in Kharkov, but it was far from established: the Soviet declaration did not lead to clear control and quick liquidation of opposing institutions as it did in Saratov.

The declaration of Soviet power in fact was only a political step in a protracted struggle in Kharkov in which an essential element was the establishing of armed supremacy. Indeed, armed confrontations would yet be necessary to make the declaration meaningful. In this process the Red Guards played a critical role, though their organization was still inadequate. As we have noted, in September considerable effort went into organizing district- and citywide Red Guard staffs. On October 22 the city staff adopted a new set of regulations based on those published by the Petrograd Bolshevik Military Organization on September 6.[64] Nevertheless, it appears that at the time of the October Revolution the Red Guard organization was still primarily local, the "city staff" rather shadowy, and the district staffs inoperative except in Petinskii.[65] In November these staffs struggled to get some grip on the situation in their districts and in the city. Despite publication of a rather elaborate scheme of organization for the Red Guards in *Donetskii proletarii* on November 12, and a series of meetings, central control was difficult to achieve, for the factory units jealously guarded their autonomy. Not until December 6 was a real central staff finally established. It had five members, all Bolsheviks, and took over from the districts responsibility for establishing patrols and for training. From about 3,000 on October 25 the Red Guards had grown to about 3,500 by the beginning of December, and they were relatively well armed and trained.[66]

The Red Guards played an active and important role in the Bolshevik consolidation of power in Kharkov, even before their organizational problems were worked out. There was not in Kharkov, as there was in Saratov, a fairly quick confrontation following news of the October Revolution in Petrograd resulting in a Bolshevik seizure of power. Rather, there was a gradual process of Bolshevik takeover of the Soviet and of Soviet takeover of the city. Moreover, it was a three-cornered affair, with the problem of support for the Ukrainian Rada being a major roadblock.* In this process there

---

* An interesting comparison with the "Kharkov October" is the "Baku October," which was even more delayed and in which nationality factors played an even greater role. See Suny, *The Baku Commune.*

were armed confrontations both within the city—in which the Bolshevik opponents were worn down, out-maneuvered, or demoralized—and outside the city—in which potential rivals to soviet power were driven off. The Red Guards, along with the soldiers of the 30th Regiment, played a critical role in the gradual accretion of armed power to the Soviet during November, and gained strength and confidence in the process. We have already made reference to their role in seizing major points during the night of October 25–26 and in defending the city against the Chuguev cadets. During November they gradually took over primary responsibility for the security of the city. The Red Guards provided the muscle to back up worker demands for a larger voice in the factories or, in some cases, workers' seizure of the factories. They also watched for "counterrevolutionary" activity: one guardsman recounts that during this period he received a report of counterrevolutionary speeches being made at a meeting of students and took the Red Guard of the garment workers' union and broke up the meeting, seizing 50 revolvers and arresting 30–40 people.[67] These were the kinds of events that, piecemeal, established Soviet—which in late November came to mean Bolshevik—control over the city.

The Kharkov Red Guards also took an active role in the area outside the city. They patrolled the railway lines in and out of the city and through this were drawn into expeditions to control the nearby small towns and stations. During the first week in November a large contingent of Red Guards from the Shimanskii Factory, KhPZ, the railroad shops, and some other factories was sent to Pavlograd, 130 miles southeast, to help suppress "pogroms" by drunken soldiers. Apparently soldiers of the garrison there broke into spirits stores on November 3; troops sent from Ekaterinoslav joined them. Finally on November 5, about 800–900 Kharkov Red Guards and soldiers of the Kharkov garrison restored order.[68] During the second week in November Red Guards from VEK, KhPZ, and other factories were engaged in efforts to control the rail lines south of the city and especially to ward off Ukrainian nationalist units. Reinforced by other Red Guards and troops, including an armored train, they became engaged in a series of fights for control of the stations. A number of casualties were suffered in the process, but the Ukrainians were pushed back and the safety of Kharkov from this direction secured.[69] (See Map 3.)

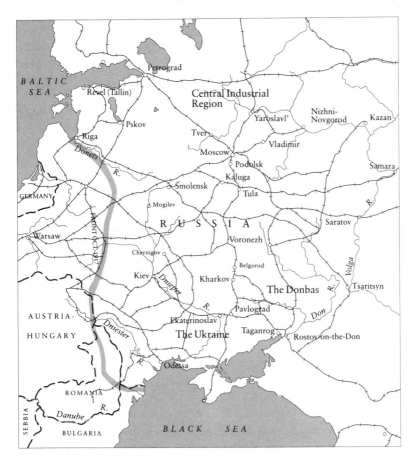

MAP 3. European Russia in 1917.

The Kharkov Red Guards also played a role in meeting a major threat from the north to leftist control of the city: the appearance at Belgorod, 52 miles to the north by railway, of "shock troops"* making their way south. These troops, about 3,000–6,000 strong (accounts vary), were trying to get south and yet avoid major leftist

* "*Udarniki*." These were special units of better disciplined soldiers created in 1917. They had played a major role as attack units in the June offensive and gener- ally were supportive of the Provisional Government and considered likely to oppose the Bolsheviks.

strongholds, and hence intended to bypass Kharkov. They were popularly thought to be connected with the efforts of General A. M. Kaledin to build an anti-Bolshevik force based on the Don region and were also confused with troops simultaneously moving southward under General Lavr Kornilov. It was feared that they might move on the city. They found their way blocked, perhaps accidentally, by pro-Bolshevik forces—a combination of sailors from both the Black Sea and Baltic fleets, soldiers, and Red Guards from Moscow and Petrograd—at the critical rail junction at Belgorod. Fighting began on November 24 and lasted in sporadic and disjointed fashion until December 6. A detachment of Kharkov Red Guards and soldiers from the 30th Regiment, numbering several hundred each, arrived and joined the fighting on the 25th. They were recalled to Kharkov on December 2 because of perceived threats from other quarters, particularly the Ukrainian nationalists. The "Kornilovite" troops were nonetheless defeated, some being disarmed and the rest forced to leave the area. This removed what was seen as a threat to leftist authority in Kharkov. The Red Guards' role in the fighting further bolstered their self-confidence.[70] Indeed, the deaths of some guardsmen in this fighting led to a ceremonial funeral on December 3 that must have had the effect of further solidifying the men's sense of determination.

What caused the Kharkov Red Guards and soldiers to be withdrawn from Belgorod to Kharkov was also the last major roadblock to Soviet—and Bolshevik—authority in the city: the growing strength of Ukrainian nationalists supporting the Central Rada in Kiev. Tensions between the Bolsheviks and the Ukrainians had risen steadily in November as the Bolsheviks had striven to get the Soviet to recognize the Council of People's Commissars in Petrograd and specifically reject the Rada, which it finally did on November 24. In turn, Ukrainian nationalists labeled the Bolsheviks "Muscovites" who had no right to decide the fate of the Ukrainian people (the charge of being "outsiders" would also apply to the Latvian members of the Red Guards). Apparently the Ukrainians decided to put pressure on Kharkov. A Ukrainian detachment was sent out along the Kiev-Kharkov railroad line, and on November 26 there was a parade of Ukrainian troops in Kharkov. At about the same time the garrison commander, Chebotarev, a Ukrainian who supported the Rada, proposed disarming the Red Guards and dispersing the 30th Regiment, both of which had a large part of their forces temporarily out of the city, at Belgorod. Since the Central Rada in Kiev was calling for the expulsion from Ukrainian soil of all non-Ukrainian soldiers, his suggestion appeared to be part of a larger design. Also, rumors spread of the imminent arrival of Ukrainian forces commanded by Simon Petlura. Although the latter did not materialize, several hundred Ukrainian soldiers did arrive in small groups: *Izvestiia iuga* of December 2 speaks of armed Ukrainian soldiers arriving daily. In addition, "free Cossack" units, volunteer Ukrainian nationalist armed bands, were being formed in the city and the surrounding villages to suppress banditry and keep order. Both the "free Cossacks" and the Ukrainian soldiers found their political expression through the Kharkov Free Ukrainian Rada, led by S. Petrenko, which backed the Central Rada in Kiev as the government for all of the Ukraine, including Kharkov.

It was against this background that the Soviet leaders felt the need to recall the Red Guards and 30th Regiment troops from Belgorod. Vigorous efforts were made to get the Red Guards better organized. There were citywide Red Guard meetings on December 3 and 6, at the latter of which a new city staff was formed under complete Bolshevik control. Here, too, a statement by M. L. Rukhimovich that the Red Guards would "not surrender a single shell" met stormy approval from the guardsmen.[71] This was a reference to Chebotarev's earlier proposal to disarm them. Thus when on December 7 Chebotarev issued an ultimatum that the Red Guards disarm in 24 hours, an armed confrontation seemed imminent. *Izvestiia iuga* of December 7 described the tension in the city: "in Kharkov machine guns stand ready and whole regiments have been sitting alert in their barracks for some nights, without sleep, in armed preparedness, as if at any moment artillery fire might begin to roar."[72]

The distribution of forces at this point was not favorable to the Bolsheviks. The largest armed force in Kharkov was the 28th Reserve Infantry Regiment, which was in the process of reorganizing itself into the 2d Ukrainian Regiment. It supported the Free Ukrainian Rada. Numbering about 3,500 officers and men, the 28th Regiment was strong enough and well-disciplined enough that no steps could be taken against it throughout November. Complicating any assessment of the situation is the fact that although Soviet historians always imply that it was hostile to the Bolsheviks, it may not have been entirely opposed to "soviet power," for on October 14 it had passed a resolution containing a number of revolutionary demands, including "all power to the soviets."[73] This underscores the fact that it is an error to equate pro-soviet-power sentiment with pro-Bolshevik sentiment, especially in an area with as complex a political and ethnic situation as Kharkov and the Ukraine. In addition to the 28th Regiment there were other Ukrainian forces, and they were growing: the steady arrival of other Ukrainian soldiers resulted in a total of as many as 8,000 Ukrainian soldiers and "free Cossacks" in Kharkov on December 8. Moreover, as commander of the garrison, Chebotarev was in a position to give military leadership to the Ukrainian troops against the Bolsheviks.[74]

To oppose the Ukrainian forces the Bolsheviks looked chiefly to about 3,500 Red Guards and the 30th Regiment, which, however, had shrunk to about 500 men. There was, in addition, the possibility of support (if not for the Bolsheviks then at least for the Soviet) from some other small units, mainly an artillery brigade and part of a sappers' regiment—perhaps a couple of hundred unenthusiastic men in all. The Red Guards, then, made up the bulk of Bolshevik armed support, and thus proposals to disarm them were especially frightening. To further confuse the military picture, an armored car unit generally described in the literature as "SR-oriented" but sometimes as pro-Ukrainian had come to the city just before the October Revolution. As tensions mounted it declared itself "neutral," but the Bolsheviks distrusted it and suspected that in a crisis it would oppose them. There do not appear to have been any other complete army units in the city after the October Revolution, which means that the garrison had shrunk during the course of 1917 to well under 10,000 men, few of them supporting the Bolsheviks.[75]

The situation changed suddenly on December 8 with the arrival in Kharkov of Bolshevik armed forces fresh from the fighting at Belgorod. This group included about 1,500 soldiers commanded by Rudolf Sivers, about 300 Baltic Fleet sailors led by N. A. Khovrin, and an unspecified number of Petrograd Red Guards commanded by A. E. Zaitsev.* Not only did the Bolsheviks suddenly find them-

---

* Sivers, a 25-year-old lieutenant, played an active role in the Bolshevik Party in 1917, organizing pro-Bolshevik armed forces after October and helping establish Bolshevik control over what remained of the old army. Khovrin was one of the Bolshevik leaders in the Baltic Fleet throughout 1917. Zaitsev's unit apparently was drawn from the Putilov Factory.

selves in a much stronger position, but Sivers pushed the local Bolsheviks to take a more aggressive stance, which the local Bolsheviks were reluctant to do. Nonetheless, the arrival of Sivers pushed both sides toward confrontation, including some maneuvering for control of railroad stations, telegraph offices, and other buildings. To try to resolve the political situation and avoid an armed clash, a meeting of all party groups was convened at 6 P.M. on December 8 at the City Duma building on the initiative of local Mensheviks and the Jewish Bund. The main purpose seems to have been to resolve a conflict between the Bolsheviks and the Ukrainians over passage of troops and goods. The Ukrainians were represented not only by Petrenko and Chebotarev, but also by Simon Petlura from Kiev. The Bolsheviks demanded the unhindered passage of food and other supplies to northern Russia and the passage of pro-Soviet troops and Red Guards to the south to fight General Kaledin's anti-Bolshevik forces in the Don region. Petlura agreed neither to hinder nor to help these movements, but in return demanded that the Bolshevik soldiers, sailors, and Red Guards move out of Kharkov. The Bolsheviks refused this demand.[76]

During the negotiations the Bolsheviks secretly laid plans for some of Sivers' troops and the Red Guards from VEK and the Shimanskii Factory to fall on and disarm the armored car unit. Part of the plan involved luring the unit's commander to the headquarters of the Military Revolutionary Committee before the attack. Around 9 P.M., Sivers' detachment set out to surround the armored car unit's barracks. At this point the local Bolshevik leaders, some of whom had opposed this action all along, became fearful; the balance of power was too delicate. Artem, who had been a hard-line advocate of soviet power, and the Kharkov Bolshevik Committee demanded that Sivers restrain himself from any kind of hostile actions against the Ukrainian regiments. Sivers assured them that he would limit himself to a show of strength and to disarming the armored car unit. Finally, just as the negotiations at the City Duma building dragged toward an end around 1 A.M., the Bolsheviks opened fire on the armored car barracks, starting with two artillery rounds. At the Duma building Petrenko and others demanded that the Bolsheviks stop all military activity lest there be extensive bloodshed, and a delegation to mediate a cease-fire was proposed. The Bolsheviks caucused. Artem again expressed doubts about the success of the action and apparently was ready to back off for fear that the Ukrainians would fall upon them from the rear. M. L. Rukhimovich, a leading Bolshevik from the 30th Regiment, assured him that precautions had been taken. Sivers declared that he would proceed no matter what the local Bolsheviks desired; events were now out of their hands. By the time a delegation was organized and sent, the armored car unit had surrendered, the only casualties being five wounded.

Flushed with success, the Bolsheviks—again with Sivers, Khovrin, and the Kharkov Red Guard commanders seemingly in the lead—now proceeded against the Ukrainians, who had remained inexplicably inactive. Around 4 A.M. the Bolsheviks surrounded the building housing the staff of the Ukrainian Military Council. The guard at the entrance withdrew into the building, followed closely by the pursuing Bolsheviks. After a short scuffle the staff was arrested, along with whatever soldiers and "free Cossacks" were there. The 28th Regiment's barracks were surrounded, and after some brief firing the troops there surrendered. Petrenko was arrested at the staff building and Chebotarev at the railroad station. No reference is made to Petlura, who presumably had left the city or else was left alone and allowed to leave later. These actions were followed up on the morning of the 9th by the closing of two "Kadet" newspapers, *Iuzhnyi krai* and *Russkaia zhizn'*. The "Kharkov October" was finally completed.

In Kharkov both the Red Guard and the Bolshevik roles were rather different than in Saratov, and Saratov seems to have conformed more closely to the Petrograd model. In Kharkov spontaneous armed bands played a lesser role in the events of the February Revolution. Afterward, however, from midsummer at least, they seem to have progressed more rapidly than in Saratov or Petrograd in forming reasonably well organized Red Guard units—and certainly were better armed. Also, Kharkov is distinctive for the greater creation of party *druzhiny*, and for the larger role played by Latvian workers. What is most distinctive, however, is "October." In Kharkov this stretched over a month and a half and involved Ukrainian nationalists and outside Bolshevik forces as well.

Kharkov is an excellent case study of the complex relationship among the Bolshevik Party, worker aspirations as reflected by the Red Guards, and the concept of soviet power. In Kharkov a sort of "soviet power" was achieved after the October Revolution in Petrograd but before the Bolsheviks gained control of the local Soviet, a soviet power that relied upon Red Guards and soldiers for support but that backed neither the Petrograd Bolsheviks and Council of People's Commissars nor their various opponents. The case of Kharkov is a good reminder that Red Guard and other worker activities were not completely under Bolshevik direction, though they clearly reflected Bolshevik involvement, for many of the Red Guard actions were in support of the Soviet before the Bolsheviks established control over it. Red Guard actions must be viewed as directed toward protecting and extending their own perceived self-interest as workers (as in the seizure of factories) or toward defense of the Soviet's authority broadly defined, which at that time was not synonymous with Bolshevik authority. It is worth emphasizing this point, for there has been a general tendency to make not only the simple equation of "soviet power" with the Bolsheviks, but also the more sophisticated argument that to support the slogan of "soviet power" meant to be pro-Bolshevik because the Bolsheviks were the only ones advocating soviet power. The latter is a dubious assertion that ignores the complexity and fluidity of 1917, and certainly was not an opinion universally held among workers in 1917: workers tended to look to the Soviet as a symbol of their own self-determination, quite aside from party positions. Often this led them to support the Bolsheviks—but not always. Indeed, sometimes they bowed to Soviet authority in 1917 even when it ran counter to their own immediate positions, as in the case of the April Red Guard Conference in Petrograd, whereas at other times they ignored the Soviet's position while still in general supporting the Soviet as the true source of legitimate political authority. Moreover, even though the workers' desire for soviet power coincided with a Bolshevik position, one must remember that there were many other issues in 1917, and that a worker could both support the idea of soviet power and oppose the Bolshevik platform in general or, conversely, support the Mensheviks or SRs on general grounds but disagree on this issue. Sometimes workers were hostile to the parties and their intelligentsia leaders altogether but still supportive of the idea of the soviet as a vehicle for the expression of proletarian interests. And here in Kharkov we have an example of "soviet power" meaning power openly and officially controlled by a Soviet that was for some weeks non-Bolshevik. There is no doubt that Bolshevik advocacy of the slogan "soviet power" brought them supporters, but not all who supported the slogan and concept backed the Bolsheviks. Only in early December did the Bolsheviks have their "October" in the sense of an armed confrontation and ouster of their opponents from the government; only then did they bring "soviet power" and "Bolshevik power" together in Kharkov.

12

The Red Guards Across Russia

"Russia, what country can compare with her in magnitude."
—M. P. Pogodin, *Letter on Russian History*

Russia was indeed a country of great magnitude, and this raises the question of the extent to which the patterns and characteristics we have identified on the local level were typical of the country as a whole. Were there important differences or local peculiarities that we have not yet seen? As it happens, the worker armed bands are a good vehicle for examining diversity and similarity in the Revolution across Russia, for here we have hundreds of organizations that sprang up and operated independently, yet that had the same general traits and purposes. Resemblances and differences among them provide good evidence both of how local conditions put a stamp on revolutionary development and also of how certain events or broad forces at work in 1917 forced analogous responses regardless of local peculiarities. A look at these issues will enhance our understanding of the Russian Revolution as a whole and provide an opportunity for some generalizations about the Red Guards.

The general chronological development of worker armed bands in the provincial cities and towns followed a rhythm of revolutionary ebb and flow closely paralleling the pattern seen in Petrograd, Saratov, and Kharkov: an initial surge to arms and self-organization; a tapering off in the spring, but with sporadic efforts at better organization; a renewed interest in the late summer and early fall resulting both from industrial unrest and from the Kornilov Affair; and then a vigorous drive to get arms and to organize and expand in the month and a half before the October Revolution (and after it, in the case of those cities that, like Kharkov, did not have their Bolshevik Revolution for some weeks after the October

Revolution in Petrograd). There were, of course, variations in this pattern—for example, much earlier and better formation of workers' guards in some places—but the general outline traced in the earlier chapters holds good. When we turn from chronological development and look at other characteristics, however, we find more striking variations. We will begin by looking at local variations in social composition of the Red Guards—age, nationality, and so forth—and then turn to political and other features.

Age is one area where the data on the Red Guards in the provinces seem to bear out the generalizations made about Petrograd—that younger workers enrolled disproportionately. Many memoirists and other writers refer to the role of younger workers in the armed bands, suggesting that this was so. Probably the most comprehensive statistical data are provided by V. P. Verkhos', who has drawn up a table, based on more specialized works and on archives, that gives figures for seven cities or districts.[1] These figures show, as did our comparison of individual factories within Petrograd, that the age distribution varied from place to place. However, lacking the ability to compare these figures to figures on the age composition of the local work force, we are left to conclude on the basis of the memoir and other nonstatistical data that overall the Red Guards probably were younger than the general work population. This is reinforced by scattered references to the fact that the Socialist Union of Young Workers and similar youth organizations often served to funnel members into the Red Guards, sometimes joining as a group. A. N. Atsarkin's study stresses this role in large and medium cities—including Petrograd, Moscow, Kharkov, Odessa, Tallin, Kazan, Samara, Tver, and Kaluga—and in many of the smaller industrial settlements across Russia.[2]

Nationality was a more important factor in the country as a whole than in our model cities, except perhaps for Kharkov. Militias and Red Guards were factory-based, and thus any given detachment tended to reflect the nationality of the factory. That in turn usually reflected the composition of the local working-class population. Thus in Great Russian areas the Red Guard was overwhelmingly Great Russian. In other areas the issue is less clear. In many non-Russian areas Russian workers made up a disproportionate part of the industrial population; we can assume that they would have made up a similarly large share of the Red Guard. What

TABLE 2
*Percentage Breakdown of Red Guard Members by Age,
Selected Cities and Regions*

City or region	No. of guardsmen counted	Age					
		Under 18	18–25	26–30	31–40	41–50	Over 50
Petrograd	3,557	8.2%	45.6%	20.5%	20.9%	4.2%	0.5%
Moscow	2,000	4.8	38.5	27.5	24.9	3.7	0.6
Central Industrial Region	400	2.5	45.3	33.5	18.0	0.8	—
Samara and Samara Province	57	8.8	42.1	15.8	28.0	3.5	1.8
Tashkent	217	3.2	31.8	17.0	30.9	15.7	1.4

SOURCE: Verkhos', *Krasnaia gvardiia*, p. 86.

NOTE: Figures for Ivanovo-Vosnesensk are as follows: of 409 Red Guard members counted, 14.6 percent were 20 and under, 44.3 percent were 21–30, 34.2 percent were 31–40, and 6.9 percent were 41–50. In Ekaterinoslav, of 523 counted, 15.9 percent were 17 and under, 55.9 percent were 18–27, 27 percent were 28–37, and 1.2 percent were over 37.

we cannot determine is whether they made up a percentage greater or less than their share of the factory population. Moreover, we do not know to what extent ethnically mixed detachments tended to be Russian- or Slavic-led, or, alternatively, to what extent Russian-dominated units excluded minority nationality groups. Contemporary sources rarely discuss nationality.

We do know that in some instances nationality groups did play a significant role. In cities where factories evacuated from the Baltic region were located Latvians played a very active role in the Red Guards, as we have seen in Kharkov and, to a lesser degree, in Saratov. The Latvians tended to form their own detachments at the factories with which they had been evacuated, and then to operate alongside units from other factories that were Russian in composition. Local workers recruited into an evacuated Latvian factory, however, were not prevented from joining the factory's Red Guard. In the cities where they were sent, the Latvians tended to take leadership roles in organizing the Red Guard. At Podolsk, for example, the Red Guard leaders seem to have had basically Latvian and Baltic names, reflecting the role of the evacuated Zemgor Factory, which was also the most Bolshevik-oriented factory in the city.[3] Indeed, in most cities where they were located the Latvian factories seem to have been among the most radical and among the first to form armed units. This probably reflected both the unsettling experience of evacuation, accompanied as it was by great hardships, and a longer tradition of industrial and proletarian experience. Besides factory organizations, Latvian, Polish, and other displaced workers sometimes had special clubs at which fighting *druzhiny* were formed.

In some places the Red Guards had a considerable nationality mix without benefit of evacuated factories. In the Donbas there was a mixture of nationalities, including prisoners of war, in the mines. Kh. Luk'ianov notes that in the Paramonovskii settlement the Red Guard included 27 Chinese and 3 Austrians, and in the Almazno settlement and others there were to be found Chinese, Germans, Czechs, Slovaks, and Poles. In Odessa, the Polish Socialist Party and the Ukrainian SDs, as well as the Russian SDs and SRs, submitted names of candidates for membership in a Red Guard of railway workers.[4] In Ekaterinoslav, according to a 1928 computation, of 408 former guardsmen still living there, 40.9 percent were Russian, 37.7 percent Ukrainian, 9.6 percent Jewish, 7.1 percent Belorussian, and 4.4 percent "other." The compiler felt that the "others," mostly Poles, Latvians, and Lithuanians evacuated there during the war, probably were a larger percentage in 1917 than this later survey indicates.[5] Thus there appears to have been considerable mixing of nationalities in the Red Guards, but some clumping by nationality when factories drew on a given area for workers.

When we look at the social composition of the Red Guards across Russia, the picture is very different than for the large cities, especially Petrograd. Indeed, entirely new types of population centers—industrial settlements and peasant villages—are introduced. Even in medium-sized provincial cities, however, the social structure of the Red Guards was different from what it was in Petrograd or large industrial cities such as Kharkov. The best overall data are provided by G. A. Tsypkin and R. G. Tsypkina, although there are difficulties with them. Remembering that 95.9 percent of the Petrograd Red Guards were workers, the figures Tsypkin and Tsypkina give present an interesting contrast.[6] We can see from Table 3 that both "employees" and peasants were more heavily represented in areas such as the Volga and the Urals. This reflects the fact that both areas were less heavily industrialized than the Moscow region. It also suggests that in the smaller towns class lines may have been

TABLE 3
Social Composition of the Red Guard

Category	Moscow and Central Indus. Region No.	Pct.	Urals No.	Pct.	Volga No.	Pct.	Total No.	Pct.
Workers	2,305	81.1%	254	75.6%	207	57.8%	2,766	78.2%
Peasants	144	5.1	34	10.1	55	15.4	233	6.6
Employees	222	7.8	35	10.4	57	15.9	314	8.9
Military	69	2.4	8	2.4	18	5.0	95	2.7
Students and others	101	3.6	5	1.5	21	5.9	127	3.6
TOTAL	2,841	100.0%	336	100.0%	358	100.0%	3,535	100.0%

SOURCE: Tsypkin and Tsypkina, p. 188.

less sharply drawn, and that the industrial workers there may have had a smaller and less confident cadre of leaders from among their own ranks and so accepted leaders (and Red Guard members) from the white-collar employees and intelligentsia more readily than elsewhere. The small percentage of student members in the Urals reflects the lack of many educational institutions there, and the large percentage of workers relative to the Volga probably reflects the large number of industrial settlements in the Urals region.

The above statistics give an overview by large areas. Two kinds of militias and Red Guards need special attention, however, both because we have not studied them thus far and because they played an important role in the Revolution across the countryside. These are the armed bands to be found in rural industrial settlements and in peasant villages. Industrial settlements were a feature of Russian industrialization and thus of the factory working class. Typically they consisted of a single large industrial enterprise established in a rural setting and a town created to house the workers and provide services for them and the factory. These settlements sometimes ran to many thousands of workers, and they had a long history of turbulent labor relations: Robert Johnson found that even in the 1890's there was more strike activity and unrest among the workers in the settlements of the Central Industrial Region than in the city of Moscow.[7]

Workers' militias were established in the industrial settlements shortly after the Revolution. The pattern and timing seem to have been reasonably close to what we have seen for the country as a whole.[8] There were some of the same problems in the early days of trying to define the separate roles of armed workers' militias and general people's militias, for the latter were also quickly established in most places. The basic task of the workers' militias was to guard the factories and provide general security in the settlements. The workers' detachments tended to grow larger as the year progressed and social tensions grew, and to become increasingly radical. The Bolsheviks were particularly active in encouraging their formation. The Kornilov Affair and the strikes and other industrial unrest of the late summer and early fall stimulated the growth of Red Guards in the industrial settlements, as they did in the large cities. Most units had from 30 to 75 members, but some numbered 300 or more.[9] They played a significant role in helping enforce worker demands during the great strike of textile workers in September–October that spread through the Central Industrial Region and that at its height involved 300,000 workers at 114 factories, many of them in these settlements. In some instances, too, workers' armed forces from the industrial settlements were used to keep order or otherwise influence events in nearby small cities. In Dmitrov district (*uezd*) of Moscow province, Red Guard units were set up at factory settlements in the villages of Iksha and Iakhroma. When disorders broke out in August in Dmitrov, the district city, the local soviet had to call for the Iksha and Iakhroma Red Guards to come and restore order.[10]

In the industrial settlements the armed worker bands were in a position to play a much more powerful role than in larger cities— after all, workers made up most of the population. If there was no army garrison nearby and the units were well organized, armed, and led, they could dominate politics locally. The Red Guards in the industrial settlements played an important role in the October Revolution in at least three ways. First, they usually were able to seize power directly in their own settlements. If the local soviet leaders were Bolshevik, then it was a simple matter to declare adherence to the October Revolution. Examples of this occurred at Liudinovo in Kaluga province and at Iartsevo in Smolensk province.[11]

Second, these Red Guards often were able to send significant armed forces to help in the seizure of power in nearby larger and more socially mixed cities. For example, the declaration of soviet power in some of the industrial settlements around Moscow—especially those astride railway lines, such as Liubertsy, Tushino, and Mytishchi—had important implications for the outcome of the struggle for power in Moscow, for these villages both contributed Red Guards for the fighting in Moscow and also blocked the arrival of any forces supporting the Provisional Government. The October Revolution in Moscow involved extensive maneuvering and fighting over several days. During that time Red Guard units entered the city not only from the nearby industrial settlements but from those in other provinces of the Central Industrial Region. R. G. Tsypkina estimates that over 1,600 Red Guards from the Moscow *uezd* (the district immediately around the city) took part in the October Revolution in Moscow, as did 4,000 Red Guards and soldiers from elsewhere in Moscow province and over 2,000 Red Guards from Vladimir province, especially from the industrial settlements there.[12] The initial Vladimir contingent consisted of a detachment of 900 Red Guards and soldiers from Shuia and Ivanovo-Vosnesensk led by M. V. Frunze (later to be an important Bolshevik general).[13] Tsypkina argues that a frequent pattern in the Central Industrial Region was for the Revolution to triumph first in the industrial settlements and then with their aid in the district towns or provincial capitals.[14]

A third role of the industrial settlement Red Guards was in stimulating the peasant village Red Guards. It is by now well established that there was a close connection and information network between industrial workers and peasant villages; this was especially true in the Central Industrial Region, and particularly for the workers in industrial settlements.[15] Workers tended to return to their villages in times of economic distress, and the slowdowns and shutdowns of industry in the summer and fall must have sent many workers back to their villages. They brought much information with them, including about forming armed bands. Their return and experiences reinforced village tendencies toward formation of village *druzhiny* and Red Guards.

A particularly good account of the formation of village constabularies and militias is given by John Rickman, a British doctor at a district hospital in Buzuluk district, Samara province. After the February Revolution, the village replaced the police with a militia of about a dozen "old men, greybeards," who kept order for a few months. Their appointment was based on the premise that they had judgment and would neither antagonize younger men nor be attacked by them. The situation changed with the appearance of deserting soldiers and as a result of "other causes," and in the summer a "military militia" appeared, apparently appointed from outside the village (perhaps by regional authorities of the Provisional Government). In the fall this militia "went away" and the village elected new constables, this time middle-aged men who were on the village council. This arrangement apparently lasted until the Civil War, when Red Army soldiers or Cossacks patrolled the village, depending on the fortunes of the competing forces.[16] The type of local constabulary described by Rickman must have been very common—perhaps general—for other scattered evidence suggests that after February the peasants often chose their own militias to replace the old police and that in the summer the Provisional Government had some success in bringing them under the control of its local representatives.[17] The purpose of these militias was mainly to keep local peace and order, but they often acted to defend or advance peasant interests in conflicts with local landowners. As early as May in the village of Nikol'skoe in Orel province (a village of about 1,000 houses), a conflict between landowners and peasants led to formation of a Red Guard on the model of the Red Guards of the capitals. This unit was still in existence in October, when it disarmed a punitive detachment and freed some prisoners being held for agrarian disorders.[18]

More politically oriented peasant armed bands also developed, especially in the late summer and fall of 1917, in part as the shock waves of the Kornilov Affair spread across Russia. They are found in the Ukraine and in Belorussia and the Great Russian provinces.[19] In general, however, politically active and purely peasant *druzhiny* were few and relatively small before the October Revolution. P. I. Garchev says that in the Ukraine few existed, and that even those that did were composed mostly of demobilized and furloughed soldiers.[20] R. G. Tsypkina, in her book on the village Red Guards in the Central Industrial Region, talks almost exclusively about industrial settlements, where the bulk of the population and the Red Guards were drawn from the factory workers; a questionnaire on the social composition of the Red Guards in 18 locations found only one that was a peasant Red Guard, two that consisted of workers and soldiers, and 15 that consisted of workers only.[21] Indeed, a later book that Tsypkina coauthored contains the straightforward statement that "in village settlements (*sel'skie mestnosti*) Red Guard detachments . . . were formed only where there was an industrial enterprise," although that is modified two pages later by the statement that "separate detachments of Red Guards, composed of peasants, existed before the October Revolution."[22] Still, most peasant Red Guards came after October.

After October the number of peasant units increased, although most came into existence only in 1918. The Bolsheviks made a special effort to encourage them. The first issue of *Derevenskaia bednota* (*Rural Poor*), published by the Bolshevik Military Organization on October 12, carried an article by Vladimir Nevskii that listed among the steps important to the peasants in gaining control of the land the formation of a peasant Red Guard "for guarding property and the security of all citizens."[23] The Bolsheviks increased their efforts after the October Revolution, relying especially on demobilized soldiers. *Soldatskaia pravda* on December 13 published an article entitled "How to Organize the Countryside," in which demobilized soldiers were urged to visit the Red Guard staff headquarters (presumably in Petrograd) to see how a Red Guard was organized, and to obtain there a copy of the Red Guard regulations, which would be helpful in setting up a Red Guard when they returned to their own villages. The Congress of Delegates of Military Units of Moscow Oblast in early December encouraged soldiers to join the Red Guards when they returned home—which presumably for most of them would mean to rural villages. Resolutions by congresses and soviets at the district level in late 1917 and early 1918 on the transfer of power to the soviets often included statements about the need to establish Red Guards.[24]

Although their role is very difficult to quantify, workers and soldiers seem to have had a vital influence in organizing armed bands in the peasant villages, before and especially after October.[25] Yet in this case, unlike that of the rural industrial settlements, the revolutionary wave—including Red Guards—rolled from the provincial and district centers out to the peasant villages, with the latter following the lead of the former.[26] The Red Guards or similar armed bands, once formed, could then provide the organized armed force to carry through the seizure of land and other social and economic changes desired by the peasantry, whether organized by the peasants spontaneously or by district leaders concerned with problems of keeping order or consolidating power.

The soldiers represent a special element in the Red Guards. Although not numerous, when they participated they did play an important role, especially in training. This was often done in an ad hoc manner, as voluntary help from sympathetic individual soldiers, but in some places, especially where the local soviet was supportive of the Red Guards or where the Red Guard staff was well organized, it was done more systematically. There were instances, however, of significant direct participation by soldiers in the Red Guards. The Belorussian cities (near the front and with large garrisons) seem to have had quite a large soldier component in their Red Guards.[27] At Veliki Luki, where there was a large garrison supporting the front, a cavalry unit on October 22 proclaimed itself the "First Cavalry Red Guard Unit," an unusual event. Further south, at Ungeny in Moldavia, the soldiers' soviet decided on October 23 to form a Red Guard from among armed revolutionary soldiers. This was less common away from the front, although at Kazan in September a Red Guard was formed from garrison soldiers and subordinated to the soldiers' section of the Kazan Soviet.[28] Generally, however, soldiers entered the Red Guards in small numbers or individually. Sometimes they gained entry through their experience in the order-keeping militias formed after February. In other instances they were attached to factories as workers and thus easily entered. Sometimes they were simply members of the garrison who volunteered to join. The Taganrog "*druzhiny* of workers' guard" (*sic*) regulations specifically provided for soldier members, but stipulated that they must have the permission of their unit committee.[29] A suggestion of the relative frequency of soldiers comes from the 18 towns and industrial settlements of the Central Industrial Region mentioned earlier that gave data on the social composition of their Red Guards; only two included soldiers.[30] The best overall figures on soldier participation are the statistics on the social composition of the Red Guard provided by the Tsypkins. They show that soldiers made up 2.4 percent of guardsmen in the Central Industrial Region (including Moscow) and the Urals, but 5 percent in the Volga region, where there were numerous large rear garrisons in the major Volga cities.[31] What is clear from all data is that the number of active-duty soldiers in the Red Guards was slight; their main value was as instructors and as a source of arms.

Women made up a component—usually minor—of the Red Guards in many places. In Moscow they made up a relatively large element—6.7 percent (as against perhaps 2 percent for Petrograd). G. A. Tsypkin attributes this high Moscow figure to the large percentage of women in the work force—a reflection of the role of the textile industry there. However, he calculates that only 2.25 percent of the Red Guards of the Central Industrial Region were women, and states that the figures for the Urals and the Volga region were similar.[32] As in Petrograd, women mainly served in first aid groups attached to Red Guard units or else as messengers, clerks, or staff providing food to guardsmen. A few women, such as R. S. Samoilova and T. F. Liudvinskaia in Moscow, took a leading role in organizing the Red Guard, but this was uncommon and seems to have occurred mostly in the course of local Bolshevik Party work.

The party orientation of the Red Guards throughout the country seems to have been pretty much the same as what we saw in Petrograd, Kharkov, and Saratov—that is, the Red Guards drew on members of all parties and of none, with the Bolsheviks assuming an increasingly prominent role as the year wore on. Most Soviet historians who give statistical breakdowns show the Bolsheviks making up about half of all guardsmen, members of other parties a small percentage, and members of no party the rest.[33] As we stated in connection with V. I. Startsev's figures for Petrograd, this does not tally with the memoir and contemporary sources. Biases in the data and in definitions—G. A. Tsypkin, for example, asserts that in Moscow the Red Guards took only Bolsheviks as members before the Kornilov Affair,[34] which simply is not so unless the term is used in some special way—explain this distortion. Some Soviet historians, however, do admit to extensive participation by adherents of other leftist parties. P. I. Garchev, in his study of the Ukraine, for example, acknowledges significant participation by members of other parties in the Red Guards of Poltava, Chernigov, Kiev, Vinnitsa, Odessa, Nikolaev, and other localities, including Sevastopol', where as late as the beginning of 1918 nearly all of the 250–400 guardsmen were Mensheviks or SRs.[35] In Sormovo, a large industrial center near Nizhnii Novgorod, both the Mensheviks and the SRs played an active role in the workers' militia; one early participant states that the SRs and Mensheviks "went about draped with bombs and revolvers," and the commander in the summer was an SR.[36] As late as December the Red Guard there had 300 Bolsheviks,

200 SRs, and 40 Maximalists.* [37] At Odessa the Red Guard at first was under SR influence and then was dominated by an anarchist, Khaim Rut, who is described as having been very popular among unemployed workers (apparently a significant element). Only later did the Red Guard come under Bolshevik influence. [38] There are examples of Mensheviks, SRs, and members of other leftist parties playing an active role in other cities, including as commanders. Though the central leaderships of the Menshevik and SR parties were hostile to the Red Guards, local leaders often supported them, as did rank-and-file members. This was true also of the Jewish Bund: in Samara the local leaders on October 28 announced support for "soviet power" and called on their supporters to join the Red Guard, upon whom "the task of accomplishing the transfer of power has fallen." [39] The outlook and activism of local party leaders were the determining factors, reflecting the intensely local orientation and origin of the armed worker bands.

The resolutions calling for the establishment of Red Guards, and even the Red Guard regulations, often stipulated multiparty participation. The statutes for the Moscow Red Guard drawn up on September 3 called for a Central Staff that included three representatives from each political party in the executive committees of the Workers' Soviet and of the Soldiers' Soviet. At the Briansk Arsenal Factory, a resolution on forming a Red Guard passed in a general meeting of the workers on August 30 specified an organizing committee including one member from each political party. In Bezhitsa, the soviet set up a revolutionary committee on August 29 that called for a *druzhina* and invited all SRs, SDs, anarchists, and trade unionists to join. [40] Such provisions were common and suggest not only that non-Bolsheviks did play a role, but that it was an accepted fact that they would.

Even when we correct for the bias of later writings, the fact remains that the Bolsheviks did play the most prominent role in the workers' militias and Red Guards and that their prominence increased as the year wore on. Many Mensheviks and SRs went over to the Bolsheviks, especially in September, and nonparty guards-

---

* The term Maximalist was used in 1917 to refer to SRs and SDs taking extreme left positions, those pushing for fulfillment of "maximum" rather than "minimum" party programs or objectives. In the provinces the reference is usually to leftist SRs; in Petrograd it was more generally used for the left wing of the political spectrum, including sometimes Bolsheviks or Menshevik-Internationalists.

men tended to join the Bolsheviks rather than other parties. In fact there seems to have been a dual process at work: Bolsheviks were joining the Red Guards (the Party often encouraged this), and non-party guardsmen were signing up as Bolsheviks, the one party that gave the Red Guards unqualified endorsement. Certainly, the same maximalist mentality, impatience, and urge to action characterized both Bolsheviks and Red Guards; such a mental set was conducive to membership in both. This notion is supported by the fact that in Moscow a disproportionately large percentage (one-third) of the Bolsheviks who joined the Red Guards had joined the Party before 1917. This suggests that the same commitment and activist—even extremist—mentality that had led them into illegal political activity in the most radical revolutionary party made the Red Guards attractive, especially since the Red Guards were the most voluntaristic form of revolutionary activity in 1917 and the one most likely to involve them in violence. Moreover, the Red Guards were semilegal in many places at different times in 1917, which would influence who joined.

Related to party membership is the matter of the existence of party *druzhiny*. As we have noted, there were few such *druzhiny* in Petrograd, and they played for the most part an unimportant role. Party *druzhiny* seem to have been more common in the provinces, where they were usually very small, were formed by a political party from its own members, and remained at the disposal of the local party leaders. Usually these *druzhiny* had limited functions, their main purpose being to provide an armed guard for party offices and meetings. Sometimes, however, their functions tended to overlap with those of the broader workers' armed units to involve general "protection of the Revolution." The Bolsheviks and SRs seem to have had the *druzhiny* most active along these lines. Bolshevik *druzhiny* existed or local committees resolved to form them in many places, including Kiev, Astrakhan, Nizhnii Novgorod, Ufa, and Pskov. There are also a number of references to SR *druzhiny* before October in Yaroslavl', Tula, Voronezh, and elsewhere.[41] Menshevik *druzhiny* seem to have been very rare, perhaps because the Mensheviks lacked both the Bolsheviks' voluntarism and the SRs' heritage of party fighting units or terrorist bands. The line between these party *druzhiny* and the Red Guards was not always distinct. Party *druzhiny* often merged into the Red Guards, especially in the fall.[42] The Bolsheviks in particular sometimes tried to limit local Red Guard units to Party members or supporters. For example, A. V. Savel'eva, at the Nizhnii Novgorod Provincial Bolshevik Conference (held from September 30 to October 2) stressed the need to limit the Red Guard "to the circle of Party comrades and to subject it to strict Party discipline."[43] Where the Bolsheviks controlled the soviet before October, the distinction between the Red Guard as a Party organization and as a soviet organization (or an organization of all the workers) sometimes became blurred.

There are some special characteristics of the Red Guards in the country as a whole not found in Petrograd, and in some instances not even found in other large cities such as Kharkov and Saratov. One such was the tendency to look to Petrograd itself (and Moscow) for guidance, inspiration, or justification in the formation of armed worker units. Though the urge to arm and organize themselves was initially spontaneous and was acted on without much knowledge of what was happening in Petrograd, the authority of Petrograd was such that by the second half of 1917 workers' militia and Red Guard organizers did look to the example of the capital. Thus the workers at the Zlokazov Chemical Factory in Ekaterinburg, in a resolution of September 5, called for arming the workers "on the example of the workers of Petrograd," and the Cheliabinsk Bolshevik organization cited the existence of a Red Guard in Petrograd in their own resolution on organizing a Red Guard in the city (September 13).[44] At Rodniki, a village in Kostroma province, the workers called for a Red Guard based on the example of "red Presna" (a militant district of Moscow).[45] The influence of Petrograd is seen clearly, too, in the tendency to adopt for local use Red Guard regulations developed there (usually the April regulations of the Vyborg District Soviet) either whole or in part. We have seen this already in Kharkov. The Vyborg regulations were adopted with a few changes in Odessa and in the Alafuzov district of Kazan in May, and in Ekaterinoslav in June.[46] The regulations adopted by the Tsaritsyn Soviet in October draw heavily on those established by the *piaterka* in August. Finally, as we noted earlier, the Saratov Soviet adopted the October regulations of the Petrograd Central Komendatura before the latter officially did so! Many of these documents were readily available in the press. Others, however, such as the *piaterka* regulations and those of the Petrograd Central Komendatura at the time the Saratov Soviet adopted them, could only have been transmitted by personal contacts. Sometimes delegates to meetings in Petrograd were instructed to look into the Red Guards while there. We have seen how the Kharkov Bolshevik organization instructed its delegates to the April Party congress to look into the workers' armed organizations in Petrograd; the Odessa Bolsheviks did the same, charging G. Achanov, a delegate to the First All-Russian Congress of Soviets at the end of March, to familiarize himself with the armed organization of the Petrograd proletariat.[47]

Another special feature of the armed workers' bands in the provinces is the role of veterans of the fighting *druzhiny* of 1905. These *druzhiny* had existed in many places in 1905 and had played a more prominent role in the provinces than in Petrograd. G. A. Tsypkin's sample of 2,000 former Moscow Red Guards showed that only 3.6 percent had participated in fighting bands in 1905; his smaller sample of former guardsmen from the Central Industrial Region showed only 2.25 percent.[48] Yet other literature suggests that these veterans played a more prominent role. In some places, especially the industrial settlements, they apparently were an important component of the 1917 armed *druzhiny*. For example, a report from Asha-Balashevo in Ufa province in October reported that a "core of fighters from 1905" was important in the organization of the Red Guard there. Indeed, in the factory and mine settlements of the Urals, where there had been extensive organization of *druzhiny* in 1905, veterans of those bands seem to have been especially active in 1917. In some parts of the Urals, especially Ufa province, a local term used in 1905 was again used in 1917 as the name for armed bands: Fighting Organizations of the Armed People (*Boevye otriady narodnogo vooruzheniia*). These Fighting Organizations seem to have been paramilitary, factory-based, and very militant. In the Central Industrial Region there had been numerous and fairly large armed detachments in 1905 in the industrial settlements, especially in Vladimir, Kostroma, and Iaroslav provinces, and memories of those and veterans from them played a role in the new armed bands in 1917.[49]

Mostly, however, the importance of 1905 and its veteran *druzhi-niki* lay in providing a source of inspiration and leadership rather than a significant number of guardsmen. At Ufa, in the Urals, two members of a *troika* set up in April to organize the local fighting *druzhina* were members of fighting detachments in 1905–6. At Orekhovo-Zuevo, a Bolshevik meeting in the spring decided to organize a fighting *druzhina*, using the lessons learned in 1905. The Central Staff for the Red Guard set up at the Moscow Workers' Soviet in May undertook to study the 1905 armed uprising there for applicable lessons. In Moscow also a 1905 brochure—"Tactics of Street Fighting," by one Vychegodskii—was recirculated.[50] Moreover, there is some similarity between the Regulations of the Workers' Fighting *Druzhina* of the Moscow Committee of the RSDRP of 1905 and the Regulations adopted by the Moscow Soviet in September of 1917. The members of 1905 *druzhiny* also were a useful source of instructors where military veterans or soldiers were unavailable. Overall, the influence of 1905 on the Red Guards seems to have been greatest in the provinces, especially the Urals, and in those few places where there had been active armed detachments in 1905. In this respect it is noteworthy that 1905 seems to have consciously influenced thinking in Moscow, where there was bitter street fighting in 1905, much more than it did in Petrograd, where there was not.

In the provinces the general impulse in organizing Red Guards came from the factory—as it did also in Petrograd, Saratov, and Kharkov—but there were some notable local variations. Two such, which overlap, are the role of trade unions and the role of the railway workers and railroad repair shop workers. In many places railway workers made up a large portion of the local proletariat. We have seen in Saratov that the railway depot and repair shop workers had one of the largest and best organized Red Guards. Sometimes the railroad workers, especially in the repair shops, formed their Red Guard through their factory committee, but at other times they formed it through their union, with the focus at a given railroad depot or repair shop. The Kornilov Affair gave special impetus to the formation of *druzhiny* among the railwaymen, for it emphasized the critical role of the railroads in moving troops for counterrevolutionary purposes. At Voronezh a meeting was held on September 1 to organize a railroad workers' fighting *druzhina* to combat counterrevolution. At Minsk two *druzhiny* were formed during the Kornilov Affair on the Aleksandrovskii Railroad. They patrolled the Minsk station and the railway lines in the city's outskirts. They continued after the Kornilov Days, numbering about

300 at the end of September and armed with an adequate supply of rifles and two machine guns. In October they merged into a larger Minsk Red Guard organization.[51] In Odessa a separate Red Guard of railway workers was established October 1 with the special function of protecting railway shops and stations. It had the unique feature of having its members drawn from lists supplied by political parties: SDs, SRs, Ukrainian SDs, and Polish Socialists. Red Guards of railwaymen were even set up in October in Irkutsk and in Novonikolaevsk.[52] The railway workers seem to have been the most active in organizing *druzhiny* by union, in part perhaps because they had one of the best organized unions and because of their political importance. There were other union-based *druzhiny* besides those of the railwaymen, although they were small in number compared to those formed at factories. Still, they played a more important role in the provinces than in the capital. In Odessa the needleworkers' union even set up a special commission to encourage other unions to organize Red Guards. In Moscow there were Red Guard units formed by the unions of leatherworkers, metalworkers, tailors, and workers in precious metals.[53]

The role of local soviets, both in forming and in directing the Red Guards, varied from place to place. In some instances the soviet supported and encouraged these Red Guard units, in others it opposed them, and in yet others its attitude was ambivalent. In many smaller cities and towns the soviet supported some sort of armed workers' organizations and often played a role in their creation. This was especially true during and after the Kornilov Affair, when a great flood of local soviet resolutions called for formation of Red Guards.[54] Even so, the soviet role in forming Red Guards was basically one of encouragement and limited assistance—the actual formation of units depended on the factories. In many places, however, the local soviet opposed formation of Red Guards, seeing them either as useless or as potential tools of opposition party elements. This was especially the case in cities where the soviet was Menshevik- and SR-dominated and suspected the Bolsheviks of being the organizers of the Red Guards. The *druzhiny* formed at the Arkhangel woodworking factories were opposed by the Arkhangel Soviet, which was Menshevik-SR–dominated: a Soviet letter of October 21 stated that the Red Guard was harmful and pointless.[55] Opposition from the local soviet leaders was no more effective in preventing Red Guard formation in the provinces than it had been in Petrograd. It deprived the Red Guards of a useful source of support and legitimacy, but it did not block them, given their factory base. Indeed, soviet opposition reflects one of the important characteristics and strengths of the Red Guards: the ability of their organizers to utilize whatever institutions were at hand, so that if the soviet did not support them, for example, they could turn to a factory committee, trade union, or party committee. Lack of soviet support probably handicapped and slowed the Red Guards, but it did not stifle them.

In many instances, the relationship between a local soviet and the *druzhiny* or Red Guards was more complex than simple support or opposition. Often units were formed in the factory or at party behest, and then the soviet was left to take a position. It was difficult actually to oppose the idea of armed workers, but at the same time the soviet leaders often mistrusted these groups. Odessa is a good case in point of how complex the relationship often was, even before the rise of the Bolsheviks became a complicating factor. There the Soviet on March 18 established a "Department for Public Order," which seems to have been intended to regulate the various workers' militias in their city guard duties. The leaders of the Department soon came into conflict with the Soviet leadership, however. On April 8 they rejected a Soviet order to carry out general safeguarding functions and refused to guard "bourgeois goods" or to work under "Kadet commissars." They also announced their transformation into a "Department for the Red Guard (Workers' Militia)." Apparently they withdrew from general guard work and began to undergo a transformation into a more political organization, which soon got them into trouble with the Soviet. On at least three occasions in the spring they engaged in activities that brought them censure from the Odessa Soviet Executive Committee, including a resolution to take away all arms and keep them locked up under the control of the Executive Committee. This failed.[56]

The Odessa conflict clearly illustrates how such popular and factory-based worker organizations could go their own way despite nominal dependence on higher political bodies such as a soviet. How much easier, then, for a factory *druzhina* that lacked even nominal direct connections. Over these the local soviet had even less control, especially if the organizers deliberately sought to avoid it. At Lys'eva (Perm province), for example, the Bolshevik organization of the Lys'eva Ironworks and Shell Factory met on October 1 to discuss organizing a Red Guard, and even read draft regulations for it. The discussion centered primarily around whether it should be created as a soviet or as a party organization. The latter view prevailed on the grounds of the danger of losing the Red Guard should the soviet become "opportunist," i.e., Menshevik or SR.[57] This discussion reveals one feature of 1917—and the Red Guards— easy to forget today. In retrospect we see an unstoppable (un-stopped, anyway) process of bolshevization. However, from the perspective of the time, even in those areas where the soviet was already Bolshevik (as this one apparently was), there could be no certainty that new developments might not result in loss of that control. Therefore, the prudent local Party leader might opt to have such a *druzhina* or Red Guard not too closely tied to the soviet. This helps explain the frequently expressed concern for Party control over or dominance in the Red Guards long before there was any conscious intent to seize power. Indeed, local party organizations— usually but not always Bolsheviks—often took a leading role in organizing Red Guard units. Normally, however, they did it through a factory or soviet rather than through the party organization itself.

The soviets did play a critical role in larger provincial cities, however, when the guardsmen sought—as they inevitably did—broader organization and a greater political role. The urge for central coordination and leadership among the many individual factory units seems to have been as strong as the contrary urge to self-assertion, self-direction, and autonomy. These two mutually exclusive sentiments kept up a tug-of-war throughout 1917. To the extent that broader organization was achieved, however, it depended almost exclusively on the soviets. In general, the role of the soviet and the degree of central organization tended to vary widely and to be determined largely by two factors: Bolshevik control of the soviet, and the presence of vigorous local Red Guard leaders. Where the Bolsheviks gained control of the soviet there tended to be more support for strengthening and coordinating the Red Guards. Even then, however, a Bolshevik soviet did not mean *effective* leadership in the Red Guard organization; that depended on the skill and vigor of local leaders in welding the factory units together. What bound the Red Guards to the soviets was the notion of "soviet power."

When a local soviet espoused that position, it was better able to organize the Red Guards around itself; when it did not, its relation to the Red Guards remained ambivalent—the guardsmen almost always accepted that the soviet was the primary spokesman for worker interests—and the Red Guards organized more around factory, trade union, or party. In general, then, as the Bolsheviks gained control of local soviets, and as the concept of soviet power became general among workers, the soviets took on a more active role in the Red Guards.

In earlier chapters we have attempted to answer the three related questions of the size, arms, and training of the Red Guards for Petrograd, Saratov, and Kharkov. To extend our estimates to the entirety of Russia is fraught with the danger of serious error, especially on the question of size, where we cannot take refuge in descriptive terms but must venture a stark and naked figure. Let us nonetheless tackle the problem and the wide range of estimates that exist. David Collins, who has traced the various estimates and tried to evaluate them, notes that there has been a tendency to scale down earlier estimates and himself calculates between 70,000 and 100,000 Red Guards.[58] V. P. Verkhos', in a recent Soviet assessment, lists the *known* Red Guards by province and comes up with a minimum count of 100,752 by October 1917.[59] These estimates seem much too low. First of all, as Verkhos' himself acknowledges, there are numerous cities and towns in which it is known that Red Guard detachments existed but for which no figures are available; their inclusion would increase the size estimates considerably. Second, the number of guardsmen was considerably larger in some places than Verkhos' suggests. We have seen that in Saratov there were about 2,700 armed guardsmen on October 27; Verkhos' lists only 1,500. Tula is an excellent example of the variety of figures available for a single locality, with estimates ranging from zero to 60 to 500 to 1,000 (in addition to an SR *druzhina* of 200 and an anarchist unit of unknown size); Verkhos' lists only 60, much too small a figure.[60] Third, there is the problem of definition, particularly the tendency of some writers to limit the term "Red Guards" to Bolshevik-led or Bolshevik-affiliated groups. As we noted in connection with Petrograd, this leaves out not only the many armed workers who were only loosely attached to any organization, if attached at all, but also many of those organized into groups calling themselves *druzhiny*, workers' militias, and so forth; moreover, it leaves out Red Guard units in places where the leadership or soviet was not Bolshevik. Many authors tend to assume the Bolshevik connection, and this leads to seriously underestimating the size of armed workers' bands. The Bolsheviks and the Red Guards, much less other armed bands, were *not* coterminous.

Some indication of how much higher the total figures might be can be found in the most recent major Soviet work on the Red Guards, that by G. A. Tsypkin and R. G. Tsypkina. Extending their earlier separate studies on Moscow and the Central Industrial Region, the Tsypkins have made an extensive count of Red Guard units in that area and a sketchier study of the Volga and Urals region. In determining size they have not only compiled an extensive chart of factories where the Red Guard was known to exist (with size where available), but calculated a total figure for all of them based on the general size of such units and the ratio of factories where the size is known to that where it is not. Thus they tally 11,500 guardsmen in the 110 factories where the size of the unit is known (or some reasonable figure exists), and by extrapolating for the other 183 factories, they estimate a total Red Guard size of 30,500.[61] By contrast, Verkhos' estimates only 14,474 for this region.[62]

What emerges from all of the above is that the figure of about 200,000 that traditionally has been used by Soviet historians may be closer to the fact than some recent downward revisions. If we take the figure of 100,752 used by Verkhos' as a minimum base, and allow a considerable increase on the basis of the findings of the Tsypkins for the Central Industrial Region alone, then we probably have over 150,000 Red Guards for the country as a whole. In addition, we must make some allowance for those workers who were in some sort of armed workers' organization not included in these figures (even the Tsypkins tend toward a narrow definition of the term "Red Guard"), not to mention those individual workers who had arms that they were willing to and would use to achieve "soviet power" during and after October. In fact, we may not be far short of the traditional 200,000. Even that figure does not include the rapid and enormous growth of the Red Guards *during* the October

Revolution. The Tsypkins estimate that in Moscow, for example, they went from 8,500 to 30,000![63]

More important than numbers, however, is how strong and influential the Red Guards were in the local context, their ability to dominate a locality physically or to threaten to do so. That ability depended on such factors as morale, leadership, and the availability of arms and of training in their use. How well armed were these workers? The answer to this varied, not surprisingly, from place to place. In some cities and localities they were well armed, whereas in others they were not; much depended upon the initiative of local leaders and the proximity of and access to arms depots or friendly troops. What is clear is that the acquisition of arms was taken very seriously and that their possession was a very important psychological factor which grew in importance as the year wore on and social tensions increased. Getting arms, especially rifles and ammunition, became a major preoccupation. The first arms, acquired during or shortly after the local "February Revolution," were taken from the old police, seized from private citizens or local stores, or received from soldiers. This last source, so important in Petrograd in the early months, was less valuable in the provinces, however, for the soldiers had not mutinied as they had in Petrograd and hence there was less opportunity or inclination to hand rifles to the workers. Until midsummer the workers' bands generally were not well armed.

During the late summer and fall, especially after Kornilov, systematic attempts to get weapons in quantity began. The methods varied, and some of them speak eloquently of the mood of the workers and the breakdown of social order. In locales where local soviets were supportive, they themselves often undertook to get arms for the *druzhiny* or Red Guards. Sometimes this took the form of appeals to the Petrograd Soviet or the All-Russian Central Executive Committee to help them, as at Ekaterinoslav, where the Soviet asked the Central Executive Committee to intercede with the Provisional Government to help it get arms.[64] This evinced a gross misunderstanding of the posture of the Menshevik-SR leadership in Petrograd on this issue. Even in Moscow the Red Guard leaders in September sent delegates to Petrograd to try to obtain arms. Other cities, ironically, appealed at the same time to Moscow for arms. Smaller communities often turned to provincial centers for help.

Thus for example the Red Guard at the factory settlement of So-
bino, 250 strong, asked for and got arms from the Vladimir Soviet.[65] The Kostroma Soviet received numerous requests from village soviets asking for arms.[66] Sometimes local forces pressured the
cities to provide support: at Kanavino, a militant industrial settlement near Nizhnii Novgorod, the Red Guard staff told the Nizhnii
Novgorod Provincial Temporary Revolutionary Committee in early
October that if the latter did not provide arms, the Kanavino Red
Guard would not respond to calls from the Committee for assistance.[67] If there was a garrison or arms factory nearby, the Red
Guard sought arms from it. For example, the Izhevsk Soviet (in
Viatka province in the Urals) demanded in late September or early
October that the local arms factory turn over 500 rifles, 75,000 cartridges, and 50 revolvers for its fighting *druzhina*. The factory
director asked the local garrison commander to guard the arms
stores, but in a telegram to the government's Main Artillery Administration (which owned the factory) he revealed that he feared the
garrison soldiers would give out the arms regardless and felt himself
helpless to prevent it. Indeed, on October 5 the Izhevsk Soviet
resolved that if the factory management continued to refuse arms
for the Red Guard, then the executive committee was authorized
"not to stop short even of organized revolutionary seizure of the
arms."[68] A similar incident occurred in Kiev in September. There
the Executive Committee of the Kiev Workers' Soviet requested
that General Oberushev, the Commander of the Kiev Military District, provide arms for the fighting *druzhiny*, implying that the
Committee would get them by "revolutionary methods" if they
could not be gotten legally.[69] This type of demand upon military
factories and arms storehouses was common.

One special feature of the provinces, reflecting perhaps a lingering respect for legality, is the frequency of offers to pay for arms.
Sometimes the local soviet offered to pay, and sometimes the workers took up a collection among themselves. Collections are found in
places as diverse as the Minin Factory in Moscow and at Iasinov in
the Donbas, which sent four workers with money to Petrograd to
purchase arms from the Sestroretsk Factory.[70] Such collections were
often the fruit of all the workers in a factory contributing a day's or
a half-day's salary, or working a Sunday with all the money going to
the fund. In other instances, such as the Lefortovo district in Mos-

cow, stage performances were held to raise money for the purchase of arms. Sometimes the workers took a sort of halfway position between paying and outright seizure of arms: General Iashcherov in Omsk reported various groups demanding weapons for arming the Red Guards and *druzhiny*, some offering money but some wanting them on credit from the state treasury! At Vichuga, in Kostroma province, as early as April 19 the local soviet resolved to organize a Red Guard and demanded that the Provisional Government arm it at public expense.[71]

Often, however, the workers themselves simply seized arms. A frequent method was a raid on a storehouse or a shipment of arms. At Sormovo, for example, in the summer a group of Red Guards slipped into the arsenal at the local fortress and made off with a store of arms.[72] In smaller towns and factory settlements a newly formed Red Guard or workers' *druzhina* often simply seized the arms of the local militia, accomplishing two goals at one stroke: obtaining arms and replacing the militia-police of the city authorities with a workers' armed force. Thus they became the only armed organization in the town (at least if there was no garrison). Normally they also took over public safety functions. At Ust-Katavsk in the Urals, for example, the workers of the railway wagon factory formed a Red Guard in September and seized all the arms of the town militia. The commander of the militia appealed to the soviet, which decided that since the Red Guard had also undertaken the guarding of the population, there was "nothing blameworthy in these actions."[73] This method sometimes was used in larger cities: in Moscow the Mar'inskii Subdistrict Soviet in October helped workers seize the rifles of the local City Militia commissariat.[74]

A major source of arms was army units, especially in the fall. Arms were acquired from them in both small and large quantities. Sometimes the local soviet undertook to get arms from the local regiment, but at other times the Red Guards themselves got them from the regiments' stores. Often arms were transferred directly from individual soldiers to individual guardsmen. This usually was a gift, but sometimes soldiers sold their own rifles or those of the regiment: in Moscow the workers of the Vtorov Factory bought six rifles from the guard at the Khamovnicheskii barracks. A variation was to seize them from soldiers. At the industrial settlement of Liubertsy, near Moscow, a special Red Guard detachment was set up at the railway station to confiscate arms from soldiers passing through the station on their way from the front. They obtained enough rifles not only to equip their own Red Guard but also to give away to nearby factories, and they also got some machine guns.[75]

In these and other ways—as in Ekaterinoslav, where city officials agreed to give arms in need of repair to the Red Guard, who could get them repaired[76]—the Red Guards and workers' *druzhiny* gradually acquired weapons. The Provisional Government and militia authorities tried to stop this flow of arms, but their orders either were ignored altogether or proved unenforceable locally. Local officials in turn often were frustrated by the lack of response from the central government when they sought guidance; General Iashcherov's (Omsk) complaint in October to General Lekhovich (head of the Main Artillery Administration in Petrograd) that he still "awaited an answer to my [earlier] inquiries" was typical.[77] Though many local soviets and Red Guard units continued to complain of arms shortages—a long list claimed inadequate arms in their response to the questionnaire filled out at the Second All-Russian Congress of Soviets—clearly there were hundreds of thousands of rifles and other arms in the hands of workers across Russia by the time of the October Revolution.

The amount of training received by these armed units varied widely across Russia. In some areas there was fairly extensive training—in the industrial settlements of the Urals, for example—whereas in others the Red Guard was little more than a poorly armed assemblage that was organized more on paper than in reality. However, some general characteristics of training emerge time and again across Russia. One is how instructors were acquired. Here the pattern we have seen in the three focal cities holds. Instructors came primarily from among workers who had had military service, and varied in quality accordingly. The second main source of instructors was soldiers from a local garrison. On occasion a deserter or absentee from the army or navy served as instructor, and sometimes in the provinces (but not in Petrograd) prisoners of war. These usually are identified as Austrian or Hungarian; references to Germans are rare. One example is the instructor at the industrial settlement of Iksha, an Austrian noncommissioned officer named Shubert, who is described as having a "strong revolutionary mood" and who trained a Red Guard in which not a single worker had prior military experience.[78] In general, local Red Guard or *druzhina* organizers seized upon whatever instructors were at hand, with whatever qualifications they could offer, although some of the better organized Red Guard staffs or local soviets made more systematic efforts to obtain qualified instructors. Sometimes local units appealed to Petrograd, Moscow, or other large cities to provide instructors. A few local Red Guard leaders attended the special school for instructors set up by the Bolsheviks' Military Organization in Petrograd in September.

The actual training itself also varied by locality. Most of the available local regulations or instructions governing Red Guard units make some sort of reference to training, and some go into considerable detail. At Taganrog the regulations provided for training twice a week on the grounds of the local garrison; at Omsk it was to be done twice a week under direction of officers and noncommissioned officers of the garrison provided by the Soldiers' Soviet.[79] Some of the regulations, and numerous soviet or factory statements on *druzhiny* and Red Guards, simply refer to training as the responsibility of the detachment commander. Training usually was done fairly openly, but sometimes it was covert, especially before September. An unusual example is the training that took place at a "club" in the Butyrskii District of Moscow, at which the guardsmen shut up the windows and played the radio loudly in an attempt—probably futile—to muffle the sound of the firing.[80] Training was handicapped by shortages of arms and, especially, cartridges. There was reluctance to squander the supply of cartridges at training sessions, yet the guardsmen needed shooting practice. The need for arms and cartridges for training purposes was a common theme in requests to army or city officials for supplies. There were even rare instances of guardsmen drilling with wooden dummy rifles.

The vigor of local leaders and the availability of arms and instructors determined the amount and quality of training in any given place. Overall, however, training increased significantly in the fall. It was based on the assumption that any improvement in military skill was desirable and that a reasonable amount could be achieved in a fairly short time. This was training not for sophisticated military operations, but for direct confrontations and overawing rivals. Even where minimal, such training would increase the confidence of the guardsmen and perhaps lessen that of their opponents. This was not an unimportant consideration, for during the October Revolution morale and bluff usually were more important than military skill or action in deciding the issue locally. Where fighting took place, whatever training and discipline the Red Guards had acquired was all the more important.

Discipline was a major concern of Red Guard leaders and organizers. It was treated as a serious matter, with both political and military implications. One of the most common charges hurled against the various workers' *druzhiny* was that they would engage in illegal and violent activities and even degenerate into robber bands. The specter of 1905, when some did turn in this direction, was frequently invoked. The organizers, however, were more concerned that tight discipline be maintained in order to insure that orders would be carried out during fighting and that there would be no looting or other arbitrary actions. As we have seen in the case of Petrograd, many of the Red Guard regulations provided for strict punishment for violation of discipline or any activity such as looting; this same pattern held in the provinces. The common range of punishments was outlined in the Samara regulations, in September, which listed four degrees of punishment: (1) comradely talk; (2) expulsion from the *druzhina*; (3) expulsion from the factory; and (4) boycott of the person.[81] It is surprising, and indicative of the willingness of the workers to impose harsh punishments on their peers for infractions of agreed-upon rules, that the regulations envision expelling the person not only from the unit but from the factory—that is, from his livelihood. In Odessa, the Red Guard regulations adopted by the Workers' Section of the Odessa Soviet on April 30 stipulated that the names of expelled guardsmen be published in the local *Izvestiia*.[82] Discipline was enforced by the workers themselves: the Odessa regulations, and others, specified that the offenders would be tried by some sort of Red Guard court or other workers' agency, such as the factory committee that sponsored the detachment.

For what purposes were these workers' militias, *druzhiny*, and Red Guards formed, armed, and trained? The reasons behind them were, in broad outline, fairly uniform across Russia and similar to those we have seen expressed in Petrograd, Saratov, and Kharkov.

Local peculiarities existed, but generally the broad purposes held and are repeated over and over in factory and soviet resolutions and in the statutes and regulations drawn up to govern the Red Guards. They fall into two broad categories: first, the defense of public order and personal security, especially among the workers; and second, the defense of the Revolution, and especially worker interests in it.

Maintaining public order and security—especially guarding factories and working-class districts—emerged as a concern of and reason for armed workers' bands during the February Revolution, in Petrograd and elsewhere. This order-keeping function remained a role for most of them, although there were exceptions (the Odessa Soviet's "Section of Public Order" declared on April 8 that it would no longer guard bourgeois goods and persons or perform police work—to the dismay of the soviet leaders). Some regulations said that the Red Guard would act to keep order only in emergencies,[83] and all mixed in a political role as well. Demands for new worker armed units in the summer and fall often cited a need for public order as a justification for their formation. At Liudinovo in Kaluga province the local soviet chairman on September 14 called for the formation of a Red Guard because irresponsible people were terrorizing the population and the militia could not cope with them.[84] The workers at the Kyrkalov Factory in Maimaks, near Arkhangel, organized a volunteer force to patrol the area at night because of the problem of theft and hooliganism. The union of workers and employees in woodworking factories in the Arkhangel area took this up on October 9 and, citing the inability of the regular militia to deal with hooliganism and theft (they said that the militia "fears to stick its nose out of the building, especially now in the long dark nights of fall"), called on the Arkhangel Soviet to help in organizing a Red Guard.[85] Often the workers' guards were seen as specifically protecting workers and their factories—their source of economic livelihood. An article by Iu. Slesarev in *Sotsial-Demokrat* (Moscow) on August 22 noted that a rash of factory fires in Moscow and elsewhere was putting workers out of jobs and argued that the workers needed to form well-armed *druzhiny* to guard the factories—perhaps even, the author hinted, against the owners themselves. Slesarev ended with an exhortation to "Guard your own factories! Arm yourselves!"

The other main set of reasons given for the Red Guard was to defend against counterrevolution, protect the gains of the Revolution, and advance worker interests. These political ideas tended to be intermingled. The statements about defending the Revolution tended to be general, but they increasingly took on a sharp we/they tone as the general crises and divisions in Russian society became more evident. Some clearly looked forward to class warfare and named the "capitalists," "bourgeoisie," or "privileged classes" as the enemy. The regulations of the Ekaterinoslav workers' guard, adopted by the soviet in late September, mentioned as one purpose to "fight together with the revolutionary army against counterrevolutionary antipeople intrigues by the governing classes." Those adopted by the Odessa Soviet as early as April 30 gave as one purpose the defense of the class interests of the proletariat in the struggle with capitalism and the bourgeoisie. At Rostov-on-Don, a meeting of factory committee representatives on September 26 decided to organize a Red Guard, one reason being that class tensions were growing and the workers must be prepared to defend themselves against counterrevolution and to fight for a socialist order.[86] References to the need for protection against pogroms, Black Hundreds, and "dark forces," which generally were lumped together with "counterrevolution," were common. Fears, vague and specific, of the threat from those who represented a conservative outlook or the old privileged order were the motivation behind these references. The weakness of the right, so clear in retrospect, should not obscure our appreciation of how greatly it was feared and how real the potential for a successful counterrevolution seemed from the perspective of 1917, especially after Kornilov.

The issue of the need to defend the Revolution often raised the question of the relationship of the Red Guard to the army. In the provinces as in Petrograd, moderate socialist leaders often tried to argue that the Red Guard was unnecessary because the "revolutionary army" was the real force defending the Revolution, against whom the Red Guard was nothing. Advocates reversed the argument, arguing that the army would soon be demobilized and then the workers would be defenseless against counterrevolution. This argument was a running theme in the debates over the Red Guard in Moscow, where the Soldiers' Soviet was separate from the Workers' Soviet, and is found in debates on the Red Guard in many places, large and small. In some instances an underlying suspicion of the soldiers manifested itself in suggestions that a Red Guard was necessary in case "counterrevolutionary officers" reasserted control over the soldiers. Generally, however, the assumed forthcoming demobilization of the army was linked with fear of counterrevolution as a justification for the Red Guard.

The range of issues is shown in a rare record of the soviet debates that produced the decision to form a Red Guard in Kolomna, in Moscow province. P. Mochalin, a local Red Guard leader (whose party ties are not identified by later Soviet editors and hence who probably was *not* a Bolshevik), spoke of the need to organize and arm the Red Guard as a force against counterrevolution, adding that the soldiers could not be relied upon for that purpose. A Soviet member named Rodin argued against him, stating that no counterrevolutionary mood existed among the people, and that if such were to develop the Red Guard would be unable to stop it. I. Petukhov, a Bolshevik, supported Mochalin, citing the example of Petrograd and Moscow as proof that the desirability of forming a Red Guard was recognized by all socialist factions (not quite an accurate statement on his part) and opposed only by Kadets and counterrevolutionary elements. One Petrushin also supported the idea of a Red Guard, citing again the impossibility of relying on the soldiers, who might be sent away and replaced by Cossacks or military cadets who could crush the unarmed workers. S. V. Sarychev argued that in all revolutions the workers had lost out because they were not armed. Moreover, he warned, the Kornilov Affair had shown the danger that still existed in the "struggle between the bourgeoisie and the proletariat for power," and the bourgeoisie might not be so easily defeated again. Therefore the Red Guard was essential. However, another Soviet member, Tsvelen'ev, argued against it on the grounds that if the army went over to the counterrevolution the Red Guard could not oppose it. He added that current economic disorder and unemployment did not allow its formation, and charged that the Bolsheviks by their policies were driving the greater part of the democratic elements from the Revolution. Mochalin responded by again stressing the need for the Red Guard, this time linking it to the need to have a force to protect the workers and poor peasants, especially after the army was demobilized. Tsvelen'ev then proposed that the Red Guard question be transferred to the political parties for organization of *druzhiny* for self-defense. Mochalin proposed that the soviet organize the Red Guard. Mochalin's resolution carried.[87]

These were typical of the main arguments made for the Red Guard. There were others, too, ones that often evolved in practice. The Red Guards protected demonstrations and meetings. Often they gave clout to worker demands on management, sometimes arresting administrators. During strikes they defended the workers. At strikes in the Urals in August and September they set up guard posts at factory gates and refused to let anyone enter.[88] During a wave of strikes in Odessa in the summer, Red Guards cleared strikebreakers from the Il'inskii Sugar Factory.[89] Ultimately, however, the deep-seated feeling of a need to have weapons and their own armed organization as an expression of self-assertion and control of their own destiny was the underlying justification for the formation of Red Guards. Nothing illustrates this more than the resolution by the workers in the Kronstadt factories in early October to form a Red Guard,[90] for in few places was a worker armed force as redundant in terms of combating counterrevolution as in this stronghold of armed sailor radicalism. Even those who were generally skeptical of the role of armed workers' bands sometimes recognized this element: I. A. Isuv, a Menshevik member of the Executive Committee of the Moscow Soviet of Workers' Deputies, in a debate on arming the workers on August 30, deprecated their fighting significance but acknowledged their importance as a "moral force."[91]

The "moral force" factor proved extremely important in the October Revolution, but the fighting role was not insignificant either. The course of "October" in the provinces depended upon a host of local conditions: the political makeup of the local soviet, the social composition of the community, the presence and attitude of army garrisons, the vigor of local political leaders, and so on, including the size and organizational level of the Red Guard. In many cities and provincial centers the transfer of power was carried out swiftly and easily, with little armed confrontation. In these instances the local soviet usually was already Bolshevik-controlled, quickly assumed full authority in its own hands, and called for the Red Guards or Red Guards and soldiers to seize key points in the city. Thus at Podolsk in Moscow province the chairman of the soviet and commander of the Red Guard, N. G. Chizhov, a Bolshevik, organized the declaration of soviet power and the Red Guard seizure of the railroad station, post office, telephone exchange, bank, and other key points on October 26. At Kolomna on the 26th the Red Guard, under orders of the Military Revolutionary Committee set up that day by the soviet, arrested the district commissar of the Provisional Government and seized the main buildings in the city and patrolled the streets.[92] Similar quick seizures of power took place in other cities and towns of Russia, especially in the industrial settlements and towns of the Central Industrial Region north and east of Moscow (e.g. Orekhovo-Zuevo, Serpukhov, Ivanovo-Vosnesensk) and in the Urals. The Tsypkins state that soviet power was achieved quickly and peacefully in 93 cities and industrial settlements of the Urals, reflecting the fact that most of the soviets were Bolshevik-controlled and the Red Guards already well established there.[93]

In many places, despite Bolshevik control of the local soviet, the enforcement of soviet power required an armed confrontation in which the Red Guards took an active role but there was little actual fighting. Saratov is a prototype of this kind of situation. In Smolensk, for example, the Bolsheviks pushed through a resolution in the Soviet on October 26 calling for soviet power, upon which the Mensheviks and some SRs went to the City Duma and helped form a Committee for the Salvation of the Fatherland and Revolution. This was followed by some minor fighting, with the anti-Soviet forces stronger than in Saratov thanks to support from Cossack units. By November 1, however, the Soviet forces had won, using troops and Red Guards. The same pattern held for the main Volga cities—Kazan, Samara, and Tsaritsyn—and for most of the larger cities of the Central Industrial Region north and east of Moscow, including Tver, Nizhnii Novgorod, and Vladimir. In many of these cities the Red Guards from nearby or suburban industrial settlements played a major role, as in the case of Sormovo and Kanavino near Nizhnii Novgorod.

In a few instances more extensive fighting was necessary during the week following October 25. The prime example is Moscow, about which, because of its importance, a few words should be said. In Moscow the Bolsheviks dominated the Workers' Soviet but not the separate Soldiers' Soviet, which left control of the soldiers in doubt and made the Red Guard more important. A Military Revolutionary Committee was formed only on October 25, and even then included for some time Mensheviks opposed to the seizure of power. Overall, the local Bolshevik leadership was not prepared for the new Revolution: their control over the garrison was not as sure as in Petrograd; the Red Guard was smaller and lacked even the degree of central leadership found in Petrograd; and many top leaders were in Petrograd at the Second All-Russian Congress of Soviets. These factors, plus hesitation among the Bolshevik leaders and firmer action among opponents in the Committee of Public Safety and especially by Colonel K. I. Riabtsev, commander of the Moscow Military District, set up a prolonged confrontation marked by alternating periods of negotiation and armed clashes.

The role of the Red Guards in the October Revolution in Moscow seems to have been significant.[94] For one thing, most of the 30,000 soldiers of the garrison played no role, and many did not have arms. At first only 5,000–6,000 could be relied on by the Bolsheviks. Even those who participated did so not as a part of units such as regiments but as individuals or in small groups, often composite soldier–Red Guard units. The Red Guard, by contrast, numbered about 8,500 on October 25 and ballooned to about 30,000 by November 1. Most of these new recruits were not trained, but they provided an overwhelming numerical superiority even if only part of them took any more active role than patrolling worker districts. In Moscow, despite the emphasis traditionally put upon the fighting there, overawing opponents was usually the key element in taking or holding strategic points (such as buildings, stations, and bridges) and whole areas. The Red Guards were especially active in this type of action. Moreover, the ability of the Red Guards to play a role was strengthened by two other developments. First, they finally got adequate arms. On October 28 a guardsman named I. T. Markin found a shipment of about 40,000 rifles at the Kazan Railroad Station, which were quickly seized and distributed. Other arms were seized at other railroad depots in the city, including wagonloads of shells. These were distributed throughout the workers' districts, so that for the first time the workers were well armed and, moreover, had an abundance of cartridges to expend (their opponents did not). Second, Red Guards from the surrounding provinces began to arrive in significant groups from October 29 on, numbering several thousand before the fighting ended. Not only did this boost morale, but the fact that these men came from a distance suggests that they were more than usually committed and determined. Indeed, they took part in the seizure of key points in the last days of the struggle.

Overall, it is clear that a huge number of armed workers took to the streets. The many accounts of the October Revolution in Moscow—like those of Petrograd—describe one strategic point being taken by soldiers, another by Red Guards, yet another by Red Guards and soldiers, leaving us with the almost impossible task of disentangling the relative importance of each component. What is clear is that the Red Guards and other armed workers were an important element. Their sheer size and their factory base made them so in the confused situation in Moscow, where local initiative by district leaders was especially important in the fighting and maneuvers, perhaps more so than directions from the Moscow Soviet and the Military Revolutionary Committee. Later histories, which rely heavily on central Party records and accounts of its leaders, tend therefore to understate the role of the armed workers and Red Guards. Indeed, the workers often showed greater militancy than the Bolshevik leaders, as demonstrated by the general strike of October 29 and the denunciation of the truce of November 2 by some workers and Red Guards who were opposed to a negotiated end to the conflict. Aside from their own direct action, the swelling ranks of the Red Guards must have contributed to the demoralization of the Committee of Public Safety's supporters, who saw their own hopes for outside reinforcements dwindle and disappear at the same time. Although the total number of dead and wounded has never been definitively established, Red Guards were perhaps the largest single group of casualties, numbering in the hundreds. This alone testifies to their vigorous and active role.

In other areas, especially in the Ukraine and in some Russian provinces south of Moscow—Tula, Tambov, and Orel in particular—the struggle for power was more protracted and similar to the Kharkov model. The struggle for control of Tula, which lasted until December, was particularly important because of the arms factory there. It is also of special interest because here we find one of the few references to workers' *druzhiny* ("armed *druzhiniki* of SRs and Mensheviks") acting in support of local political forces opposing the declaration of soviet power. In Tula both the City Duma and the Soviet were controlled by the Mensheviks and SRs, the former party being unusually strong in the factories at this late date. There were several *druzhiny* and Red Guard units before the October Revolution, organized both on a party basis and at factories (Tula was an important metalworking and arms-producing center), but there was no significant central direction from the Tula Soviet. The Bolsheviks responded to the news from Petrograd by forming a Military Revolutionary Committee. Soviet and other local organizations opposed the declaration of soviet power in Petrograd and formed a coalition government, the Committee for the People's Struggle with Counterrevolution. From late October to early December Tula appears to have gone through a process similar to Kharkov's: Bolshevik agitation among workers and soldiers to change the orientation of the Soviet; the formation and expansion of armed worker detachments; a maneuvering for position among the various groups; and, finally, on December 7 the establishment of soviet power and adherence to the Petrograd regime. There appears to have been little or no fighting (Soviet sources generally pass over November in Tula quickly), but the Tula Red Guards did utilize their strategic position to block the movement of supporters of the anti-Bolshevik forces in Moscow and to send arms from local factories to pro-Bolshevik forces. A similar process of bolshevization took place elsewhere, especially in the Ukraine.[95]

Whether the local October Revolution was quick or slow in resolving itself, the Red Guards played an important and usually underestimated role that depended to a great extent on their size and degree of organization, the existence and size of a local garrison, their leadership, and the amount of opposition they faced. This makes simple generalizations about them difficult, for in some places the Red Guards played a critical role, and in others a very minor one. Overall, however, the Red Guards were important in providing both armed force and psychological and moral force for the establishment of soviet power in late 1917. Four factors made their role of great—often decisive—importance, even where they were small in size and weak in organization and training. First, once the issue of "soviet power" was forced by the actions in Petrograd, workers in general defended it with various degrees of active or passive support; those in the Red Guards took an especially active role, even to the point of armed confrontation, to defend the whole array of aspirations and images that soviet power embodied. Second, in almost every situation the number of people, especially armed people, actively engaged in the local struggle for power in October and November was small. Third, since in most instances there was a common desire to avoid bloodshed, morale, psychological pressure, and the ability to overawe or outmaneuver rivals usually counted for more than fighting ability or the actual use of force. In this the supporters of a new order had a distinct advantage over a generally discredited regime for which few people could summon much enthusiasm and for which almost no one was ready to die or even shed blood. Fourth, there was a willingness among many, especially the intelligentsia, to let the Bolsheviks try their hand at government, since they were confident that they would quickly fail. This has often been noted of the Bolsheviks' opponents in Petrograd, nonsocialists as well as socialists. The same was true in the countryside. Indeed, there was a dual psychology at work: among political opponents there existed feelings that perhaps the Bolsheviks had some right to try governing; among workers and other supporters there existed a feeling that their time had come to establish soviet power. In this psychological setting the Red Guards provided the physical threat in a confrontation that their opponents were loath to push to the point of extensive fighting and bloodshed. These factors made the Red Guards, however well or poorly organized and however numerous, a key element in the October Revolution in the provinces.

Epilogue: The Red Guards After October

"The culminating point in the history of the Red Guard was the moment of the October overturn. . . . [Afterward], despite the fact that with the increasingly rapid self-demobilization of the old army the Red Guard become almost the only significant armed force, its importance began to decline."

— *Vladimir Malakhovskii*

"Without the 'red guards' the triumph of Soviet power would have been impossible in the south against Kaledin, Kornilov, and against the venal Central Rada in Kiev. . . . The [Petrograd and Moscow Red Guards] were the best fighting units of the revolutionary detachments that fought under my general command."

— *V. A. Antonov-Ovseenko*

Malakhovskii's statement, though seemingly paradoxical, is a succinct and accurate description of the later history of the Red Guards.[1] Despite their importance in establishing and defending soviet power in the first days and weeks after the October Revolution, the Red Guards were not suitable as a long-range military or militia force. Moreover, in their new role as the defenders of a state order their very character and structure began to change. Fundamental to the Red Guards in 1917 were several features: their voluntary, self-formed, and self-directed nature; their intensely local, usually factory, orientation; their hostile attitude toward established political authority; and their volatile and crisis-oriented membership. Now they had to become an ongoing *supporter* of an existing political system, which required a dramatic shift in structure and mentality. Their voluntaristic and localistic character, a source of strength when faced with hostile governmental pressure, became a liability when the government tried to mobilize them for regular and continuing armed support. Thus Malakhovskii's paradox, that the moment of success for the Red Guards—the achievement of "soviet power" and of a worker-oriented government—marked the beginning of their obsolescence. Indeed, the very issues we have traced to this point are, after October, replaced by new problems of mobilizing a reliable governmental military and police force. Yet the Red Guards still had a critical role to play for some months, as the quotation from Antonov-Ovseenko makes clear, and this chapter will be devoted to a brief account of their activities between the October Revolution and their gradual disappearance by about the middle of 1918.

The Second All-Russian Congress of Soviets, which convened in Petrograd the evening of October 25 and lasted until the morning of October 27, approved the Bolshevik seizure of power and the formation of the Council of People's Commissars (Sovnarkom) as the new government. Led by Lenin, the new regime immediately turned to the problem of consolidating its position. In the short run, this involved suppressing an uprising by opponents inside the capital and defeating an attempt by deposed Minister-President Kerensky and General N. P. Krasnov to bring troops to the city to oust the Bolsheviks. The Red Guards played a prominent role in frustrating both counterrevolutionary attempts.

The first armed threat took the form of an uprising led by Colonel G. P. Polkovnikov and some of the members of the Committee for the Salvation of the Fatherland. The latter was formed on October 26, primarily by Mensheviks and SRs from the Petrograd City Duma, the Soviet of Peasants' Deputies, and the old Central Executive Committee. The uprising was to rely primarily upon cadets from the military schools and to be coordinated with the expected effort of Kerensky and Krasnov to retake the city with troops from the front. Plans for the uprising became known when one of the plotters was captured by a Red Guard patrol with details of the plan on him. Once Soviet leaders learned the news they called on the district soviets, party organizations, factories, and military units to mobilize to suppress the uprising. Forced to commence action on the morning of October 29, earlier than planned, the rebels seized the telephone exchange and a few other points. However, they were quickly surrounded and disarmed by Red Guards, soldiers, and sailors. The main fighting, bloodier than any in the October Revolution, came at the Vladimir Cadet School. Surrounded by large numbers of Red Guards, soldiers, and sailors, the cadets fought back. Over 200 men were killed or wounded before the fighting ended late on the afternoon of the 29th. Other military schools that had not participated and some Cossack and shock troop units who were considered potential threats were disarmed also. In this process, the Red Guards took a prominent role: V. I. Startsev, who tends to be very cautious in asserting the importance of the Red Guards in comparison to military units, claims that they provided the main strength of the Military Revolutionary Committee in the struggle.[2]

Even before the fighting ended, the Soviet Government was also calling for help in meeting the advance of Krasnov's forces, which since October 28 had been just outside the city at Tsarskoe Selo awaiting reinforcements. Though numbering only about 700–1,000 Cossacks, Krasnov's forces represented a major threat for a regime that had doubts about the reliability of its own supporters and that could not be confident about the behavior of the many army units in the area. Calls for support had already gone out to army units, Red Guards, and sailors as early as the 27th.[3] The force that assembled on Pulkovo Heights was composed mostly of workers and sailors, with the former arriving first. The workers included not only armed Red Guards but others who built barricades and dug trenches. Most of these workers came straight from the factory, and they came as whole units, small groups, and individuals. Although their morale was high (as apparently was their readiness to fight—unlike the soldiers, many of whom abandoned the heights before the fighting), they were ill-prepared for any prolonged engagement. Having assembled hastily and directly from work, they lacked field kitchens and other support supplies. Moreover, they lacked organized leadership. Nonetheless, they quickly dug themselves in and prepared to meet Krasnov's Cossacks.[4] When Krasnov surveyed the scene on the 30th, prior to launching his attack, he saw "all the slopes of Pulkovo Heights were dug up with trenches and black with Red Guards."[5] The Red Guards occupied the center, the sailors the flanks. Krasnov launched a futile attack and then, under pressure of a counterattack, withdrew. Soon thereafter Kerensky fled and Krasnov's troops surrendered. In all, between 8,000 and 10,000 armed Red Guards took an active part in the Pulkovo defense and another 4,000–5,000 Red Guards were engaged against the uprising inside Petrograd.[6] (An additional 20,000 or so workers dug trenches.) Thus the defense of the Revolution elicited an enormous outpouring of voluntary effort by the Petrograd Red Guards, many of whom were engaged not in these two major actions but in guarding various strategic points and buildings and in patrol duties. Clearly, most of the Petrograd Red Guard, estimated at about 32,000 at this time, was active in these days.

After the suppression of the immediate challenge to the new regime in Petrograd, the role of the Red Guards began to change; both their strengths and their weaknesses became much clearer in the process. The activities of the Red Guards after October can be discussed in three broad categories. First, there is their role as an internal "militia" or police, as keepers of the new order and guardians of worker interests—an extension in modified form of an old role into a new era. Second, there is their activities as expeditionary forces to extend Bolshevik power and to resist the first efforts at counterrevolution in the countryside. Third, there is their role in the formation of the Red Army. All of these functions evolved out of a constantly changing mixture of idealism and pragmatism, and out of a welter of competing ideas about the kind of armed forces needed for the new republic and the role of workers in the new state (as against that of other social groups, particularly the peasants and soldiers). Moreover, all were affected by the institutional confusion that marked the first months of the new regime.

One of the major functions of the Red Guards after the October Revolution was to take over the general responsibility for maintaining public security, broadly defined. That included taking action not only against thieves but against suspected counterrevolutionaries as well, requisitioning food, protecting liquor stores from looters, and even participating in the beginnings of the Cheka, the political police. In effect, the Red Guards functioned as a replacement for the old city militias, which disappeared after the October Revolution—suddenly in some places, gradually in most. Workers' armed bands, sailors, and soldiers filled the vacuum. Although the Bolshevik leaders had vague theories of arming all the people and of general militia service,[7] and although the new Peoples' Commissariat of Internal Affairs decreed on October 28 that all soviets of workers' and soldiers' deputies should establish workers' militias,[8] there does not appear to have been any clear plan of how this was to happen at first. Rather it was an organic process, accompanied by decisions by local officials to use the Red Guards for this purpose. Popular opinion played a role also, especially in industrial centers, where sentiment for patrols of armed workers was especially strong. In December and January, more systematic attention finally resulted in a series of decrees formally abolishing what was left of the old city public militias in the Petrograd and Moscow regions, and replacing them with the Red Guards or other workers' *druzhiny*.[9]

The Red Guards became engaged in all kinds of general militia activities, including manning guard posts and mounting general patrols. They were charged with preventing "hooliganism," especially in the markets. They were particularly active in combating "counterrevolutionary activities"—arresting those suspected of speculation, for example, and closing down presses. Their activities were ill-defined and varied. For example, in early 1918 the assistant commissar for military affairs, Mikhail Kedrov, asked the Vasil'evskii Island District Soviet to send 50 Red Guards to help in searches and arrests among prisoners of war in Petrograd. On March 2 the Executive Committee of employees of the Commissariat of Trade and Industry asked the same soviet to send Red Guards to arrest people carrying on counterrevolutionary activity in the building. Even after the government had moved to Moscow, Commissar for Foreign Affairs Georgii Chicherin on March 18 asked the Vasil'evskii Island District Soviet to send to Moscow an additional ten Red Guards from the Simens-Shukkert Factory to provide security for the commissariat. Guardsmen of this factory evidently had provided security for the commissariat while it was in Petrograd, for Chicherin referred to needing men familiar with the "life and needs of the commissariat."[10] Meanwhile, various government agencies made use of the Red Guards as their enforcement arm. On November 24 the Sovnarkom authorized local soviets to use the Red Guards in collecting taxes. The People's Commissariat of Justice on December 19 made the Red Guards and workers' militias responsible for enforcing decrees of its Investigating Commission. In a Sovnarkom decree of February 21 written by Lenin and entitled "The Socialist Fatherland Is in Danger," the Red Guards were given the duty of supervising work in trench-digging battalions by "all able-bodied members of the bourgeois class, men and women," and were told to shoot those who resisted;[11] one imagines that they took to the task with some enthusiasm.

One of the major areas of activity for the Red Guards after October was to guard wine stores and, when break-ins did occur, to put a stop to the resulting riots and pogroms. Late November and the first half of December saw a rash of drunken disorders in Petrograd—many involving soldiers—in the suppression of which the Red Guards played a major role, along with sailors and reliable soldiers. Because of the involvement of soldiers, these incidents sometimes resulted in shooting, as at the Petrov Vodka Factory in early December, when the Red Guards had to use an armored car against soldiers from the Semenov Guard Regiment and three Red Guards and eight soldiers were killed. These conflicts, plus the use of Red Guards to disarm undisciplined army units, fueled tensions between soldiers and workers, which reached a high level in December. On December 6 a great meeting of soldier, sailor, and Red Guard representatives was held, the main thrust of which was to assure the soldiers that the Red Guards were not receiving any special privileges (rumors to that effect had circulated) and to stress the importance of forming composite units to deal with drunken riots so that neither soldiers nor workers could charge the others with misdeeds in this area. The Red Guard leaders, especially V. N. Pavlov and K. K. Iurenev, were at such pains to reassure the soldiers that they were less than honest in their statements about the Red Guards (claiming, for example, that they were made up largely of evacuated soldiers and that only 3,000–4,000 had arms—both simply untrue).[12]

The Red Guards also fulfilled special revolutionary functions related to general public security and police activity. Some of these were extensions of pre-October activities—for instance, enforcing worker control of factories or guarding the railroads. Not only were special Red Guard railroad detachments and water transport detachments formed, but as early as November Red Guards in special food detachments were used in Petrograd to search out food stores and in the provinces to secure foodstuffs and ensure their shipment to the industrial centers. Often Red Guards accompanied food and supply trains as special guards. Some later joined the special "food supply requisition army," formed in the summer of 1918 under G. M. Zusmanovich, and got involved in the upheaval in the countryside. Among the guardsmen who lost their lives in the process was one of the main figures of the Petrograd Red Guard, A. A. Skorokhodov.[13] Indeed, these requisition activities took up so much energy at a time when the regime was trying to mount expeditionary forces of Red Guards to send to the various "fronts" that they posed a major dilemma and were the subject of debates over how much of the available Red Guard and soldier resources to use for which purpose.[14]

The activities of the Red Guards as an internal police, whether in keeping order, in enforcing the new revolutionary decrees, or in such special tasks as requisitioning food, led some members to enter the new security organs of the state once they were set up. As local soviets began to regularize order keeping, not unnaturally they often turned to local Red Guard commanders to head their new militias and drew on some of the guardsmen as members. They were backed in this by officials of the central government, who regularly encouraged the local Red Guards to take on militia functions. Participation in the Red Guards led some members into a very different police activity, however—the Cheka. Combating "counterrevolution" had been a purpose of the Red Guards from the beginning, and this role had increased after October. Thus, when the Sovnarkom created the Cheka in a resolution of December 7 it is not surprising that the Red Guards were drawn in. One of the most important Petrograd Red Guard leaders, Evgenii Trifonov, was sent from the General Staff of the Red Guard to participate in establishing the Cheka. About 30 picked guardsmen were assigned to the first Cheka armed formations in Petrograd. In January, the General Staff of the Red Guard ordered all district Red Guard staffs in Petrograd to provide guardsmen to fill out Cheka units. In other cities the Red Guards worked closely with the local Cheka, and in some instances special Red Guard units were organized to work with them. As the Cheka became better and more fully organized in the summer, some of these Red Guard units were reformed into Cheka units.[15]

The militia and police activities caused serious problems for the Red Guards. They considered themselves regular workers who volunteered to take up arms and stations in times of crisis. They were neither free for nor inclined to long-term continuous duty. Thus

they might be called out to put down a riot or guard against a suspected counterrevolutionary demonstration, but frequent calls on
them or requests that they take up long-term guard duty caused difficulties and strained their resources. Also, the question of pay for
time spent on militia duty remained an unresolved problem, caus-
ing friction among guardsmen, factory managements, and the new
government. Moreover, the increased level of demand on the Red
Guards is cited by several authors as the reason for a morale problem in late 1917, and for excesses on the one hand (such as arbitrary arrests and thefts during searches) and refusal to perform
guard duty on the other.[16] Indeed, the Red Guards themselves appear to have been less inclined to do militia duty, especially general
order keeping, than the political authorities were to use them for
this purpose. Symbolic of the different attitudes was the situation
in Moscow, where after the Red Guard Central Staff drafted new
regulations on December 4 that deleted earlier references to maintaining public order as a purpose of the Red Guards the Moscow
Bolshevik Party organization on December 10 resolved that the
Red Guards must carry on this duty until the regular militia was
reorganized.[17]

The demands on the Red Guards, both for militia-police duties
and for service in expeditionary forces, led to proposals to impose a
general militia service obligation. The General Staff of the Red
Guard (Petrograd) adopted a resolution on general service that was
adopted in turn by the City Duma. It was a complex scheme, written by Evgenii Trifonov, for rotating Red Guard service among
workers and "all who support Soviet power." A similar resolution
was adopted in Moscow in December by the Red Guard organization and the Moscow Bolshevik Party Committee, and in January
by the Moscow Regional (Oblast) Party Conference.[18] Such a general service scheme was never in fact instituted—it was unrealistic
as well as contrary to the whole voluntary and self-formed nature of
the Red Guard—but its discussion shows how hard-pressed the
Bolshevik and Red Guard leaders were in December and January
and how much uncertainty and debate there was over what kind of
an armed force the new regime should have. Rather than the old
idea of a general militia service, the Soviet state, under the pressure
of harsh reality, turned to the idea of a new permanent, uniformed,
salaried professional militia. This at first was advanced cautiously,

as in an article by V. Tikhomirov about why such a force was needed and why neither the Red Guards nor the Red Army could substitute for it.[19] Eventually, in the late spring and early summer of 1918, a new militia force did come into being that gradually took over the militia-police functions of the Red Guards and other irregular armed bands.[20]

The second major role of the Red Guards after the October Revolution was to participate in expeditionary forces sent to assist local leaders in establishing "soviet power" and to fight the various opponents of the regime as they appeared (often the two were blended together). The main focus at first was in three geographic directions. One was to the south, where Red Guards were sent to fight both the forces of General Kaledin, who was organizing opposition in the Don Cossack region, and those of the Ukrainian Rada, which sought to detach the western Ukraine from the Russian state. Expeditions to the south were sent first to Kharkov, which the Bolsheviks controlled and where V. D. Bonch-Bruevich set up headquarters in December; from there, often after reorganization or reoutfitting, Red Guard forces proceeded southeast to the Don region or westward into the Ukraine toward Kiev. The second main geographic area was west to the military headquarters at Mogilev and the Belorussian region generally, where the regime needed to establish firm control if it was to take command of what remained of the old army and maintain some semblance of a front against Germany. The third main arena for expeditionary forces was Finland. The Red Guard units used for all these expeditions came from Petrograd, Moscow, and other industrial centers, especially of the Central Industrial Region. Unfortunately, many of the earliest of these ventures are poorly documented in the historical literature. (See Map 3, p. 267.)

The Petrograd Red Guards played an especially important role, and the one best documented. The earliest expeditionary activities by Red Guard units were part of the process of establishing and consolidating soviet power. Red Guard units, from Petrograd and elsewhere, often went to other cities to help out, as we have seen in the case of Kharkov, where some Petrograd Red Guards under the leadership of Zaitsev were active in the first week of December. (The problem with documentation is shown by the fact that the Kharkov expedition is not mentioned in histories of the Petrograd

Red Guard.) Even earlier, around November 11, a Petrograd Red Guard force of about 500 led by V. N. Pavlov, one of the old *piaterka*, went to Mogilev, supreme military headquarters. Its purpose was to help secure Bolshevik control there, for General Nikolai Dukhonin was resisting the policies of the new government, especially the appointment of Nikolai Krylenko as the new supreme commander.[21]

The main Petrograd expeditionary forces, however, were sent out from mid-December onward. On December 11 the Red Guard General Staff instructed all Petrograd district staffs to make preparations to send out "expeditionary corps of Red Guards." This was to include one-third of all the guardsmen of the city, those who were not needed for patrol and guard duty and who could be spared from their factories. They were to report to the specified gathering point on December 14. A force consisting of one-third of the Petrograd Red Guards meant about 10,000 men. The debate in the Vyborg District Soviet shows that many had misgivings about the order, but at least the more militant districts undertook to comply. Although the figure of 10,000 was not reached, this mobilization marked the beginning of serious efforts by the central authorities to raise large expeditionary forces among the Red Guards.[22]

Initially, two battalions of 600–800 men each were sent to Moscow and then on to the Ukraine. The 1st Petrograd Marching Battalion, drawn mainly from the Vyborg district and commanded by K. A. Lifonov, whom we met earlier as a soldier training Red Guards in September at the New Parviainen Factory, left on the evening of December 16. The 2d Battalion, drawn primarily from Vyborg also and commanded by I. P. Vorob'ev, a worker from the Aivaz Factory, left four days later. The two units joined forces in Moscow and on January 6 left for the Ukraine, where they helped establish Soviet control along the Kharkov-Kiev railway line and then joined in the attack on Kiev, entering the city on January 27. In early February part of this force returned to Petrograd (from whence some elements were sent to fight in Finland); the remainder stayed on for fighting in the south.[23] Also in mid-December another force, the 2d Composite Detachment of the Petrograd Red Guard, was formed primarily from Vasil'evskii Island factories. Consisting of about 1,500 men and commanded by Evgenii Trifonov, it left on December 19 for Moscow and proceeded on December 30 to

Kharkov. It participated in fighting to the south, toward Rostov-on-the-Don. That it retained a connection to its home base is shown by the fact that at least once, on February 16, one of its members returned and reported in person to the Vasil'evskii Island District Soviet on its activities. The 2d Composite Detachment returned to Moscow on March 11 and soon afterward entered the new Red Army with almost its full complement. Other units went south during the winter, including the "Second Southern Expedition of the Petrograd Red Guard," a body of about 500–600 men that fought in the Don region and the Ukraine. On this unit's return to Petrograd in early April, some of its members joined the Red Army and 46 men entered the Cheka.

Smaller expeditionary forces were sent west to Belorussia. In addition to the 500 sent to Mogilev in November, a force of about 700 Red Guards left Petrograd around December 12–14. This latter unit, named the 1st Petrograd Fighting Battalion, was composed of Red Guards from 36 factories and was commanded by P. A. Ol'gin, a worker from the New Lessner Factory.[24] Additional detachments left for Belorussia in early January. One, the 2d Fighting Battalion of the Petrograd Workers' Red Guard, also organized by V. N. Pavlov, was the focus of a grand send-off on January 1, at which Lenin spoke. As other units followed, a total of about 1,500 guardsmen from Petrograd came to be involved in Belorussia, where they were concerned primarily with two tasks: disarming unreliable military units, and opposing the "Polish Legion" of General I. P. Dovbor-Musnitskii. Battles with the latter resulted in the Red Guards suffering heavy losses and having to appeal back to the district Red Guard staffs in Petrograd for replacements.[25] In addition, some small detachments of 100–200 men were sent to cities of the northwestern region—Novgorod, Vologda, and others. In all, well over 5,000 Red Guards were sent out from Petrograd in December and January on expeditions to the Don, the Ukraine, Belorussia, and the northwest.[26]

The Petrograd Red Guards also became involved in Finland during this time. Eino Rakh'ia and other Finns organized a Petrograd Finnish Red Guard, with Rakh'ia as commissar and A. Duvva as commander. There were many Finns in the work force of the Vyborg district and in nearby Sestroretsk, both radical strongholds. Thus it was easy, after October, to organize a Red Guard for action in Finland. Officially, this unit at first was attached to the Finnish Railroad Line, which was forced to pay its members' salaries. In January and February increasing numbers of Red Guards from Petrograd and Sestroretsk—mostly Finns apparently—went to Finland to join in the struggle there. Reverses at the hands of Finnish White Guards and the Germans led to more Petrograd Red Guards being sent, some in units recently returned from the Ukraine and more heavily Russian in composition. In a major battle in March lasting nine days, the Petrograd Red Guards and Finnish Red Guards were decisively beaten, with heavy casualties, and forced to pull back from Finland. Between 5,000 and 5,500 Petrograd Red Guards were engaged in Finland between December and April.[27] Allowing for duplication of men who served in both the Ukraine and Finland, V. I. Startsev estimates that 8,000 to 9,000 Petrograd guardsmen served in these expeditionary forces up to April, with over half of them—more than 5,000—going out during the second half of December.[28] E. Pinezhskii, who was active in organizing these detachments, says that virtually all of them had machine gun units, some had artillery (some factories organized special artillery batteries), and most had medical units.[29]

Red Guard expeditionary units were sent from other cities than just Petrograd. Indeed, the 1st Moscow Revolutionary Detachment of Red Guards left Moscow to oppose General Kaledin in the Don region on December 6, well before similar units left Petrograd. This detachment was composed of about 600 men drawn from various districts of the city and commanded by P. V. Egorov. It was followed by a second unit of about 500 men on December 15, which the Moscow Bolshevik Committee exhorted not to allow generals and landlords to cut off food and fuel supplies from the south. Other expeditionary units were formed composed of Red Guards only, of soldiers and Red Guards, and of soldiers only. G. A. Tsypkin estimates that about 4,000 men were sent from Moscow against Kaledin, but he does not indicate how many were Red Guards.[30] Some Red Guard units were sent from other cities and industrial settlements of the Central Industrial Region, including such worker strongholds as Ivanovo-Vosnesensk and Orekhovo-Zuevo. In the later stages of the fight against Kaledin, before his final defeat in late February, Red Guard units from other cities, including Saratov, Sevastopol', and Riazan, joined in the campaign.[31] At the same time, Red Guard units from these and other cities also were being sent into the Ukraine to help establish Soviet control there and defeat the Ukrainian nationalists.

Kharkov served as the funnel into which the Red Guards from Petrograd, Moscow, and other northern centers flowed, and from which they were then sent against Kaledin, the Ukrainian Rada, and other opponents. The exact role of the Red Guard units in the successful winter efforts in the south cannot be gauged exactly but was significant, perhaps decisive. Though some of the Red Guard units, ill-prepared and poorly trained, performed badly, most fought well: R. F. Sivers, who continued to command Soviet expeditionary forces in the south after his role in the Kharkov seizure of power, asked in early 1918 that some Red Guard echelons being sent to the rear be disarmed because of their demoralization, but he noted also that the guardsmen in general had conducted themselves heroically.[32] One early writer and commander, N. Skrypnik, observed that there was a significant difference in Red Guard units according to place of origin: the Petrograd and Moscow units generally were the best disciplined and organized and performed well as expeditionary forces; those from the Ukraine, even from industrial centers such as Kharkov and Ekaterinoslav, performed well close to home but not as expeditionary forces.[33] V. A. Antonov-Ovseenko is especially emphatic about the role of the Red Guards as the key to the regime's survival in the first months. Antonov-Ovseenko was one of the "commanders" at Pulkovo Heights and later was in overall charge of the southern expeditions from his base in Kharkov. He wrote in 1920, in a military journal, that though a few celebrated bolshevized units of the old army and fleet (such as the Latvian Riflemen and the Baltic sailors) were important, "the main fighting strength of the October insurrection and first campaigns was the *Red Guard*."[34]

Though the campaigns against General Kaledin and the Ukrainian Rada in the south and for control of the western regions were especially important, the Red Guards were involved in operations all across Russia, a few of which were smaller-scale versions of the Denikin struggle—i.e., struggles to defeat organized military resistance to the new government. One important example took place in the Urals against General A. I. Dutov, who like Denikin relied on the Cossacks. Here the Red Guard units came primarily from the cities and industrial settlements of the Urals and Volga River region. An effort to defeat Dutov in December failed, in no small part because the Red Guard units were poorly trained and armed, as well as too few. In mid-January a force of about 10,000, a large portion of them Red Guards, finally seized Orenburg and defeated Dutov.[35]

In his study of the composition of the Petrograd Red Guards, V. I. Startsev discovered that disproportionate numbers of younger men volunteered for the expeditionary forces. His figures, based on the Vyborg, Vasil'evskii Island, and Petrogradskii districts, are dramatic: 62.4 percent of Red Guards in expeditionary forces were 22 and under, whereas only 38.5 percent of the Red Guards overall were in that age group.[36] The lack of family responsibilities among many young workers, and the greater likelihood of such workers having fewer skills than older workers and thus being less needed at the factory or simply unemployed, are two possible explanations for the decided age skew in the expeditionary forces. We have seen that unemployment was a serious problem in Petrograd from the summer of 1917 on, and there is evidence that Red Guard recruiters actively sought to enlist the unemployed for expeditions—at least this was specifically mentioned in the debate in the Vyborg District Soviet on December 14 on how to meet the government's call for 10,000 men.[37] Also, pay to unemployed guardsmen turns up regularly in the fiscal records of the district Red Guard staffs in Petrograd.[38]

The youth of the expeditionary forces of the Red Guards also affected their party composition, for the Bolsheviks were less well represented in them than in the Petrograd Red Guards as a whole. Bolsheviks were 42.7 percent of the Petrograd Red Guards but only 37.9 percent of those going to the Ukraine, 40.4 percent of those going to the "Kaledin front," and 39.9 percent of those going to the Belorussian region.[39] The disparity is not as sharp as in age, however, which suggests both that young Bolshevik Red Guards volunteered especially heavily and that younger men were less likely to be members of political parties.

These generalizations about who went to the "fronts" and who stayed are the more intriguing when compared to who participated in the October events *in* Petrograd—the October seizure of power, the military cadet uprising, and the Krasnov-Kerensky attack. The figures for the same three districts show that in the 22-and-under age category only 35.7 percent participated (this category was 38.5 percent of the guards)—and this was before mobilization for expeditions depleted their numbers. Thus the more mature Red Guards, in their later 20's and 30's, participated very actively in those events near home despite their reluctance to join expeditions.[40]

The age discrepancy pattern manifested itself again when recruitment for the Red Army began: among those who had joined expeditions (younger men) there were many volunteers for the Red Army, whereas among those still in the city (older men) there were widespread resignations from the Red Guard upon hearing of possible mobilization into the army. With the younger men away on expeditions, the Red Guards remaining in Petrograd by February must have included disproportionate numbers of mature family men—men willing to turn out from their homes to do guard and patrol duty and even to defend the Revolution in a moment of crisis, but not men willing to go off on long-term expeditions or into a regular army, not even a "new" one. Since Startsev argues that about 10,000 Petrograd guardsmen had joined the new Red Army by March 1918,[41] and since the figure of 10,000 is only a little larger than that of the expeditionary forces, who tended to go over into the Red Army en masse, this suggests that relatively few Red Guards went into the Red Army without first volunteering for the expeditionary forces. In other words, among the Red Guards, who already represented the more adventuresome and activist workers, there was probably a stratum of younger, more adventuresome, more militant, and perhaps disproportionately unemployed men who both joined the expeditions and made up the initial enlistment of guardsmen in the Red Army.

The evolving role of the Red Guards was closely linked to the great debate about what kind of permanent armed force the new Soviet state should have. The Bolsheviks had consistently demanded the abolition of the standing army and its replacement with an arming of all the people. Though a useful slogan and ideological posture—and one shared in principle by other socialist parties—it left the Bolsheviks with little in the way of concrete ideas about what to do with the real military problems facing them, both from the Germans and from opponents within the country. Indeed, it probably delayed the development of the Red Army, for it created ideological roadblocks to the establishment of a new but more or less regular type of army. These roadblocks had to be overcome, as did opposition by some of the Bolsheviks and Left SRs who were most dedicated to the idea of an entirely new type of armed force and who viewed the workers' Red Guards as the embryo of such a force. Thus the period up to the end of 1917 was one of debate and searching as the Bolshevik chieftains sorted out and tested their ideas.

The efforts of the People's Commissariat for Military Affairs and other organizations concerned with the military were at first directed primarily toward ensuring some control over the rapidly disintegrating old army (or, perhaps more critical, ensuring that no opponents exercised any control over it) and maintaining some semblance of a front against Germany. By mid-December, however, three basic positions had emerged about how to build a new armed force: (1) use units of the old army; (2) create special Red Guard corps; and (3) create a new type of army, what some proponents called a "socialist guard."[42] The third idea was close to the Red Guard concept in that it envisioned drawing upon the industrial workers as the core element, but it differed significantly in its goal of a single, centrally organized force rather than one composed of many local and autonomous Red Guard units. It received important support when Nikolai Krylenko, the Bolshevik army supreme commander, on December 25 issued an order to create a new army of the armed people, the "Revolutionary People's Guard," the "embryo of which is the Red Guard of the Working Class."[43] Others were simultaneously calling for or organizing—in Petrograd and elsewhere—new armed forces called by such various names as the Socialist Army, the Red People's Guard, and the Revolutionary Red Army. All of these developments pointed in the same direction— toward the creation of a new army, but one relying heavily on the existing Red Guards as a reliable core and bolstered by new volunteers, including soldiers of the old army. Still, there was plenty of room for disagreement over such issues as the social composition of the army, the degree of voluntarism, and universality of service.

Practical events were pushing in the same direction. A new collapse on the German front in December led the Bolsheviks to rush as many Red Guards forward as possible, especially from Petrograd and Moscow, as well as to try to raise new forces. This pointed up the problem with using the Red Guards: quite aside from their military training and quality, their size was inherently limited, and they had already been drawn upon heavily for expeditionary forces, especially of their most adventuresome members and those most readily spared from militia guard duties and factory production. They could not provide the numbers envisioned now: 300,000 men in the next 8–10 days had been called for on December 22 to meet the German-Austrian threat alone; more were needed to fight internal enemies and establish control in areas such as the Ukraine. Faced with harsh reality, the Sovnarkom on January 15, 1918, issued a decree calling for the formation of a "Workers' and Peasants' Red Army"; three days later it formed an "All-Russian Collegium for the Organization and Administration of the Worker-Peasant Red Army." The All-Russian Collegium was headed by five men: N. V. Krylenko, K. A. Mekhonoshin, N. I. Podvoiskii, V. A. Trifonov, and K. K. Iurenev. The latter two had a long and close association with the Red Guards and were drawn from its General Staff. The Red Guards and their leaders expected to play a key role in creating the new Red Army and had asked the Sovnarkom to insure that the Red Guard leaders would have a voice equal to that of the military men.[44]

The decree of January 15 creating the Red Army left the role of the Red Guards ambiguous, neither calling for their disbandment nor incorporating them directly into the new Red Army. The latter policy was not feasible for two reasons. First, there was an economic limit to the number of workers who could be taken out of production, just as there was a political limit to the number of Red Guards who could be spared from militia and other police duties. Second, the organizers of the new army had to face the unpleasant reality that among the guardsmen who remained after recruitment for expeditions there was significant resistance to being mobilized for expeditions or the front. Many were willing to serve in the Red Guards at home but not to be incorporated into any army, old or new. From recruiting records we find that on February 19 in the Vasil'evskii Island district there was an "exit from the ranks of the Red Guard after [the] announcement of the possibility of transforming the Red Guard into [a Red] Army"; a week later in the Obukhov district (site of the Obukhov Steel Mill) half the Red Guards "laid down [their] arms and dispersed" after learning of the mobilization plans. There were similar problems in provincial cities.[45] Nor was it feasible to disband the Red Guards. For one thing, until the Red Army was formed they were a critical source of armed support. For another, it was ideologically unthinkable at the time to disband them, for the idea of the Red Guards as the first step in the abolition of armies and the arming of all the people had not yet died. Indeed, the idea of a universal Red Guard obligation on the part of all workers had been formally proposed by Vladimir Trifonov in late November, was still alive, and was endorsed by the Moscow Regional (Oblast) Bolshevik Party Conference as late as March 10.[46] Moreover, the regime probably could not have abolished the Red Guards even if it wished to, given their local orientation, and indeed had some difficulty when it later decided to disband them. And finally, many local leaders interpreted the decrees on the Red Army as meaning either that the Red Guards' functions would be broadened or that the two entities would exist side by side.

The official decrees on the Red Army may have left the status of the Red Guards uncertain, but there was no uncertainty on the part of the Red Army organizers about the potential usefulness of the Red Guard staffs in the mobilization tasks they faced. They realized that the staffs were an invaluable resource and quickly moved to use them. In early February the All-Russian Collegium and the Petrograd Defense Committee ordered the establishment in Petrograd of district Red Army staffs, including a recruiting commission made up of two representatives from district soviets, two from the Red Guards, and one from the All-Russian Collegium.[47] Although there was some resistance, this marked the beginning of the use of the Red Guard apparatus to staff the Red Army and of the merging of the two staffs. On March 2 the Petrograd Defense Committee ordered the district soviets of Petrograd not only to organize district Red Army staffs but also to oblige their Red Guard staffs to enter and participate in them. In the Vyborg district almost all of the Red Guard staff entered the new district Red Army staff. On March 3, representatives from the General Staff of the Petrograd Red Guard, the district Red Guard staffs, the Petrograd Military District Staff, and the Petrograd Defense Committee met and decided (according to a circular of the Vyborg district Red Guard) to merge all Red Guards into the Red Army—both staffs and members. The district

Red Guard staffs began to dissolve themselves, turning their duties over to the Red Army staffs—often the same people—and the Petrograd Red Guard General Staff ended its own existence on March 21.[48] A similar process took place in Moscow and other cities. For example, the Central Staff of the Red Guards of the Donbas announced on February 17 that it henceforth was the Central Staff of the Red Army of the Donets Basin, and the Mariunopol district military commissar stated on March 20 that the local Red Guard Staff was now renamed the Red Army Staff.[49] There are many other such examples. One problem, however, was that Red Guard leaders and staff members often were eager to participate in the expeditionary detachments, thus disrupting the work of local staffs; the Moscow Central Staff of the Red Guard found it necessary to order staff members to stay at their posts.[50]

The rank and file of the Red Guard also entered the new Red Army, although the process was slow and varied from place to place. Some guardsmen, as we have noted, were not willing to enter the Red Army, and some were needed in other capacities. Still, many—probably most—entered. Some transitions were spectacular, as whole Red Guard units, especially expeditionary forces, were transformed into Red Army units: for example, the 2d Petrograd Composite Detachment of the Red Guard (men from Vasil'evskii Island and the Baltic Factory especially) became the 2d Vasil'evskii Battalion of the Red Army. Individuals usually were allowed to opt out when these mass conversions took place, but there was great peer pressure not to do so. Sometimes the local soviet decreed the reorganization, as at Tambov on April 5.[51] This was by no means always a smooth process, however. At a meeting of the 2d Petrograd Composite Detachment of the Red Guard to discuss reorganization into the Red Army, anarchist members strongly opposed the idea of *any* army-type organization and supported a continued Red Guard organization with elected commanders.[52]

Some local soviet and political leaders dragged their feet in merging the Red Guards into the Red Army, and the distinction between the two remained subject to local interpretation. In many places the local soviet encouraged enlistment in the Red Army simultaneously with formation of new Red Guard units or enlargement of existing ones. This was in part the result of confusion and uncertainty about what was happening. Many names and titles for armed units ex-

isted, including variant names for the Red Army, so it is hardly surprising that local leaders, engaged in the day-to-day struggle to establish and defend themselves, organized armed detachments to do
what they felt needed to be done without worrying overmuch about
proper titles. The continued enlistment of men in the Red Guards as
well as the Red Army, however, was also deliberate: sometimes
local soviets and Party organizations continued to organize Red
Guard units as well as enlist men in the Red Army because they
identified the two as fulfilling different roles. The Red Army was
seen as a force to serve elsewhere, but the Red Guards would serve
primarily at home, where they would protect against counterrevolutionaries, perform guard duty, and function as an emergency
reserve for the Red Army. Acting on their own interpretation of
what was needed—and lacking clear policies from above—local
leaders worked out their own course of action on the Red Guards
and the Red Army, and not surprisingly they often emphasized the
importance of the Red Guards to the locality. Resolutions and policies adopted in the late winter and early spring of 1918 commonly
conceded that the local Red Guards must be a reserve for the Red
Army but insisted that they were not a standing armed force and
were to be mobilized only in times of direct danger. The continuing
strength of worker self-assertiveness and of local leaders' desire to
retain some armed forces under their control (i.e., Red Guards)
rather than under central control (the Red Army) is reflected in the
fact that as late as May the Red Guards in about half the country
retained their former form, and in only 47 districts out of 310 had
merged even in part into the Red Army.[53]

Despite the reluctance of some guardsmen and local leaders, the
process of incorporating the Red Guards into the Red Army proceeded. It was pretty well accomplished in Petrograd by the beginning of April, although some Red Guards lingered on into May.
About 10,000 Petrograd Red Guard members (out of a total of
about 30,000) had gone directly into the Red Army by the end of
March, and over 5,000 more entered eventually.[54] In Moscow the
process of transformation took longer, and in most of the rest of the
country longer still, not being completed until late spring and summer (not until early 1919 in the Far East, and October 1919 in Tur-
kestan).[55] The actual physical process was complicated, taking
different paths and forms according to local conditions, and in

many instances only occurring under the pressure of actual fighting against the Whites or Czechoslovaks. It included transforming Red Guard detachments into Red Army ones by decree as well as by voluntary reorganization. Perhaps most of all, it featured Red Guards forming the kernel of new Red Army units. One of the key distinctive features of the transformation of Red Guard into Red Army, as one Soviet historian recently put it, was that the former did not "flow into" (*vlivalis'*, the term commonly used in Soviet accounts) the latter, or "join" it, but rather provided its "kernel," its social base and organizational cell, as well as much of its command staff and Party-political workers. Overall, this historian argues, the Red Guards united worker and peasant volunteers around themselves and provided not only a core but also a new *esprit de corps* and the first traditions of a new Red Army.[56]

Although the nature of the Revolution and the forces of self-assertion it had let loose ensured the continuation of some self-formed and self-directed autonomous bands, the resolution taken at the Fifth All-Russian Congress of Soviets on June 10 formally abolishing such bands not only stripped them of moral as well as legal authority, but can be taken as marking their passing as a significant force in the Revolution. This resolution, which asserted that "the period of casual formations, of self-willed detachments, of amateurish construction, must be considered as over,"[57] reflected both the regime's growing recognition of hard political and military facts and its success in reorganizing the army apparatus.

Still, the ideals of a citizenry in arms and of a militia-type armed force for which the Red Guards would provide the nucleus lingered on, as shown in the creation in 1918 of a special commission to work on creating a "militia army" or "socialist army."[58] The debate between proponents of a new type of decentralized militia army and proponents of a traditional army reemerged vigorously in 1920 as the Soviet leaders struggled with the question of what kind of post–Civil War army the country should have. Ironically, Leon Trotsky, a vigorous proponent of centralized control and command during the Civil War, emerged as the sponsor of a new plan for a decentralized militia system. Adopted at the Ninth Party Congress, which met between March 29 and April 6, 1920, it called for the creation of territorial militias based on industrial enterprises and their agrarian peripheries, with local industrial, trade-union, or other economic personnel providing the leadership cadre. This scheme was vigorously opposed by proponents of a more traditional army structure, including such celebrated Civil War heroes as generals M. N. Tukhachevskii and M. V. Frunze. Moreover, the debate got involved in other political and economic issues such as labor policy, political attacks on Trotsky, and the general turbulence of 1920–21 (including the rebellion of the Kronstadt sailors).[59] Eventually, the ideal of a decentralized, militia-type army, based partly on the Red Guard experience, faded in the face of both the general effort to strengthen central Party control over all branches of government following the Tenth Party Congress in 1921 and the gathering struggle for power, which undermined Trotsky, the most prominent proponent of the militia concept.

Reference Matter

Notes

Complete authors' names, titles, and publishing data for sources cited in the Notes are given in the Bibliography, pp. 361–80.

INTRODUCTION

1. Wade, "The Rajonnye Sovety," pp. 226–40.
2. Shliapnikov, vol. 1, p. 168.
3. Haimson, *The Russian Marxists and the Origins of Bolshevism*.
4. Hasegawa, "The Problem of Power," pp. 613–14.
5. For an example of the eclectic pattern, see Verkhos', *Krasnaia gvardiia v Oktiabr'skoi revoliutsii*.
6. The only books focusing on a single city are Suny, *The Baku Commune, 1917–1918*, and Koenker, *Moscow Workers and the 1917 Revolution*. However, there is a doctoral dissertation on one of the cities treated in this study: Raleigh, "The Russian Revolutions of 1917 in Saratov."

CHAPTER ONE

1. The following material on the districts of Petrograd is drawn from a large number of sources, as well as from the author's experience tramping around Leningrad, a city in which many of the physical features of 1917 are still evident. Probably the three most important specific sources, however, are the introductions to the minutes of the district soviets found in *Raionnye sovety Petrograda v 1917 godu*, Bater's extremely valuable and informative *St. Petersburg: Industrialization and Change*, and the six volumes of *Ocherki istorii Leningrada*.
2. *Rech'*, Mar. 9, 1917.
3. Bater makes this point especially well.
4. Baedeker, p. 173. There is a charming description of Vasil'evskii Island in Almedingen's *I Remember St. Petersburg*, a memoir of her childhood there before the Revolution.
5. Baedeker, p. 177.
6. Rashin, p. 171.
7. Gaponenko, p. 71.
8. *Ibid*.

9. Freidlin, p. 26; Stepanov, *Rabochie Petrograda*, pp. 25–26.
10. Stepanov, *Rabochie Petrograda*, pp. 27–32; Gaponenko, p. 105.
11. Stepanov, *Rabochie Petrograda*, p. 28.
12. Leiberov, "Petrogradskii proletariat v gody pervoi mirovoi voiny," pp. 467–69.
13. Freidlin, pp. 23–24, 28; Gaponenko, pp. 71–72.
14. Keep, pp. 44–45.
15. *Ibid.*, p. 48.
16. Leiberov, "Petrogradskii proletariat v gody pervoi mirovoi voiny," pp. 473–74.
17. *Ibid.*, pp. 467–68.
18. Hamm, p. 190.
19. Stepanov, *Rabochie Petrograda*, p. 44.
20. *Ibid.*, pp. 44–45.   21. Liapin, p. 97.
22. Keep, pp. 43–44.   23. *Ibid.*, p. 49.
24. Senchakova, pp. 186–91.
25. There are numerous accounts of the *druzhiny* by participants. Senchakova gives a general survey of the fighting units in 1905–6, as do the authors of two early works on the Red Guard, G. P. Georgievskii and S. Ventsov and S. Belitskii.
26. See, for example, the biographies in *Geroi Oktiabria*.
27. For example, Georgievskii, p. 64; Ventsov and Belitskii, pp. 5, 12; *Pravda*, May 2, 1917; Kaiurov, pp. 225–27; and Malakhovskii, *Iz istorii Krasnoi gvardii*, p. 10.
28. Tsypkin, p. 108.
29. *Ibid.* Tsypkin maintains this, and the various memoir accounts and biographical materials support it, although these are admittedly unrepresentative of the guardsmen as a whole.
30. Lenin, *Collected Works*, vol. 23, p. 253.
31. The material on the following pages is based on the author's general study of the Revolution over the years. In composing it, however, I drew especially on Hasegawa, *The February Revolution: Petrograd, 1917*, which is probably the best and most detailed account available; I wish to thank Professor Hasegawa in particular for his generosity in lending me his manuscript before publication. The best Soviet history is Burdzhalov, *Vtoraia russkaia revoliutsiia: vosstanie v Petrograde*, parts of which are available in translation in *Soviet Studies in History*, vol. 18, no. 1 (Summer 1979). Of all the many memoirs, one must single out Sukhanov's detailed and colorful rendering, in either the Russian or the abridged English version.
32. Hasegawa makes this especially clear in *The February Revolution*.
33. Hasegawa explores this problem in his article "The Problem of Power in the February Revolution." Wildman, pp. 178–79, makes the same point about the role of the Duma in helping block opposition inside Petrograd and in bringing over some wavering units.

CHAPTER TWO

1. Burdzhalov, *Vtoraia . . . v Petrograde*, pp. 138–39.
2. Leiberov, "Petrogradskii proletariat vo vseobshchei," pp. 42–43.
3. Mitel'man, Glebov, and Ul'ianskii, p. 552.
4. Burdzhalov, *Vtoraia . . . v Petrograde*, pp. 152–54; Shliapnikov, vol. 1, p. 109.
5. Shliapnikov, vol. 1, p. 109.
6. Rafes, p. 187. Linde was active in later crises, but was not a party member.
7. Sukhanov, *Zapiski*, vol. 1, pp. 96–97.
8. P. A. Lur'e, p. 101.
9. Gundorov, pp. 317–20. The Obukhov "revolutionary committee" gives an interesting picture of revolutionary self-organization in February. A young woman student showed up at headquarters and offered to type whatever was needed, thus providing a secretariat. The first typed order was to the cooperative store for bread, butter, tea, and sugar for headquarters. A. S. Gundorov signed it as chairman of the "Revolutionary Committee of the Nevskii District" and, to make it look official, used the seal of the Kornilov (Workers') School, whose premises they were using. With the supplies came a group of women who set up a buffet. Thus encouraged, the committee sent another order, this time to the directorate of the nearby Aleksandrovskii Factory for mattresses to sleep on. The director complied, which made a tremendous impression on all of them: they could order the factory management to do something and be obeyed!
10. Sukhanov, *Zapiski*, vol. 1, pp. 121, 132, 151; Aleksandrov, p. 130.
11. *Izvestiia*, Feb. 28; Shliapnikov, vol. 1, p. 125; Sukhanov, *Zapiski*, vol. 1, p. 155; *Petrogradskii sovet . . . protokoly*, p. 287. There were two issues of *Izvestiia* published on the 28th. The first carried only the general appeal to rally to the Revolution and to organize for its defense—in broad terms and with no mention of a militia. The second issue came out during the afternoon and included the instructions on forming militias. For times, see Sukhanov, *Zapiski*, vol. 1, pp. 150, 155.
12. Sukhanov, *Zapiski*, vol. 1, p. 155.
13. Shliapnikov, vol. 1, p. 126.
14. *Ibid.*, p. 124; Peshekhonov, pp. 220–21. Peshekhonov soon discovered that Surin was a police agent and personally went to the Tauride Palace to arrest him. Ironically, "Peshekhonov" had been used by Surin as a police code name.

15. Iurii Trifonov, p. 64.   16. *Izvestiia*, Mar. 1.
17. *Ibid.*   18. Kel'son, part 1, p. 171.
19. Georgievskii, p. 65.
20. Malakhovskii, *Iz istorii Krasnoi gvardii*, p. 10.
21. Kel'son, part 1, pp. 162–63; *Rech'*, Mar. 5; *Izvestiia petrogradskoi gorodskoi dumy*, 1917, nos. 3–4, p. 212.
22. Kel'son, part 1, p. 162.
23. *Ibid.*, pp. 174–75.

24. *Ibid.*, pp. 163–65.
25. *Ibid.*, part 2, pp. 159–60.
26. *Ibid.*
27. Browder and Kerensky, vol. 1, p. 50; Zenzinov, p. 217.
28. *Izvestiia revoliutsionnoi nedeli,* Mar. 1.
29. "Fevral'skaia revoliutsiia v Petrograde," pp. 72–102.
30. The report of the Organizational Committee filed with the Petrograd Soviet on Mar. 1 was received by Shliapnikov and retained by him. It is in his book, vol. 1, pp. 181–82. See also "Fevral'skaia revoliutsiia v Petrograde," p. 96, and *Izvestiia,* Mar. 1.
31. From the report given in Shliapnikov, vol. 1, pp. 181–82. See also *Izvestiia,* Mar. 1 and 3.
32. "Iz istorii Krasnoi gvardii Petrograda," p. 121.
33. *Ibid.*, pp. 121–22.
34. Kel'son, part 2, pp. 159–60.
35. Peshekhonov, pp. 266–68.
36. Peshekhonov, esp. pp. 289–96; Arzub'ev, "Na sluzhbe u novago rezhima," *Rech',* Mar. 18. Arzub'ev was one of Peshekhonov's assistants, pressed into service largely because he was on the spot and available.
37. Peshekhonov, p. 289; Shakh is also mentioned in Kel'son, part 2, p. 163, and Startsev, *Ocherki,* p. 45.
38. Peshekhonov, pp. 306–7.
39. *Ibid.*, pp. 288–89, 304–6.
40. Ganichev, p. 306.
41. Startsev, *Ocherki,* pp. 44–45.
42. Liapin, p. 93.
43. *Izvestiia,* Mar. 3.
44. Shliapnikov, vol. 1, pp. 130, 167–69, 193.
45. Kaiurov, p. 230.
46. Startsev, *Ocherki,* pp. 43–44. See also Gavrilov, "Krasnaia gvardiia v Vyborgskom raione," *Krasnaia letopis',* p. 93, and Vinogradov, pp. 162–63.
47. *Izvestiia,* Mar. 2; Shliapnikov, vol. 1, pp. 169–70; Kel'son, part 2, pp. 159–60.
48. *Izvestiia,* Mar. 5. This ill-defined region included the area on the east bank of the Neva formerly called the Okhta district.
49. *Raionnye sovety,* vol. 3, p. 179.
50. Aleksandrov, p. 134.
51. Kel'son, part 2, pp. 159–61.
52. Sukhanov, *Zapiski,* vol. 1, p. 215.

CHAPTER THREE

1. Browder and Kerensky, vol. 1, pp. 126, 135.
2. Schapiro, p. 113.
3. This figure is given by Kel'son, part 2, p. 158. He probably was in the

best position to make a reasonable estimate, although he most likely would err on the low side. Startsev accepts his figure and provides some partial data to support it.

4. Kel'son, part 1, p. 167. It is a bit puzzling, but indicative of both the great confusion of the time and the paucity of sources, that Shliapnikov does not mention the efforts of Piatiev and Chernev, and that Kel'son does not discuss Shliapnikov's activities.

5. Kel'son, part 1, p. 174.

6. Shliapnikov, vol. 2, pp. 134–35.

7. *Izvestiia*, Mar. 6.

8. *Petrogradskii sovet . . . protokoly*, p. 24.

9. *Rabochaia gazeta*, Mar. 9; *Izvestiia*, Mar. 10.

10. *Rech'*, Mar. 8, reported that the council of the City Duma had set up a committee including four professors to draw up a draft on a city police. This is probably the committee referred to here; it may also have produced the above-mentioned draft.

11. *Rabochaia gazeta*, Mar. 9; *Izvestiia*, Mar. 9; Shliapnikov, vol. 2, pp. 135–36.

12. *Izvestiia*, Mar. 9; *Rabochaia gazeta*, Mar. 9.

13. *Petrogradskii sovet . . . protokoly*, p. 28.

14. *Izvestiia*, Mar. 12; Matveev, pp. 35–37.

15. "Iz istorii Krasnoi gvardii Petrograda," pp. 122–23.

16. *Raionnye sovety*, vol. 2, p. 96.

17. A good analysis of worker demands—economic and other—in March is in Ferro, *La Révolution de 1917*, pp. 170–84. Worker dignity is discussed in Sobolev, esp. pp. 69–72, and in Devlin, pp. 53–56.

18. Worker control is discussed in virtually every Soviet book on the working class or economy in 1917. Extensive material in English is to be found in Devlin's dissertation and in two articles by Avrich: "The Bolshevik Revolution and Workers' Control in Russian Industry," and "Russian Factory Committees in 1917." See also Rosenberg, "Workers' Control on the Railroads."

19. Kel'son, part 2, pp. 160–61.　　20. Kel'son, part 3, pp. 224–25.

21. Lenskii, pp. 265–70.　　22. Kel'son, part 1, p. 179.

23. Startsev, *Ocherki*, pp. 55–58.

24. *Ibid.*, pp. 57–58.

25. Vinogradov, "Krasnaia gvardiia," pp. 162–63.

26. *Fabrichno-zavodskie komitety . . . Protokoly*, p. 91.

27. The rules are in Pinezhskii, 2d ed., p. 154. See also Rostov, pp. 169–70.

28. N. A. Bogdanov, p. 34.　　29. *Pervyi legal'nyi*, pp. 8, 10.

30. *Ibid.*, p. 36.　　31. *Ibid.*, pp. 71–88 *passim*.

32. *Pravda*, Mar. 26.

33. Both realization of their responsibility to the workers and their actual ignoring of it is reflected especially in Podvoiskii, "Voennaia organizatsiia," esp. pp. 64–65.

CHAPTER FOUR

1. *Izvestiia*, Mar. 10.
2. *Izvestiia*, Mar. 15.
3. Startsev, *Ocherki*, p. 72.
4. Shliapnikov, vol. 2, p. 137; *Izvestiia*, Mar. 21.
5. *Izvestiia*, Mar. 21.
6. *Raionnye sovety*, vol. 1, pp. 72–74.
7. *Pravda*, Mar. 26; *Revoliutsionnoe dvizhenie v Rossii posle sverzheniia samoderzhaviia*, pp. 132–48.
8. *Pervyi legal'nyi*, pp. 71, 88; *Pravda*, Mar. 31 and Apr. 11; *Moskovskaia zastava v 1917*, pp. 181–82; *Revoliutsionnoe dvizhenie v Rossii v aprele 1917*, p. 34.
9. "Iz istorii Krasnoi gvardii Petrograda," p. 123.
10. *Raionnye sovety*, vol. 1, p. 94; Startsev, *Ocherki*, p. 107.
11. *Izvestiia*, Apr. 15; *Pravda*, Apr. 21; *Revoliutsionnoe dvizhenie v Rossii v aprele 1917*, p. 393.
12. M. L. Lur'e, *Petrogradskaia Krasnaia gvardiia*, p. 28.
13. *Raionnye sovety*, vol. 2, pp. 144–45.
14. Rostov, pp. 169–70.
15. *Ibid.*, p. 170, and M. L. Lur'e, *Petrogradskaia Krasnaia gvardiia*, p. 29. The protocol of the meeting, with editorial commentary, is in "Pervoe sobranie po organizatsii Krasnoi gvardii," pp. 178–79.
16. For a brief summary of the April Crisis see Wade, *The Russian Search for Peace*, pp. 37–43. Documents on the crisis are in Browder and Kerensky, vol. 2, pp. 1096–1101, and vol. 3, pp. 1236–48.
17. *Pravda*, Apr. 23; *Delo naroda*, Apr. 26; "Manifestatsii," p. 22.
18. Rostov, p. 174. This seems to be the same confrontation described in Mitel'man, pp. 603–4.
19. TsGAOR, Fond 6935, opis' 6, ed. khr. 77, l. 19.
20. Information on the meeting is in Rostov, pp. 171–72; Pinezhskii, 2d ed., pp. 22–23; M. L. Lur'e, *Petrogradskaia Krasnaia gvardiia*, p. 30; *Revoliutsionnoe dvizhenie v Rossii v aprele 1917*, pp. 412–14. Both sets of regulations are in Pinezhskii, 2d ed., pp. 154–55.
21. Pinezhskii, 2d ed., p. 23.
22. Proclamation reproduced in Rostov, pp. 172–73, and *Moskovskaia zastava v 1917*, p. 156.
23. *Soldatskaia pravda*, Apr. 26 and 27; *Raionnye sovety*, vol. 2, pp. 44–45; *Istoriia Leningradskoi gosudarstvennoi . . .*, p. 150; M. L. Lur'e, *Petrogradskaia Krasnaia gvardiia*, p. 28.
24. Rostov, pp. 176–77; M. L. Lur'e, *Petrogradskaia Krasnaia gvardiia*, p. 31.
25. Rostov, pp. 175–76.
26. *Ibid.*
27. Account in *Rech'*, Apr. 29; Rostov, p. 177.
28. *Rech'*, Apr. 29; Rostov, pp. 177–79.

29. Rostov, pp. 179–80; Fleer, p. 27; *Revoliutsionnoe dvizhenie v Rossii v aprele 1917*, p. 864.

30. Rostov, p. 180.

31. *Pravda*, May 3.

32. *Raionnye sovety*, vol. 1, pp. 135–36.

33. Pinezhskii, 1st ed., p. 19. This statement in the 1929 edition is omitted in the 1933 version, even though the latter generally is fuller and more detailed as a result of information provided by former Red Guard members in response to the first edition.

CHAPTER FIVE

1. Kel'son, part 1, p. 176.

2. *Soldatskaia pravda*, June 17; *Pravda*, June 8; *Raionnye sovety*, vol. 1, p. 199.

3. *Pravda*, June 16, June 22.

4. Liapin, p. 94.

5. Gessen, p. 54. Gessen's article is largely devoted to this question, and is based on the archives of the Society and of various factories.

6. TsGIA, Fond 150, opis' 1, ed. khr. 559, l. 3; ed. khr. 563, l. 3.

7. *Ibid.*, ed. khr. 563, ll. 4, 7, 11, 12.

8. *Ibid.*, l. 14

9. *Ibid.*, l. 29.

10. Fleer, pp. 28–30; *Narvskaia zastava v 1917*, p. 187; Vasilii Vinogradov, "Krasnaia gvardiia," p. 165.

11. See particularly the discussion at a district conference of factory management in the Vyborg district, June 6, in "Iz istorii Krasnoi gvardii Petrograda," pp. 126–27.

12. *Vestnik Petrogradskogo obshchestva zavodchikov i fabrikantov*, June 3.

13. TsGIA, Fond 150, opis' 1, ed. khr. 563, l. 29.

14. Gessen, p. 64.

15. See, for example, the four factories whose factory committee protocols are printed in *Fabrichno-zavodskie komitety . . . Protokoly*.

16. *Raionnye sovety*, vol. 2, pp. 171–72.

17. Kel'son, part 1, pp. 176–77; Malakhovskii, "Kak sozdavalas'," p. 51; Vasilii Vinogradov, "Krasnaia gvardiia," p. 167; Liapin, p. 95; Vasil'ev, part 1, p. 103.

18. Cited in Startsev, *Ocherki*, p. 85.

19. Baklanova, pp. 31–39, 62.

20. TsGAOR, Fond 6935, opis' 6, ed. khr. 77, contains many reports on this theme, from Petrograd and the rest of the country.

21. As cited in *ibid.*, p. 53.

22. Pinezhskii, 1st ed., pp. 23–24.

23. Rosenberg, "Workers' Control on the Railroads," p. D1186.

24. *Revoliutsionnoe dvizhenie . . . v mae–iiune*, p. 291; *Fabrichno-zavodskie komitety . . . Protokoly*, p. 71.

25. TsGIA, Fond 150, opis' 1, ed. khr. 564, l. 30.
26. *Rech'*, May 9.
27. Voitsekhovskii, p. 112.
28. Vasil'ev, part 1, p. 101.
29. Startsev, *Ocherki*, pp. 72–73; *Revoliutsionnoe dvizhenie . . . v mae–iiune*, p. 60.
30. Erykalov, "Krasnaia gvardiia Petrograda," p. 74.
31. Part of the resolution and discussion is in *ibid.*, p. 75. See also Startsev, *Ocherki*, pp. 74–75, and Vasil'ev, part 1, p. 102.
32. *Raionnye sovety*, vol. 1, pp. 199–200; Startsev, *Ocherki*, pp. 74–75.
33. Vasil'ev, part 1, pp. 102–4; Startsev, *Ocherki*, pp. 82–83; *Pervyi legal'nyi*, p. 109.
34. Lenin, *Collected Works*, vol. 23, pp. 287–329 *passim*, and vol. 24, pp. 23–70.
35. This has been commented on also by David Collins in "The Russian Red Guard of 1917 and Lenin's Utopia," where he makes the point that it is really only after the October Revolution that Lenin and the central Bolshevik leaders began to think more precisely about the role of the Red Guard and other proletarian militias in performing police, military, and administrative duties.
36. E. Trifonov, p. 95.
37. Rabinowitch, *Prelude to Revolution*, especially pp. 100–102.
38. *Rech'*, June 6.
39. The account of the Council's activities basically is from Startsev, *Ocherki*, pp. 83–84, who uses mostly archival sources, including memoirs of its members. See also Kel'son, part 1, p. 176.
40. *Rech'*, June 13.
41. Vinogradov, p. 166; Startsev, *Ocherki*, p. 86. On the anarchists in the Durnovo Villa, see Rabinowitch, *Prelude to Revolution*, pp. 64–66, 107–8.
42. For the ideas behind the government's decision to launch an offensive and the Soviet leadership's support, see Wade, *The Russian Search for Peace*, pp. 69–73, 88–92.
43. The best account of the attempt to mount a demonstration on June 10, and of the maneuvering leading to the June 18th demonstration, is in Rabinowitch, *Prelude to Revolution*, pp. 54–106.
44. *Rabochaia gazeta*, June 22, as translated in Browder and Kerensky, eds., vol. 3, p. 1326.
45. *Pervyi legal'nyi*, pp. 185–86.
46. *Novaia zhizn'*, July 4; Znamenskii, pp. 61–63; "Piterskie rabochie ob iiul'skikh dniakh," pp. 19–41; Rabinowitch, *Prelude to Revolution*, pp. 135–76.
47. See Znamenskii, pp. 69–75; Rabinowitch, *Prelude to Revolution*, p. 171; *Rabochii i Soldat*, July 29.
48. The role of the Bolsheviks in the July Days is the main focus of

Rabinowitch's excellent *Prelude to Revolution*, which details the actions of and divisions among the Bolsheviks. The following information is based on that source, especially pp. 161–66 and 174–84.

49. Iurii Trifonov, p. 45; Mitel'man et al., pp. 168–69.

50. See the account of the demonstration's collapse and the assessment of its causes in Rabinowitch, *Prelude to Revolution*, pp. 191–200.

51. Znamenskii, p. 106.

52. Startsev, *Ocherki*, pp. 89–90.

53. Shakhov-Lankovskii, p. 49.

54. Startsev, *Ocherki*, pp. 88–89. Unfortunately, Startsev is the only source of information on the role of the Council of the Petrograd People's Militia. He based his account on archival records, mostly memoirs and biographical sketches of the Council members.

55. Gessen, p. 68.

56. Startsev, *Ocherki*, pp. 94–95, gives numerous examples of searches.

57. Ganichev, p. 315.

58. Liapin, p. 96.

59. *Raionnye sovety*, vol. 3, pp. 268–70; M. L. Lur'e, *Petrogradskaia Krasnaia gvardiia*, pp. 60–61; Wade, "The Rajonnye Sovety," p. 235; *Fabrichno-zavodskie komitety . . . Protokoly*, pp. 142, 300–302; Rabinowitch, *Prelude to Revolution*, p. 223.

60. Startsev, *Ocherki*, pp. 90–92; Barikhovskii, p. 148; *Fabrichno-zavodskie komitety . . . Protokoly*, p. 188.

61. *Izvestiia*, July 14; *Rabochaia gazeta*, Aug. 5.

62. Tsereteli, vol. 2, p. 362. See also Roobol, pp. 156–57.

63. Gessen, pp. 67–69; "Iz istorii Krasnoi gvardii Petrograda," pp. 127–29; TsGIA, Fond 150, opis' 1, ed. khr. 563, ll. 1, 27.

64. Startsev, *Ocherki*, p. 93.

65. *Ibid.*; *Istoriia . . . 'Skorokhod'*, pp. 172–74; Gessen, pp. 70–71; "Iz istorii Krasnoi gvardii Petrograda," pp. 128–30; Chechkovskii, p. 160.

66. Bortnik, p. 274.

67. *Fabrichno-zavodskie komitety . . . Protokoly*, p. 458.

68. Wade, "The Rajonnye Sovety," pp. 234–40.

69. Malakhovskii, *Iz istorii Krasnoi gvardii*, pp. 15–19; Pinezhskii, 1st ed., p. 33.

70. Fleer, p. 28.

71. The records of the *piaterka* were found by Startsev in the Central Museum of the Soviet army, where they had been deposited, and were reprinted in his study of the Red Guard (*Ocherki*, pp. 294–99). The following account is based mainly on those records and some material provided by Iurii Trifonov in the biography of his father, especially pages 6–8 and 69–80.

CHAPTER SIX

1. The most thorough and recent account of the Kornilov Affair is to be found in Rabinowitch, *The Bolsheviks Come to Power*, pp. 94–150. See

also the three excellent articles by Abraham Ascher, Harvey Asher, and J. D. White that examine the Kornilov Affair in detail.

2. *Izvestiia*, Aug. 29, no. 156.

3. *Raionnye sovety*, vol. 3, pp. 292−93; Wade, "The Rajonnye Sovety," pp. 237−39.

4. *Raionnye sovety*, vol. 3, pp. 293−97.

5. *Raionnye sovety*, vol. 2, p. 252, vol. 3, pp. 254−55; Gorin, p. 359; Korchagin, "Razgrom," p. 162; *Revoliutsionnoe dvizhenie v Rossii v avguste 1917 g.*, p. 496.

6. Startsev, *Ocherki*, p. 155; M. L. Lur'e, *Petrogradskaia Krasnaia gvardiia*, p. 78; Chechkovskii, pp. 162−63; *Rabochii*, Aug. 31, no. 9; *Soldat*, Aug. 30, no. 14; *Raionnye sovety*, vol. 1, pp. 224−27; Gorin, p. 360.

7. *Izvestiia*, Sept. 1, no. 159, and Sept. 5, no. 162; *Rabochii*, Aug. 30, no. 8.

8. *Rabochii*, Aug. 30, no. 8; *Izvestiia*, Aug. 31, no. 158; *Rabochii put'*, Sept. 3, no. 1; Rozanov, p. 391; *Moskovskaia zastava*, p. 158; "Iz istorii Krasnoi gvardii Petrograda," p. 133; *Istoriia . . . 'Skorokhod'*, p. 184.

9. Korchagin, "Razgrom," p. 162; M. L. Lur'e, *Petrogradskaia Krasnaia gvardiia*, p. 78; Chechkovskii, p. 164.

10. See Rosenberg, *Liberals in the Russian Revolution*, pp. 175−260.

11. *Vestnik Vremennogo pravitel'stva*, Sept. 3, no. 145; *Raionnye sovety*, vol. 3, p. 298.

12. *Delo naroda*, Sept. 5, no. 14; Pinezhskii, 2d ed., p. 47.

13. *Raionnye sovety*, vol. 3, pp. 303−4; Wade, "The Rajonnye Sovety," pp. 238−39.

14. *Rabochii put'*, Sept. 3, no. 1.

15. *Rabochee dvizhenie*, pp. 266−67.

16. The situation is described in many places. Some of the examples here are drawn from *Oktiabr'skoe vooruzhennoe vosstanie: semnadtsatyi god v Petrograde*, vol. 1, pp. 72−82, and the documents in *Ekonomicheskoe polozhenie Rossii*, vol. 2, particularly pp. 351−53, the report of a conference on supplies held on Oct. 15.

17. *Ekonomicheskoe polozhenie*, vol. 2, pp. 163−64.

18. *Fabrichno-zavodskie komitety . . . Protokoly*, pp. 490−92.

19. Stepanov, *Rabochie Petrograda*, p. 143.

20. Devlin, pp. 236−37, 239−40.

21. Stepanov, *Rabochie Petrograda*, p. 144.

22. *Revoliutsionnoe dvizhenie v Rossii v sentiabre 1917 g.*, pp. 361−64.

23. *Pervyi legal'nyi*, pp. 285−87.

24. Pinezhskii, 1st ed., p. 50.

25. *Protokoly Tsentral'nogo komiteta RSDRP(b)*, p. 53.

26. Avvakumov, pp. 49−50.

27. Regulations are appended to Pinezhskii, 1st ed., p. 109.

28. See Startsev, *Ocherki*, p. 151.

29. His report, filed the next day, is reprinted in Fleer, pp. 36−37.

30. The resolution is in *Soldat*, Sept. 19, no. 29.

31. Pinezhskii, 2d ed., p. 49.
32. *Raionnye sovety*, vol. 3, p. 311.
33. Pinezhskii, 2d ed., p. 49.
34. Pinezhskii, 1st ed., pp. 42–43, 2d ed., pp. 50–51.
35. Chechkovskii, p. 163; Vasil'ev, part 1, p. 104; Baklanova and Stepanov, p. 94; Sergeev, pp. 194–95.
36. "Iz istorii Krasnoi gvardii Petrograda," pp. 137–38.
37. M. L. Lur'e, *Petrogradskaia Krasnaia gvardiia*, pp. 211–13. See also Startsev, "Ustavy," p. 200, about its date.
38. Malakhovskii, *Iz istorii Krasnoi gvardii*, p. 16; Startsev, *Ocherki*, pp. 179–80; *Soldat*, Oct. 13, no. 50. The following description of the conference is from its protocol, published in *Soldat*.
39. Appended to Malakhovskii, *Iz istorii Krasnoi gvardii*, pp. 48–50.
40. *Oktiabr'skoe vooruzhennoe vosstanie v Petrograde: Dokumenty*, pp. 203–4, 209–10.
41. Malakhovskii, *Iz istorii Krasnoi gvardii*, pp. 20–21; Startsev, "Voenno-revoliutsionnyi komitet," pp. 110–11.
42. M. L. Lur'e, *Petrogradskaia Krasnaia gvardiia*, p. 112. Startsev dates it to October 18, on the basis of a document from the commandant of the Peterhof workers' fighting *druzhiny* about a meeting of *druzhiny* representatives to discuss organization (Startsev, *Ocherki*, p. 182; the memo is in *Oktiabr'skoe vooruzhennoe vosstanie v Petrograde*, p. 211). However, it is not clear from this brief memo that it is the first meeting or the one which adopted the regulations. Indeed, Startsev also states in his work that the drafters of a citywide workers' guard regulation had at their disposal at the beginning of October the "draft of the regulations" for the Narva-Peterhof guards. It also is quite possible that the October meeting was to elect delegates to the citywide workers' guard meeting, for such meetings were being held at this time. Thus, it seems likely that the conference took place in early October, about the same date as the Vyborg conference.
43. *Raionnye sovety*, vol. 3, p. 120.
44. Tsukerman, p. 59.
45. M. L. Lur'e, *Petrogradskaia Krasnaia gvardiia*, p. 113; Chechkovskii, p. 167.
46. Pinezhskii, 1st ed., pp. 46–47, 2d ed., pp. 57–60; E. Trifonov, p. 96; Iurenev, pp. 75–76.
47. Startsev, *Ocherki*, p. 167; Chechkovskii, p. 167.
48. Startsev, *Ocherki*, p. 184, from *Rabochii put'*, Oct. 13.
49. *Rabochii put'*, Oct. 25; Pinezhskii, 2d ed., p. 65; Startsev, *Ocherki*, pp. 184–85.
50. The following account is based on Pinezhskii, 2d ed., pp. 67–70, and Malakhovskii, *Iz istorii Krasnoi gvardii*, pp. 16–17.
51. Pinezhskii, 2d ed., pp. 160–62.
52. Iurii Trifonov, p. 80.

CHAPTER SEVEN

1. Pinezhskii, 2d ed., p. 54; Startsev, *Ocherki*, pp. 163–64.
2. *Soldat*, Oct. 13; M. L. Lur'e, *Petrogradskaia Krasnaia gvardiia*, p. 106.
3. *Pervyi legal'nyi*, p. 286; E. Trifonov, p. 91.
4. Ratner, p. 244.
5. Startsev, *Ocherki*, p. 195.
6. Tsinis, p. 101.
7. Tsybul'skii, "Arsenal revoliutsii," p. 250.
8. Matveev, p. 35.
9. Tsybul'skii, "Arsenal revoliutsii," p. 251.
10. Kaiurov, p. 230.
11. Kel'son, part 1, p. 174.
12. Mints, vol. 1, p. 538.
13. Zlokazov, *Petrogradskii sovet* . . . *(fevral'–iiun' 1917 g.)*, p. 55.
14. Kel'son, part 1, p. 175.
15. See the protocols of the *piaterka*, published in Startsev, *Ocherki*, pp. 197–98.
16. M. L. Lur'e, *Petrogradskaia Krasnaia gvardiia*, pp. 77–78; Korchagin, "Narod pobezhdaet," p. 195.
17. Chechkovskii, pp. 166–67.
18. Georgievskii, p. 68.
19. Startsev, "Voenno-revoliutsionnyi komitet," pp. 115, 121; Baklanova and Stepanov, p. 94.
20. Rozanov, p. 400.
21. Korchagin, "Narod pobezhdaet," p. 195.
22. *Ibid.*
23. Startsev, "Voenno-revoliutsionnyi komitet," pp. 135–36.
24. Sergeev, p. 195.
25. *Pervyi legal'nyi*, p. 286.
26. Pinezhskii, 2d ed., pp. 254–55.
27. *Pervyi legal'nyi*, pp. 285–87, 313–16.
28. Tsinis, p. 101.
29. Fleer, p. 29.
30. M. L. Lur'e, *Petrogradskaia Krasnaia gvardiia*, p. 108.
31. Chechkovskii, p. 158.
32. Tsinis, pp. 100–103.
33. Leiberov, "Petrogradskii proletariat v gody pervoi mirovoi voiny," p. 468.
34. Freidlin, p. 31.
35. Malakhovskii, *Iz istorii Krasnoi gvardii*, pp. 11–12.
36. "K istorii Petrogradskoi Krasnoi gvardii," p. 35.
37. Pinezhskii, 1st ed., p. 44; Chechkovskii, p. 166; Podvoiskii, "Voennaia organizatsiia," p. 35.
38. Devlin, p. 310.
39. "Iz istorii Krasnoi gvardii Petrograda," p. 140.

40. Baklanova and Stepanov, pp. 91–92; M. Bogdanov, pp. 22–23.
41. "K istorii Petrogradskoi Krasnoi gvardii," p. 36.
42. Ratner, p. 244; Gavrilov, p. 96.
43. Tsinis, p. 102.
44. M. L. Lur'e, *Petrogradskaia Krasnaia gvardiia*, p. 107.
45. Vasil'ev, part 1, p. 105.
46. Malakhovskii, *Iz istorii Krasnoi gvardii*, p. 13.
47. "K istorii Petrogradskoi Krasnoi gvardii," pp. 36–37.
48. Sondak, p. 182.
49. Podvoiskii, "Voenaia organizatsiia," p. 12.
50. Trotsky, vol. 3, pp. 234–35.
51. Nesterenko, p. 32.
52. Ganichev, pp. 315–16; Vasil'ev, part 1, p. 108.
53. Malakhovskii, "Sanitarnaia chast' Krasnoi gvardii."
54. Nesterenko, pp. 120–21.
55. "K istorii Petrogradskoi Krasnoi gvardii," p. 37.
56. Pasiukov, p. 65.
57. "K istorii Petrogradskoi Krasnoi gvardii," pp. 36–39.
58. Stepanov, *Rabochie Petrograda*, pp. 34–35.
59. Kazakova, p. 201.

CHAPTER EIGHT

1. Startsev discusses his use of these records and general methodology in *Ocherki*, pp. 249–54. We cannot approach his data or his findings uncritically, however. For one thing, his sample runs to January 1918, so that it includes some people who joined the Red Guard after the Bolshevik Revolution. Since our concern is with the Red Guard up to October, and the nature and composition of the Red Guard changed after October, we will have to keep this fact in mind in certain instances. A more serious problem is determining just who Startsev and the Commission meant by the term Red Guard. Startsev sometimes tends to make too sharp a distinction among various workers' armed organizations, especially between Red Guards and workers' militias. Similarly, it is not clear what criteria the Commission used—whether it accepted anyone who belonged to a workers' armed band, militia, or *druzhina*, or only members of organizations specifically named "Red Guard." Startsev's figures show that some registrants had joined in March 1917; but since there were no organizations named Red Guards that early, we cannot be certain whether they later did belong to something called a Red Guard but dated their membership back to their first joining of an armed band, or whether the Commission accepted membership in any workers' armed band as meeting the definition. Nonetheless, it seems that most of the age, origin, and other characteristics—though not all, as we will see—apply whether Red Guard is defined in a narrow or a broad sense, and these records are extremely valuable to any effort to obtain a social profile of these groups.

2. Pinezhskii, 1st ed., p. 26; Rozanov, p. 405; Liapin, pp. 95–97; A. I. Afanas'ev, p. 125; Petrov and Lur'e, p. 285.
3. Startsev, *Ocherki*, pp. 265–67.
4. *Ibid.*, pp. 267–68.
5. Haimson, "The Problems of Social Stability in Urban Russia," part 1, p. 634.
6. Startsev, *Ocherki*, p. 266.
7. Stepanov, *Rabochie Petrograda*, p. 38.
8. *Ibid.*, p. 25.
9. Haimson, "The Problem of Social Stability in Urban Russia," part 1, pp. 634–36.
10. Startsev, *Ocherki*, p. 268.
11. Liapin, p. 95.
12. The figures for the Red Guard are from Startsev, *Ocherki*, pp. 254–58, and those on the general work force are from Stepanov, *Rabochie Petrograda*, pp. 29, 34. Stepanov's base is not exactly the same as Startsev's, but it is close enough for our purposes.
13. Tikhomirov, p. 62.
14. Stepanov, *Rabochie Petrograda*, pp. 41–42.
15. Tsinis, p. 103.
16. TsGAOR, Fond 6935, opis' 6, ed. khr. 114, l. 19.
17. *Revoliutsionnoe dvizhenie v Rossii v avguste 1917 g.*, p. 510.
18. Startsev, *Ocherki*, pp. 260, 263–64.
19. Ganichev, p. 315; Vasil'ev, part 1, pp. 103–4; *Geroi Oktiabria*, vol. 1, p. 703.
20. A. S., "Pervyi partizanskii otriad petrogradskikh pechatnikov," p. 166; *Revoliutsionnoe dvizhenie v Rossii v sentiabre 1917 g.*, p. 335.
21. Pinezhskii, 1st ed., pp. 24–25.
22. Skuratov, pp. 112–13.
23. *Geroi Oktiabria*, vol. 2, pp. 69–71.
24. Liapin, p. 97.
25. Rozanov, pp. 261–64.
26. Vasil'ev, part 1, p. 104; Bortnik, p. 271; *Geroi Oktiabria*, vol. 2, pp. 704, 706.
27. *Revoliutsionnoe dvizhenie v Rossii v avguste 1917 g.*, p. 485.
28. Liapin, p. 96.
29. "Iz istorii Krasnoi gvardii Petrograda," p. 133.
30. Avrich, *The Russian Anarchists*, pp. 145–46.
31. Kanev, p. 59; Collins, "Origins," p. 99.
32. Gorin, pp. 358–59; Rozanov, p. 264; Startsev, "Voenno-revoliutsionnyi komitet," p. 125; Startsev, *Ocherki*, p. 159; *Petrogradskii voenno-revoliutsionnyi komitet: Dokumenty i materialy*, vol. 1, pp. 40–41.
33. Malakhovskii, *Iz istorii Krasnoi gvardii*, p. 12.
34. Especially to be noted in this respect is Keep, *The Russian Revolution: A Study in Mass Mobilization*.
35. Vasil'ev, part 1, esp. pp. 105–6.
36. Tsinis, p. 103.

37. Vinogradov, "Dorozhe otchego doma," pp. 90, 95-96; Iurkin, p. 259.

38. *Geroi Oktiabria*, vol. 1, pp. 149-50.

39. *Ibid.*, vol. 2, pp. 138-39.

40. *Raionnye sovety*, vol. 3, pp. 12-161 *passim*; *Geroi Oktiabria*, vol. 2, p. 698.

41. Vasil'ev, part 1, pp. 105-6.

42. For the *piaterka*, see especially Iurii Trifonov, pp. 6-11, 70-75; Iurkin, pp. 259-63, and the members' respective biographical entries in *Geroi Oktiabria*.

43. Lenin, *Polnoe sobranie sochinenii*, vol. 51, p. 74. Emphasis in the original.

44. These connections and the role of the activists have not been given much attention in historical studies and are poorly understood. Soviet historians rarely discuss them except indirectly and inadvertently, as in biographies. Western historians have given a little attention to them. Aside from the book by Keep mentioned in n. 34 above, see especially Uldricks, "The Crowd in the Russian Revolution: Towards Reassessing the Nature of Revolutionary Leadership"; Pethybridge, *The Spread of the Russian Revolution*, notably pp. 167-70; and Hasegawa, "The Problem of Power in the February Revolution of 1917 in Russia."

CHAPTER NINE

1. Trotsky's speech is in Browder and Kerensky, vol. 3, pp. 1,728-29.

2. *Ekonomicheskoe polozhenie Rossii*, vol. 2, pp. 351-53.

3. Cited in Browder and Kerensky, vol. 3, p. 1,642.

4. See Rabinowitch, *The Bolsheviks Come to Power*, pp. 208-16.

5. See, for example, *Den'*, Oct. 24.

6. *Velikaia Oktiabr'skaia sotsialisticheskaia revoliutsiia . . . v Petrograde*, p. 229.

7. M. L. Lur'e, *Petrogradskaia Krasnaia gvardiia*, p. 122. This is the same order given in Kaiurov, p. 234, but not dated.

8. Quoted in Tsukerman, no. 3, p. 64.

9. Shabalin, p. 296; Podvoiskii, *Krasnaia gvardiia*, p. 53; M. L. Lur'e, *Petrogradskaia Krasnaia gvardiia*, pp. 116, 122-23.

10. Rabinowitch, *The Bolsheviks Come to Power*, pp. 151-272; see also Ferro, *October, 1917*, pp. 224-68. The first major challenge to the old view of a carefully planned and executed Bolshevik takeover was Daniels, *Red October*.

11. *Pervyi legal'nyi*, pp. 307-19.

12. On the origins and functioning of the MRC, see Rabinowitch, *The Bolsheviks Come to Power*, pp. 224-48.

13. *Petrogradskii voenno-revoliutsionnyi komitet*, vol. 1, pp. 109, 115.

14. *Raionnye sovety*, vol. 1, p. 151-52; M. L. Lur'e, *Petrogradskaia Krasnaia gvardiia*, p. 24.

15. Podvoiskii, *Krasnaia gvardiia*, p. 63.

16. *V boiakh: Sbornik vospominanii* . . . , pp. 37–38.

17. Ganichev, p. 318; Baklanova and Stepanov, pp. 95, 99; Sergeev, p. 196; Chechkovskii, p. 168; Egorov, p. 36.

18. Podvoiskii, *Krasnaia gvardiia*, p. 27.

19. Reed, p. 99.

20. Startsev, "Voenno-revoliutsionnyi komitet," p. 137.

21. News of the bridges—important to all the population—is one of the best reported parts of the October Revolution in the contemporary press. See especially *Novaia zhizn'* and *Rech'* for October 25 and 26. See also Startsev, "Voenno-revoliutsionnyi komitet," pp. 131–36, and Baklanova and Stepanov, pp. 101–4. The struggle for the bridges is described in numerous memoirs. For the crossing of the Palace Bridge under fire, see Vasil'ev, part 1, pp. 109–10.

22. Mukhtar-Londarskii, p. 208; Startsev, "Voenno-revoliutsionnyi komitet," p. 133.

23. Startsev, "Voenno-revoliutsionnyi komitet," pp. 133–35; Baklanova and Stepanov, p. 102; Sergeev, p. 196.

24. Baklanova and Stepanov, p. 102.

25. Sergeev, p. 196.

26. *Raionnye sovety*, vol. 2, p. 285; Startsev, "Voenno-revoliutsionnyi komitet," p. 137.

27. Startsev, "Voenno-revoliutsionnyi komitet," p. 137.

28. The contemporary press and many memoirs give accounts of the events of October 24–25. Good summaries of the actions, and of sources, are in Startsev, "Voenno-revoliutsionnyi komitet," pp. 132–36, and Baklanova and Stepanov, pp. 101–4.

29. The troop estimates are from Ilin-Zhenevskii, p. 222, based on notes taken at the time, and Erykalov, *Oktiabr'skoe vooruzhennoe vosstanie v Petrograde*, table on p. 435.

30. Eremeev, "Osada," pp. 177–78; Dzenis, p. 203.

31. Vasil'ev, part 1, pp. 106–10.

32. Eremeev, "Osada," p. 175.

33. Quoted in *Oktiabr'skoe vooruzhennoe vosstanie: semnadtsatyi god v Petrograde*, vol. 2, p. 336.

34. Reed, p. 99.

35. The role of the Red Guard in the final act of the seizure of power, the siege and taking of the Winter Palace, has been pieced together from a large number of sources, no one of which presents any sort of comprehensive view. Listing them would take pages; most are in the Bibliography. The most useful secondary accounts in English are Rabinowitch, *The Bolsheviks Come to Power*, pp. 273–304 (especially on the difficulties of the Bolsheviks in getting the whole thing organized); Daniels, *Red October* (focusing on the role of accident in the Revolution); and Ferro, *October, 1917*. A useful Soviet account, written collectively but including a number of the best Soviet historians on the Revolution, including Startsev, is *Oktiabr'skoe vooruzhennoe vosstanie: semnadtsatyi god v Petrograde*.

CHAPTER TEN

1. Lebedev, p. 250; Z. Petrov, p. 6.
2. Raleigh, "The Russian Revolutions of 1917 in Saratov," pp. 1–49.
3. This summary is drawn primarily from *ibid.*, pp. 50–99.
4. Vasil'ev-Iuzhin, pp. 9–11; F. Morozov, "Fevral'skaia revoliutsiia," p. 25.
5. Antonov-Saratovskii, "Saratov s fevralia," pp. 157–61, gives a protocol of the meeting. Vasil'ev-Iuzhin, pp. 11–14, and F. Morozov, "Fevral'skaia revoliutsiia," pp. 25–26, give accounts also.
6. See *Izvestiia Saratovskogo Soveta*, Mar. 14, no. 6; *1917 god v Saratovskoi gubernii*, p. 580; Rumiantsev, "Rabochaia militsiia," p. 8; Medvedev, pp. 50–51. On this, as on so many issues in Saratov and Kharkov, we are almost completely dependent upon Bolshevik sources. This suggests the need for special caution, for our knowledge of the origins and workings of the Petrograd Soviet—the best known—would be very different if we were as heavily dependent upon Bolshevik memoirists and later Soviet historians there as we are in the provinces. The same is true of other aspects of the Revolution, especially where the question of Bolshevik leadership is concerned.
7. Vasil'ev-Iuzhin, pp. 16–17; Antonov-Saratovskii, "Saratov s fevralia," p. 161; Rumiantsev, "Rabochaia militsiia," p. 45; F. Morozov, "Fevral'skaia revoliutsiia," p. 28; *Saratovskii Sovet*, pp. 3–4 (protocols of the Saratov Soviet); Z. Petrov, p. 6; Gerasimenko and Rashitov, pp. 9–10.
8. Listed by Rumiantsev in "Rabochaia militsiia," p. 48.
9. Vasil'ev-Iuzhin, pp. 18–20; F. Morozov, "Fevral'skaia revoliutsiia," pp. 28–29; Rumiantsev, "Rabochaia militsiia," pp. 44, 47; Chepenko, p. 132.
10. *Izvestiia Saratovskogo Soveta*, Mar. 15, no. 7; Mar. 17, no. 8.
11. Rumiantsev, "Rabochaia militsiia," pp. 46 47, 51.
12. *Izvestiia Saratovskogo Soveta*, Mar. 15, no. 7.
13. *Saratovskii Sovet*, p. 9; Rumiantsev, "Rabochaia militsiia," p. 52.
14. Lebedev, p. 237; Rumiantsev, "Rabochaia militsiia," p. 52.
15. *Izvestiia Saratovskogo Soveta*, Mar. 14, no. 6; Vas'kin, pp. 101–3.
16. Martsinovskii, pp. 82–83.
17. *Saratovskii Sovet*, pp. 7–9; Rumiantsev, "Rabochaia militsiia," pp. 52–53.
18. *Saratovskii Sovet*, pp. 29, 47. *Saratovskii listok*, Mar. 7, no. 52; Rumiantsev, "Rabochaia militsiia," pp. 58–59.
19. *Saratovskii listok*, Mar. 17, no. 60; Rumiantsev, "Rabochaia militsiia," pp. 59–64.
20. Rumiantsev, "Rabochaia militsiia," p. 67.
21. *Izvestiia Saratovskogo Soveta*, Mar. 22, no. 12.
22. Rumiantsev, "Fabrichno-zavodskaia militsiia," p. 79.
23. *Saratovskii Sovet*, protocols, pp. 4, 67.
24. Rumiantsev, "Rabochaia militsiia," p. 68.
25. Razgon, pp. 116–17; *Khronika revoliutsionnykh sobytii v Saratov-*

skom Povolzh'e, pp. 27–29. See also Gerasimenko and Rashitov, pp. 25–26.

26. Gerasimenko and Rashitov, p. 51; *Revoliutsionnoe dvizhenie v Rossii v mae–iiune 1917*, pp. 201–2; Vas'kin, p. 214. Two sets of figures exist, but they are close.

27. Levinson, p. 81. There exists an erroneous set of figures, first used in Antonov-Saratovskii, "Oktiabr'skie dni v Saratove," p. 279, and repeated by many later writers.

28. Both figures are in *Izvestiia Saratovskogo Soveta*, June 28. See also Gerasimenko and Rashitov, p. 51.

29. Antonov-Saratovskii, "Saratov s fevralia," p. 190.

30. Medvedev, p. 67; Antonov-Saratovskii, *Pod stiagom proletarskoi bor'by*, pp. 291–94.

31. *Revoliutsionnoe dvizhenie v Rossii v mae–iiune 1917*, pp. 201–2; Lebedev, p. 241.

32. Lebedev, p. 241.

33. *Khronika revoliutsionnykh sobytii v Saratovskom Povolzh'e*, p. 84.

34. Rumiantsev, "Rabochaia militsiia," p. 65.

35. Raleigh, "The Russian Revolutions of 1917 in Saratov," pp. 214–22, 287–95.

36. Rumiantsev, "Rabochaia militsiia," pp. 77–109.

37. *Sotsial-Demokrat* (Saratov), May 7, no. 13.

38. *1917 god v Saratovskoi gubernii*, p. 100.

39. Khodakov, pp. 273–74.

40. *Proletarii povolzh'ia*, July 19, no. 38.

41. As quoted in Rumiantsev, "Rabochaia militsiia," p. 94.

42. *Ibid.*, p. 164.

43. *Proletarii povolzh'ia*, Sept. 1, no. 76.

44. *1917 god v Saratovskoi gubernii*, p. 137.

45. Rumiantsev, "Rabochaia militsiia," p. 268.

46. On the "Tsaritsyn Republic," see Raleigh, "Revolutionary Politics."

47. *Sotsial-Demokrat* (Saratov), Sept. 3, no. 63.

48. Z. Petrov, p. 10.

49. Raleigh, "The Russian Revolutions of 1917 in Saratov," pp. 328–36, 366–70.

50. *Sotsial-Demokrat* (Saratov), Sept. 10, no. 65; *1917 god v Saratovskoi gubernii*, pp. 147–48; A. V. Afanas'ev, "Iz istorii," p. 141–42; Rumiantsev, "Rabochaia militsiia," pp. 185, 205–7; Chepenko, pp. 134–35.

51. Fedorov, p. 112; Krasichkov, p. 120; Chugunov, p. 130; Z. Petrov, p. 13; *Proletarii povolzh'ia*, Sept. 24, no. 97, and Oct. 6, no. 106; Rumiantsev, "Rabochaia militsiia," pp. 185, 204–5.

52. Rumiantsev, "Rabochaia militsiia," p. 188.

53. *Ibid.*, p. 224; Medvedev, p. 81.

54. *Saratovskii Sovet*, pp. 196–97.

55. *Izvestiia Saratovskogo Soveta*, Sept. 12, no. 81.

56. Rumiantsev, "Rabochaia militsiia," p. 170, citing the account in *Saratovskii vestnik*.

57. *Izvestiia Saratovskogo Soveta*, Sept. 19, no. 83; Rumiantsev, "Rabochaia militsiia," pp. 186–87.

58. Z. Petrov, p. 11; Gerasimenko and Rashitov, p. 85.

59. A. V. Afanas'ev, "Iz istorii," pp. 145–46; Rumiantsev, "Rabochaia militsiia," pp. 188–89, 207–8.

60. Medvedev, p. 81.

61. "Khronika Oktiabr'skoi revoliutsii v Saratove," part 1, pp. 33, 35.

62. Lebedev, p. 250; Rumiantsev, "Rabochaia militsiia," pp. 228–29.

63. *1917 god v Saratovskoi gubernii*, pp. 164, 168, 265; Gerasimenko and Rashitov, p. 93; Rumiantsev, "Rabochaia militsiia," p. 248.

64. Krasichkov, pp. 120–21; Medvedev, p. 81.

65. Raleigh, "The Russian Revolutions of 1917 in Saratov," pp. 385–88.

66. The following account of the October Revolution, unless otherwise noted, is a composite of the following sources: *Godovshchina sotsial'noi revoliutsii v Saratove*, pp. 3–8; *Khronika revoliutsionnykh sobytii v Saratovskom Povolzh'e*, pp. 134–51; Lebedev, pp. 250–61; Vasil'ev-Iuzhin, pp. 23–45; Antonov-Saratovskii, "Oktiabr'skie dni v Saratove," pp. 279–92; Gerasimenko and Rashitov, pp. 101–14. There is a general agreement among these sources—all of which are Bolshevik.

67. Lebedev, p. 250, for example.

68. Nedostupov, pp. 7–8.

69. "Khronika Oktiabr'skoi revoliutsii v Saratove," part 2, p. 120.

70. See the accounts of Chugunov, p. 130; Chepenko, p. 135; Krasichkov, p. 121; Fedorov, p. 112; Shcherbakov, p. 97.

71. Lebedev, pp. 258–59.

72. Shcherbakov, p. 97.

CHAPTER ELEVEN

1. Buzdalin, "Oktiabr'skaia revoliutsiia v Khar'kove," p. 35.

2. Smolinchuk, p. 179.

3. Most of the following material on Kharkov up to 1917 comes from Kurman and Lebedinskii, and from *Istoriia gorodov i sel Ukrainskoi SSR; Khar'kovskaia oblast'*, pp. 9–32, 77–97. The most useful information on the transfer of Latvian workers to Kharkov is in Mel'nik and Raevs'kii, pp. 80–86.

4. Kurman and Lebedinskii, pp. 121–23.

5. Palij, p. 26.

6. For an account of the first days of the February Revolution in Kharkov, see the account from the Kharkov *Izvestiia* in *Khar'kov i Khar'kovskaia guberniia*, pp. 11–12; Lobakhin, pp. 9, 13.

7. *Izvestiia* account in *Khar'kov i Khar'kovskaia guberniia*, p. 12; Lobakhin, p. 10.

8. *Izvestiia* summary in *Khar'kov i Khar'kovskaia guberniia*, p. 14.

9. *Ibid.*, pp. 13–15.

10. *Ibid.*, p. 12.

11. Pavliuk, pp. 15–16.

12. Lobakhin, pp. 27–28; Pavliuk, p. 14; Gritsenko, "Rol' fabzav-komov," p. 159.

13. Lobakhin, pp. 18–21.

14. *Khar'kov i Khar'kovskaia guberniia*, pp. 9–10.

15. Garchev, "Sozdanie," pp. 38–39.

16. Miroshnichenko, p. 134.

17. *Velikaia Oktiabr'skaia sotsialisticheskaia revoliutsiia na Ukraine*, vol. 1, pp. 193–94.

18. *Ibid.*, pp. 194–95.

19. Miroshnichenko, p. 136.

20. *Proletarii* (Kharkov), May 17, no. 44.

21. Simkin, p. 160.

22. *Ibid.*; Simkin and Silin, p. 130; "Petinskii (Krasnozavodskii) raion," p. 213; Onufrienko, p. 16; Pavliuk, p. 31. Garchev, "Sozdanie," pp. 39–40. Garchev questions that the meeting ever took place, but the evidence is strongly in its favor. There are conflicting dates, but as the difference is the same between the two calendar systems I suspect that is the source of the confusion.

23. "Petinskii (Krasnozavodskii) raion," p. 213; Simkin and Silin, p. 130.

24. Garchev, "Sozdanie," p. 39.

25. Simkin, p. 158; Simkin and Silin, pp. 130–31; Smil'tnik, p. 198.

26. Simkin and Silin, p. 130; Miroshnichenko, pp. 137–38.

27. Miroshnichenko, p. 138; Simkin, p. 161.

28. On labor unrest see especially Leshchenko, pp. 428–30, and newspaper accounts.

29. *Izvestiia iuga*, Aug. 29, no. 145. The Kharkov Soviet newspaper added the term *iuga* ("south") to its name in the summer.

30. For an account of these activities, see *Revoliutsionnoe dvizhenie v Rossii v sentiabre 1917 g.*, pp. 584–85.

31. Popov, pp. 18–19; *Velikaia Oktiabr'skaia sotsialisticheskaia revoliutsiia na Ukraine*, vol. 1, pp. 564–66.

32. Quoted in Leshchenko, p. 425.

33. Kondufor, p. 214.

34. Pavliuk, p. 41. Regulations repeated in *Revoliutsionnoe dvizhenie v Rossii v sentiabre 1917 g.*, pp. 357–58.

35. Kondufor, pp. 216–17; Miroshnichenko, p. 142; Chepurnov, pp. 57–58.

36. Miroshnichenko, pp. 142–43; Chepurnov, p. 58.

37. Garchev, *Chervona gvardiia Ukraini*, p. 42.

38. TsGAOR, opis' 6, ed. khr. 114, ll. 2, 4, 15–16; Voskresenskii, p. 184; Pavliuk, pp. 44–51; Leshchenko, pp. 428–30; Usatenko, p. 38; Goncharenko, p. 187; *Podgotovka . . . na Ukraine*, p. 686.

39. Simkin and Silin, pp. 131–32; "Petinskii (Krasnozavodskii) raion," p. 214; Miroshnichenko, p. 143; Leshchenko, p. 426.

40. "Petinskii (Krasnozavodskii) raion," p. 214; Simkin, p. 163; Pavliuk, p. 52.

41. Onufrienko, p. 73; Pavliuk, p. 52.

42. Simkin, p. 161.

43. Garchev, *Chervona gvardiia Ukraini*, p. 170.

44. Leshchenko, pp. 434–35.

45. *Proletarii*, Sept. 14, no. 129.

46. Kondufor, p. 204; Leshchenko, p. 427; *Khar'kov i Khar'kovskaia guberniia*, pp. 165–66.

47. Morgunov, "Vospominaniia," p. 209.

48. *Izvestiia iuga*, Sept. 23, no. 165.

49. Garchev, *Chervona gvardiia Ukraini*, p. 42.

50. Kin, p. 70; Simkin, p. 159; Pokko, p. 44; Onufrienko, p. 16; Chepurnov, p. 55.

51. "Petinskii (Krasnozavodskii) raion," p. 214. Buzdalin, "Oktiabr'skaia revoliutsiia," p. 35, suggests that the figure for arms might be smaller, but he is vague.

52. Poliakov, pp. 73–74.

53. Pokko, p. 44; "Petinskii (Krasnozavodskii) raion," pp. 213–14; Simkin and Silin, p. 130; Simkin, pp. 158–59; Krivonos, p. 170.

54. Simkin, p. 159.

55. *Izvestiia iuga*, Oct. 13, no. 180.

56. Pipes, p. 61.

57. Pipes, pp. 69–73, 114–27; Reshetar, pp. 82–94.

58. Miroshnichenko, p. 144; Pavliuk, p. 347; Korolivskii, Rubach, and Suprunenko, p. 294.

59. On the Committee, see the accounts in Leshchenko, p. 435; Smolinchuk, pp. 174–75; Korolivskii, Rubach, and Suprunenko, pp. 294–96; *Khar'kov i Khar'kovskaia guberniia*, p. 23; *Bol'shevistskie organizatsii Ukrainy v period ustanovleniia*, pp. 141–42.

60. Leshchenko, pp. 438–39; Smolinchuk, p. 175; Korolivskii, Rubach, and Suprunenko, p. 297.

61. Pokko, p. 45; Chepurnov, p. 60; Miroshnichenko, p. 146; Leshchenko, p. 439; *Khar'kov i Khar'kovskaia guberniia*, p. 236.

62. Smolinchuk, pp. 175–77; Korolivskii, Rubach, and Suprunenko, pp. 296–98; *Khar'kov i Khar'kovskaia guberniia*, pp. 263–64.

63. Korolivskii, Rubach, and Suprunenko, pp. 338–39; Smolinchuk, p. 178; *Khar'kov i Khar'kovskaia guberniia*, pp. 304–5.

64. Onufrienko, p. 89.

65. Garchev, *Chervona gvardiia Ukraini*, pp. 98–99.

66. *Pobeda . . . na Ukraine*, p. 206; *Khar'kov i Khar'kovskaia guberniia*, p. 279; Pavliuk, pp. 58, 66–67. Some estimates of size are higher, but these are the commonly accepted figures and seem the best.

67. Miroshnichenko, pp. 145–48; Chepurnov, pp. 60–62; Garchev, *Chervona gvardiia Ukraini*, pp. 67–68; Morgunov, "Vospominaniia," p. 209.

68. Garchev, "Pitannia," p. 4.
69. Goncharenko, pp. 189–92; Garchev, "Pitannia," p. 5.
70. Accounts of the fighting around Belgorod contain considerable discrepancies. The best accounts, however, are in Garchev, "Pitannia," pp. 5–7, and Polikarpov, pp. 282–306. See also Loza, pp. 83–84; Pavliuk, pp. 65–66; Miroshnichenko, pp. 145–46; Smil'tnik, p. 199.
71. *Donetskii proletarii*, Dec. 9, no. 31.
72. Garchev, *Chervona gvardiia Ukraini*, p. 206.
73. *Podgotovka . . . na Ukraine*, p. 703.
74. Garchev, *Chervona gvardiia Ukraini*, p. 186.
75. *Ibid.*; Antonov-Ovseenko, *Zapiski*, vol. 1, pp. 55–56.
76. The major sources for the negotiations and takeover described here and in the following paragraphs are the accounts of Pokko, one of the participants; Garchev, "Pitannia," pp. 11–12; and Antonov-Ovseenko, *Zapiski*, vol. 1, pp. 55–56 (who received his account on arrival two days later from one of Sivers' staff members, Volynskii). See also Kin, p. 70; Smil'tnik, p. 199.

CHAPTER TWELVE

1. Verkhos', *Krasnaia gvardiia*, p. 86.
2. Atsarkin, pp. 324, 361, 430–31.
3. Chaadaeva, part 1, pp. 46–47.
4. Luk'ianov, pp. 25–26; *Revoliutsionnoe dvizhenie v Rossii nakanune*, pp. 337–38.
5. Cited in Garchev, *Chervona gvardiia*, p. 174. For some reason, 0.3 percent are not accounted for.
6. Tsypkin and Tsypkina, p. 118.
7. Johnson, esp. pp. 146–47.
8. Tsypkina presents the most detailed study of the Red Guards in the industrial settlements. See especially pp. 7–57.
9. See the chart in Tsypkin and Tsypkina, pp. 280–341.
10. Tsypkin and Tsypkina, p. 83; Tsypkina, p. 35.
11. Tsypkina, p. 66.
12. *Ibid.*, pp. 66–68.
13. N. A. Golubev, "Krasnaia gvardiia," pp. 71–72.
14. Tsypkina, pp. 69–71.
15. See Johnson.
16. Gorer and Rickman, pp. 70–75.
17. Tikhomirov, pp. 69–70, using reports of the Provisional Government's Main Militia Administration.
18. Verkhos', "Partiia bol'shevikov," p. 51.
19. *Ibid.*; Reshod'ko, p. 97.
20. Garchev, *Chervona gvardiia Ukraini*, p. 169.
21. Tsypkina, p. 80.
22. Tsypkin and Tsypkina, pp. 109, 111.
23. Tsypkina, pp. 51–52.

24. *Ibid.*, p. 82; Gerasimenko, *Nizovye krest'ianskie organizatsii,* p. 253.

25. Tsypkin and Tsypkina, p. 111; Verkhos', "Partiia bol'shevikov," p. 52.

26. See especially the detailed studies of the Volga region by Gerasimenko, *Nizovye krest'ianskie organizatsii,* pp. 215–62, and of the Central Industrial Region by Tsypkina, pp. 63–70.

27. On this point see Khokhlov.

28. Tsypkin and Tsypkina, p. 94; Collins, "The Origins," pp. 158, 171–72.

29. *Krasnaia gvardiia Taganroga,* p. 29.

30. Tsypkina, p. 80.

31. Tsypkin and Tsypkina, p. 118.

32. Verkhos', *Krasnaia gvardiia,* p. 91; Tsypkin, pp. 108–9; Tsypkin and Tsypkina, p. 119.

33. Tsypkin, p. 109; Verkhos', *Krasnaia gvardiia,* pp. 82–84.

34. Tsypkin, p. 108.

35. Garchev, *Chervona gvardiia Ukraini,* pp. 170–72.

36. Chaadaeva, part 1, p. 43.

37. Tsypkina, p. 80.

38. Iaroshevskii, p. 6.

39. Collins, "The Origins," p. 221.

40. *Ibid.,* p. 152.

41. Gagin, p. 191; Collins, "The Origins," p. 156.

42. Rumiantsev, "Rabochaia militsiia," p. 148.

43. *Oktiabr'skoe vooruzhennoe vosstanie v Petrograde: dokumenty i materialy,* p. 126.

44. *Revoliutsionnoe dvizhenie v Rossii v sentiabre 1917 g.,* pp. 368–69; *Bor'ba za Sovetskuiu vlast' na Iuzhnom Urale,* p. 152.

45. N. A. Golubev, "Krasnaia gvardiia," p. 64.

46. Onufrienko, pp. 83–84; Tagirov, "Iz istorii," p. 205.

47. Gritsenko, "Rol' fabzavkomov," p. 160.

48. Tsypkin, pp. 107–8.

49. *Revoliutsionnoe dvizhenie v Rossii nakanune,* p. 39; Ventsov and Belitskii, p. 31; N. A. Golubev, "Rost i ukreplenie," pp. 35–36.

50. Tsypkin and Tsypkina, pp. 49–54.

51. I. P. Golubev, "Krasnogvardeitsy-zheleznodorozhniki," pp. 91–92.

52. *Revoliutsionnoe dvizhenie v Rossii nakanune,* pp. 337–38, 342; Ioganson, p. 152.

53. *Revoliutsionnoe dvizhenie v Rossii nakanune,* pp. 351–52; Tsypkin, p. 202.

54. See, for example, *Revoliutsionnoe dvizhenie v Rossii v sentiabre 1917 g.,* pp. 147, 355–77.

55. Verkhos', *Krasnaia gvardiia,* p. 47.

56. Iaroshevskii, pp. 2–5.

57. *Revoliutsionnoe dvizhenie v Rossii nakanune,* pp. 331–32.

58. Collins, "A Note," p. 280.
59. Verkhos', *Krasnaia gvardiia*, pp. 244-56.
60. Collins, "A Note," p. 277; Collins, "The Origins," pp. 135-43.
61. Tsypkin and Tsypkina, pp. 114-15, 280-341.
62. Verkhos', *Krasnaia gvardiia*, pp. 244-48.
63. Tsypkin and Tsypkina, p. 113.
64. *Revoliutsionnoe dvizhenie v Rossii v sentiabre 1917 g.*, pp. 385-86.
65. Verkhos', *Krasnaia gvardiia*, p. 146.
66. N. A. Golubev, "Iz istorii Krasnoi gvardii," p. 109.
67. *Revoliutsionnoe dvizhenie v Rossii nakanune*, p. 346.
68. *Ibid.*, pp. 335, 336-37.
69. Sivtsov, p. 22.
70. *Iz istorii moskovskoi rabochei Krasnoi gvardii*, p. 183; Luk'ianov, p. 22.
71. N. A. Golubev, "Rost i ukreplenie," p. 41; *Revoliutsionnoe dvizhenie v Rossii nakanune*, p. 338.
72. Chaadaeva, part 1, p. 44.
73. *Bor'ba za sovetskuiu vlast' na Iuzhnom Urale*, p. 145.
74. Nefedov, p. 58.
75. Verkhos', *Krasnaia gvardiia*, p. 149; Tsypkin, p. 84; Tsypkina, pp. 50-51.
76. *Revoliutsionnoe dvizhenie v Rossii nakanune*, p. 346.
77. *Ibid.*, p. 338.
78. Tsypkina, p. 35.
79. *Krasnaia gvardiia Taganroga*, p. 31; *Omskie bol'sheviki*, pp. 36-37.
80. Tsypkin and Tsypkina, p. 46; Tsypkin, p. 53.
81. *Revoliutsionnoe dvizhenie v Rossii v sentiabre 1917 g.*, pp. 386-87.
82. "Instruksiia Krasnoi Gvardii . . . Odesse," pp. 207-9.
83. Iaroshevskii, p. 4.
84. *Revoliutsionnoe dvizhenie v Rossii v sentiabre 1917 g.*, p. 374; Tsypkin, p. 45.
85. *Revoliutsionnoe dvizhenie v Rossii nakanune*, p. 340.
86. *Revoliutsionnoe dvizhenie v Rossii v sentiabre 1917 g.*, pp. 383-85; "Instruksiia Krasnoi Gvardii . . . Odesse," pp. 207-9.
87. *Revoliutsionnoe dvizhenie v Rossii v sentiabre 1917 g.*, pp. 377-78. Unless otherwise indicated, party affiliations are unknown. There are other examples of such debates, as at the Moscow Workers' Soviet on August 30, but most date from the time of the Kornilov Affair, which temporarily changed the nature of the debates.
88. Rychkova, pp. 26-27.
89. Gritsenko, "Rol' fabzavkomov," p. 163.
90. Startsev, "Voenno-revoliutsionnyi komitet," p. 113.
91. *Revoliutsionnoe dvizhenie v Rossii v avguste 1917 g.*, p. 477.
92. Tsypkin and Tsypkina, p. 148.
93. *Ibid.*, pp. 147-52, 166-71.

94. The following account of the Revolution in Moscow is a composite of many sources, both general ones and specific accounts of the role of the Red Guards, including a large number of memoir articles. General Soviet histories include Grunt, pp. 266–349, and Mints, vol. 3, pp. 189–307. An extensive and informative account is the memoir-history by one of the Moscow Red Guard leaders, Ia. Peche, pp. 50–159. A valuable non-Bolshevik account is Mel'gunov, pp. 277–383. A brief account with a good analysis of worker attitudes is in Koenker, pp. 336–46.

95. Tsypkin, pp. 150–52; Collins, "The Origins," pp. 133–43; Garchev, *Chervona gvardiia Ukraini*, pp. 68–89; Luk'ianov, pp. 27–47.

EPILOGUE

1. Malakhovskii, "Kak sozdavalas'," pp. 31–32.

2. Startsev, *Ocherki*, pp. 198–99. See also Artemov, "Bol'sheviki," pp. 5–16.

3. "Iz istorii Krasnoi gvardii Petrograda," pp. 144–45.

4. See especially the accounts of Pinezhskii, 2d ed., pp. 81–84; Malakhovskii, *Iz istorii Krasnoi gvardii*, pp. 26–27; Bonch-Bruevich, p. 54; Artemov, "Uchastie petrogradskoi Krasnoi gvardii," pp. 17–28.

5. Krasnov, p. 166.

6. Startsev, *Ocherki*, pp. 200, 295; Pinezhskii, 2d ed., p. 82; Verkhos', *Krasnaia gvardiia*, p. 194.

7. Collins, "The Russian Red Guard of 1917 and Lenin's Utopia," pp. 3–5.

8. *Vestnik narodnogo komissariata vnutrennykh del*, Dec. 27.

9. Molodtsygin, p. 35; Tsypkin, *Krasnaia gvardiia*, p. 172.

10. Pinezhskii, 2d ed., pp. 125–29.

11. Lenin, *Polnoe sobranie sochinenii*, vol. 35, pp. 357–58.

12. Pinezhskii, 2d ed., pp. 124–32, devotes extensive attention to these problems. See also Bonch-Bruevich, p. 191, and Iurenev, p. 79, on the efforts to stop riots at liquor stores.

13. Konev, *Krasnaia gvardiia*, pp. 117–40.

14. *Ibid.*, p. 120.

15. Molodtsygin, pp. 34–35.

16. Malakhovskii, *Iz istorii Krasnoi gvardii*, p. 33; Morozov, p. 44; Startsev, *Ocherki*, pp. 241–43.

17. *Iz istorii moskovskoi rabochei Krasnoi gvardii*, pp. 75, 81; Tsypkin, *Krasnaia gvardiia*, pp. 170–72.

18. Pinezhskii, 2d ed., pp. 145–48; Tsypkin, *Krasnaia gvardiia*, pp. 172–73; Startsev, *Ocherki*, pp. 239–41.

19. In *Vestnik narodnogo komissariata vnutrennykh del*, Apr. 24, 1918.

20. Collins, "The Russian Red Guard of 1917 and Lenin's Utopia," p. 8.

21. Konev, *Krasnaia gvardiia*, pp. 76–78.

22. Startsev, *Ocherki*, p. 220; *Triumfal'noe shestvie Sovetskoi vlasti*, vol. 1, pp. 198–99; *Raionnye sovety*, vol. 1, pp. 169–70.

23. Startsev, *Ocherki*, pp. 222–26.

24. Konev, *Krasnaia gvardiia*, pp. 78–79; Startsev, *Ocherki*, pp. 220–26.
25. Startsev, *Ocherki*, pp. 226–28.
26. *Ibid.*, p. 228.
27. *Ibid.*, pp. 228–32.
28. *Ibid.*, pp. 232–33.
29. Pinezhskii, 2d ed., pp. 139–42.
30. Morozov, *Ot Krasnoi gvardii k Krasnoi armii*, pp. 51–52; Tsypkin, *Krasnaia gvardiia*, pp. 182–85; *Voennye voprosy v resheniiakh KPSS*, pp. 503–5.
31. Tsypkin, *Krasnaia gvardiia*, pp. 182–85; Verkhos', *Krasnaia gvardiia*, pp. 206–9.
32. Cited in Morozov, *Ot Krasnoi gvardii k Krasnoi armii*, p. 46.
33. Skrypnik, p. 43.
34. Antonov-Ovseenko, "Krasnaia gvardiia–narodnaia militsia," pp. 5–6 (emphasis in the original). This article is also the source of Antonov-Ovseenko's statement about the Red Guards in the epigraph to this chapter.
35. Verkhos', *Krasnaia gvardiia*, pp. 210–11.
36. Startsev, *Ocherki*, p. 280.
37. *Raionnye sovety*, vol. 1, p. 170.
38. Pinezhskii, 2d ed., pp. 165–71.
39. Startsev, *Ocherki*, p. 277.
40. *Ibid.*, pp. 281–82.
41. *Ibid.*, pp. 233–36, 346–47.
42. Erickson, "The Origins of the Red Army," p. 232.
43. *Oktiabr'skaia revoliutsiia i armiia*, pp. 309–11.
44. Pinezhskii, 2d ed., pp. 150–51.
45. Molodtsygin, p. 38.
46. Pinezhskii, 2d ed., p. 178; Morozov, *Ot Krasnoi gvardii k Krasnoi armii*, p. 71.
47. Erickson, "The Origins of the Red Army," p. 241.
48. Startsev, *Ocherki*, pp. 245–46; Malakhovskii, "Perekhod," p. 9.
49. Verkhos', *Krasnaia gvardiia*, p. 231.
50. Konev, *Krasnaia gvardiia*, p. 166.
51. *Ibid.*, p. 154.
52. Borisov, p. 53.
53. Molodtsygin, pp. 39–41.
54. Startsev, *Ocherki*, pp. 233–36, 346–47.
55. Molodtsygin, p. 42; Konev, *Krasnaia gvardiia*, pp. 163–65.
56. Molodtsygin, p. 42.
57. Cited in *ibid.*
58. Erickson, "The Origins of the Red Army," pp. 242–43.
59. Erickson, *The Soviet High Command*, pp. 48–49, 109, 115–18.

Bibliography

ARCHIVES

Tsentral'nyi gosudarstvennyi arkhiv Oktiabr'skoi revoliutsii i sotsialisticheskogo stroitel'stva SSSR (TsGAOR). Fond 6935: Komissiia po izucheniiu professional'nogo dvizheniia (istprof).
Tsentral'nyi gosudarstvennyi istoricheskii arkhiv SSSR (TsGIA). Fond 150: Petrogradskoe obshchestvo zavodchikov i fabrikantov.

NEWSPAPERS (1917)

Delo naroda. Petrograd. Newspaper of the Socialist Revolutionary Party.
Den'. Petrograd. Independent socialist newspaper, Right Menshevik oriented.
Donetskii proletarii. Kharkov. Bolshevik newspaper.
Gorodskoe delo. Petrograd.
Iuzhnyi krai. Kharkov. Liberal newspaper.
Izvestiia iuga. Kharkov. Later name for the newspaper of the Kharkov Soviet.
Izvestiia Khar'kovskogo Soveta rabochikh i soldatskikh deputatov.
Izvestiia Moskovskogo Soveta rabochikh deputatov.
Izvestiia Petrogradskogo Soveta rabochikh i soldatskikh deputatov.
Izvestiia petrogradskoi gorodskoi dumy.
Izvestiia revoliutsionnoi nedeli: izdanie komiteta petrogradskikh zhurnalistov. Published during the first week of the Revolution in Petrograd.
Izvestiia Saratovskogo Soveta rabochikh i soldatskikh deputatov.
Novaia zhizn'. Petrograd. Independent socialist newspaper, Left Menshevik oriented.
Pravda. Petrograd. Central Bolshevik Party newspaper.
Proletarii. Kharkov. Bolshevik newspaper.
Proletarii. Petrograd. Published Aug. 14–24 in place of *Pravda.*
Proletarii Povolzh'ia. Saratov. Menshevik newspaper.
Rabochaia gazeta. Petrograd. Central Menshevik newspaper.
Rabochii. Petrograd. Published Aug. 25–Sept. 2 in place of *Pravda.*
Rabochii i soldat. Petrograd. Published July 23–Aug. 9 as replacement for *Soldatskaia pravda.*

Rabochii put'. Petrograd. Published Sept. 3–Oct. 6 as replacement for *Pravda*.

Rech'. Petrograd. Newspaper of the Kadet Party.

Saratovskii listok. Newspaper associated with the Kadet Party.

Saratovskii vestnik. Moderate socialist newspaper.

Soldat. Petrograd. Published Aug. 13–Oct. 26 in place of *Soldatskaia pravda*.

Soldatskaia pravda. Petrograd. Newspaper of the Bolshevik Military Organization.

Sotsial-Demokrat. Moscow. Bolshevik newspaper.

Sotsial-Demokrat. Saratov. Bolshevik newspaper.

Vestnik narodnogo komissariata vnutrennykh del.

Vestnik Petrogradskogo obshchestva zavodchikov i fabrikantov. Petrograd. Publication of the Society of Manufacturers.

Vestnik Vremennogo pravitel'stva. Petrograd. Daily official publication of the Provisional Government.

BOOKS AND ARTICLES

Afanas'ev, A. I. "Klub molodezhi," in *Narvskaia zastava v 1917 godu v vospominaniiakh i dokumentakh*. Leningrad, 1960.

Afanas'ev, A. V. "Iz istorii organizatsii Krasnoi gvardii v g. Saratove (sentiabr'–oktiabr' 1917 g.)," *Povolzhskii krai* (Saratov), 1975, no. 2, pp. 135–48.

Aleksandrov, P. P. *Za Narvskoi zastavoi; vospominanii starogo rabochego*. Leningrad, 1963.

Almedingen, E. M. *I Remember St. Petersburg*. London, 1969.

Andreev, A. M. *Sovety rabochikh i soldatskikh deputatov nakanune Oktiabria, mart–oktiabr' 1917 g*. Moscow, 1967.

Antonov-Ovseenko, V. A. "Krasnaia gvardiia–narodnaia militsiia," *K novoi armii*, 1920, no. 16, pp. 5–7.

———. "Oktiabr'skaia buria," in *Oktiabr'skoe vooruzhennoe vosstanie v Petrograde. Vospominaniia aktivnykh uchastnikov revoliutsii*. Leningrad, 1956.

———. "Stroitel'stvo Krasnoi armii v revoliutsii," in *Za 5 let (1917–1922). Sbornik*. Moscow, 1922.

Antonov-Saratovskii, V. P. "Oktiabr'skie dni v Saratove," *Proletarskaia revoliutsiia*, 1924, no. 10, pp. 278–98.

———. *Pod stiagom proletarskoi bor'by. Otryvki iz vospominanii o rabote v Saratove za vremia s 1915 g. do 1918*. Moscow-Leningrad, 1925.

———. "Saratov s fevralia–po oktiabr'," *Proletariskaia revoliutsiia*, 1924, no. 2, pp. 144–71; no. 4, pp. 178–210.

Anulov, F. "Krasnaia gvardiia v ee ustavakh," *Krasnaia armiia. Vestnik Voenno-nauchnogo obshchestva pri Voennoi akademii*, 1922, nos. 18–19, pp. 21–44.

———. "Oktiabr' v stolitsakh," *Krasnaia armiia. Vestnik Voenno-nauchnogo obshchestva pri Voennoi akademii*, 1922, nos. 18–19, pp. 8–20.

Artemov, A. A. "Bol'sheviki—organizatory razgroma miatezha iunkerov v Petrograde," *Vestnik Leningradskogo universiteta*, 1964, no. 20, pp. 5–16.

———. "Uchastie petrogradskoi Krasnoi gvardii v razgrome kontrrevoliutsionnogo miatezha Kerenskogo-Krasnova," *Vestnik Leningradskogo universiteta*, 1964, no. 8, pp. 17–28.

Arzub'ev, P. "Na sluzhbe u novago rezhima," *Rech'*, Mar. 12, 1917, no. 61; Mar. 16, 1917, no. 64; Mar. 18, 1917, no. 66.

Ascher, Abraham. "The Kornilov Affair," *Russian Review*, Oct. 1953, pp. 235–52.

Asher, Harvey. "The Kornilov Affair," *Russian Review*, July 1970, pp. 286–300.

Atsarkin, A. N. *Zhizn' i bor'ba rabochei molodezhi v Rossii (1901 g.–Oktiabr' 1917 g.)*. Moscow, 1965.

Avrich, Paul. "The Bolshevik Revolution and Workers' Control in Russian Industry," *Slavic Review*, 22, no. 1 (Mar. 1963), pp. 47–63.

———. *The Russian Anarchists*. Princeton, N. J., 1967.

———. "Russian Factory Committees in 1917," *Jahrbücher fur Geschichte Osteuropas*, 1963, no. 11, pp. 161–82.

———. "The Russian Revolution and the Factory Committees." Ph.D. diss., Columbia Univ., 1961.

Avvakumov, S. I. "Bor'ba petrogradskikh bol'shevikov za osushchestvlenie leninskogo plana Oktiabr'skogo vosstaniia," in *Oktiabr'skoe vooruzhennoe vosstanie v Petrograde: Sbornik statei*. Moscow-Leningrad, 1957.

Babushkin, V. F. *Dni velikikh sobytii*. Saratov, 1932.

Baedeker, Karl. *Russia: A Handbook for Travelers*. New York, 1971 (facsimile of the 1914 edition).

Baklanova, I. A. *Rabochie Petrograda v period mirnogo razvitiia revoliutsii (mart–iiun' 1917 g.)*. Leningrad, 1978.

Baklanova, I. A., and Z. V. Stepanov. "Rabochie-metallisty Petrograda v dni Velikogo Oktiabria," in *Oktiabr'skoe vooruzhennoe vosstanie v Petrograde: Sbornik statei*. Moscow-Leningrad, 1957.

Barikhovskii, F. G. "Raionnaia duma," in *Vyborgskaia storona*. Leningrad, 1957.

Bastiony revoliutsii. Sbornik materialov iz istorii leningradskikh zavodov v 1917 godu. Leningrad, 1957.

Bater, James H. *St. Petersburg: Industrialization and Change*. Montreal, 1976.

Bogdanov, M. "Krasnogvardeitskie ataki," *Voennyi vestnik*, 1957, no. 10, pp. 22–24.

Bogdanov, N. A. "Po zovu partii," in *Oktiabr' i profsoiuzy*. Moscow, 1967.

Boll, Michael M. *The Petrograd Armed Workers Movement in the February Revolution (February–July 1917): A Study in the Radicalization of the Petrograd Proletariat*. Washington, D. C., 1979.

Bol'shevistskie organizatsii Ukrainy v period podgotovki i provedeniia Velikoi Oktiabr'skoi sotsialisticheskoi revoliutsii (mart–noiabr' 1917 g.). Sbornik dokumentov i materialov. Kiev, 1957.

Bol'shevistskie organizatsii Ukrainy v period ustanovleniia i ukrepleniia sovetskoi vlasti (noiabr' 1917–aprel' 1918 gg.). Sbornik dokumentov i materialov. Kiev, 1962.

Bonch-Bruevich, V. D. *Na boevykh postakh fevralskoi i oktiabr'skoi revoliutsii.* Moscow, 1936.

Bor'ba za sovetskuiu vlast' na Iuzhnom Urale. Sbornik dokumentov i materialov. Cheliabinsk, 1957.

Borisov, M. "S oruzhiem v rukakh," in *V boiakh. Sbornik vospominanii, posviashennyi geroicheskoi bor'be vasileostrovtsev za 15 let, 1917–1932.* Leningrad, 1932.

Bortnik, M. "Na Trubochnom zavode," in *Professional'noe dvizhenie v Petrograde v 1917 g.* Leningrad, 1922.

Browder, Robert P., and Alexander F. Kerensky, eds. *The Russian Provisional Government of 1917: Documents.* 3 vols. Stanford, Calif., 1961.

Burdzhalov, E. N. *Vtoraia russkaia revoliutsiia: Moskva, front, periferiia.* Moscow, 1971.

————. *Vtoraia russkaia revoliutsiia: Vosstanie v Petrograde.* Moscow, 1967.

Buzdalin, S. F. "Fevral'skaia revoliutsiia v Khar'kove," *Letopis' revoliutsii,* 1927, no. 1, pp. 17–22.

————. "Oktiabr'skaia revoliutsiia v Khar'kove," *Letopis' revoliutsii,* 1922, no. 1, pp. 35–38.

Chaadaeva, O. N. "Vooruzhenie proletariata v 1917 g.," *Istoriia proletariata SSSR,* 1932, no. 11, pp. 15–58 (part 1); 1932, no. 12, pp. 21–49 (part 2).

Chechkovskii, A. "Krasnaia gvardiia Moskovskoi zastavy," in *Moskovskaia zastava v 1917 g.* Leningrad, 1959.

Chepenko, V. I. "Bol'sheviki zavoda Beringa," in *Za vlast' Sovetov. Vospominaniia uchastnikov revoliutsionnykh sobytii 1917 goda v Saratovskoi gubernii.* Saratov, 1957.

Chepurnov, P. I. "Krasnaia gvardiia Khar'kova," in *Khar'kov v 1917 godu. Vospominaniia aktivnykh uchastnikov Velikoi Oktiabr'skoi sotsialisticheskoi revoliutsii.* Kharkov, 1957.

Chirkov, P. M. "Bor'ba bol'shevistskikh organizatsii Tsentral'nogo promyshlennogo raiona za sozdanie Krasnoi gvardii (fevral'–noiabr' 1917 g.)," in *Kommunisticheskaia partiia v bor'be za pobedu Oktiabria. Sbornik statei.* Moscow, 1959.

————. "Fabzavkomy i profsoiuzy v bor'be za sozdanie rabochei Krasnoi gvardii," *Sbornik nauchnykh trudov kafedr obshchestvennykh nauk MEIS,* 1961, vyp. 1, pp. 183–234.

Chugunov, T. K. "Za vlast' sovetov," in *Za vlast' Sovetov. Vospominaniia uchastnikov revoliutsionnykh sobytii 1917 goda v Saratovskoi gubernii.* Saratov, 1957.

Collins, David N. "A Note on the Numerical Strength of the Russian Red Guard in October 1917," *Soviet Studies,* 24, no. 2 (Oct. 1972), pp. 270–80.

————. "The Origins, Structure, and Role of the Russian Red Guard." Ph.D. diss., Univ. of Leeds, 1975.

————. "The Russian Red Guard of 1917 and Lenin's Utopia," *Journal of Russian Studies*, 1976, no. 32, pp. 3–12.

————. "The Russian Red Guards of 1917–1919: A Bibliographical Survey," *Soviet Armed Forces Annual*, 3 (1979), pp. 300–316.

Daniels, Robert V. *Red October: The Bolshevik Revolution of 1917*. New York, 1967.

Deiateli revoliutsionnogo dvizheniia v Rossii. 5 vols. Moscow, 1927–33.

Devlin, Robert J., Jr. "Petrograd Workers and Workers' Factory Committees in 1917: An Aspect of the Social History of the Russian Revolution." Ph.D. diss., SUNY Binghamton, 1976.

Dmitriev, N. "Petrogradskie fabzavkomy v 1917 g.," *Krasnaia letopis'*, 1927, no. 2, pp. 62–101.

Doneseniia komissarov Petrogradskogo voenno-revoliutsionnogo komiteta. Moscow, 1957.

Dubenko, P. E. *Iz nedr tsarskogo flota k velikomu Oktiabriu*. Moscow, 1928.

Dzenis, O. "Kak my brali Zimnii dvorets," in *Oktiabr'skoe vooruzhennoe vosstanie v Petrograde: Vospominaniia aktivnykh uchastnikov revoliutsii*. Leningrad, 1956.

Egorov, A. "Kak my borolis' za Oktiabr'," in *V boiakh za Oktiabr'. Vospominaniia ob Oktiabre za Nevskoi zastavoi*. Leningrad, 1932.

Ekonomicheskoe polozhenie Rossii nakanune Velikoi Oktiabr'skoi sotsialisticheskoi revoliutsii. A. L. Sidorov et al., eds. 2 vols. Moscow, 1957.

Eremeev, K. "Nachalo Krasnoi armii," *Proletarskaia revoliutsiia*, 1928, no. 4, pp. 154–68.

————. "Osada Zimnego dvortsa," in *Oktiabr'skoe vooruzhennoe vosstanie v Petrograde: Vospominaniia aktivnykh uchastnikov revoliutsii*. Leningrad, 1956.

Erickson, John. "The Origins of the Red Army," in Richard Pipes, ed., *Revolutionary Russia*. Cambridge, Mass., 1968.

————. *The Soviet High Command, 1918–1941*. New York, 1962.

Erykalov, E. F. "Krasnaia gvardiia Petrograda v period podgotovki Velikoi Oktiabr'skoi sotsialisticheskoi revoliutsii," *Istoricheskie zapiski*, 47 (1954), pp. 58–92.

————. *Krasnaia gvardiia v bor'be za vlast' Sovetov*. Moscow, 1957.

————. *Oktiabr'skoe vooruzhennoe vosstanie v Petrograde*. Leningrad, 1966.

————. "Petrogradskie Krasnogvardeitsy v bor'be za razgrom kontrrevoliutsionnykh ochagov (noiabr' 1917–fevral' 1918 gg.)," *Trudy Leningradskogo vysshego voenno-pedagogicheskogo instituta*, 1951, no. 5, pp. 214–40.

Erykalov, E. F., and Yu. I. Korablev. "Nekotorye novye materialy o III Petrogradskoi obshchegorodskoi konferentsii RSDRP(b)," *Voprosy istorii KPSS*, 1966, no. 7, pp 28–35.

Evseev, F. Z. "V Petrograde v 1917 godu," *Sovety deputatov trudiashchikhsia*, 1957, no. 1, pp. 91–94.

Ezergailis, Andrew. *The 1917 Revolution in Latvia*. New York, 1974.

Fabrichno-zavodskie komitety Petrograda v 1917 godu. Protokoly. I. I. Mints et al., eds. Moscow, 1979.

Fedorov, A. A. "Sorok let tomu nazad," in *Za vlast' Sovetov. Vospominaniia uchastnikov revoliutsionnykh sobytii 1917 godu v Saratovskoi gubernii.* Saratov, 1957.

Ferro, Marc. *October, 1917.* London, 1980.

———. *La Révolution de 1917: La chute du tsarisme et les origines d'Octobre.* Paris, 1967.

———. *The Russian Revolution of February 1917.* Englewood Cliffs, N. J., 1972. Translation of previous entry.

"Fevral'skaia revoliutsiia v Petrograde (28 fevralia–1 marta 1917 g.)," *Krasnyi arkhiv,* 1930, no. 4–5, pp. 62–102.

Fleer, M. "Rabochaia Krasnaia gvardiia v Fevral'skuiu revoliutsiiu," *Krasnaia letopis',* 1926, no. 1 (16), pp. 23–43.

Fraiman, A. L. *Revoliutsionnaia zashchita Petrograda v fevrale–marte 1918 g.* Moscow, 1964.

———. "Revoliutsionnyi Petrograd i bor'ba za pobedu Sovetskoi vlasti na Iuge Rossii," in *Oktiabr' i grazhdanskaia voina v SSSR. Sbornik k 70-letiiu akademika I. I. Mintsa.* Moscow, 1966.

Freidlin, B. M. *Ocherki istorii rabochego dvizheniia v Rossii v 1917 g.* Moscow, 1967.

Gagin, I. "Boevye budni iaroslavskikh krasnogvardeitsev," *Literaturnyi Iaroslavl',* 1958, vyp. 9, pp. 191–97.

Gamrets'kii, Iu. M. "Chervona gvardiia Ukraini v radians'ki istoriografii," *Ukrains'kii istoricheskii zhurnal,* 1959, no. 6, pp. 119–28.

———. *Radi robitnichikh deputativ Ukraini v 1917 rotsi (period dvovladdia).* Kiev, 1966.

Ganichev, L. "Rozhdenie Krasnoi gvardii (Iz istorii zavoda voenno-vrachebnykh zagotovlenii, nyne zavoda krasnogvardeets)," in *Bastiony revoliutsii. Sbornik materialov iz istorii leningradskikh zavodov v 1917 godu.* Leningrad, 1957.

Gaponenko, L. S. *Rabochii klass Rossii v 1917 godu.* Moscow, 1917.

Garchev, P. I. *Chervona gvardiia na Sumshchini.* Sumy, 1957.

———. *Chervona gvardiia Ukraini u Zhovtnevii revoliutsii.* Kharkov, 1969.

———. "Krasnaia gvardiia Ukrainy v bor'be za diktaturu proletariata," in *Proletariat Rossii puti k Oktiabriu 1917 goda. Oblik, bor'ba, gegemoniia.* Odessa, 1967.

———. "Pitannia istorii Ukraini. Chervona gvardiia Khar'kova v borot'bi za peremogu radians'koi vladi," *Vesnik Kharkivs'kogo Universitetu. Istorichna seriia,* 1967, vyp. 2, pp. 3–13.

———. "Sozdanie Krasnoi gvardii na Ukraine v period dvoevlastie," *Vestnik Khar'kovskogo gosudarstvennogo universiteta. Seriia istoriia KPSS i istorii naradov SSSR,* 1965, vyp. 2, pp. 33–44.

Gavrilov, I. G. "Krasnaia gvardiia v Vyborgskom raione," *Krasnaia letopis',* 1926, no. 6, pp. 93–102.

―――. "Krasnaia gvardiia v Vyborgskom raione (Vospominaniia o 1917–1918 gg.)," *Iunyi proletarii*, 1935, no. 21, pp. 23–28.

Georgievskii, G. P. *Ocherki po istorii Krasnoi gvardii*. Moscow, 1919.

Gerasimenko, G. A. *Nizovye krest'ianskie organizatsii v 1917—pervoi polovine 1918 godov; Na materialiakh Nizhnego Povolzh'ia*. Saratov, 1974.

―――. *Partiinaia bor'ba v sovetakh Nizhnego Povolzh'ia*. Saratov, 1966.

―――. *Pobeda Oktiabr'skoi revoliutsii v Saratovskoi gubernii*. Saratov, 1968.

Gerasimenko, G. A., and F. Rashitov. *Sovety Nizhnego Povolzh'ia v Oktiabr'skoi revoliutsii*. Saratov, 1972.

Geroi Oktiabria. Biografii aktivnykh uchastnikov podgotovki i provedeniia Oktiabr'skogo vooruzhennogo vosstaniia v Petrograde. 2 vols. Moscow, 1967.

Gessen, V. Iu. "Krasnaia gvardiia i petrogradskie promyshlenniki v 1917 g.," *Krasnaia letopis'*, 1928, no. 3, pp. 52–90.

Gill, Graeme J. *Peasants and Government in the Russian Revolution*. New York, 1979.

Godovshchina sotsial'noi revoliutsii v Saratove. Saratov, 1918.

Golovin, I. G. "Krasnaia gvardiia," in *V ogne revoliutsii i grazhdanskoi voiny; Vospominaniia uchastnikov*. Omsk, 1959.

Golubev, I. P. "Krasnogvardeitsy-zheleznodorozhniki," in *V bor'be za Oktiabr' v Belorussii i Zapadnom fronte*. Minsk, 1957.

Golubev, N. A. "Iz istorii Krasnoi gvardii," *Voprosy arkhivovedeniia*, 1964, no. 3, pp. 106–12.

―――. "Krasnaia gvardiia Ivanovo-Kineshemskogo raiona," *Uchenye zapiski. Moskovskii gosudarstvennyi pedagogicheskii institut im. V. I. Lenina*, no. 299 (1964), pp. 55–80.

―――. "Rost i ukreplenie riadov Krasnoi gvardii Vladimirskoi, Kostromskoi i Iaroslavskoi gubernii v kontse 1917–nachale 1918 g.," in *Iz istorii rabochego klassa SSSR*. Ivanovo, 1964.

Golubtsov, V. S. *Memuary kak istochnik po istorii Sovetskogo obshchestva*. Moscow, 1970.

Goncharenko, I. "Krasnogvardeiskii otriad parovozostroitel'nogo zavoda," *Letopis' revoliutsii*, 1928, no. 1, pp. 186–97.

Gorer, Geoffrey, and John Rickman. *The People of Great Russia; A Psychological Study*. London, 1949.

Gorin, P. O., ed. *Organizatsiia i stroitel'stvo sovetov rabochikh i soldatskikh deputatov v 1917 godu. Sbornik dokumentov*. Moscow, 1928.

Graf, T. "Ob oktiabr'skoi revoliutsii," *Krasnaia letopis'*, 1923, no. 6, pp. 164–69.

Gritsenko, A. P. "Rol' fabzavkomov v sozdanii Krasnoi gvardii na Ukraine," in *Oktiabr' i grazhdanskaia voina v SSSR. Sbornik statei k 70-letiiu akademika I. I. Mintsa*. Moscow, 1966.

―――. "Struktura i sklod promislovogo proletariatu Ukraini v 1917 r.," in *Velikii Zhovten' i gromadians'ka viina na Ukraini*. Kiev, 1973.

Grunt, A. I. *Moskva 1917-i; revoliutsii i kontrrevoliutsiia.* Moscow, 1976.
Gundorov, A. S. "Za Nevskoi zastavoi," in *V ogne revoliutsionnykh boev (Raionny Petrograda v dvukh revoliutsiiakh 1917 g.). Sbornik vospominanii starykh bol'shevikov-pitertsev.* Moscow, 1967.
Haimson, Leopold. "The Problems of Social Stability in Urban Russia, 1905–1917," *Slavic Review,* 23, no. 4 (Dec. 1964), pp. 619–42 (part 1); 24, no. 1 (Mar. 1965), pp. 1–22 (part 2).
———. *The Russian Marxists and the Origins of Bolshevism.* Cambridge, Mass., 1955.
Hamm, Michael F. "The Breakdown of Urban Modernization: A Prelude to the Revolutions of 1917," in Michael F. Hamm, ed., *The City in Russian History.* Lexington, Ky., 1976, pp. 182–200.
Hasegawa, Tsuyoshi. *The February Revolution: Petrograd, 1917.* Seattle, 1981.
———. "The Formation of the Militia in the February Revolution: An Aspect of the Origins of Dual Power," *Slavic Review,* 32, no. 2 (June 1973), pp. 303–22.
———. "The Problem of Power in the February Revolution of 1917 in Russia," *Canadian Slavonic Papers,* 14, no. 4 (1972), pp. 611–33.
Hunzak, Taras, ed. *The Ukraine, 1917–1921: A Study in Revolution.* Cambridge, Mass., 1977.
Iaroshevskii, P. "Iz istorii Odesskoi Krasnoi gvardii," *Letopis' revoliutsii,* 1924, no. 3, pp. 1–12.
Ilin-Zhenevskii, A. F. *Ot fevralia k zakhvatu vlasti: vospominaniia o 1917 g.* Leningrad, 1927.
"Instruksiia Krasnoi Gvardii Ispolnital'nogo Komiteta Soveta Rabochikh Deputatov v gor. Odesse," *Letopis' revoliutsii,* 1924, no. 3, pp. 207–9.
Ioganson, O. I. "Krasnogvardeitsy Krasnogo kresta v bor'be za vlast' Sovetov," in *Kak my borolis' za vlast' Sovetov v Irkutskoi gubernii.* Irkutsk, 1957.
"Istoki Chrezvychainoe sobranie upolnomochennykh fabrik i zavodov g. Petrograda (mart 1918 g.)," *Kontinent,* 1955, no. 2, pp. 383–419.
Istoriia gorodov i sel Ukrainskoi SSR. Khar'kovskaia oblast'. Kiev, 1976.
Istoriia Leningradskoi gosudarstvennoi ordena Lenina i ordena Trudovogo Krasnogo znameni obuvnoi fabriki 'Skorokhod' imeni Ia. Kalinina. Leningrad, 1969.
Istoriia Sovetskogo obshchestva v vospominaniiakh sovremennikov 1917–1957. Annotirovannyi ukazatel' memuarnoi literatury. 2 vols. Moscow, 1958, 1967.
Iurenev, I. [K. K.] "Krasnaia gvardiia," *Krasnoarmeets,* 1919, no. 10–15, pp. 73–79.
Iurkin, A. A. "Krasnaia gvardiia," in *Petrograda v dni Velikogo Oktiabria. Vospominaniia uchastnikov revoliutsionnykh sobytii v Petrograda v 1917 godu.* Leningrad, 1967.
"Iz istorii Krasnoi gvardii Petrograda," *Istoricheskii arkhiv,* 1957, no. 5, pp. 119–45.

Iz istorii moskovskoi rabochei Krasnoi gvardii. Materialy i dokumenty. G. D. Kostomarov and V. F. Malakhovskii, eds. Moscow, 1930.

Johnson, Robert Eugene. *Peasant and Proletarian: The Working Class of Moscow in the Late Nineteenth Century.* New Brunswick, N. J., 1979.

"K istorii Petrogradskoi Krasnoi gvardii," *Sovetskie arkhivy,* 1966, no. 3, pp. 35–40.

Kabanov. "Krasnaia gvardiia i profsoiuzy," in *Leningradskie profsoiuzy za desiat let. 1917–1927.* Leningrad, 1927.

Kaiurov, V. "Iz istorii Krasnoi gvardii Vyborgskogo raiona v 1917 g.," *Proletarskaia revoliutsiia,* 1927, no. 10, pp. 224–37.

Kamenev, S. S. *Zapiski o grazhdanskoi voine i voennom stroitel'stve.* Moscow, 1963.

Kanev, S. N. "Krakh russkogo anarkhizma," *Voprosy istorii,* 1968, no. 9, pp. 50–75.

Kazakova, M. N. "Na 'Treugol'nike'," in *V ogne revoliutsionnykh boev (Raiony Petrograda v dvukh revoliutsiiakh 1917 g.). Sbornik vospominanii starykh bol'shevikov-pitertsev.* Moscow, 1967.

Keep, John L. H. *The Russian Revolution: A Study in Mass Mobilization.* London, 1974.

Kel'son, Z. S. "Militsiia Fevral'skoi revoliutsii," *Byloe,* 1925, no. 1, pp. 161–79 (part 1); no. 2, pp. 151–75 (part 2); no. 5, pp. 220–35 (part 3).

Khar'kov i Khar'kovskaia guberniia v Velikoi Oktiabr'skoi sotsialisticheskoi revoliutsii. Dokumenty i materialy. Khar'kov, 1957.

Khodakov, G. F. *Ocherki istorii Saratovskoi organizatsii KPSS: Chast' 1, 1898–1918.* Saratov, 1968.

Khokhlov, A. G. *Krasnaia gvardiia Belorussii v bor'be za vlast' Sovetov (mart 1917–mart 1918 g.).* Minsk, 1965.

"Khronika Oktiabr'skoi revoliutsii v Saratove," *Kommunisticheskii put'* (Saratov), 1927, no. 19, pp. 29–36 (part 1); no. 20, pp. 111–25 (part 2).

Khronika revoliutsionnykh sobytii v Saratovskom Povolzh'e, 1917–1918. Saratov, 1968.

Kin, P. A. "Khar'kovskaia Krasnaia gvardiia," *Letopis' revoliutsii,* 1923, no. 3, pp. 70–72.

Kir'ianov, Iu. U. *Rabochie iuga Rossii, 1914–fevral' 1917 g.* Moscow, 1971.

Koenker, Diane. *Moscow Workers and the 1917 Revolution.* Princeton, N. J., 1981.

Kogan, Ts. A. "V te istoricheski dni," in *Za vlast' Sovetov. Vospominaniia uchastnikov revoliutsionnykh sobytii 1917 goda v Saratovskoi gubernii.* Saratov, 1957.

Kondufor, Iu. Iu. *Proletariat Khar'kova v predoktiabr'skie dni. Uchenye zapiski Khar'kovskogo universiteta,* 88 (1957), pp. 201–21.

Konev, A. M. "Deiatel'nost' partii po ispol'zovaniiu Krasnoi gvardii v sozdanii Krasnoi armii," *Voprosy istorii KPSS,* 1978, no. 7, pp. 88–100.

————. *Krasnaia gvardiia na zashchite Oktiabria.* Moscow, 1978.

————. "Krasnaia gvardiia posle Oktiabria v Sovetskoi istoriografii," in *Iz istorii grazhadanskoi voiny i interventsii 1917–1922 gg. Sbornik statei.* Moscow, 1974.

Korchagin, S. M. "Narod pobezhdaet," in *Narvskaia zastava v 1917 godu, v vospominaniiakh i dokumentakh.* Leningrad, 1960.

————. "Razgrom general'skoi avantiury," in *Narvskaia zastava v 1917 godu, v vospominaniiakh i dokumentakh.* Leningrad, 1960.

Kornatovskii, N. A. "Ot Krasnoi gvardii k Krasnoi armii," *Krasnaia letopis'*, 1933, no. 1, pp. 46–53.

Korolivskii, S. M., M. A. Rubach, and N. I. Suprunenko. *Pobeda sovetskoi vlasti na Ukraine.* Moscow, 1967.

Kovalenko, D. A. "Bor'ba fabrichno-zavodskikh komitetov Petrograda za rabochikh kontrol' nad proizvodstvom (mart–oktiabr' 1917 g.)," *Istoricheskie zapiski*, 61 (1957), pp. 66–111.

Kozlov, T. S. *Krasnaia gvardiia i armii v Turkestane. Istoricheskaia spravka ob organizatsii i etapakh.* Ashkhabad, 1928.

————. *Krasnaia gvardiia i armii v Turkmenii.* Ashkhabad, 1922.

Krasichkov, V. N. "V Saratovskikh zheleznodorozhnykh masterskikh," in *Za vlast' Sovetov. Vospominaniia uchastnikov revoliutsionnykh sobytii 1917 goda v Saratovskoi gubernii.* Saratov, 1957.

Krasnaia gvardiia Taganroga. K. V. Gubarev, ed. Taganrog, 1928.

Krasnov, P. "Na vnutrennem fronte," *Arkhiv russkoi revoliutsii*, 1922, no. 1, pp. 97–190.

Krivonos, G. M. "30-i polk i Krasnaia gvardiia (vospominaniia)," in *1917 g. v Khar'kove. Sbornik vospominanii.* Kharkov, 1927.

Kuliapin, S. I. "Iz istorii Krasnoi gvardii Urala," in *Iz istorii partiinykh organizatsii Urala (1917–1967).* Perm, 1967.

————. "Osnovnyi etapy sozdaniia Krasnoi gvardii na Urale (mart 1917–iiun' 1918 g.)," in *Iz istorii sotsialisticheskogo stroitel'stva na Urale. Sbornik.* Perm, 1969.

Kurman, M. V., and I. V. Lebedinskii. *Naselenie bol'shogo sotsialisticheskogo goroda.* Moscow, 1968.

Kushnev, P. *Krasnaia gvardiia, ee istoriia i zaslugi pered nashei revoliutsei.* Moscow-Leningrad, 1927.

Lebedev, P. "Fevral'–Oktiabr' v Saratove (vospominaniia)," *Proletarskaia revoliutsiia*, 1922, no. 10, pp. 237–77.

Leiberov, I. P. "Petrogradskii proletariat v gody pervoi mirovoi voiny," in *Istoriia rabochikh Leningrada.* Vol. 1. Leningrad, 1972.

————. "Petrogradskii proletariat vo vseobshchei politicheskoi stachke 25 fevralia 1917 g.," in *Oktiabr' i grazhdanskaia voina v SSSR. Sbornik 70-letiiu akademika I. I. Mintsa.* Moscow, 1966.

Lenin, V. I. *Collected Works.* 45 vols. Moscow, 1960–70.

————. *Polnoe sobranie sochinenii.* 55 vols. Moscow, 1958–65. 5th ed.

Leningradskie profsoiuzy za desiat' let. 1917–1927. Sbornik vospominanii. Leningrad, 1927.

Leningradskie rabochie v bor'be za vlast sovetov. Leningrad, 1924.

Lenskii, N. A. "Gorodskaia militsiia, eia organizatsiia i kompetentsiia," *Gorodskoe delo*, 1917, no. 7 (Apr.), pp. 265–70.

Leshchenko, A. P. "Bor'ba za ustanovlenie Sovetskoi vlasti v Khar'kove," in *Ustanovlenie sovetskoi vlasti na mestakh v 1917–1918 godakh. Sbornik statei.* Moscow, 1953. Vyp. 1.

Levinson, M. "Krest'ianskoe dvizhenie v Saratovskoi gubernii v 1917 godu," in *1917 god v Saratove.* Saratov, 1927.

Liapin, I. M. "Iz vospominanii byvshego nachal'nika Krasnoi gvardii 1-go gorodskogo raiona Petrograda," *Istoriia proletariata SSSR*, 1932, no. 11, pp. 91–100.

Lobakhin, V. "Khar'kovskii sovet rabochikh i soldatskikh deputatov v marte i aprele 1917 goda," *Letopis' revoliutsii*, 1929, no. 4, pp. 7–42.

Loza, G. A. "Soldaty party," in *Oktiabr' i profsoiuzy.* Moscow, 1967.

Luk'ianov, Kh. *Krasnaia gvardiia Donbassa.* Stalino, 1958.

Lur'e, M. L. "Kak zarozhdalas' Krasnaia gvardiia," *Krasnaia letopis'*, 1937, no. 3, pp. 67–87.

———. "Kolomenskii (2e Gorodskoi) raionnyi Sovet rabochikh i soldatskikh deputatov v proletarskoi revoliutsii 1917 g.," *Krasnaia letopis'*, 1931, no. 5–6, pp. 30–67.

———. *Petrogradskaia Krasnaia gvardiia (fevral' 1917–fevral' 1918).* Leningrad, 1938.

Lur'e, P. A. "Listaia dnevnik 1917 g.," in *V ogne revoliutsionnykh boev (Raiony Petrograda v dvukh revoliutsiiakh 1917 g.). Sbornik vospominanii starykh bol'shevikov-pitertsev.* Moscow, 1971.

Malakhovskii, V. "Istoricheskii smysl i znachenie rabochei Krasnoi gvardii," *Staryi bol'shevik*, 1933, no. 4 (7), pp. 14–83.

———. *Iz istorii Krasnoi gvardii. Krasnogvardeitsy Vyborgskogo raiona, 1917 g.* Leningrad, 1925.

———. "Kak sozdavalas' rabochaia Krasnaia gvardiia," *Proletarskaia revoliutsiia*, 1929, no. 10, pp. 27–79.

———. "Literatura o rabochei Krasnoi gvardii 1917 goda," *Proletarskaia revoliutsiia*, 1928, no. 6, pp. 340–51.

———. "Perekhod ot Krasnoi gvardii k Krasnoi armii," *Krasnaia letopis'*, 1928, no. 3, pp. 5–51.

———. "Sanitarnaia chast' Krasnoi gvardii v 1917 g.," *Proletarskaia revoliutsiia*, 1927, no. 11, pp. 195–201.

"Manifestatsii rabochikh 22-go aprelia," in *Leningradskie rabochie v bor'be za vlast' sovetov.* Leningrad, 1924.

Martsinovskii, A. *Zapiski rabochego-bol'shevika.* Saratov, 1923.

Matveev, F. P. *Iz zapisnoi knizhki deputata 176 pekhotnogo polka. Petrogradskii Sovet r.i.s.d. mart–mai 1917 goda.* Moscow-Leningrad, 1932.

Mawdsley, Evan. *The Russian Revolution and the Baltic Fleet; War and Politics, February 1917–April 1918.* New York, 1978.

Medvedev, V. K. "Saratovskii sovet ot fevralia k oktiabriu," in *Uchenye zapiski Saratovskaia oblastnaia partiinaia shkoly*, Saratov, 1948, vyp. 1.

Mel'gunov, S. P. *Kak bol'sheviki zakhvatili vlast'; Oktiabr'skii perevorot 1917 goda*. Paris, 1953.

Mel'nik, S. K., and V. R. Raevs'kii. "Uchast' Latis'kikh proletariv u borot'bi za vstanovlennia Radians'koi vladi na Ukraini," *Ukrainskyi istorychnyi zhurnal*, 1977, no. 12, pp. 80–91.

Minailenko, F. Z. "Krasnogvardeitsy idut v boi," in *Skvoz grozy i buri*. Kharkov, 1969.

Minichev, A. "Boevye dni. Iz vospominanii," *Krasnaia letopis'*, 1923–24, no. 9, pp. 5–10.

Mints, I. I. *Istoriia Velikogo Oktiabria*. 3 vols. Moscow, 1967.

Miroshnichenko, V. "Boevye druzhiny i Krasnaia gvardiia v Khar'kove," in *1917 g. v Khar'kov. Sbornik vospominanii*. Kharkov, 1927.

Mitel'man, M., B. Glebov, and A. Ul'ianskii. *Istoriia Putilovskogo zavoda, 1801–1917*. Moscow, 1961.

Molodtsygin, M. A. "Krasnaia gvardiia posle Oktiabria," *Voprosy istorii*, 1980, no. 10, pp. 25–43.

Morgunov, V. R. "Organizatsiia i bor'ba Krasnoi gvardii v 1917–1918 gg.," *Letopis' revoliutsii*, 1923, no. 5, pp. 159–66.

———. "Vospominaniia uchastnikov Velikogo Oktiabria," *Istoricheskii arkhiv*, 1957, no. 5, pp. 207–9.

Morozov, F. "Fevral'skaia revoliutsiia v Saratove," in *Fevral'. Sbornik vospominanii v 1917 g.* Saratov, 1922.

Morozov, V. F. *Ot Krasnoi gvardii k Krasnoi armii*. Moscow, 1958.

Moskovskaia zastava v 1917; stat'i i vospominaniia. Leningrad, 1959.

Mukhtar-Londarskii, M. I. "Boevaia druzhina Krasnoi gvardii Putilovskogo zavoda," *Istoricheskii arkhiv*, 1957, no. 1, pp. 205–12.

"Nakanune Oktiabr'skogo vooruzhennogo vosstaniia," *Voprosy istorii KPSS*, 1981, no. 11, pp. 80–88.

Narvskaia zastava v 1917 godu, v vospominaniiakh i dokumentakh. Leningrad, 1960.

Nedostupov, N. "Oktiabr' v Saratove," in *V boiakh za diktaturu proletariata. Sbornik vospominanii*. Saratov, 1933.

Nefedov, N. "Sushchevsko-Mar'inskii raion v Oktiabr'," in *Oktiabr' na Krasnoi Presne. Vospominanii*. Moscow, 1922.

Nenarokov, A. P. *1917. Velikii Oktiabr': Kratkaia istoriia, dokumenty, fotografii*. Moscow, 1977.

Nesterenko, A. I. *Bol'sheviki-organizatory sanitarnykh otriadov v revoliutsionnom Petrograde*. Leningrad, 1969.

Nevskii, V. "V Oktiabre," in *Oktiabr'skoe vooruzhennoe vosstanie v Petrograde. Vospominaniia aktivnykh uchastnikov revoliutsii*. Leningrad, 1956.

Ocherki istorii Leningrada. 6 vols. Moscow-Leningrad, 1955–1970.

Oktiabr' na Krasnoi Presne. Vospominanii. Moscow, 1922.

Oktiabr'skaia revoliutsiia i armiia. 25 oktiabria 1917 g.–mart, 1918 g. Sbornik dokumentov. Moscow, 1963.

Oktiabr'skoe vooruzhennoe vosstanie: semnadtsatyi god v Petrograde. 2 vols. Leningrad, 1967.

Oktiabr'skoe vooruzhennoe vosstanie v Petrograde: Dokumenty i materialy. Moscow, 1957.

Oktiabr'skoe vooruzhennoe vosstanie v Petrograde: Sbornik statei. Moscow-Leningrad, 1957.

Oktiabr'skoe vooruzhennoe vosstanie v Petrograde. Vospominaniia aktivnykh uchastnikov revoliutsii. Leningrad, 1956.

Omskie bol'sheviki v bor'be za vlast Sovetov (1917–1920). Sbornik dokumental'nykh materialov. Omsk, 1952.

Onufrienko, M. Ia. "Krasnaia gvardiia v bor'be za ustanovlenie Sovetskoi vlasti na Ukraine." Diss., Kiev Univ., 1955.

Orov, K. "Boevoi otriad soiuza transportnikov," in *Leningradskie profsoiuzy za desiat let.* 1917–1927. Leningrad, 1927.

Palij, Michael. *The Anarchism of Nestor Makhno, 1918–1921.* Seattle, 1976.

Pasiukov, F. V. "Organizatsiia meditsinskoi pomoshchi uchastnikam sturma Zimnego dvortsa," *Sovetskoe zdravookhranenie,* 1960, no. 4, pp. 63–67.

Pavliuk, P. *Kharkivs'ka Chervona gvardiia (Liutii 1917 g.–berezen' 1918 r.).* Kiev, 1948.

Peche, Ia. *Krasnaia gvardiia v Moskve v boiakh za Oktiabr'.* Moscow, 1929.

"Pervoe sobranie po organizatsii Krasnoi gvardii (17 aprelia 1917 g.)," *Istoricheskii arkhiv,* 1961, no. 6, pp. 178–79.

Pervyi legal'nyi Peterburgskii komitet bol'shevikov v 1917 godu: Sbornik materialov i protokolov zasedanii Peterburgskogo komiteta RSDRP(b) i ego Ispolnitel'noi komissii za 1917 g. P. F. Kudelli, ed. Moscow-Leningrad, 1927.

"Pervyi partizanskii otriad petrogradskikh pechatnikov." *Leningradskie profsoiuzy za desiat let. 1917–1927.* Leningrad, 1927, pp. 166–68.

Peshekhonov, A. P. "Pervyia nedeli (Iz vospominanii o revoliutsii)," *Na chuzhoi storone,* 1923, no. 1, pp. 255–319.

Pethybridge, Roger. *The Spread of the Russian Revolution: Essays on 1917.* London, 1972.

"Petinskii (Krasnozavodskii) raion g. Khar'kova v Oktiabre'," *Letopis' revoliutsii,* 1927, nos. 5–6, pp. 208–18.

Petrogradskii sovet rabochikh i soldatskikh deputatov; protokoly zasedanii Ispolnitel'nogo komiteta i buiro I. K. Moscow, 1925.

Petrogradskii voenno-revoliutsionnyi komitet: Dokumenty i materialy. D. A. Chugaev, ed. 3 vols. Moscow, 1966.

Petrov, G. F., and P. A. Lur'e. "Rabochaia molodezh' Vasil'evskogo ostrova g. Petrograda v 1917–1918 gg.," in *V ogne revoliutsionnykh boev (Raiony Petrograda v dvukh revoliutsiiakh 1917 g.). Sbornik vospominanii starykh bol'shevikov-pitertsev.* Moscow, 1967.

Petrov, Z. "Saratovskii proletariat v bor'be za vlast'," in *1917 god v Saratove.* Saratov, 1927.

Pinezhskii, E. *Krasnaia gvardiia. Ocherk istorii piterskoi Krasnoi gvardii 1917 g.* Moscow, 1st ed., 1929; 2d ed., 1933.

Pipes, Richard. *The Formation of the Soviet Union; Communism and Nationalism, 1917–1921.* New York, 1968.

"Piterskie rabochie ob iiul'skikh dniakh," *Krasnaia letopis'*, 1924, no. 9, pp. 19–41.

Pobeda Velikoi Oktiabr'skoi sotsialisticheskoi revoliutsii i ustanovlenie Sovetskoi vlasti na Ukraine. Sbornik dokumentov i materialov. Kiev, 1951.

Podgotovka i pobeda Oktiabr'skoi revoliutsii v Moskve. Dokumenty i materialy. Moscow, 1957.

Podgotovka Velikoi Oktiabrskoi sotsialisticheskoi revoliutsii na Ukraine. Sbornik dokumentovi materialov. Kiev, 1955.

Podvoiskii, N. I. *Krasnaia gvardiia v Oktiabr'skie dni (Leningrad i Moskva).* Moscow-Leningrad, 1927.

————. "Krasnaia gvardiia v Oktiabr'skie dni v Moskve," *Proletarskaia revoliutsiia*, 1927, no. 11, pp. 74–102.

————. "Voennaia organizatsiia TsK RSDRP(b) i voenno-revoliutsionnyi komitet 1917 g.," *Krasnaia letopis'*, 1923, no. 6, pp. 64–97; no. 8, pp. 7–43.

Pokko, S. "Organizatsiia i bor'ba Krasnoi gvardii v Khar'khove," *Letopis' revoliutsii*, 1922, no. 1, pp. 44–48.

Poliakov, I. A. "Kakim putem bylo, glavnym obrazom, dostignuto vooruzhenie obrazovavsheisia v Khar'kove Krasnoi gvardii," *Letopis' revoliutsii*, 1923, no. 3, pp. 73–74.

Polikarpov, V. D. *Prolog grazhdanskoi voiny v Rossii, oktiabr' 1917–fevral' 1918.* Moscow, 1976.

Popov, N. "Ocherki revoliutsionnykh sobytii v Khar'kove," *Letopis' revoliutsii*, 1922, no. 1, pp. 17–20.

Potekhin, M. N. "Krasnaia gvardiia," in *Vyborgskaia storona: Sbornik statei i vospominanii.* Leningrad, 1957.

Protokoly Tsentral'nogo komiteta RSDRP(b): Avgust 1917–fevral' 1918. Moscow, 1958.

Rabinovich, S. "K voprosu o krest'ianskoi Krasnoi gvardii," *Tolmachevets*, 1926, no. 7.

Rabinowitch, Alexander. *The Bolsheviks Come to Power; The Revolution of 1917 in Petrograd.* New York, 1976.

————. *Prelude to Revolution: The Petrograd Bolsheviks and the June 1917 Uprising.* Bloomington, Ind., 1968.

Rabochee dvizhenie v 1917 godu. V. L. Meller and A. M. Pankratova, eds. Moscow-Leningrad, 1926.

Rafes, M. "Moi vospominaniia," *Byloe*, 1922, no. 19, pp. 177–97.

Raionnye sovety Petrograda v 1917 godu. 3 vols. Moscow-Leningrad, 1965.

Raleigh, Donald J. "Dvoevlastie in the Provinces: A Case Study of Saratov." Unpublished paper.

————. "Revolutionary Politics in Provincial Russia: The Tsaritsyn 'Republic' in 1917," *Slavic Review*, 40, no. 2 (Summer 1981), pp. 198–209.

————. "The Russian Revolutions of 1917 in Saratov." Ph.D. diss., Indiana Univ., 1979.

Rashin, A. G. *Formirovanie rabochego klassa Rossii. Istoriko-ekonomicheskie ocherki.* Moscow, 1958.

Ratner, B. A. "Vasil'evskii ostrov," in *V ogne revoliutsionnykh boev (Raiony Petrograda v dvukh revoliutsiiakh 1917 g.). Sbornik vospominanii starykh bol'shevikov-pitertsev.* Moscow, 1967.

Razgon, A. I. "O sostave sovetov Nizhnego Povolzh'ia v marte–aprele 1917 goda," in *Sovety i soiuzy rabochego klassa i krest'ianstva v Oktiabr'skoi revoliutsii. Sbornik statei.* Moscow, 1964.

Reed, John. *Ten Days That Shook the World.* New York, 1919.

Reiman, Mikhail. *Russkaia revoliutsiia. 23 fevralia–25 oktiabria 1917.* Prague, 1968.

Rempel', L. I. *Krasnaia gvardiia v Krymu 1917–1918 gg.* Simferopol, 1931.

Reshetar, John. *The Ukrainian Revolution, 1917–1920.* Princeton, N.J., 1952.

Reshod'ko, P. F. "Chervona gvardiia v selakh Livoberezhnoi ukraini (listopad 1917–sichen' 1918 rr.)," *Ukrains'kyi istorychnyi zhurnal,* 1966, no. 11, pp. 95–102.

Revoliutsionnoe dvizhenie v Rossii nakanune Oktiabr'skogo vooruzhennogo vosstaniie. Moscow, 1962.

Revoliutsionnoe dvizhenie v Rossii posle sverzheniia samoderzhaviia. Moscow, 1957.

Revoliutsionnoe dvizhenie v Rossii v aprele 1917. Aprel'skii krizis. Moscow, 1958.

Revoliutsionnoe dvizhenie v Rossii v avguste 1917 g.: Razgrom Kornilovskogo miatezha. Moscow, 1959.

Revoliutsionnoe dvizhenie v Rossii v iiule 1917 g.: Iul'skii krizis. Moscow, 1959.

Revoliutsionnoe dvizhenie v Rossii v mae iiune 1917. Iiun'skaia demostratsiia. Moscow, 1959.

Revoliutsionnoe dvizhenie v Rossii v sentiabre 1917 g.: Obshchenatsional'nyi krizis. Moscow, 1961.

Roobol, W. H. *Tsereteli—A Democrat in the Russian Revolution; A Political Biography.* The Hague, 1976.

Rosenberg, William G. "The Democratization of Russia's Railroads in 1917," *American Historical Review,* 1981, no. 5, pp. 983-1008.

———. *Liberals in the Russian Revolution. The Constitutional Democratic Party, 1917–1921.* Princeton, N.J., 1974.

———. "The Russian Municipal Duma Elections of 1917: A Preliminary Computation of Returns," *Soviet Studies,* 21 (1969), pp. 131–63.

———. "Workers' Control on the Railroads and Some Suggestions Concerning Social Aspects of Labor Politics in the Russian Revolution," *Journal of Modern History,* 49, no. 2 (June 1977), pp. D1181-D1219.

Rostov, N. (Kogan). "Vozniknovenie Krasnoi gvardii," *Krasnaia nov',* 2, no. 2 (1927), pp. 168–80.

Rozanov, M. D. *Obukhovtsy. Istoriia zavoda "Bolshevik" 1863–1938.* Leningrad, 1938.

Rumiantsev, E. D. "Fabrichno-zavodskaia militsiia i ee deiatel'nost v Povolzh'e (mart–leto 1917 g.)," in *Ocherki istorii narodov Povolzh'ia i Priural'ia.* Vyp. 4. Kazan, 1972.

————. "Istochniki izucheniia istorii rabochei militsii i Krasnoi gvardii v Povolzh'e," in *Oktiabr' v Povolzh'e i Priural'e. Istochniki i voprosy istoriografii.* Kazan, 1972.

————. "Rabochaia militsiia i Krasnaia gvardiia Povolzh'ia v bor'be za vlast Sovetov." Diss., Kazan Univ., 1971.

————. "V. I. Lenin o vooruzhenii proletariata. Ot rabochikh druzhin k Krasnoi gvardii," in *Nekotorye voprosy otechestvennoi istorii v trudakh V. I. Lenina. Iz istorii obshchestvennoi mysli i revoliutsionnogo dvizheniia v Rossii.* Kazan, 1971.

Rychkova, G. *Krasnaia gvardiia na Urale.* Sverdlovsk-Moscow, 1933.

Saratovskii Sovet rabochikh deputatov (1917–1918). Sbornik dokumentov. V. P. Antonov-Saratovskii, ed. Moscow-Leningrad, 1931.

Saul, Norman. *Sailors in Revolt: The Russian Baltic Fleet in 1917.* Lawrence, Kans., 1978.

Schapiro, Leonard. "The Political Thought of the First Russian Provisional Government," in Richard Pipes, ed., *Revolutionary Russia* (Cambridge, Mass., 1968), pp. 97–113.

Sed'maia (Aprel'skaia) Vserossiiskaia konferentsiia RSDRP (bol'shevikov); Petrogradskaia obshchegorodskaia konferentsiia RSDRP (bol'shevikov), aprel' 1917 goda. Protokoly. Moscow, 1958.

Senchakova, L. T. *Boevaia rat' revoliutsii; ocherk o boevykh organizatsiiakh RSDRP i rabochikh druzhinakh 1905–1907 gg.* Moscow, 1975.

Senderskii, A. I. "Krasnaia gvardiia Kieva v bor'be za pobedu Sovetskoi vlasti na Ukraine (fevral' 1917–fevral' 1918)," in *Uchenye zapiski Instituta povysheniia kvalifikatsii prepodavatelei obshchestvennykh nauk pri Kievskom universitete.* Kiev, 1958.

Sergeev, N. "Na Vyborgskoi storone (Iz istorii Petrogradskogo, nyne Leningradskogo, Metallicheskogo zavoda)," in *Bastiony revoliutsii. Sbornik materialov iz istorii leningradskikh zavodov v 1917 godu.* Leningrad, 1957.

Shabalin, B. "Ot Fevralia–k Oktiabriu (Iz istorii zavoda 'Treugol'nik,' nyne 'Krasnyi Treugol'nik')," in *Bastiony revoliutsii. Sbornik materialov iz istorii leningradskikh zavodov v 1917 godu.* Leningrad, 1957.

Shakhov-Lankovskii, K. "Iunost' boevaia," *Kommunist* (Vilnius), 1957, no. 6, pp. 48–50.

Shcherbakov, P. K. "Dni velikikh svershenii," in *Za vlast' Sovetov. Vospominaniia uchastnikov revoliutsionnakh sobytii 1917 goda v Saratovskoi gubernii.* Saratov, 1957.

Shliapnikov, A. G. *Semnadtsatyi god.* 4 vols. Moscow, 1923–31.

Shus, O. I. "Stvorennia Rad soldatskikh deputatov u tilovikh garnizonakh v 1917 r.," in *Velikii Zhovten' i gromadians'ka viina na Ukraini.* Kiev, 1973.

Simkin, S. "Krasnogvardeitsy zavoda VEK," in *1917 g. v Khar'kove. Sbornik vospominanii*. Kharkov, 1921.

Simkin, S., and Silin (Birznek). "Kak rodilas' Khar'kovskaia Krasnaia gvardiia," *Letopis' revoliutsii*, 1926, no. 1, pp. 130–35.

Sivtsov, A. *Kievskaia Krasnaia gvardiia v bor'ba za vlast Sovetov*. Kiev, 1927.

Skalov, S. "27 fevralia 1917 v Peterburge," *Krasnaia nov'*, 1931, no. 3, pp. 115–21.

Skrypnik, N. "Organizatsii Krasnoi gvardii i Krasnoi armii na Ukraine v 1917–1918 gg.," *Armiia i revoliutsii*, 1923, nos. 3–4, pp. 38–47.

Skuratov, P. D. "Vospominaniia byvshego krasnogvardeits, rabochego Putilovskogo zavoda Pavla Dmitrievicha Skuratova," *Istoriia proletariata SSSR*, 1932, no. 11, pp. 109–16.

Smil'tnik, Zh. "Otriad Krasnoi gvardii zavoda VEK," *Letopis' revoliutsii*, 1928, no. 1, pp. 198–201.

Smolinchuk, A. I. *Bol'sheviki Ukrainy v bor'be za Sovety (mart 1917– ianvar' 1918 gg.)*. L'vov, 1969.

Snow, Russell. *The Bolsheviks in Siberia*. Rutherford, N.J., 1977.

Sobolev, G. L. *Revoliutsionnoe soznanie rabochikh i soldat Petrograda v 1917 g. Period dvoevlastiia*. Leningrad, 1973.

Sokolov, S. F. "Rabochaia Krasnaia gvardiia na frontakh grazhdanskoi voiny. Krasnogvardeitsy Vasileostrovskogo raiona," *Krasnaia letopis'*, 1926, no. 4, pp. 27–55.

Sondak, I. L. "Novolessnerovtsy," in *Vyborgskaia storona (Iz istorii bor'by rabochego klassa za pobedu Velikoi Oktiabr'skoi sotsialisticheskoi revoliutsii). Sbornik statei i vospominanii*. Leningrad, 1957.

Startsev, V. I. "K voprosu o sostave Krasnoi gvardii Petrograda," *Istoriia SSSR*, 1962, no. 1, pp. 136–41.

———. "Krasnogvardeitsy Petrograda v bor'be za ustanovlenie sovetskoi vlasti na strane," in *Ot Oktiabria k stroitel'stvu kommunizma. Sbornik statei*. Moscow, 1967.

———. "O metodike izucheniia sostava Krasnoi gvardii Petrograde," in *Nauchanaia sessiia po istorii rabochego klassa Leningrade, 22–27 dekabria 1961 g*. Leningrad, 1961.

———. *Ocherki po istorii petrogradskoi Krasnoi gvardii i rabochei militsii (mart 1917–aprel' 1918)*. Moscow-Leningrad, 1965.

———. "Ustavy rabochei Krasnoi gvardii Petrograda," in *Voprosy istoriografii i istochnikovedeniia istorii SSSR*. Moscow-Leningrad, 1963.

———. "Voenno-revoliutsionnyi komitet i Krasnaia gvardiia v Oktiabr'skom vooruzhennom vosstanii," in *Oktiabr'skoe vooruzhennoe vosstanie v Petrograde: Sbornik statei*. Moscow-Leningrad, 1957.

Stepanov, Z. V. "Fabrichno-zavodskie komitety v podgotovke vooruzhennykh sil petrogradskogo proletariata nakanune vosstaniia," in *Lenin i Oktiabr'skoe vooruzhennoe vosstanie v Petrograde; materialy Vsesoiuznoi nauchnoi sessii sostoiavsheisia 14–16 noiabria 1962 g. v Leningrade*. Moscow, 1964.

———. *Rabochie Petrograda v period podgotovki i provedeniia Oktiabr'skogo vooruzhennogo vosstaniia.* Moscow-Leningrad, 1965.

Sukhanov, N. N. *The Russian Revolution, 1917.* London, 1955. Translation of the following entry.

———. *Zapiski o revoliutsii.* 7 vols. Berlin, St. Petersburg, and Moscow, 1922.

Suny, Ronald G. *The Baku Commune, 1917–1918.* Princeton, N. J., 1972.

Tagirov, I. R. "Iz istorii sozdaniia vooruzhennykh otriadov kazanskogo proletariata v 1917 godu," in *Ocherki istorii Povolzh'ia i Priural'ia. Sbornik statei.* Kazan, 1969.

———. "K voprosy ob osobennostiakh vooruzhennogo vosstaniia v Kazane," in *Itogovaia nauchnaia aspirantskaia konferentsiia za 1964 god. Tezisy dokladov.* Kazan, 1964.

Tikhomirov, K. A. "Bol'sheviki v bor'be za Krasnuiu gvardiiu posle razgroma kornilovshchiny," in *Trudy Gor'kovskogo politekhnicheskogo instituta im. A. A. Zhdanova, Obshchestvenno-ekonomicheskie nauki.* Gor'kii, 1958. Tom 14, vyp. 4.

Tiushkevich, S. A., V. G. Kolychev, et al. *Vooruzhennye sily Velikogo Oktiabria.* Moscow, 1977.

Trifonov, E. "Kak vooruzhalsia proletariat (Petrogradskaia Krasnaia gvardiia)," *Katorga i ssylka,* 1932, no. 11–12, pp. 94–98.

Trifonov, Iurii. *Otblesk kostra.* Moscow, 1968.

Triumfal'noe shestvie Sovetskoi vlasti. 2 vols. Moscow, 1963.

Trotsky, Leon. *The History of the Russian Revolution.* 3 vols. New York, 1936.

Trukan, G. A. *Oktiabr' v Tsentral'noi Rossii.* Moscow, 1967.

Tsereteli, I. G. *Vospominaniia o fevral'skoi revoliutsii.* 2 vols. Paris, 1963.

Tsinis, M. P. "Vospominaniia rabochego-bol'shevika Martina Petrovicha Tsinisa o fevral'skikh dniakh i o Krasnoi gvardii," *Istoriia proletariata SSSR,* 1932, no. 11, pp. 100–103.

Tsukerman, S. I. "Petrogradskii raionnyi sovet rabochikh i soldatskikh deputatov v 1917 godu," *Krasnaia letopis',* 1932, nos. 1–2, pp. 69–101; no. 3, pp. 44–75.

Tsybul'skii, V. A. "Arsenal revoliutsii (Iz istorii Sestroretskogo oruzheinogo, nyne instrumental'nogo zavoda imeni S. P. Voskova)," in *Bastiony revoliutsii.* Leningrad, 1957.

———. "Rabochie Sestroretskogo zavoda v 1917 g.," *Istoriia SSSR,* 1957, no. 4, pp. 141–54.

———. "S. P. Voskov," *Istoriia SSSR,* 1959, no. 5, pp. 68–75.

Tsypkin, G. A. *Krasnaia gvardiia v bor'be za vlast' sovetov.* Moscow, 1967.

Tsypkin, G. A., and R. G. Tsypkina. *Krasnaia gvardiia—udarnaia sila proletariata v Oktiabr'skoi revoliutsii.* Moscow, 1962.

Tsypkina, R. G. *Sel'skaia Krasnaia gvardiia v Oktiabr'skoi revoliutsii; po materialam gubernii tsentral'nogo promyshlennogo raiona.* Moscow, 1970.

Tvorchestvo revoliutsionnykh rabochikh Vtorogo Gorodskogo raiona. Petrograd, 1918.

"U istokov Krasnoi armii (vospominaniia)," *Letopis' revoliutsii* (Kharkov), 1926, no. 1, pp. 129–51.

Uldricks, Teddy J. "The Crowd in the Russian Revolution: Towards Reassessing the Nature of Revolutionary Leadership," *Politics and Society*, 1974, no. 3, pp. 397–413.

Usatenko, A. V. "V riadakh Krasnoi gvardii," in *Skvoz grozy i buri.* Kharkov, 1969.

Ushakov, M. I. "Krasnaia gvardiia Khar'kova v boiakh za pobedu Sovetskoi vlasti na Ukraine," in *Trudy Khar'kovskogo vyshego aviatsionno-inzhenernogo voenno uchilishcha.* Kharkov, 1957. No. 94.

Ustanovlenie sovetskoi vlasti na mestakh v 1917–1918 gg. Sbornik statei. 2 vols. Moscow, 1953, 1959.

V boiakh: Sbornik vospominanii, posviashchennyi geroicheskoi bor'be vasileostrovtsev za 15 let. Leningrad, 1932.

V boiakh za Oktiabr'. Vospominaniia ob Oktiabre za Nevskoi zastavoi. Leningrad, 1932.

V ogne revoliutsionnykh boev (Raiony Petrograda v dvukh revoliutsiiakh 1917 g.). Sbornik vospominanii starykh bol'shevikov-pitertsev. Moscow, 1967.

V ogne revoliutsionnykh boev (Raiony Petrograda v dvukh revoliutsiiakh 1917 g.). Sbornik vospominanii starykh bol'shevikov-pitertsev. Moscow, 1971.

Vargin, N. F. "Partiia bol'shevikov i sozdanie Krasnoi gvardii," *Voprosy istorii KPSS*, 1968, no. 3, pp. 114–22.

Vasil'ev, A. "Moe uchastie v Krasnoi gvardii i Oktiabr'skoi revoliutsii," *Katorga i ssylka*, 1932, nos. 11–12, pp. 99–110 (part 1); 1933, no. 2, pp. 122–34 (part 2).

Vasil'ev-Iuzhin, M. I. "1917 god v Saratove," in *Za vlast' Sovetov. Vospominaniia uchastnikov revoliutsionnykh sobytii 1917 goda v Saratovskoi gubernii.* Saratov, 1957.

Vas'kin, V. V. "Iz istorii bor'by za bol'shevizatsiiu Saratovskogo garnizona v 1917 godu," in *Materialy k nauchnoi konferentsii aspirantov i molodykh nauchnykh sotrudnikov.* Saratov, 1965.

Velikaia Oktiabr'skaia sotsialisticheskaia revoliutsiia na Ukraine. Fevral' 1917–aprel' 1918. Sbornik dokumentov i materialov. 3 vols. Kiev, 1957.

Velikaia Oktiabr'skaia sotsialisticheskaia revoliutsiia: Oktiabr'skoe vooruzhennoe vosstanie v Petrograde. Dokumenty i materialy. Moscow, 1957.

Ventsov, S., and S. Belitskii. *Krasnaia gvardiia.* Moscow, 1924.

Verkhos', V. P. *Krasnaia gvardiia v Oktiabr'skoi revoliutsii.* Moscow, 1976.

———. "Partiia bol'shevikov i krest'ianskaia Krasnaia gvardiia," *Voprosy istorii KPSS*, 1967, no. 7, pp. 50–57.

Vinogradov, V. P. "Dorozhe otchego doma," in *Petrograda v dni Velikogo*

Oktiabria. Vospominaniia uchastnikov revoliutsionnykh sobytii v Petrograde v 1917 godu. Leningrad, 1967.
Vinogradov, Vasilii. "Krasnaia gvardiia Petrogradskogo Metallicheskogo zavoda," *Krasnaia letopis'*, 1927, no. 2, pp. 162–72.
Voennye voprosy v resheniiakh KPSS, 1903–1917 gg. Sbornik dokumentov. Moscow, 1969.
Voitsekhovskii, M. A. "Rozhdenie Krasnoi gvardii," in *Narvskaia zastava v 1917 godu, v vospominaniiakh i dokumentakh.* Leningrad, 1960.
Volobuev, P. V. *Ekonomicheskaia politika Vremennogo pravitel'stva.* Moscow, 1962.
Von Laue, Theodore. *Why Lenin? Why Stalin?* New York, 1964.
Voskresenskii, A. A. *Revoliutsionnaia bor'ba rabochikh Khar'kovskogo parovozostroitel'nogo zavoda (1895–1917 gg.).* Kharkov, 1958.
"Vospominaniia uchastnikov Velikogo Oktiabria," *Istoricheskii arkhiv*, 1957, no. 5, pp. 186–220.
Vyborgskaia storona (Iz istorii bor'by rabochego klassa za pobedu Velikoi Oktiabr'skoi sotsialisticheskoi revoliutsii). Sbornik statei i vospominanii. Leningrad, 1957.
Wade, Rex A. "The Rajonnye Sovety of Petrograd: The Role of Local Political Bodies in the Russian Revolution," *Jahrbücher fur Geschichte Osteuropas*, 20, no. 2 (June 1972), pp. 226–40.
———. *The Russian Search for Peace, February–October, 1917.* Stanford, Calif., 1969.
———. "Spontaneity in the Formation of the Workers' Militia and Red Guards, 1917," in Ralph Carter Elwood, ed., *Reconsiderations on the Russian Revolution.* Cambridge, Mass., 1976.
White, J. D. "The Kornilov Affair: A Study in Counterrevolution," *Soviet Studies*, July 1970, pp. 3–23.
Wildman, Allan K. *The End of the Russian Imperial Army; The Old Army and the Soldier's Revolt (March–April 1917).* Princeton, N. J., 1980.
Za vlast' Sovetov. Vospominaniia uchastnikov revoliutsionnykh sobytii 1917 goda v Saratovskoi gubernii. Saratov, 1957.
Zenzinov, V. M. "Fevral'skie dni," *Novyi Zhurnal*, 1953, no. 34, pp. 118–211; no. 35, pp. 208–40.
Zlodeev, N. I. *Krasnaia Gvardiia.* Moscow, 1957.
Zlokazov, G. I. *Petrogradskii sovet na puti k Oktiabriu.* Moscow, 1978.
———. *Petrogradskii sovet rabochikh i soldatskikh deputatov v period mirnogo razvitiia revoliutsii (fevral'–iiun' 1917 g.).* Moscow, 1969.
Znamenskii, O. N. *Iul'skii krizis 1917 goda.* Moscow-Leningrad, 1964.
1917 god v Khar'kove. Sbornik vospominanii. Kharkov, 1927.
1917 god v Saratove. Saratov, 1927.
1917 god v Saratovskoi gubernii. Sbornik dokumentov (Fevral' 1917–dekabr' 1918 gg.). Saratov, 1957.

Index